THE ENCYCLOPAEDIA OF ISLAM

INDEX OF SUBJECTS

THE ENCYCLOPAEDIA OF ISLAM

NEW EDITION

INDEX OF SUBJECTS

to Volumes
I-XI
and to the Supplement, Fascicules
1-6

COMPILED BY

P. J. BEARMAN

BRILL
LEIDEN · BOSTON
2003

The paper in this book meets the guidelines for permanence and durability of the Committee on Production Guidelines for Book Longevity of the Council on Library Resources.

Library of Congress Cataloging-in-Publication Data

Bearman, P.J.
The Encyclopaedia of Islam, new edition. Index of Subjects = Encyclopédie de l'islam, nouvelle édition. Index des matières compiled by P.J. Bearman.
p. cm.
French.
ISBN 9004097392 (alk. paper)
1. Encyclopaedia of Islam—Indexes. 2. Islam—Indexes. 3. Islamic countries—Indexes. I. Title. II. Title: Encyclopédie de l'islam, nouvelle édition. Index des matières.
DS35.53.E533B4 1992
909'.097671—dc20 92-31738
CIP
Rev.

ISBN 90 04 12759 3

PRINTED IN THE NETHERLANDS

TABLE OF CONTENTS

PREFACE TO THE FIFTH EDITION

This edition of the Index of Subjects indexes Volumes I through XI and fascicules 1 through 6 (the first 423 pages) of the Supplement. The final volume of the main text of the *Encyclopaedia of Islam* was published in June 2002. The remaining pages of the Supplement will be published in 2003.

A List of Entries precedes the actual subject index. The List of Entries refers the reader to single articles in the *Encyclopaedia of Islam*. For an overview of what the *Encyclopaedia* offers on a larger subject, the reader should consult the Index of Subjects proper. Thus, in order to find the entry on chess in the *Encyclopaedia*, one would look in the List of Entries, which refers one to S͟haṭrand͟j, while reference to this article in its larger context can be found in the Index of Subjects under the heading RECREATION.GAMES.

Comments and suggestions for improvement of this Index are welcome.

September 2002

Peri Bearman

LIST OF ENTRIES

References are given here either to the main article in the *Encyclopaedia* or to the Index of Subjects proper, which groups all articles concerned with the subject under one heading (e.g. Clove → Ḳaranful; but Spices → CUISINE.FOOD). The Index of Subjects follows the List of Entries on p. 21. Countries and names of dynasties or caliphates, which are included *in extenso* in the Index of Subjects, are not given in the following list.

A

Abbreviations [in Suppl.] Abbreviations

Ablution → ABLUTION

Abridgement Mukhtaṣar

Abstinence Istibrāʾ

Academy Madjmaʿ ʿIlmī

Accident ʿAraḍ

Accounting → FINANCE

Acquisition Kasb

Acrobat Djānbāz

Act ʿAmal; Fiʿl

Addax Mahāt

Administration → ADMINISTRATION

Admiral Ḳapudan Pasha

Adoption → ADOPTION

Adultery → ADULTERY

Advance guard Ṭalīʿa

Adverb Ẓarf

Aesthetics ʿIlm al-Djamāl

Agency Wakāla

Agriculture → AGRICULTURE

Album Muraḳḳaʿ

Alchemy → ALCHEMY

Alfa-grass Ḥalfāʾ

Algebra → MATHEMATICS

Almanac Taḳwīm

Alms → ALMS

Aloe Ṣabr

Alphabet → ALPHABET

Amazement Taʿadjdjub

Amber Kahrubā

Ambergris ʿAnbar

Americas → NEW WORLD

Amplification (of poetry) Takhmīs

Amulet Tamīma

Analogy Ḳiyās

Anatomy → ANATOMY

Anecdote Nādira

Anemone Shaḳīḳat al-Nuʿmān

Angel → ANGELOLOGY

Animal → ANIMALS

Ant Naml

Antelope → ANIMALS

Anthology Mukhtārāt

Anthropomorphism → ANTHROPOMORPHISM

Antinomianism Ibāḥa (II)

Antithesis Ṭibāḳ

Apostasy → APOSTASY

Appeal Istiʾnāf

Apple Tuffāḥ

Apricot Mishmish

Aqueduct → ARCHITECTURE.MONUMENTS

Arabian peninsula → ARABIAN PENINSULA

Arabic → ALPHABET; LANGUAGES.AFRO-ASIATIC; LINGUISTICS
Arabicisation Taʿrīb
Arabism → PANARABISM
Arachnoids → ANIMALS
Arbitration Taḥkīm
Arbitrator Ḥakam
Archaeology → ARCHAEOLOGY
Architecture → ARCHITECTURE
Archives → ADMINISTRATION
Arithmetic → MATHEMATICS
Army → MILITARY
Arsenal Dār al-Ṣināʿa
Art → ART
Artemisia Shīḥ
Article Maḳāla
Artisans → PROFESSIONS.CRAFTSMEN AND TRADESMEN
Ascendent al-Ṭāliʿ
Ascensions al-Maṭāliʿ
Asceticism → ASCETICISM
Assignation Ḥawāla
Association Andjuman; Djamʿiyya
Associationism Shirk
Astrolabe Asṭurlāb
Astrology → ASTROLOGY
Astronomical handbook Zīdj
Astronomy → ASTRONOMY
Atheism Kāfir
Atomism Djuzʾ
Attributes Ṣifa
Avarice Bukhl

B

Bābism → SECTS
Bacchism → WINE.BACCHIC POETRY
Backgammon Nard
Bahais → BAHAIS
Balance al-Mīzān
Balance of powers Tawāzun al-Sulutāt
Bamboo sugar Ṭabāshīr
Band → MILITARY.BAND
Banking → FINANCE
Barber [in Suppl.] Ḥallāḳ
Bargaining Sawm
Barley Shaʿīr
Barracks Ṭabaḳa
Barter Muʿāwaḍa
Basques → BASQUES
Bat Waṭwāṭ
Bath → ARCHITECTURE.MONUMENTS
Battalion Ṭabūr
Battle → MILITARY.BATTLES
Beauty ʿIlm al-Djamāl
Bedding Mafrūshāt; Mifrash
Bedouin → BEDOUINS
Bee Naḥl
Beggar Sāsān
Belles-lettres → LITERATURE
Belomancy Istiḳsām
Ben-nut Bān
Bequest Waṣiyya
Berbers → BERBERS
Betrothal Khiṭba
Bible → BIBLE
Bibliography → BIBLIOGRAPHY
Bier Djanāza
Biography → LITERATURE.BIO-GRAPHICAL
Bird → ANIMALS
Birth control → LIFE STAGES. CHILDBIRTH.PREGNANCY
Bitumen Mūmiyāʾ
Blacksmith Ḳayn
Blessing Baraka

Blockprinting → WRITING.MANUSCRIPTS AND BOOKS
Blood [in Suppl.] Dam
Blood-letter [in Suppl.] Faṣṣād
Blood-vengeance Ḳiṣāṣ; Thaʾr
Boar, wild Khinzīr
Boat Safīna
Body Djism
Book Kitāb
Bookbinding → WRITING
Bookseller Warrāḳ
Booktitle ʿUnwān.2(=3)
Boon-companion Nadīm
Booty → MILITARY
Botany → BOTANY
Boundaries Takhṭīṭ al-Ḥudūd
Bow Ḳaws
Bowing → PRAYER
Brand Tamgha; Wasm
Bread Khubz
Bribery → PAYMENTS
Brick Labin
Bridge → ARCHITECTURE.MONUMENTS
Brigand Ṣuʿlūk
Broadcasting Idhāʿa
Broker Dallāl
Buddhism → BUDDHISM
Buffalo [in Suppl.] Djāmūs
Building Bināʾ
Butcher [in Suppl.] Djazzār
Butter al-Samn
Byzantines → BYZANTINE EMPIRE

C

Calendar → TIME
Caliph Khalīfa
Caliphate → CALIPHATE
Call to prayer Adhān
Calligraphy → ART; WRITING.SCRIPTS
Camel → ANIMALS
Camel-driver [in Suppl.] Djammāl
Camomile [in Suppl.] Bābūnadj
Camphor Kāfūr
Canal Ḳanāt
Candle Shamʿa
Candle-maker Shammāʿ
Cannon Ṭop
Capitulations Imtiyāzāt
Caravan → TRANSPORT
Carmathians → SHIITES.BRANCHES
Carpet → ART.TAPESTRY
Cart ʿAdjala; Araba
Cartography → CARTOGRAPHY
Cattle Baḳar
Cause ʿIlla
Cedar-oil Ḳaṭrān
Cemetery Maḳbara
Ceramics → ART.POTTERY
Cession Ḥawāla
Chair Kursī
Chamber, underground Sardāb
Chamberlain Ḥādjib
Chameleon Ḥirbāʾ
Chancellery → DOCUMENTS
Charity → ALMS
Charms → CHARMS
Cheetah Fahd
Cheiropters Waṭwāṭ
Chemistry → ALCHEMY
Chess Shaṭrandj
Chest → ANATOMY
Child → LIFE STAGES
Childbirth → LIFE STAGES
Childhood → LIFE STAGES
Chintz Ḳalamkārī

Chirognomy al-Kaff
Christianity → CHRISTIANITY
Christians Naṣārā
Chronogram Taʾrīkh.III
Church Kanīsa
Cinema Cinema
Cinnamon [in Suppl.] Dār Ṣīnī
Circumcision → CIRCUMCISION
Cistern Ḥawḍ
Citizen Muwāṭin
Citrus fruits Nārandj
Civilisation Medeniyyet
Clan Āl
Clay Ṭīn
Cleanliness Ṭahāra
Clime Iḳlīm
Cloak Khirḳa
Clock Sāʿa
Clothing → CLOTHING
Clove Ḳaranful
Cock Dīk
Codes → CRYPTOGRAPHY
Codification (of the law) Tashrīʿ
Coffee Ḳahwa
Coinage → NUMISMATICS
Coitus Bāh
Coitus interruptus ʿAzl
Colour → COLOUR
Column ʿAmūd
Comedians → HUMOUR
Commentary Sharḥ; *and* → KORAN
Commerce → FINANCE
Communications → COMMUNICATIONS
Communism → COMMUNISM
Community, Muslim Umma
Companions (of the Prophet) → MUḤAMMAD, THE PROPHET
Compass Maghnāṭīs.2; al-Ṭāsa
Concealment (of belief) Taḳiyya
Concubinage → WOMEN
Conference Muʾtamar
Confessionalism Ṭāʾifiyya
Congress Muʾtamar
Conjunction Ḳirān
Constellation → ASTRONOMY
Constitution Dustūr
Consul Consul
Consultation Shūrā
Contraception Tanẓīm al-Nasl
Contract → LAW.LAW OF OBLIGATIONS
Cook Ṭabbākh
Cooking → CUISINE
Cooperatives Taʿāwun
Copper Nuḥās; *and see* Malachite
Copts → CHRISTIANITY.DENOMINATIONS
Copyist Warrāḳ
Coral Mardjān
Cornelian ʿAḳīḳ
Corpse Djanāza
Corpse-washer [in Suppl.] Ghassāl
Corsair → PIRACY
Corundum Yāḳūt
Cosmetics → COSMETICS
Cosmography → COSMOGRAPHY
Cotton Ḳuṭn
Country Waṭan
Court (of law) Maḥkama
Court Ceremony → COURT CEREMONY
Courtier Nadīm
Couscous Kuskusū
Cowrie Wadaʿ
Craftsmanship → PROFESSIONS
Creation → CREATION
Creditor Ghārim
Creed ʿAḳīda
Crescent Hilāl
Criticism, literary → LITERATURE
Crocodile Timsāḥ
Cross al-Ṣalīb
Crow Ghurāb

Crown Tādj
Crucifixion Ṣalb
Crusades → CRUSADE(R)S
Crustaceans → ANIMALS
Cryptography → CRYPTOGRAPHY
Crystal *see* Rock-crystal
Cubit Dhirāʿ
Cuckoo Wāḳwāḳ.4
Cuisine → CUISINE
Cumin Kammūn
Cupper [in Suppl.] Faṣṣād
Currants Zabīb
Custody Ḥaḍāna
Custom → CUSTOM
Customary law → LAW
Cymbal Ṣandj

D

Dactylonomy Ḥisāb al-ʿAḳd
Dam → ARCHITECTURE.MONUMENTS
Dance Raḳṣ
Dandy Ẓarīf
Date Nakhl
Day → TIME
Death → DEATH
Debt [in Suppl.] Dayn
Debtor Ghārim
Deception (in law) Taghrīr
Declension Iʿrāb
Declination al-Mayl
Decoration → ARCHITECTURE; ART.DECORATIVE; MILITARY
Decree, divine al-Ḳaḍāʾ wa 'l-Ḳadar
Decree of ruler Tawḳīʿ
Deer Ayyil
Definition Taʿrīf
Delegations Wufūd
Delusion Wahm
Demography [in Suppl.] Demography
Demon Djinn
Dentistry → MEDICINE
Deposit Wadīʿa
Deputisation Wakāla
Dervish → MYSTICISM
Description Waṣf
Desert → DESERTS
Devil Iblīs; Shayṭān
Devotions Wird
Dialect → LANGUAGES.AFRO-ASIATIC.ARABIC; LINGUISTICS.PHONETICS
Diamond Almās
Dictionary → DICTIONARY
Dill Shibiththth
Diplomacy → DIPLOMACY
Disease → ILLNESS
Disputation → THEOLOGY
Dissolution Faskh
Ditch Khandaḳ
Divination → DIVINATION
Divorce → DIVORCE
Documents → DOCUMENTS
Dog Kalb
Donative coins Yādgār
Donkey Ḥimār
Double entendre Tawriya
Doubt Shakk
Dove Ḥamām
Dowry → MARRIAGE
Dragon al-Tinnīn
Dragoman Tardjumān
Drama → LITERATURE
Drawing → ART
Dreams → DREAMS
Dress → CLOTHING

Dressmaker Khayyāṭ
Drinks → CUISINE
Dromedary → ANIMALS.CAMEL
Drugs → DRUGS
Druggist al-ʿAṭṭār
Drum Darabukka; Ṭabl
Drummer Ṭabbāl
Druze → DRUZES
Dualism → RELIGION
Dulcimer Sanṭūr
Duress [in Suppl.] Ikrāh
Dwelling Bayt; Dār
Dye → DYEING
Dyer → DYEING
Dynasty → DYNASTIES

E

Eagle ʿUḳāb
Earthquakes → EARTHQUAKES
Ebony Abanūs
Eclipse Kusūf
Ecliptic Minṭaḳat al-Burūdj
Economics → ECONOMICS
Edict Farmān
Education → EDUCATION
Elative Tafḍīl
Elegy Marthiya
Elephant Fīl
Elixir al-Iksīr
Eloquence Balāgha; Bayān; Faṣāḥa
Emancipation → EMANCIPATION
Embalming Ḥināṭa
Emblem of sultan Tughra
Emerald Zumurrud
Emigration → EMIGRATION
Emphatic phonemes Tafkhīm
Encyclopaedia Mawsūʿa
Endive [in Suppl.] Hindibāʾ
Endowment, charitable Waḳf
Enjambment Taḍmīn
Ephemeris Taḳwīm
Epic Ḥamāsa
Epidemic Wabāʾ
Epigraphy → EPIGRAPHY
Epistolography → LITERATURE.EPISTOLARY
Epithet → ONOMASTICS
Equation (astronomical) al-Taʿdīl; Taʿdīl al-Zamān
Equator Istiwāʾ
Equines → ANIMALS
Eroticism → LOVE.EROTIC
Error Khaṭaʾ
Error, writing *see* Mistakes
Eschatology → ESCHATOLOGY
Esoteric sense al-Ẓāhir wa ʾl-Bāṭin
Espionage *see* Spy
Estate Ḍayʿa
Eternity Abad; Ḳidam
Ethics → ETHICS
Ethnicity → ETHNICITY
Ethnology → TRIBES
Etiquette → ETIQUETTE
Etymology Ishtiḳāḳ
Eulogy Madīḥ
Eunuch → EUNUCH
Europeanisation Tafarnudj
Evidence Bayyina
Ewer [in Suppl.] Ibrīḳ
Exception Istithnāʾ
Executor Waṣiyya
Exegesis Tafsīr
Existence Wudjūd
Exoteric sense Ẓāhir; al-Ẓāhir wa ʾl-Bāṭin
Expedition → MILITARY
Expiation Kaffāra

Extremism Taṭarruf

Eye → Anatomy; Evil Eye

F

Faculty Kulliyya
Faïence Kāshī
Faith → Faith
Faith, profession of *see* Profession of faith
Falconry → Falconry
Family ʿĀʾila
Family planning Tanẓīm al-Nasl
Fan Mirwaḥa
Farming → Agriculture
Fasting → Fasting
Fate → Predestination
Fauna → Animals
Felines → Animals
Felt Lubūd
Female circumcision Khafḍ
Fennec-fox Fanak
Fennel [in Suppl.] Basbās
Festival → Festival
Fief Iḳṭāʿ
Fig Tīn
Film Cinema
Finance → Finance
Fine Djurm
Fire Nār
Firefighter Ṭulumbadji̊
Fiscal system → Taxation
Fish → Animals
Fishing Samak.3
Five Khamsa
Flag ʿAlam; Sandjaḳ
Flamingo Nuḥām
Flax Kattān
Fleet, naval Usṭūl
Flora → Flora
Flower poetry Zahriyyāt
Flowers → Flora
Fly Dhubāb
Folklore → Custom; Divination; Legends
Food → Cuisine
Forest Ghāba
Foreword Muḳaddima
Forgery (of coins) Tazyīf
Forgery (of writings) Tazwīr
Form, legal Waṣf.2
Formulas → Islam
Fortress → Architecture.monuments.strongholds
Foundling Laḳīṭ
Fountain Shadirwān
Fowl Dadjādja
Fox Thaʿlab; *and see* Fennec-fox
Fraction Kasr
Frankincense Lubān
Fraud Taghrīr
Free will → Predestination
Freedom Ḥurriyya; [in Suppl.] Āzādī
Freemasonry [in Suppl.] Farāmūsh-khāna; Farmāsūniyya
Fruit → Cuisine.food
Fundamentalism → Reform.politico-religious.militant
Funeral Djanāza
Fur Farw
Furnishings → Furnishings
Furniture [in Suppl.] Athāth
Fürstenspiegel Naṣīḥat al-Mulūk

G

Gain Kasb
Gambling → Gambling
Games → Recreation
Garden → Architecture.monuments.gardens
Gate → Architecture.monuments
Gazehound Salūḳī
Gazelle Ghazāl
Gemstones → Jewelry
Gender studies → Women
Genealogy → Genealogy
Generation, spontaneous Tawallud
Geography → Geography
Geometry → Mathematics
Gesture Ishāra
Gift → Gifts
Giraffe Zarāfa
Girdle Shadd
Glass → Art
Gloss Hāshiya
Goats [in Suppl.] Ghanam
God Allāh; Ilāh
Gods, pre-Islamic → Pre-Islam
Gold Dhahab
Goldsmith Ṣāʾigh
Gospels Indjīl
Government Ḥukūma
Grains → Cuisine.food
Grammar → Linguistics
Gratitude Shukr
Greeks Yūnān
Greyhound *see* Gazehound
Grocer Baḳḳāl
Guardianship Ḥaḍāna
Guild → Guilds
Gum resins Ṣamgh
Gunpowder Bārūd
Gymnasium Zūrkhāna
Gynaecology → Life Stages
Gypsies → Gypsies

H

Hadith → Literature.tradition-literature
Hagiography → Hagiography
Hair → Anatomy
Hairdresser [in Suppl.] Ḥallāḳ
Hamito-Semitic Ḥām
Hand, right Yamīn
Handbook Tadhkira
Handbook, astronomical Zīdj
Handicrafts → Art
Handkerchief Mandīl
Harbour Mīnāʾ
Hare [in Suppl.] Arnab
Headware → Clothing
Health → Medicine
Heart Ḳalb
Heaven Samāʾ
Hedgehog Ḳunfudh
Hell → Hell
Hemerology Ikhtiyārāt
Hemp Ḥashīsh
Hempseed Shahdānadj
Henbane Bandj
Henna Ḥinnāʾ
Heraldry → Heraldry
Herbs → Cuisine.food
Hereafter → Eschatology
Heresy → Heresy
Hippopotamus [in Suppl.] Faras al-Māʾ
Hire, contract of → Law
Historiography → Literature.

HISTORICAL
Holiness Ḳadāsa
Holy War Dj̲ihād
Homeland Waṭan
Homicide Ḳatl
Homonym Aḍdād
Homosexuality Liwāṭ
Honour ʿIrḍ
Hoopoe Hudhud
Horn Būḳ
Horse Faras
Horseback rider Fāris
Horseback riding Furūsiyya
Horticulture → ARCHITECTURE.MONUMENTS.GARDENS; FLORA
Hostelry → HOSTELRY
Houris Ḥūr
House *see* Dwelling
Humour → HUMOUR
Hunting → HUNTING
Hydrology → HYDROLOGY
Hydromancy Istinzāl
Hyena [in Suppl.] Ḍabuʿ
Hymn Nas̲h̲īd
Hyperbole Mubālag̲h̲a
Hypnotism Sīmiyāʾ.1
Hypocrisy Riyāʾ

I

Ice-seller T̲h̲allād̲j̲
Iconography → ART
Idol → IDOLATRY.IDOLS
Idolatry → IDOLATRY
Illness → ILLNESS
Illumination ʿUnwān.2
Image Ṣūra
Impurity Dj̲anāba; Ḥadat̲h̲
Incubation Istik̲h̲āra
Independence Istiḳlāl
Indigo Nīl
Individual S̲h̲ak̲h̲ṣ
Industry → INDUSTRY
Infanticide Waʾd al-Banāt
Infantryman Yaya
Infidel Kāfir
Inflection Imāla
Inheritance → INHERITANCE
Inimitability (of Ḳurʾān) Iʿd̲j̲āz
Injustice Ẓulm
Ink Midād
Ink-holder [in Suppl.] Dawāt
Inner dimension al-Ẓāhir wa ʾl-Bāṭin
Innovation Bidʿa
Inscriptions → EPIGRAPHY
Insects → ANIMALS
Insignia → MILITARY.DECORATIONS; MONARCHY.ROYAL INSIGNIA
Inspection (of troops) Istiʿrāḍ
Instrument Āla
Instrument, musical → MUSIC
Insulting verse Hid̲j̲āʾ
Intellect ʿAḳl
Intercession S̲h̲afāʿa
Intercourse, sexual Bāh
Intercourse, unlawful sexual Zinā
Interdiction Ḥad̲j̲r
Interest Ribā
Interpolation (astronomical) al-Taʿdīl bayn al-Saṭrayn
Interpreter Tard̲j̲umān
Interrogation Istifhām
Interruption Ḳaṭʿ
Introduction Ibtidāʾ; Muḳaddima
Inventions → INVENTIONS
Invocation Duʿāʾ
Ipseity Huwiyya
Iris Sūsan

Iron al-Ḥadīd
Irrigation → IRRIGATION
Islam → ISLAM
Ivory ʿĀdj

J

Jackal Ibn Āwā
Jade Yashm
Janissaries Yeñi Čeri
Japan(ese) al-Yabānī
Jasmine Yāsamīn
Javelin Djerīd
Jerboa Yarbūʿ
Jewelry → JEWELRY
Jews Banū Isrāʾīl; Yahūd
Journalism → PRESS
Judaism → JUDAISM
Judge Ḳāḍī
Jujube ʿUnnāb
Juncture Waṣl
Jurisconsult → LAW.JURIST
Jurisprudence → LAW
Jurist → LAW
Justice ʿAdl

K

King Malik; Shāh
Kingdom Mamlaka
Kinship Ḳarāba
Kitchen Maṭbakh
Knowledge ʿIlm; Maʿrifa
Kohl al-Kuḥl
Koran → KORAN
Kurdish → KURDS

L

Labour *see* Trade union
Labourers → PROFESSIONS.CRAFTSMEN AND TRADESMEN
Lakes → GEOGRAPHY.PHYSICAL GEOGRAPHY.WATERS
Lamentation → LAMENTATION
Lamp Sirādj
Land → LAND
Landowner Zamīndār
Language → LANGUAGES
Largesse coins Yādgār
Law → LAW
Leader Zaʿīm
Leasing Kirāʾ
Leather Djild
Legacy Waṣiyya
Legatee Waṣī
Legend → LEGENDS
Lemon Nārandj
Lemon balm Turundjān
Leprosy [in Suppl.] Djudhām
Lesbianism Siḥāḳ
Letter(s) Ḥarf; Ḥurūf al-Hidjāʾ; *and for* letters of the alphabet → ALPHABET
Lexicography → LEXICOGRAPHY
Library → EDUCATION.LIBRARIES
Lice Ḳaml
Licorice Sūs
Life → LIFE STAGES

Light Nūr
Lighthouse → ARCHITECTURE.MONUMENTS
Lily Sūsan
Linen Kattān; Khaysh
Linguistics → LINGUISTICS
Lion al-Asad
Literature → LITERATURE
Lithography → PRINTING
Liver Kabid
Lizard Ḍabb
Locust Djarād
Lodge Zāwiya
Logic → PHILOSOPHY
Longevity Muʿammar
Louse *see* Lice
Love → LOVE
Lute Sāz; ʿŪd
Lyre Ḳithāra

M

Mace Dūrbāsh
Madman Madjnūn
Magic → MAGIC
Magnet Maghnāṭīs.1
Malachite al-Dahnadj
Malaria Malāryā
Man Insān
Man-of-war Usṭūl
Mandrake Sirādj al-Ḳuṭrub; Yabrūḥ
Manichaeism → RELIGION.DUALISM
Manifestation Tadjallī
Manners → CUISINE; ETIQUETTE; VIRTUES AND VICES
Manumission → SLAVERY
Manuscript Nuskha
Map Kharīṭa
Marches al-Thughūr; Udj
Market Sūḳ
Marquetry Zalīdj
Marriage → MARRIAGE
Martyr Shahīd
Martyrdom → MARTYRDOM
Marxism Mārk(i)siyya
Masonry Bināʾ
Mathematics → MATHEMATICS
Matter Hayūlā; Ṭīna
Mausoleum → ARCHITECTURE.MONUMENTS.TOMBS
Mayor Raʾīs
Measurements → WEIGHTS AND MEASUREMENTS
Mechanics → MECHANICS
Mediation Shafāʿa
Medicine → MEDICINE
Melilot [in Suppl.] Iklīl al-Malik
Melissa Turundjān
Memorandum Tadhkira
Menstruation Ḥayḍ
Merchants → PROFESSIONS.CRAFTSMEN AND TRADESMEN
Mercury Ziʾbaḳ
Messenger Rasūl
Messiah al-Masīḥ
Metallurgy → METALLURGY
Metalware → ART
Metamorphosis → ANIMALS.TRANSFORMATION INTO
Metaphor Istiʿāra
Metaphysics → METAPHYSICS
Metempsychosis Tanāsukh
Meteorology → METEOROLOGY
Metonymy Kināya
Metre Wazn.2
Metrics → METRICS
Migration → EMIGRATION
Militancy → REFORM.POLITICO-

RELIGIOUS.MILITANT
Military → MILITARY
Milky Way al-Madjarra
Mill Ṭāḥūn
Miller Ṭaḥḥān
Millet [in Suppl.] Djāwars
Minaret Manāra
Mineralogy → MINERALOGY
Miniatures → ART.PAINTING
Mint [in Suppl.] Fūdhandj
Mint (money) Dār al-Ḍarb
Miracle → MIRACLES
Mirage Sarāb
Mirror Mirʾāt
"Mirror for princes" *see* Fürstenspiegel
Misfortune Shakāwa
Misrepresentation (in law) Tadlīs.1
Mistakes, writing Taṣḥīf
Modernism → REFORM
Modes, musical Maḳām
Molluscs → ANIMALS
Monarchy → MONARCHY
Monastery → CHRISTIANITY
Monasticism Rahbāniyya
Money → NUMISMATICS
Mongols → MONGOLIA
Mongoose Nims
Monk Rāhib
Monkey Ḳird
Monogram, imperial Tughra
Monotheism Tawḥīd
Months → TIME
Moon Hilāl; al-Ḳamar
Morphology Ṣarf; Taṣrīf
Mosaics → ART
Mosque → ARCHITECTURE.MONUMENTS
Mountain → MOUNTAINS
Mountain goat Ayyil
Mulberry Tūt
Mule Baghl
Municipality Baladiyya
Murder Ḳatl
Music → MUSIC
Musk Misk
Mussel Ṣadaf
Myrobalanus [in Suppl.] Halīladj
Myrtle [in Suppl.] Ās
Mystic → MYSTICISM
Mysticism → MYSTICISM
Myths → LEGENDS

N

Name Ism
Narcissus Nardjis
Narcotics → DRUGS
Nationalisation Taʾmīm
Nationalism → NATIONALISM
Natron [in Suppl.] Bawraḳ
Natural science → NATURAL SCIENCE
Nature → LITERATURE.POETRY.NATURE
Navigation → NAVIGATION
Navy → MILITARY
Nephrite Yashm
New World → NEW WORLD
Newspaper Djarīda
Nickname Laḳab
Night Layl and Nahār
Night watch ʿAsas
Nightingale Bulbul
Nilometer Miḳyās
Nomadism → NOMADISM
Nomen unitatis *see* Noun of unity
Noun Ism
Noun of unity Waḥda.1

Nourishment → CUISINE
Novel Ḳiṣṣa
Nullity Fāsid wa Bāṭil
Number → NUMBER
Numerals → NUMBER
Numismatics → NUMISMATICS
Nunation Tanwīn

O

Oak ʿAfṣ
Oasis Wāḥa
Oath Ḳasam; Yamīn
Obedience (to God) Ṭāʿa
Obelisk → ARCHITECTURE.MONUMENTS
Oboe Ghayṭa
Obscenity → OBSCENITY
Observatory → ASTRONOMY
Obstetrics → MEDICINE
Ocean → OCEANS AND SEAS
Octagon Muthamman
Oil → CUISINE.FOOD; OIL
Olive Zaytūn
Olive oil Zayt
Omen Faʾl
Oneiromancy → DREAMS
Oneness Waḥda.2
Oneness of being Waḥdat al-Wudjūd
Oneness of witnessing Waḥdat al-Shuhūd
Onomastics → ONOMASTICS
Onomatomancy Ḥurūf, ʿIlm al-
Ophthalmology → MEDICINE
Opium Afyūn
Opposites Aḍdād; Ḍidd
Optics → OPTICS
Orange Nārandj
Orchestra Mehter; *and* → MILITARY.BAND
Order, military → MILITARY.DECORATIONS
Order, mystical → MYSTICISM
Organ Urghan
Organs, body → ANATOMY
Orientalism Mustashriḳūn
Ornament Zakhrafa
Ornithomancy ʿIyāfa
Orphan Yatīm
Orthodoxy Sunna
Oryx Lamṭ; Mahāt
Ostentation Riyāʾ
Ostrich Naʿām
Ottoman Empire → OTTOMAN EMPIRE
Outward meaning Ẓāhir; al-Ẓāhir wa ʾl-Bāṭin
Ownership Milk

P

Paediatrics → LIFE STAGES
Paganism → PRE-ISLAM
Painting → ART
Palace → ARCHITECTURE.MONUMENTS
Palaeography → EPIGRAPHY; WRITING
Palanquin Maḥmal
Paleography *see* Palaeography
Palm Nakhl
Palmoscopy Ikhtilādj
Panarabism → PANARABISM

Pandore Ṭunbūr
Panegyric Madīḥ
Panislamism → PANISLAMISM
Pantheism → RELIGION
Panther Namir
Panturkism → PANTURKISM
Paper Kāg̲h̲ad
Paper seller Warrāḳ
Papyrology → PAPYROLOGY
Papyrus Papyrus
Paradise → PARADISE
Parakeet Babbag̲h̲āʾ
Parasol Miẓalla
Parchment Raḳḳ
Parliament Mad̲j̲lis
Paronomasia Muzāwad̲j̲a; Tad̲j̲nīs
Parrot Babbag̲h̲āʾ
Partnership S̲h̲arika
Party, political → POLITICS
Passion play Taʿziya
Past Māḍī
Pastimes → RECREATION
Pasture Marʿā
Pastures, summer Yaylaḳ
Pastures, winter Ḳi̊s̲h̲laḳ
Patriotism Waṭaniyya
Patronymic Kunya
Pauper Faḳīr; Miskīn
Pavilion → ARCHITECTURE.MONUMENTS
Pay → PAYMENTS
Peace Ṣulḥ
Peacock Ṭāwūs
Peacock throne Tak̲h̲t-i Ṭāwūs
Pearl al-Durr; Luʾluʾ
Pedagogy Tarbiya
Pediatrics *see* Paediatrics
Pen Ḳalam
Pen-name Tak̲h̲alluṣ
Penal law → LAW
People Ḳawm; S̲h̲aʿb
Performers → PROFESSIONS.CRAFTSMEN AND TRADESMEN
Perfume → PERFUME
Periodicals → PRESS
Persian → LANGUAGES.INDO-EUROPEAN.IRANIAN; LINGUISTICS
Person S̲h̲ak̲h̲ṣ
Personal status → LAW
Petroleum → OIL
Pharmacology → PHARMACOLOGY
Philately → PHILATELY
Philology → LINGUISTICS
Philosophy → PHILOSOPHY
Phlebotomist [in Suppl.] Faṣṣād
Phonetics → LINGUISTICS
Photography → ART
Physician → MEDICINE
Physiognomancy Ḳiyāfa
Physiognomy → PHYSIOGNOMY
Pickpocket Ṭarrār
Piety Waraʿ
Pig K̲h̲inzīr
Pigeon Ḥamām
Pilgrimage → PILGRIMAGE
Pillar Rukn
Pillars of Islam → ISLAM
Piracy → PIRACY
Pirate → PIRACY
Plague → PLAGUE
Planet → ASTRONOMY
Plants → FLORA
Plaster D̲j̲iṣṣ
Platonic love → LOVE
Pleasure-garden → ARCHITECTURE.MONUMENTS.GARDENS
Pledge Rahn
Plough Miḥrāt̲h̲
Plural D̲j̲amʿ
Poem → LITERATURE.GENRES.POETRY
Poet S̲h̲āʿir
Poetry → LITERATURE
Poison Summ

Pole al-Ḳuṭb
Police → MILITARY
Politics → POLITICS
Poll-tax Djizya
Polytheism Shirk
Pomegranate blossom [in Suppl.] Djullanār
Porcupine Ḳunfudh
Port Mīnāʾ
Porter Ḥammāl
Possession (by spirits) Zār
Postal history → PHILATELY
Postal service → TRANSPORT
Potash al-Ḳily
Pottery → ART
Powers, balance of Tawāzun al-Sulutāt
Prayer → PRAYER
Prayer direction Ḳibla
Prayer niche Miḥrāb
Pre-emption Shufʿa
Pre-Islam → PRE-ISLAM
Preacher Wāʿiẓ
Precious stones → JEWELRY
Predestination → PREDESTINATION
Preface Muḳaddima
Pregnancy → LIFE STAGES
Presentation issues (coinage) Yādgār
Press → PRESS
Primary school Kuttāb
Principles of grammar Uṣūl
Principles of jurisprudence Uṣūl al-Fiḳh
Principles of religion Uṣūl al-Dīn
Printing Maṭbaʿa
Printing, block → WRITING.MANUSCRIPTS AND BOOKS
Prison Sidjn
Prisoner → MILITARY
Procedure, legal → LAW
Processions Mawākib
Profession of faith Shahāda
Professions → PROFESSIONS
Profit Kasb
Prologue Ibtidāʾ
Property → PROPERTY
Property owner *see* Landowner
Prophecy → PROPHETHOOD
Prophet → MUḤAMMAD, THE PROPHET; PROPHETHOOD
Prophethood → PROPHETHOOD
Prose → LITERATURE
Proselytism → ISLAM
Prosody → LITERATURE.POETRY; METRICS; RHYME
Prostitution [in Suppl.] Bighāʾ
Protection Ḥimāya; Idjāra
Proverb → LITERATURE; PROVERBS
Pulpit Minbar
Punishment → (DIVINE) PUNISHMENT; LAW.PENAL LAW
Punning Tadjnīs
Purity Ṭahāra
Pyramid Haram

Q

Qat Ḳāt
Quadrant Rubʿ
Quail Salwā
Queen mother Wālide Sulṭān
Quicksilver Ziʾbaḳ
Quiddity Māhiyya
Quotation Taḍmīn
Qurʾān → KORAN

R

Rabies   *see* Dog
Radicalism   Taṭarruf
Raid   → RAIDS
Railway   → TRANSPORT
Rain prayer   Istiskāʾ
Rain stone   Yada Tas̲h̲
Rainbow   Ḳaws Ḳuzaḥ
Raisins   Zabīb
Ransoming   [in Suppl.] Fidāʾ
Reading (Koranic)   → KORAN
Recitation   → KORAN.READING
Reconnaissance force   Ṭalīʿa
Records   → ADMINISTRATION
Recreation   → RECREATION
Reed   Ḳaṣab
Reed-pen   Ḳalam
Reed-pipe   G̲h̲ayṭa; Mizmār
Reflection   Fikr
Reform   → REFORM
Register   → ADMINISTRATION. RE-
    CORDS
Religion   → RELIGION
Renewal   Tad̲j̲dīd
Renewer   Mud̲j̲addid
Renunciation   Zuhd
Repentance   Tawba
Representation, legal   Wilāya.1
Reptiles   → ANIMALS
Republic   D̲j̲umhūriyya

Repudiation   Ṭalāḳ
Resemblance   S̲h̲ubha
Resurrection   Ḳiyāma
Retaliation   Ḳiṣāṣ
Retreat   K̲h̲alwa
Revelation   Ilhām; Waḥy
Revolt   T̲h̲awra
Revolution   T̲h̲awra
Rhapsodomancy   Ḳurʿa
Rhetoric   → RHETORIC
Rhinoceros   Karkaddan
Rhyme   → RHYME
Rice   al-Ruzz
Riddle   Lug̲h̲z
Ritual (Islamic)   ʿIbādāt
Rituals   → RITUALS
River   → RIVERS
Road   S̲h̲āriʿ
Robbery, highway   Sariḳa
Robe of honour   K̲h̲ilʿa
Rock-crystal   Billawr
Rod   ʿAṣā; Ḳaḍīb
Rodents   → ANIMALS
Rooster   *see* Cock
Roots   Uṣūl; Uṣūl al-Dīn; Uṣūl al-Fiḳh
Rosary   Subḥa
Rose   Gul; Ward
Ruby   Yāḳūt
Rug   → ART.TAPESTRY

S

Saddle, horse   Sard̲j̲
Saffron   Zaʿfarān
Saint   → SAINTHOOD
Sal-ammoniac   al-Nūs̲h̲ādir
Salamander   Samandal
Sale, contract of   → LAW
Salt   Milḥ

Sand   Raml
Sandalwood   Ṣandal
Sandgrouse   Ḳaṭā
Sappan wood   Baḳḳam
Satire   Hid̲j̲āʾ
Saturn   Zuḥal
Scanning   Wazn.2

Scapulomancy Katif
Scholars ʿUlamāʾ
School, primary Kuttāb
Science → SCIENCE
Scorpion ʿAḳrab
Scribe Kātib; Yazi̊dji̊; [in Suppl.] Dabīr
Scripts → WRITING
Scripture Zabūr
Scripture, tampering with Taḥrīf
Scrupulousness Waraʿ
Sea → OCEANS AND SEAS
Seafaring → NAVIGATION
Seal Khātam; Muhr
Secretary Kātib; [in Suppl.] Dabīr
Sectarianism Ṭāʾifiyya
Semitic languages Sām.2
Sense Ḥiss; Maḥsūsāt
Sermon Khuṭba
Sermoniser Ḳāṣṣ
Servant Khādim
Sesame Simsim
Seven Sabʿ
Seveners → SHIITES.BRANCHES
Sex Djins
Sexuality → SEXUALITY
Shadow play Ḳaragöz; Khayāl al-Ẓill
Shawm Zurna
Sheep [in Suppl.] Ghanam
Sheep-herder Shāwiya
Shell Wadaʿ.2
Shiism → SHIITES
Ship → NAVIGATION
Shrine Zāwiya
Sickness → ILLNESS
Siege warfare Ḥiṣār
Siegecraft Ḥiṣār; Mandjanīḳ
Signature of ruler Tawḳīʿ
Silk Ḥarīr
Silver Fiḍḍa
Silver coinage Wariḳ
Simile Tashbīh
Sin Khaṭīʾa
Singer → MUSIC
Singing → MUSIC.SONG
Skin blemish Shāma
Slander Ḳadhf
Slaughterer [in Suppl.] Djazzār
Slave ʿAbd
Slavery → SLAVERY
Snail Ṣadaf
Snake Ḥayya
Snake-charmer Ḥāwī
Snipe Shunḳub
Soap Ṣābūn
Socialism Ishtirākiyya
Society Djamʿiyya
Soda al-Ḳily; *and see* Natron
Sodium Naṭrūn; *and see* Natron
Sodomy Liwāṭ
Son Ibn
Song → MUSIC
Sorcery → MAGIC
Soul Nafs
Sphere Falak; al-Kura
Spices → CUISINE.FOOD
Spider ʿAnkabūt
Sport → ANIMALS.SPORT; RECREATION
Spouse Zawdj
Springs → GEOGRAPHY.PHYSICAL GEOGRAPHY
Spy Djāsūs
Squares, magical Wafḳ
Stable Iṣṭabl
Stamps → PHILATELY
Standard Sandjaḳ; Sandjaḳ-i Sherīf
Star → ASTRONOMY
Statecraft Siyāsa
Stone Ḥadjar
Stone, rain Yada Tash
Stool Kursī
Story Ḥikāya

Storyteller Ḳāṣṣ; Maddāḥ
Straits → GEOGRAPHY.PHYSICAL GEOGRAPHY.WATERS
Street S̲h̲āriʿ
Stronghold → ARCHITECTURE.MONUMENTS
Substance D̲j̲awhar
Succession (to the caliphate) Walī al-ʿAhd
Successors (of the Companions) Tābiʿūn
Suckling → LIFE STAGES
Sufism → MYSTICISM
Sugar Sukkar
Sugar-cane Ḳaṣab al-Sukkar
Suicide Intiḥār
Sulphur al-Kibrīt
Sultan-fowl [in Suppl.] Abū Barāḳis̲h̲.2
Summer quarters Yaylaḳ
Sun S̲h̲ams
Sundial Mizwala
Sunshade Miẓalla
Superstition → SUPERSTITION
Surety-bond Kafāla
Surgeon D̲j̲arrāḥ
Swahili → KENYA
Sweeper Kannās
Syllable reduction Ziḥāf
Symbolism Ramz.3

T

Tablet Lawḥ
Tailor K̲h̲ayyāṭ
Talisman Tamīma, Tilsam
Tambourine Duff
Tampering (with Scripture) *see* Scripture
Tanner [in Suppl.] Dabbāg̲h̲
Tapestry → ART
Tar Mūmiyāʾ
Tattooing al-Was̲h̲m
Taxation → TAXATION
Tea Čay
Tea-house [in Suppl.] Čāy-k̲h̲āna
Teaching → EDUCATION
Teak Sād̲j̲
Teeth → MEDICINE.DENTISTRY
Tent K̲h̲ayma
Tenth *see* Tithe
Textiles → ART; CLOTHING.MATERIALS
Thankfulness S̲h̲ukr
Theatre → LITERATURE.DRAMA
Theft Sariḳa
Theology → THEOLOGY
Theophany Maẓhar; Tad̲j̲allī
Thief Liṣṣ
Thistle S̲h̲ukāʿā
Thought Fikr
Tide al-Madd wa ʾl-D̲j̲azr
Tiles → ART
Tiller Miḥrāt̲h̲
Time → TIME
Timekeeping → TIME
Tithe ʿUs̲h̲r
Titulature → ONOMASTICS.TITLES
Tobacco → DRUGS.NARCOTICS
Tomb → ARCHITECTURE.MONUMENTS
Toothbrush Miswāk
Tooth-pick Miswāk
Torah Tawrāt
Tower Burd̲j̲
Town Ḳarya; Ḳaṣaba
Toys → RECREATION.GAMES
Trade → FINANCE.COMMERCE; INDUSTRY; NAVIGATION
Trade union Niḳāba

Tradition → LITERATURE.TRADITION-LITERATURE
Transcendentalism Tas͟hbīh wa-Tanzīh
Transition (in poetry) Tak͟hallus̱
Transitivity Taʿaddī
Translation → LITERATURE
Transport → TRANSPORT
Travel → TRAVEL
Treasury → TREASURY
Treaty → TREATIES
Trees → FLORA
Triangle Mut͟hallat͟h
Tribal chief Sayyid
Tribe → TRIBES
Tribute → TREATIES
Trinity, divine Tat͟hlīt͟h
Trope Mad͟jāz
Trousers Sirwāl
Trumpet Būḳ
Trust, charitable Waḳf
Tuareg Ṭawāriḳ
Turban Tulband
Turkic languages → LANGUAGES
Turquoise Fīrūzad͟j
Turtle Sulaḥfā
Twelvers → SHIITES.BRANCHES
Twilight al-S͟hafaḳ
Tyranny Ẓulm

U

Uncle K͟hāl
Underground chamber Sardāb
University D͟jāmiʿa
Uprising T͟hawra
Urban milieux → URBANISM
Usurpation G͟haṣb
Usury Ribā

V

Vehicle → TRANSPORT.WHEELED VEHICLES
Veil → CLOTHING.HEADWARE
Ventilation → ARCHITECTURE.URBAN
Venus Zuhara
Verb Fiʿl
Vernacular → LANGUAGES.AFRO-ASIATIC.ARABIC.ARABIC DIALECTS; LITERATURE.POETRY.VERNACULAR
Verse Āya
Veterinary science → MEDICINE
Vices → VIRTUES AND VICES
Vigils, night Tahad͟jd͟jud
Vikings al-Mad͟jūs
Villa, seashore Yali̊
Village Ḳarya
Vine Karm
Viol Rabāb
Viper Afʿā
Virtues → VIRTUES AND VICES
Vizier Wazīr
Volcanoes → GEOGRAPHY.PHYSICAL GEOGRAPHY
Vow Nad͟hr
Voyage → TRAVEL
Vulture Humā; Nasr

W

Wadis → GEOGRAPHY.PHYSICAL GEOGRAPHY
Wagon *see* Cart
Walnut [in Suppl.] D̲j̲awz
War Ḥarb
Wardrobe → CLOTHING
Washer [in Suppl.] G̲h̲assāl
Washing → ABLUTION
Washing (of the dead) G̲h̲usl
Water Māʾ
Water-carrier Saḳḳāʾ
Waterhouse → ARCHITECTURE. MONUMENTS
Waterways → GEOGRAPHY.PHYSICAL GEOGRAPHY
Waterwheel Nāʿūra
Weapon → MILITARY
Weasel Ibn ʿIrs
Weather → METEOROLOGY
Weaver al-Nassād̲j̲; [in Suppl.] Ḥāʾik
Weaver-bird [in Suppl.] Abū Barāḳis̲h̲.1
Weaving → ART.TEXTILES
Wedding ʿUrs
Week → TIME
Weighing (of coinage) Wazn.1
Weights → WEIGHTS AND MEASUREMENTS
Welfare Maṣlaḥa
Well → ARCHITECTURE.MONUMENTS
Werewolf Ḳuṭrub
Wheat Ḳamḥ
Wild Waḥs̲h̲; Waḥs̲h̲ī
Wind → METEOROLOGY
Wine → WINE
Winter quarters Ḳi̊s̲h̲laḳ
Wisdom Ḥikma
Witness S̲h̲āhid
Wolf D̲h̲iʾb
Women → WOMEN
Wood K̲h̲as̲h̲ab
Wool Ṣūf
World ʿĀlam
Wormwood Afsantīn
Wrestling Pahlawān; Zūrk̲h̲āna
Writing → WRITING

Y

Yoghourt Yog̲h̲urt
Young Ottomans Yeñi ʿOt̲h̲mānli̊lar
Young Turks → TURKEY.OTTOMAN PERIOD

Z

Zaydis → SHIITES
Zero al-Ṣifr
Zodiac Minṭaḳat al-Burūd̲j̲
Zoology → ZOOLOGY
Zoroastrianism → ZOROASTRIANS

INDEX OF SUBJECTS

The Muslim world in the Index of Subjects is the world of today. What once was the greater realm of Persia is given here under Central Asia, Caucasus and Afghanistan, just as part of the region once governed by the Ottoman Empire is covered by individual countries in Eastern Europe and in the Near East. States established in the past century, such as Jordan and Lebanon, are given right of place. Countries with a long history of Islam, e.g. Egypt and Syria, have a subsection "modern period", where *Encyclopaedia* articles covering the 19th and 20th centuries have been brought together.

The *mīlādī* year of death has been used for dating purposes. Thus, when an individual is listed as "15th-century", the dating refers to his/her year of death C.E. This method of dating is regrettably inaccurate in some cases, e.g. when an individual died in the first years of a new century.

References in regular typeface are to *Encyclopaedia* articles; those printed in boldface type indicate the main article. Entries in capitals and following an arrow refer to lemmata in the Index of Subjects itself. Thus, in the case of

> BEDOUINS **Badw**; Biʾr; Dawār; Ghanīma; Ghazw; al-Hidjar; Thaʾr
> *see also* Liṣṣ; ʿUrf.2.I; *and* → LAW.CUSTOMARY; NOMADISM; SAUDI ARABIA; TRIBES.ARABIAN PENINSULA

Badw; Biʾr; Dawār; Ghanīma; Ghazw; al-Hidjar, Thaʾr refer to articles in the *Encyclopaedia* that deal primarily with Bedouins, Badw being *the* article on Bedouins; Liṣṣ and ʿUrf.2.I refer to an article or section of an article in the *Encyclopaedia* that contains information of interest relating to Bedouins; and LAW.CUSTOMARY; NOMADISM; SAUDI ARABIA; TRIBES.ARABIAN PENINSULA refer the reader to analogous entries in the Index of Subjects.

Below is the Index of Subjects proper, in which all *Encyclopaedia* articles are grouped under one or more general entries. For facility in finding a specific word or topic (e.g. "abstinence" or "sports"), the reader is referred to the List of Entries on p. 1.

A

ʿABBĀSIDS → CALIPHATE

ABLUTION **Ghusl**; Istindjāʾ; Istinshāḳ; al-Masḥ ʿalā ʾl-Khuffayn; Tayammum; **Wuḍūʾ**
see also Djanāba; Ḥadath; Ḥammām; Ḥawḍ; Ḥayḍ; Ṭahāra

ABYSSINIA → ETHIOPIA

ADMINISTRATION Barīd; Bayt al-Māl; Daftar; Diplomatic; **Dīwān**; Djizya; Kātib; [in Suppl.] Demography.I
see also al-Ḳalḳashandī.1; al-Ṣūlī; ʿUmar (I) b. al-Khaṭṭāb; *for specific caliphates or dynasties* → CALIPHATE; DYNASTIES; OTTOMAN EMPIRE; *and* → ANDALUSIA.ADMINISTRATION
diplomatic → DIPLOMACY
financial ʿAṭāʾ; Bayt al-Māl; Daftar; Dār al-Ḍarb; Ḳānūn.ii and iii; Kasb; Khāzin; Khaznadār; Makhzan; Muṣādara.2; Mustawfī; Rūznāma; Siyāḳat; Zimām
see also Dhahab; Fiḍḍa; Ḥisba; Tadbīr.1; Waḳf; *and* → NUMISMATICS; OTTOMAN EMPIRE.ADMINISTRATION; PAYMENTS
fiscal → TAXATION
functionaries ʿĀmil; Amīn; Amīr; Amīr al-Ḥādjdj; ʿArīf; Dawādār; Djahbadh; Ḥisba; Īshīk-āḳāsī; Kalāntar; Kātib; Khāzin; Mushīr; Mushrif; Mustakhridj; Mustawfī; Parwānačī; Raʾīs; Ṣāḥib al-Madīna; Wālī; Wazīr; [in Suppl.] Dabīr
see also Barīd; Consul; Fatwā; Fuyūdj; Kōtwāl; Malik al-Tudjdjār; Mawlā; Muwādaʿa.2; Waẓīfa.1; *and* → LAW.OFFICES; MILITARY.OFFICES; OTTOMAN EMPIRE
geography → GEOGRAPHY.ADMINISTRATIVE
legal → LAW
military → MILITARY
Mongol → MONGOLIA.MONGOLS
Ottoman → OTTOMAN EMPIRE
records **Daftar**.I; Ḳānūn.iii
and → DOCUMENTS; OTTOMAN EMPIRE.ADMINISTRATION
archives Dār al-Maḥfūẓāt al-ʿUmūmiyya; Geniza
and → OTTOMAN EMPIRE.ADMINISTRATION

ADOPTION [in Suppl.] ʿĀr
see also ʿĀda.iii; Yatīm.2.iii

ADULTERY Ḳadhf; Liʿān; **Zinā**
see also al-Marʾa.2
punishment of Ḥadd

AFGHANISTAN Afghān; **Afghānistān**
architecture → ARCHITECTURE.REGIONS
dynasties Aḥmad Shāh Durrānī; Ghaznawids; Ghūrids; Kart
see also Zunbīl; *and* → DYNASTIES.AFGHANISTAN AND INDIA

historians of Sayfī Harawī

language → LANGUAGES.INDO-IRANIAN.IRANIAN

modern period Djāmiʿa; Dustūr.v; Khaybar; Madjlis.4.B; Maṭbaʿa.5

see also Muhādjir.3

statesmen ʿAbd al-Raḥmān Khān; Ayyūb Khān; Dūst Muḥammad; Ḥabīb Allāh Khān; Muḥammad Dāwūd Khān; Shīr ʿAlī; [in Suppl.] Amān Allāh

see also [in Suppl.] Faḳīr of Ipi

physical geography Afghānistān.i

mountains Hindū Kush; Kūh-i Bābā; Safīd Kūh

see also Afghānistān.i

waters Dehās; Hāmūn; Harī Rūd; Kābul.1; Ḳunduz.1; Kurram; Murghāb; Pandjhīr; [in Suppl.] Gūmāl

see also Afghānistān.i; Zirih

population Abdālī; Čahār Aymak; Durrānī; Ghalča; Ghalzay; Moghols; Mohmand; Türkmen.3; [in Suppl.] Demography.III; Hazāras

see also Afghān.i; Afghānistān.ii; Khaladj; Özbeg.1.d; Wazīrīs; [in Suppl.] Djirga

toponyms

ancient Būshandj; Bust; Dihistān; Djuwayn.3; Farmūl; Fīrūzkūh.1; Khōst; Khudjistān; Marw al-Rūdh; al-Rukhkhadj; Ṭālaḳān.1; Ṭukhāristān; Walwālīdj; Zābul; Zamīndāwar

present-day

districts Andarāb.1; Bādghīs; Farwān; Ḳūhistān.3; Lamghānāt

regions Badakhshān; Dardistān; Djūzdjān; Ghardjistān; Ghūr; Kāfiristān; Khōst; Nangrahār; Sīstān; Zābul; [in Suppl.] Hazāradjāt

see also Pandjhīr; Turkistān.2

towns Andkhūy; Balkh; Bāmiyān; Djām; Farāh; Faryāb.1; Gardīz; Ghazna; Girishk; Harāt; Kābul.2; Ḳandahār; Karūkh; Khulm; Ḳunduz.2; Maymana; Mazār-i Sharīf; Rūdhbār.1; Sabzawār.2; Sar-i Pul; Shibarghān; Ṭālaḳān.3; [in Suppl.] Djalālābād

AFRICA Lamlam; Zandj

Central Africa Cameroons; Congo; Gabon; [in Suppl.] Čad

see also Muḥammad Bello; al-Murdjibī; Waḳf.VIII; [in Suppl.] Demography.V

for individual countries → CHAD; CONGO; ZAIRE

literature Hausa.iii; Kano; Shāʿir.5 and 6; Shiʿr.7; Taʾrīkh.II.5

physical geography

deserts Sāḥil.2

population Kanuri; Kotoko; Shuwa; Ṭawāriḳ; Tubu; Zaghāwa

East Africa Djibūtī; Eritrea; Ḥabesh; Ḳumr; Madagascar; Mafia; Somali; Sūdān; Tanzania; Uganda; Zandjibār

see also Emīn Pasha; Muṣāḥib; Nikāḥ.II.5; al-Nudjūm; Shīrāzī; Zandj.1; Zār.1; [in Suppl.] Djarīda.viii
for individual countries → DJIBOUTI, REPUBLIC OF; ETHIOPIA; KENYA; MADAGASCAR; MALAWI; SOMALIA; SUDAN; TANZANIA
architecture Manāra.3; Masdjid.VI; Mbweni; Minbar.4
see also Shungwaya
festivals Mawlid.2; Nawrūz.2
languages Eritrea.iv; Ḥabash.iv; Kūsh; Nūba.3; Somali.5; Sūdān.2; Swahili; Yao
see also Ḳumr; Madagascar
literature Miʿrādj.3; Somali.6; Taʾrīkh.II.6
see also Kitābāt.6; *and* → KENYA.SWAHILI LITERATURE
mysticism Ṭarīḳa.II.3; Ziyāra.10
physical geography
waters Atbara; Baḥr al-Ghazāl.1; Shebelle
see also Baḥr al-Hind; Baḥr al-Zandj
population ʿAbābda; ʿĀmir; Antemuru; Bedja; Beleyn; Bishārīn; Danḳalī; Djaʿaliyyūn; Galla; Māryā; Mazrūʿī; Oromo; Somali.1; Yao; [in Suppl.] Demography.V
see also Diglal; Lamlam; al-Manāṣir
North Africa Algeria; Ifrīḳiya; Lībiyā; Maghāriba; al-Maghrib (2x); Mashāriḳa; Tunisia
see also al-ʿArab.v; ʿArabiyya.A.iii.3; Badw.II.d; Djaysh.iii; Ghuzz.ii; Ḥawz; Kharbga; Kitābāt.4; Lamṭ; Leo Africanus; Libās.ii; Maḥalla; Mānū; Ṣaff.3; Sipāhī.2; ʿUrf.2.I.B; Waḳf.II.3; [in Suppl.] ʿĀr; *and* → DYNASTIES.SPAIN AND NORTH AFRICA
for individual countries → ALGERIA; LIBYA; MOROCCO; TUNISIA
architecture → ARCHITECTURE.REGIONS
modern period Baladiyya.3; Djamāʿa.ii; Djarīda.B; Hilāl; Ḳawmiyya.ii
and → ALGERIA; LIBYA; MOROCCO; TUNISIA
mysticism Ṭarīḳa.II.2; Walī.2; Zāwiya.2
see also Ziyāra.4; *and* → MYSTICISM.MYSTICS
physical geography Atlas; Reg; Rīf; Sabkha; al-Ṣaḥrāʾ; Shaṭṭ; Tall; Tasili; Wādī.2
and → *the section Physical Geography under individual countries*
population Ahaggar; Berbers; Dukkāla; Khulṭ; al-Maʿḳil; Shāwiya.1; Ṭawāriḳ; Tubu; [in Suppl.] Demography.IV
see also Khumayr; Kūmiya; al-Manāṣir; Mandīl; Moors; *and* → BERBERS
Southern Africa Mozambique; South Africa
see also [in Suppl.] Djarīda.ix
for individual countries → MOZAMBIQUE
West Africa Côte d'Ivoire; Dahomey; Gambia; Ghana; Guinea; Liberia; Mali;

Mūrītāniyā; Niger; Nigeria; Senegal; Sierra Leone; Togo
see also Azalay; Kitābāt.5; Ḳunbi Ṣāliḥ; al-Maghīlī; Malam; Murīdiyya; Sūdān (Bilād al-).2; Sulṭān.3; Tādmakkat; Takfīr.2; Takidda; Takrūr; ʿUlamāʾ.7; Waḳf.VIII
for individual countries → Benin; Guinea; Ivory Coast; Mali; Mauritania; Niger; Nigeria; Senegal; Togo
architecture Ḳunbi Ṣāliḥ; Masdjid.VII
empires Mande; Oyo; Songhay.3
see also Muḥammad b. Abī Bakr; Samori Ture; Takrūr; ʿUthmān b. Fūdī
languages Hausa.ii; Nūba.3; Shuwa.2; Songhay.1; Sūdān (Bilād al-).3
see also Fulbe; Kanuri; Senegal.1; *and* → Languages.afro-asiatic.arabic
literature → Africa.central africa
mysticism Walī.9; Zāwiya.3; Ziyāra.9
and → Mysticism.mystics
physical geography
deserts Sāḥil.2
mountains Fūta Djallon; Tibesti
oases Wāḥa.2
waters Niger
population Fulbe; Ḥarṭānī; Hausa.i; Ifoghas; Kunta; Songhay.2; Ṭawāriḳ; Tukulor; Wangara; Yoruba; [in Suppl.] Demography.V
see also Lamlam; Mande; Takrūr

Agriculture **Filāḥa**; Marʿā; Raʿiyya
see also Mazraʿa; Mughārasa; Musāḳāt; Muzāraʿa; Taḳdīr.2; Taḳwīm.2; [in Suppl.] Akkār; *and* → Botany; Flora; Irrigation
agricultural cooperatives **Taʿāwun**
products Ḳahwa; Ḳamḥ; Karm; Ḳaṣab al-Sukkar; Khamr.2; Ḳuṭn; Nakhl; Nārandj; al-Ruzz; Shaʿīr; [in Suppl.] Djāwars; Hindibāʾ
see also Ḥarīr; *and* → Cuisine.foods
terms Āgdāl; Baʿl.2.b; Čiftlik; Ghūṭa; Maṭmūra
tools Miḥrāth
treatises on Abu ʾl-Khayr al-Ishbīlī; Ibn Wāfid; Ibn Waḥshiyya; al-Ṭighnarī

Albania **Arnawutluḳ**; Iskender Beg; Ḳarā Maḥmūd Pasha
see also Muslimūn.1.B.4; Sāmī; *and* → Ottoman Empire
toponyms Aḳ Ḥiṣār.4; Awlonya; Delvina; Drač; Elbasan; Ergiri; Korča; Krujë; Lesh; Tiran

Alchemy Dhahab; Fiḍḍa; al-Iksīr; al-Kibrīt; **al-Kīmiyāʾ**; Ziʾbaḳ
see also Ḳārūn; Maʿdin; al-Nūshādir; Takwīn; *and* → Metallurgy; Mineralogy

alchemists D̲j̲ābir b. Ḥayyān; Ibn Umayl; Ibn Waḥs̲h̲iyya; al-Rāzī, Abū Bakr; al-Ṭug̲h̲rāʾī; [in Suppl.] Abu ʾl-Ḥasan al-Anṣārī; al-D̲j̲ildakī
  see also Hirmis; K̲h̲ālid b. Yazīd b. Muʿāwiya; [in Suppl.] al-D̲j̲awbarī, ʿAbd al-Raḥīm; Findiriskī; Ibn Daḳīḳ al-ʿĪd
equipment al-Anbīḳ; al-Ut̲h̲āl
terms Rukn.2; Ṭabīʿa.3; Zuḥal; Zuhara

ALGERIA **Algeria**
  see also ʿArabiyya.A.iii.3; ʿArs̲h̲; Ḥalḳa; Zmāla.3; *and* → BERBERS; DYNASTIES. SPAIN AND NORTH AFRICA
architecture → ARCHITECTURE.REGIONS.NORTH AFRICA
dynasties ʿAbd al-Wādids; Fāṭimids; Ḥammādids; Rustamids
  and → DYNASTIES.SPAIN AND NORTH AFRICA
literature Ḥawfī; Malḥūn
modern period D̲j̲āmiʿa; D̲j̲arīda.i.B; Ḥizb.i; Ḥukūma.iv; Maʿārif.2.B; Mad̲j̲lis. 4.A.xx
  reform Ibn Bādīs; (al-)Ibrāhīmī; Salafiyya.1(b)
    see also Fallāḳ
Ottoman period (1518-1830) ʿAbd al-Ḳādir b. Muḥyī al-Dīn; Algeria.ii.(2); ʿArūd̲j̲; Ḥasan Ag̲h̲a; Ḥasan Baba; Ḥasan Pas̲h̲a; al-Ḥusayn; Ḥusayn Pas̲h̲a, Mezzomorto; K̲h̲ayr al-Dīn Pas̲h̲a
  see also Sipāhī.2
physical geography Algeria.i
  mountains ʿAmūr; Atlas; Awrās; Bībān; D̲j̲urd̲j̲ura; Kabylia; Wans̲h̲arīs
    see also Tasili
  salt flats Tag̲h̲āza
population Ahaggar; Algeria.iii; Berbers; Zmāla.1
  see also Kabylia; *and* → BERBERS
religion Algeria.iii; S̲h̲āwiya.1
  mystical orders ʿAmmāriyya; Raḥmāniyya
    see also Darḳāwa; Ziyāniyya; *and* → MYSTICISM
toponyms
  ancient Ars̲h̲gūl; As̲h̲īr; al-Manṣūra; Sadrāta; [in Suppl.] Hunayn
  present day
    oases Biskra; Ḳanṭara.1; al-Ḳulayʿa.2.1; Laghouat; Sūf; Wargla; [in Suppl.] Gourara
    regions Ḥuḍna; Mzāb; Sāḥil.1.b; Tuwāt; Zāb
    towns Adrar.1; al-ʿAnnāba; Ārzāw; ʿAyn Temus̲h̲ent; Bid̲j̲āya; Biskra; Bulayda; Colomb-Béchar; al-D̲j̲azāʾir; Djidjelli; G̲h̲ardāya; Ḳalʿat Banī ʿAbbās; Ḳalʿat Huwwāra; al-Ḳulayʿa.2.2; Ḳusṭanṭīna; Laghouat; al-Madiyya; Masīla; Milyāna; al-Muʿaskar; Mustag̲h̲ānim; Nadrūma; Saʿīda; S̲h̲ars̲h̲al; Sīdī Bu ʾl-ʿAbbās; Tadallīs; Tāhart; Tanas; Tebessa;

Tilimsān; Tindūf; Ṭubna; Tuggurt; Wahrān; Wargla

ALMS Khayr; **Ṣadaḳa**; **Zakāt**
see also Waḳf

ALPHABET **Abdjad**; Ḥarf; Ḥisāb; **Ḥurūf al-Hidjāʾ**
see also Djafr; Khaṭṭ; [in Suppl.] Budūḥ; *and* → WRITING.SCRIPTS
for the letters of the Arabic and Persian alphabets, see Ḍād; Dāl; Dhāl; Djīm; Fāʾ; Ghayn; Hāʾ; Ḥāʾ; Hamza; Kāf; Ḳāf; Khāʾ; Lām; Mīm; Nūn; Pāʾ; Rāʾ; Ṣād; Sīn and Shīn; Tāʾ and Ṭāʾ; Thāʾ; Wāw; Yāʾ; Ẓāʾ; Zāy
secret → CRYPTOGRAPHY

ANATOMY Djism; Katif; **Tashrīḥ**; [in Suppl.] Aflīmūn
see also Ishāra; Khiḍāb; Ḳiyāfa; Shāma; [in Suppl.] Dam
body parts
chest **Ṣadr**
eye **ʿAyn**; al-Kuḥl; Manāẓir; Ramad
see also Zaʿfarān.2; *and* → MEDICINE.OPHTHALMOLOGY; OPTICS
hair ʿAfṣ; Afsantīn; Ḥinnāʾ; Liḥya-yi Sherīf; **Shaʿr**
see also [in Suppl.] Ḥallāḳ
limb Yamīn
organs Kabid; Ḳalb
teeth → MEDICINE.DENTISTRY
treatises on
Turkish Shānī-zāde
and → MEDICINE.MEDICAL HANDBOOKS/ENCYCLOPAEDIAS

ANDALUSIA **al-Andalus**; Gharb al-Andalus; Moriscos; Mozarab; Mudéjar; Sharḳ al-Andalus
see also Kitābāt.3; Libās.ii; Māʾ.7; al-Madjūs; Moors; Muwallad.1; Safīr.2.b; Ṣāʾifa.2; al-Thughūr.2; *and* → DYNASTIES.SPAIN AND NORTH AFRICA; SPAIN
administration Dīwān.iii; Ḳūmis; Ṣāḥib al-Madīna; Ẓahīr
see also Fatā; Waḳf.II.4
architecture → ARCHITECTURE.REGIONS
conquest of al-Andalus.vi.1; Mūsā b. Nuṣayr; Ṭāriḳ b. Ziyād
dynasties al-Murābiṭūn.4; al-Muwaḥḥidūn; Umayyads.In Spain; Zīrids.2; [in Suppl.] ʿAzafī
see also al-Andalus.vi; (Banū) Ḳasī; Ṭawīl, Banu; ʿUmar b. Ḥafṣūn; *and* → DYNASTIES.SPAIN AND NORTH AFRICA
reyes de taifas period (11th century) ʿAbbādids; Afṭasids; ʿĀmirids; Dhu ʾl-Nūnids; Djahwarids; Ḥammūdids; Hūdids; **Mulūk al-Ṭawāʾif**.2; Razīn, Banū; Ṭāhirids.2; Tudjīb

see also Balansiya; Dāniya; G̲h̲arnāṭa; Ibn G̲h̲albūn; Ibn Ras̲h̲īḳ, Abū Muḥammad; Is̲h̲bīliya; Ḳurṭuba; Mud̲j̲āhid, al-Muwaffaḳ; Parias; al-Sīd; Zuhayr

governors until Umayyad conquest   ʿAbd al-Malik b. Ḳaṭan; ʿAbd al-Raḥmān al-G̲h̲āfiḳī; Abu ʾl-K̲h̲aṭṭār; al-Ḥurr b. ʿAbd al-Raḥmān al-T̲h̲aḳafī; al-Ḥusām b. Ḍirār; Tud̲j̲īb; ʿUbayd Allāh b. Ḥabḥāb; Yūsuf b. ʿAbd al-Raḥmān al-Fihrī
   see also al-Andalus.vi.2; Kalb b. Wabara; Mūsā b. Nuṣayr; al-Ṣumayl

literature   Aljamía; ʿArabiyya.B.Appendix; Fahrasa; Zad̲j̲al
   and → ANDALUSIA.SCHOLARS.HISTORIANS; LITERATURE.POETRY.ANDALU-SIAN

mysticism   → MYSTICISM.MYSTICS

physical geography   → SPAIN

scholars

   astronomers   Abu ʾl-Ṣalt Umayya (*and* Umayya, Abu ʾl-Ṣalt); al-Biṭrūd̲j̲ī; D̲j̲ābir b. Aflaḥ; Ibn al-Ṣaffār; Ibn al-Samḥ; al-Mad̲j̲rīṭī; Muḥammad b. ʿUmar; al-Zarḳālī
      see also Zīd̲j̲.iii.4

   grammarians   Abū Ḥayyān al-G̲h̲arnāṭī; al-Baṭalyawsī; D̲j̲ūdī al-Mawrūrī; Ibn al-ʿArīf, al-Ḥusayn; Ibn ʿĀṣim; Ibn al-Iflīlī; Ibn K̲h̲ātima; Ibn al-Ḳūṭiyya; Ibn Maḍāʾ; Ibn Mālik; Ibn Sīda; al-Rabaḥī; al-S̲h̲alawbīn; al-S̲h̲antamarī; al-S̲h̲arīf al-G̲h̲arnatī; al-S̲h̲arīs̲h̲ī; al-Zubaydī; [in Suppl.] Ibn His̲h̲ām al-Lak̲h̲mī
      see also al-S̲h̲āṭibī, Abū Isḥāḳ; *and* → *the section Lexicographers below*

   geographers   Abū ʿUbayd al-Bakrī; Ibn ʿAbd al-Munʿim al-Ḥimyarī; Ibn G̲h̲ālib; al-Idrīsī; al-ʿUd̲h̲rī; al-Warrāḳ, Muḥammad; al-Zuhrī, Muḥammad

   historians   al-Ḍabbī, Abū D̲j̲aʿfar; Ibn al-Abbār, Abu ʿAbd Allāh; Ibn ʿAbd al-Malik al-Marrākus̲h̲ī; Ibn Bas̲h̲kuwāl; Ibn Burd.I; Ibn al-Faraḍī; Ibn G̲h̲ālib; Ibn Ḥayyān; Ibn ʿId̲h̲ārī; Ibn al-K̲h̲aṭīb; Ibn al-Ḳūṭiyya; Ibn Saʿīd al-Mag̲h̲ribī; al-Maḳḳarī; al-Rus̲h̲āṭī; al-Warrāḳ, Muḥammad
      see also al-S̲h̲aḳundī; al-ʿUd̲h̲rī; *and* → DYNASTIES.SPAIN AND NORTH AFRICA

   jurists   al-Bād̲j̲ī; al-Dānī; al-Ḥumaydī; Ibn Abī Zamanayn; Ibn ʿĀṣim; Ibn al-Faraḍī; Ibn Ḥabīb, Abū Marwān; Ibn Ḥazm, Abū Muḥammad; Ibn Maḍāʾ; Ibn Rus̲h̲ayd; ʿĪsā b. Dīnār; ʿIyāḍ b. Mūsā; al-Ḳalaṣādī; al-Ḳurṭubī, Abū ʿAbd Allāh; al-Ḳurṭubī, Yaḥyā; (al-)Mund̲h̲ir b. Saʿīd; S̲h̲abṭūn; al-Ṭulayṭulī; al-Ṭurṭūs̲h̲ī; al-ʿUtbī, Abū ʿAbd Allāh; al-Wakkas̲h̲ī; Yaḥyā b. Yaḥyā al-Layt̲h̲ī; [in Suppl.] Ibn Rus̲h̲d
      see also al-K̲h̲us̲h̲anī; Mālikiyya; Ṣāʿid al-Andalusī; S̲h̲ūrā.2; S̲h̲urṭa.2; [in Suppl.] Ibn al-Rūmiyya

   lexicographers   Ibn Sīda; al-Zubaydī

toponyms → SPAIN

ANGELOLOGY **Malāʾika**
see also ʿAdhāb al-Ḳabr; Dīk; Iblīs; Ḳarīn; Rūḥāniyya; Siḥr
angels ʿAzāzīl; Djabrāʾīl; Hārūt wa-Mārūt; Isrāfīl; ʿIzrāʿīl; Mīkāl; Munkar wa-Nakīr; Riḍwān
see also al-Zabāniyya

ANIMALS Dābba; **Ḥayawān**
see also Badw; (Djazīrat) al-ʿArab.v; Farw; Hind.i.l; Khāṣī; Marbaṭ; [in Suppl.] Djazzār; *and* → ZOOLOGY
and art al-Asad; Fahd; Fīl; Ḥayawān.6; Karkaddan; Maʿdin; Namir and Nimr; [in Suppl.] Arnab
see also Zakhrafa
and proverbs Ḥayawān.2; Mathal
and see articles on individual animals, in particular Afʿā; Dhiʾb; Fahd; Ghurāb; Ḳaṭā; Khinzīr; Ḳird; Lamṭ; Naml; Yarbūʿ
animals
antelopes Ghazāl; Lamṭ; Mahāt
arachnoids ʿAḳrab; ʿAnkabūt
bats **Waṭwāṭ**
birds Babbaghāʾ; Dadjādja; Dīk; Ghurāb; Ḥamām; Hudhud; Humā; Ḳaṭā; Naʿām; Nasr; Nuḥām; al-Rukhkh; Salwā; Shunḳub; **al-Ṭāʾir**; Ṭāwūs; Ṭoghrïl; ʿUḳāb; Wāḳwāḳ.4; [in Suppl.] Abū Barāḳish
see also Bayzara; Bulbul; ʿIyāfa; al-Ramādī; Sonḳor; Timsāḥ
camels **Ibil**
see also (Djazīrat) al-ʿArab.v; Badw.II.c and d; Kārwān; Raḥīl; Wasm; [in Suppl.] Djammāl; *and* → TRANSPORT.CARAVANS
canines Dhiʾb; Fanak; Ibn Āwā; Kalb; Salūḳī; Thaʿlab; [in Suppl.] Ḍabuʿ
crustaceans **Saraṭān**
domesticated Baḳar; Fīl; Ibil; Kalb; Khinzīr; Nims; [in Suppl.] Djāmūs; Ghanam
see also Shāwiya.2; *and* → ANIMALS.EQUINES
equines Badw.II; Baghl; **Faras**; Ḥimār; **Khayl**
see also Fāris; Furūsiyya; Ḥazīn; Ibn Hudhayl; Ibn al-Mundhir; Iṣṭabl; Marbaṭ; Maydān; Mīr-Ākhūr; Sardj
felines ʿAnāḳ; al-Asad; Fahd; Namir and Nimr; Sinnawr
fish **Samak**
see also al-Ṭāʾir
insects Dhubāb; Djarād; Ḳaml; Naḥl; Naml; Nāmūs.2; **al-Ṭāʾir**
molluscs **Ṣadaf**

reptiles Afʿā; Ḍabb; Ḥayya; Ḥirbāʾ; Samandal; Sulaḥfā; Timsāḥ
see also Ādam; Almās
rodents Yarbūʿ; [in Suppl.] Faʾr
sport Bayzara; Fahd; Furūsiyya; Ḥamām; Khinzīr; Mahāt; [in Suppl.] Ḍabuʿ
see also Čakïrdjï-bashï; Doghandjï; Kurds.iv.C.5; *and* → HUNTING
transformation into Ḥayawān.3; Ḳird; **Maskh**
wild *in addition to the above, see also* Ayyil; Fanak; Fīl; Ibn ʿIrs; Karkaddan; Ḳird; Ḳunfudh; Zarāfa; [in Suppl.] Arnab; Faras al-Māʾ
see also Waḥsh; *and* → HUNTING

ANTHROPOMORPHISM Ḥashwiyya; Karrāmiyya; **Tashbīh wa-Tanzīh**
see also Bayān b. Samʿān al-Tamīmī; Djism; Hishām b. al-Ḥakam; Ḥulmāniyya; al-Muḳannaʿ

APOSTASY Mulḥid; Murtadd
see also Ḳatl; *and* → HERESY

ARABIAN PENINSULA → BAHRAIN; KUWAIT; OMAN; QATAR; SAUDI ARABIA; UNITED ARAB EMIRATES; YEMEN; *and the section Arabian Peninsula under* ARCHITECTURE.REGIONS; DYNASTIES; PRE-ISLAM; TRIBES

ARCHAEOLOGY → ARCHITECTURE.REGIONS; EPIGRAPHY; *and the section Toponyms under individual countries*
Turkish archaeologists ʿOthmān Ḥamdī

ARCHITECTURE **Architecture**; Bināʾ
see also Kitābāt; *and* → MILITARY
architects Ḳāsim Agha; Khayr al-Dīn; Sinān
decoration Fusayfisāʾ; Kāshī; Khaṭṭ; Parčīn-kārī; Tughra.2(d)
materials Djiṣṣ; Labin
see also Bināʾ
monuments
aqueducts Ḳanṭara.5 and 6
see also Faḳīr; Sinān
baths **Ḥammām**; Ḥammām al-Ṣarakh
bridges **Djisr**; Djisr Banāt Yaʿḳūb; Djisr al-Ḥadīd; Djisr al-Shughr
see also Dizfūl; Ḳanṭara; Sayḥān
churches → CHRISTIANITY
dams **Band**
see also Dizfūl; Sāwa.2.i; Shushtar; [in Suppl.] Abū Sinbil; *and* → HYDROLOGY
gardens **Būstān**; Ḥāʾir

see also Bostāndjï; Gharnāṭa.B; Ḥawḍ; Māʾ.12; Srīnagar.2; Yalï; *and* → FLORA; LITERATURE.POETRY.NATURE

gates **Bāb**; Bāb-i Humāyūn; Ḥarrān.ii.d

lighthouses **Manār**; al-Nāẓūr

mausolea → ARCHITECTURE.MONUMENTS.TOMBS

mills **Ṭāḥūn**

monasteries → CHRISTIANITY; MYSTICISM

mosques Ḥawḍ; Külliyye; Manāra; **Masdjid**; Miḥrāb; Minbar

see also ʿAnaza; Bāb.i; Bahw; Balāṭ; Dikka; Khaṭīb; Muṣallā.2; Zāwiya.1

individual mosques Aya Sofya; al-Azhar; Ḥarrān.ii.(b); Ḥusaynī Dālān; Kaʿba; al-Ḳarawiyyīn; Ḳubbat al-Ṣakhra; Ḳuṭb Mīnār; al-Masdjid al-Aḳṣā; al-Masdjid al-Ḥarām; Zaytūna.1

see also Anḳara; Architecture; Bahmanīs; Dhār.2; Djām; Edirne; Ḥamāt; Ḥimṣ; Kāẓimayn; Ḳazwīn; Maʿarrat al-Nuʿmān; Makka.4; Sinān

obelisks **Misalla**

palaces **Sarāy**

see also Balāṭ

individual palaces Čirāghān; Ḳaṣr al-Ḥayr al-Gharbī; Ḳaṣr al-Ḥayr al-Sharḳī; Kayḳubādiyya; Khirbat al-Mafdjar; Khirbat al-Minya; Ḳubādābād; Maḥall; al-Mushattā; Ṭopḳapï Sarāyï; al-Ukhayḍir; Yïldïz Sarāyï; [in Suppl.] Djabal Says

see also Gharnāṭa.B; Khirbat al-Bayḍāʾ; Ḳubbat al-Hawāʾ; Lashkar-i Bāzār

pavilions Köshk

see also Yalï

strongholds Burdj; Ḥiṣār; **Ḥiṣn**; Ḳaṣaba; Sūr

see also al-ʿAwāṣim; Bāb.ii; al-Ḳalʿa; Ribāṭ; al-Thughūr; Udj

individual strongholds Abū Safyān; Āgra; Alamūt.i.; Alindjaḳ; ʿAmādiya; Anadolu Ḥiṣārï; Anamur; Anapa; Asīrgarh; Atak; Bāb al-Abwāb; Bālā Ḥiṣār; Balāṭunus; Barzūya; Baynūn; Bhakkar; Čanděrī; Čirmen; al-Dārūm; Djaʿbar; al-Djarbāʾ; Gaban; Gāwilgaŕh; Ghumdān; Gök Tepe; Golkonďā; Ḥadjar al-Nasr; Hānsī; Ḥarrān.ii.(a); Ḥiṣn al-Akrād; Ḥiṣn Kayfā; Iṣṭakhr; Kakhtā; Ḳalʿat Nadjm; Ḳalʿat al-Shaḳīf; Ḳalāwdhiya; Ḳalʿe-i Sefīd; Ḳandahār; Kanizsa; al-Karak; Kawkab al-Hawāʾ; Kharāna; Khartpert; Khěrla; Khotin; Khunāṣira; Kilāt-i Nādirī; Ḳoron; Ḳoyul Ḥiṣār; Lanbasar; Lüleburgaz; Mānďū; Manōhar; al-Marḳab; Muďgal; Narnālā; Parendā; al-Rāwandān; Rōhtās; Rūm Ḳalʿesi; Rūmeli Ḥiṣārï; Ṣahyūn; Shalbaṭarra; Softa; al-Ṣubayba; Umm al-Raṣāṣ; Yeñi Ḳalʿe; [in Suppl.] Bādiya; Bubashtru; al-Dīkdān; Firrīm

see also Ashīr; Bahmanīs; Bīdar; Dawlatābād; Diyār Bakr; Ḥimṣ;

Kawkabān.2; Khursābād; Maḥall; Māhūr; Thādj

tombs **Ḳabr**; **Ḳubba**; **Maḳbara**; Mashhad; **Turba**

see also Muthamman; Walī.4, 5 and 8; Zāwiya; Ziyāra

individual buildings Baḳīʿ al-Gharḳad; Golkondá; Ḥarrān.ii.(c); Maklī; Nafīsa; Rādkān; Sahsarām; Tādj Maḥall

see also Abarḳūh; Abū Ayyūb al-Anṣārī; Abū Madyan; Āgra; Aḥmad al-Badawī; Aḥmad Yasawī; Bahmanīs; Barīd Shāhīs.II; Djahāngīr; Ghāzī Miyān; Gunbadh-i Ḳābūs; Ḥimṣ; Imāmzāda; Karak Nūḥ; Ḳarbalāʾ; Ḳazwīn; al-Khalīl; Ḳubbat al-Hawāʾ; Maʿarrat al-Nuʿmān; al-Madīna; Sulṭāniyya.2

water-houses **Sabīl**.2

fire-pumps Ṭulumbadjï

fountains Shadirwān

wells Bāʾolī; **Biʾr**; Biʾr Maymūn; Zamzam

see also Ḥawḍ

regions

Afghanistan and Indian subcontinent Āgra; Bahmanīs; Barīd Shāhīs.II; Bharōč; Bīdar; Bīdjāpūr; Bihār; Čāmpānēr; Dawlatābād; Dihlī.2; Djūnāgaŕh; Ghaznawids; Ghūrids; Golkondá; Hampī; Hānsī; Ḥaydarābād; Hind.vii; Ḥusaynī Dālān; Ḳuṭb Mīnār; Lahore; Lakhnaw; Maḥall; Mahisur; Māndú.2; Mughals.7; Multān.2; Nāgawr; Sind.4; Srīnagar.2; Tādj Maḥall; Tughluḳids.2; Uččh.2

see also Burdj.iii; Bustān.ii; Imām-bārā; Lashkar-i Bāzār; Māʾ.12; Maḳbara.5; Maklī; Manāra.2; Masdjid.II; Miḥrāb; Minbar.3; Miẓalla.5; Muthamman; Parčīn-kārī; Pīshṭāḳ

Africa → AFRICA; *for North African architecture, see below*

Andalusia al-Andalus.ix; Burdj.II; Gharnāṭa; Ishbīliya; Ḳurṭuba; Naṣrids.2

see also al-Nāẓūr

Arabian peninsula al-Ḥidjr; Kaʿba; al-Masdjid al-Ḥarām

see also Makka.4; Ṣanʿāʾ; Ṭāhirids.3.2

Central Asia Bukhārā; Ḥiṣn.iii; Īlkhāns; Samarḳand.2; Tīmūrids.3.b

see also Miḥrāb

Egypt Abu ʾl-Hawl; al-Azhar; Haram; al-Ḳāhira; Mashrabiyya.1; Nafīsa

see also Miḥrāb; Misalla; Miṣr; Saʿīd al-Suʿadāʾ; al-Uḳṣur; [in Suppl.] Abū Sinbil

Fertile Crescent Baghdād; Dimashḳ; Ḥarrān.ii; Ḥimṣ; ʿIrāḳ.vii; Ḳubbat al-Ṣakhra; al-Ḳuds; Maʿarrat al-Nuʿmān; al-Marḳab.3; al-Masdjid al-Aḳṣā; al-Raḳḳa; al-Ukhayḍir; [in Suppl.] Bādiya; Dār al-Ḥadīth.I

see also Ḳaṣr al-Ḥayr al-Gharbī; Ḳaṣr al-Ḥayr al-Sharḳī; Khirbat al-Mafdjar; Miḥrāb; al-Rāwandān

Iran Ḥiṣn.ii; Iṣfahān.2; Iṣṭakhr; Ḳazwīn; Khursābād; Mashrabiyya.2; Rādkān; al-Rayy.2; Ṣafawids.V; Saldjūḳids.VI; Sāmānids.2(b); Sulṭāniyya.2;

Tabrīz.2; Tihrān.I.3.b.ii; Ṭūs.2; Warāmīn.2; Zawāra
see also Ḳaṣr-i Shīrīn; Miḥrāb; Ribāṭ-i Sharaf; Yazd.1
North Africa Fās; Fāṭimid Art; Ḥiṣn.i; Ḳalʿat Banī Ḥammād; al-Ḳarawiyyīn; Zaytūna.1
see also ʿAnaza; Bidjāya; Miḥrāb
Southeast Asia Ḥiṣn.iv; Indonesia.v; Masdjid.III-V
Turkey Adana; Anḳara; Aya Sofya; Diwrīgī; Diyār Bakr; Edirne; Ḥarrān.ii; Ḥiṣn Kayfā; Istanbul; Konya.2; Lāranda; ʿOthmānli̊.V
see also Ḳapli̊dja; Ḳāsim Agha; Khayr al-Dīn; Köshk; Miḥrāb; Rūm Ḳalʿesi; Sinān; Yali̊
terms ʿAmūd; ʿAnaza; Bahw; Balāṭ; Īwān; Muḳarbaṣ; Muḳarnas; Muthamman; Pīshṭāḳ; Riwāḳ; Sarāy; Sardāb; Shadirwān; Ṭirāz.3
urban Bāb; Dār; Funduḳ; Ḥammām; Īwān; Ḳaysāriyya; Khān.II; Madrasa.III; Masdjid; Muṣallā.2; Rabʿ; Selāmli̊ḳ; Shāriʿ; Sūḳ; Sūr
see also Kanīsa; Sarāy; *and* → SEDENTARISM
fountains → ARCHITECTURE.MONUMENTS.WATER-HOUSES
ventilation Mirwaḥa; [in Suppl.] Bādgīr
see also Khaysh; Sardāb; Sind.4

ARMENIA **Armīniya**; Rewān; Shimshāṭ
and → CAUCASUS

ART Arabesque; Fann; Fusayfisāʾ; Kāshī; Khaṭṭ; Khazaf; Kitābāt; Lawn; Maʿdin.4; Parčīn-kārī; Rasm; Taṣwīr; Ṭirāz; Zakhrafa; Zalīdj; Zudjādj
see also Architecture; Billawr; Dhahab; Fiḍḍa; ʿIlm al-Djamāl; Khātam; Muhr; Ṣūra; *and* → ANIMALS.AND ART; ARCHITECTURE
calligraphy **Khaṭṭ**; Tughra
see also ʿAlī; İnal; Ḳum(m)ī; Muraḳḳaʿ; Nuskha; Tazwīr; Tīmūrids.3.a; *and* → WRITING
calligraphers ʿAlī Riḍā-i ʿAbbāsī; Ḥamza al-Ḥarrānī; Ibn al-Bawwāb; Ibn Muḳla; Muḥammad Ḥusayn Tabrīzī; Müstaḳīm-zāde; Yāḳūt al-Mustaʿṣimī
ceramics → ART.POTTERY
decorative ʿĀdj; al-Asad; Djiṣṣ; Fahd; Ḥayawān.6; Hilāl.ii; Īlkhāns; al-Ḳamar.II; Mashrabiyya; Parčīn-kārī; Shams.3; Tawrīḳ; Ṭirāz; ʿUnwān.2; Yashm.2; Zakhrafa
see also Kāshī; Maʿdin.4
drawing **Rasm**
glass al-Ḳily; ʿOthmānli̊.VII.d; Sāmānids.2(a); **Zudjādj**
handicrafts Ḳalamkārī; [in Suppl.] Bisāṭ; Dawāt
see also Ḥalfāʾ
illumination ʿUnwān.2

metalware Bīdar; Īlkhāns; Maʿdin.4; ʿOthmānli̊.VII.b; Sāmānids.2(a); Tīmūrids.3.d; [in Suppl.] Ibrīḳ

mosaics **Fusayfisāʾ**; Kāshī; Zalīdj

painting **Taṣwīr**.1

miniatures Īlkhāns; Mughals.9; Naḳḳāsh-khāna; ʿOthmānli̊.VIII

see also Fīl; Kalīla wa-Dimna.16; Māndū.3; Miʿrādj.5; al-Mīzān.3; Muraḳḳaʿ; Rustam.2; Sāḳī.3; Tīmūrids.3.a; [in Suppl.] Djawhar; *and* → ANIMALS.AND ART; ART.DRAWING

miniaturists Bihzād; Manṣūr; Maṭrāḳči̊; Naḳḳāsh Ḥasan (Pasha); Riḍā ʿAbbāsī; Riḍāʾī; Siyāh-ḳalem

see also ʿAlī; Luḳmān b. Sayyid Ḥusayn

modern painting **Taṣwīr**.3

and → ART.DRAWING

painters Djabrān Khalīl Djabrān; ʿOthmān Ḥamdī; Sipihrī; [in Suppl.] Dinet; Eyyūboghlu, Bedrī

photography **Taṣwīr**.2

pottery Anadolu.iii.6; al-Andalus.ix; **Fakhkhār**; Īlkhāns; Iznīḳ; Ḳallala; **Khazaf**; Mināʾī; ʿOthmānli̊.VII.a; Sāmānids.2(a); Ṣīnī; Tīmūrids.3.c; Ṭīn.2

regional and period al-Andalus.ix; Berbers.VI; Fāṭimid Art; Īlkhāns; ʿIrāḳ.vii; Mughals.8 and 9; ʿOthmānli̊.VII; Saldjūḳids.VI; Sāmānids.2(a); Tīmūrids.3.a

silhouette-cutting Fakhrī

tapestry Anadolu.iii.6; ʿOthmānli̊.VI; Sadjdjāda.2; ʿUshāḳ.2; [in Suppl.] **Bisāṭ**

see also Karkaddan; Mafrūshāt; Mifrash; Mīlās.2

textiles Ḥarīr; Ḳumāsh; Ṭirāz; [in Suppl.] Ḥāʾik

see also Ḳalamkārī; Ḳaṣab; Kattān; Ḳurḳūb; Mandīl; al-Nassādj; *and* → CLOTHING.MATERIALS

production centres al-Andalus.ix; al-Bahnasā; Dabīḳ; Tinnīs

see also Bursa; Īlkhāns; Mughals.8; ʿOthmānli̊.VI; al-Rayy.2; Sāmānids.2(a); Yazd.1; *and* → ART.TAPESTRY

tiles **Kāshī**

see also Anadolu.iii.6

ASCETICISM Bakkāʾ; Malāmatiyya; **Zuhd**

see also Khalwa; Manāḳib; [in Suppl.] Asad b. Mūsā b. Ibrāhīm; *for ascetics* → MYSTICISM.MYSTICS; SAINTHOOD

poetry **Zuhdiyya**

ASIA Almali̊gh; Baikal

see also Baraba; Mogholistān

Central → CENTRAL ASIA

East Čam; Djāwī; Indochina; Indonesia; Ḳimār; Malay Peninsula; Malaysia; Patani; Philippines; al-Shīlā; al-Ṣīn; Singapore; Thailand; Tubbat; al-

Yabānī; [in Suppl.] Brunei

see also Kitābāt.8; Ṣanf; S̲h̲āh Bandar.2; ʿUlamāʾ.5; Waḳf.VII.ii-vi; Wāḳwāḳ; Walī.7; Zābad̲j̲; [in Suppl.] Demography.VIII; *and* → ARCHITECTURE.REGIONS.SOUTHEAST ASIA; LAW.IN SOUTHEAST ASIA; ONOMASTICS.TITLES

for individual countries → CHINA; INDONESIA; MALAYSIA; MONGOLIA; THAILAND; *for Japan, see* al-Yabānī; *for Tibet, see* Tubbat

Eurasia → EUROPE

South Burma; Ceylon; Hind; Laccadives; Maldives; Mauritius; Minicoy; Nepal; Nicobars; Seychelles

see also Ruhmī; Waḳf.VII.i

for individual countries → BANGLADESH; BURMA; INDIA; NEPAL; PAKISTAN; SRI LANKA

ASSYRIA   K̲h̲ursābād; Nimrūd; Nīnawā.1; Zind̲j̲irli; [in Suppl.] At̲h̲ūr

ASTROLOGY   Ik̲h̲tiyārāt; Ḳaws Ḳuzaḥ; al-Kayd; Ḳirān; Minṭaḳat al-Burūd̲j̲; Munad̲j̲d̲j̲im; **Nud̲j̲ūm (Aḥkām al-)**; al-Tasyīr

see also K̲h̲aṭṭ; Zāʾird̲j̲a; Zīd̲j̲; *and* → ASTRONOMY.CELESTIAL OBJECTS

astrologers Abū Maʿs̲h̲ar al-Balk̲h̲ī; al-Bīrūnī; Ibn Abi ʾl-Rid̲j̲āl, Abu ʾl-Ḥasan; Ibn al-K̲h̲aṣīb, Abū Bakr; al-Ḳabīṣī; al-K̲h̲ayyāṭ, Abū ʿAlī; Mās̲h̲āʾ Allāh; ʿUṭārid b. Muḥammad

see also Baṭlamiyūs; *and* → ASTRONOMY; DIVINATION

terms al-D̲j̲awzahar; Ḥadd; Ḳaṭʿ; Mut̲h̲allat̲h̲; Saʿd wa-Naḥs (*and* al-Saʿdānⁱ; S̲h̲aḳāwa); al-Sahm.1.b; al-Ṭāliʿ.2; al-Tinnīn

ASTRONOMY   Anwāʾ; Asṭurlāb; Falak; Hayʾa; **ʿIlm al-Hayʾa**; al-Ḳamar.I; al-Kayd; Kusūf; al-Ḳuṭb; al-Madd wa ʾl-D̲j̲azr; al-Mad̲j̲arra; al-Manāzil; Minṭaḳat al-Burūd̲j̲; al-Nud̲j̲ūm; Zīd̲j̲

see also D̲j̲ug̲h̲rāfiyā; Ḳibla.ii; al-Ḳubba; al-Kura; Makka.4; Mīḳāt.2; Mizwala

astronomers ʿAbd al-Raḥmān al-Ṣūfī; Abu ʾl-Ṣalt Umayya (*and* Umayya, Abu ʾl-Ṣalt); ʿAlī al-Ḳūs̲h̲d̲j̲ī; al-Badīʿ al-Asṭurlābī; al-Battānī; al-Bīrūnī; al-Biṭrūd̲j̲ī; D̲j̲ābir b. Aflaḥ; al-D̲j̲ag̲h̲mīnī; al-Farg̲h̲ānī; Ḥabas̲h̲ al-Ḥāsib al-Marwazī; Ibn Amād̲j̲ūr; Ibn al-Bannāʾ al-Marrākus̲h̲ī; Ibn ʿIrāḳ; Ibn al-Ṣaffār; Ibn al-Samḥ; Ibn Yūnus; al-Kās̲h̲ī; al-K̲h̲ʷārazmī, Abū D̲j̲aʿfar; al-K̲h̲āzin; al-K̲h̲azīnī; al-K̲h̲ud̲j̲andī; Kus̲h̲iyār b. Labān; Ḳuṭb al-Dīn S̲h̲īrāzī; al-Mad̲j̲rīṭī; al-Mārdīnī; al-Marrākus̲h̲ī; Muḥammad b. ʿĪsā al-Māhānī; Muḥammad b. ʿUmar; al-Nayrīzī; al-S̲h̲ayzarī; Taḳī al-Dīn; T̲h̲ābit b. Ḳurra; al-Ṭūsī, Naṣīr al-Dīn; ʿUmar K̲h̲ayyām; ʿUṭārid b. Muḥammad; al-Zarḳālī; [in Suppl.] ʿAbd al-Salām b. Muḥammad

see also Baṭlamiyūs; al-Falakī; Falakī S̲h̲irwānī; Ibn al-Hayt̲h̲am; Ḳusṭā b. Lūḳā; Sindhind; [in Suppl.] Ibn al-Ad̲j̲dābī; *and* → ASTROLOGY

celestial objects
comets **al-Nudjūm**.III.b
planets al-Ḳamar.I; al-Mirrīkh; al-Mushtarī; **al-Nudjūm**.II; ʿUṭārid; Zuḥal; Zuhara
see also Minṭaḳat al-Burūdj; Ruʾyat al-Hilāl; al-Saʿdān[i]; Taḳwīm.1; al-ʿUzzā; Zīdj
stars and constellations ʿAḳrab; ʿAnāḳ; al-Asad; Dadjādja; Fard.e; Kalb; Ḳird; Mahāt; Minṭaḳat al-Burūdj; Muthallath; Naʿām; Nasr; **al-Nudjūm**; Radīf.1; al-Sahm.1.c; Samak.9; Saraṭān.6; Shams.2; al-Shiʿrā; Tādj; Thaʿlab; al-Tinnīn; ʿUḳāb; Zarāfa; [in Suppl.] Arnab; Ghanam
see also al-Kayd; Saʿd wa-Naḥs (*and* al-Saʿdān[i]; Shaḳāwa); al-Sāḳ; Sulaḥfā; al-Ṭāʾir
chronology **Taʾrīkh**.I.2
observatory Marṣad
see also Udjdjayn; Ulugh Beg; ʿUmar Khayyām
terms al-Djawzahar; Istiḳbāl; al-Maṭāliʿ; al-Maṭlaʿ; al-Mayl; Muḳābala.1; Muḳanṭarāt; Niṣf al-Nahār; Radīf.1; Rubʿ; Ruʾyat al-Hilāl; al-Sāḳ; al-Samt; Shakkāziyya; Ṭabīʿa.4; al-Taʿdīl; al-Taʿdīl bayn al-Saṭrayn; Taʿdīl al-Zamān; Taḳwīm.1; al-Ṭāliʿ.1; Zīdj

AUSTRIA Beč; **Nemče**
see also Muslimūn.2.ii

B

BĀBISM → SECTS

BAHAIS Bāb; Bābīs; Bahāʾ Allāh; **Bahāʾīs**; Mashriḳ al-Adhkār; Naḳḍ al-Mīthāḳ; Shawḳī Efendi Rabbānī
see also Lawḥ; Maẓhar; [in Suppl.] Anṣārī

BAHRAIN **al-Baḥrayn**; āl-Khalīfa; Madjlis.4.A.x; Maḥkama.4.ix
see also Ḳarmaṭī; ʿUṣfūrids; ʿUtūb
toponyms al-Manāma; al-Muḥarraḳ; Yabrīn
see also al-Mushaḳḳar

BALKANS **Balkan**; **Rūmeli**; al-Ṣaḳāliba
see also Ṭarīḳa.II.6; Walī.4; Wardar; Woyvoda; *and* → EUROPE
and Ottoman military Eflāḳ; Martolos; Woynuḳ; *and* → MILITARY.OTTOMAN

BANGLADESH **Bangāla**; Madjlis.4.C

see also Bengali; Nadhr al-Islām; Satya Pīr; [in Suppl.] Djarīda.vii
literature → LITERATURE.IN OTHER LANGUAGES
toponyms Bāḳargandj; Bangāla; Bōgrā; Chittagong; Ḍhākā; Dīnādjpur; Djassawr; Farīdpur; Sātgā'on; Silhet; Sundarban
see also Ruhmī; Sonārgā'on

BASQUES **al-Bashkunish**
see also Ibn Gharsiya

BEDOUINS **Badw**; Bi'r; Dawār; Ghanīma; Ghazw; al-Hidjar; Tha'r
see also Liṣṣ; ʿUrf.2.I; Wasm;; *and* → LAW.CUSTOMARY; NOMADISM; SAUDI ARABIA; TRIBES.ARABIAN PENINSULA
writings on Rzewuski

BENIN Kandi; Kotonou; Kouandé

BERBERS **Berbers**; Judaeo-Berber
see also Ḥimāya.ii.II; Imẓad; al-Irdjānī; Ḳallala; Ḳiṣṣa.8; Leff; Libās.ii; Lithām; Mafākhir al-Barbar; Ṣaff.3; Shāwiya.1; Ṣufriyya.2; *and* → ALGERIA
customary law ʿĀda.ii; Ḳānūn.iv
see also ʿUrf
dynasties ʿAbd al-Wādids; ʿAmmār; Marīnids; Midrār; al-Murābiṭūn; al-Muwaḥḥidūn; Razīn, Banū; Zīrids
language → LANGUAGES.AFRO-ASIATIC
religion al-Badjalī; Berbers.III; Ḥā-Mīm; Ṣāliḥ b. Ṭarīf
resistance Berbers.I.c; al-Kāhina; Kusayla; Maysara
tribes al-Barānis; Barghawāṭa; Birzāl; al-Butr; Djazūla; Ghāniya; Ghubrīnī; Ghumāra; Glāwā; Gudāla; Ḥāḥā; Hargha; Hawwāra; Hintāta; Ifoghas; Īfran; Iraten; Kutāma; Lamṭa; Lamtūna; Lawāta; Maghīla; Maghrāwa; Malzūza; Maṣmūda; Māssa; Maṭghara; Maṭmāṭa; Mazāta; Midyūna; Misrāta; al-Nafūsa; Nafza; Nafzāwa; Ṣanhādja; Ṭawāriḳ; Zanāta; [in Suppl.] Awraba

BIBLE **Indjīl**; **Tawrāt**
and → CHRISTIANITY; JUDAISM
biblical personages Ādam; ʿAmālīḳ; Ayyūb; Āzar; ʿAzāzīl; Balʿam; Bilḳīs; Binyāmīn; Bukht-naṣ(ṣ)ar; Dāniyāl; Dāwūd; Djabrā'īl; Djālūt; Firʿawn; Ḥābīl wa-Ḳābīl; Ḥām; Hāmān; Hārūn b. ʿImrān; Hārūt wa-Mārūt; Ḥawwā'; Ḥizḳīl; Ibrāhīm; Ilyās; ʿImrān; Irmiyā; ʿĪsā; Isḥāḳ; Ismāʿīl; Kanʿān; Ḳārūn; Ḳiṭfīr; Kūsh; Lamak; Lazarus; Lūṭ; Maryam; al-Masīḥ; Mūsā; Namrūd; Nūḥ; Rāḥīl; Sām.1; al-Sāmirī; Sāra; Shamsūn; Shamwīl; Shaʿyā; Shīth; Sulaymān b. Dāwūd; Ṭālūt; ʿŪdj; Yāfith; Yaḥyā b. Zakariyyā'; Yaʿḳūb; Yūnus; Yūshaʿ b. Nūn; Yūsuf; Zakariyyā'

see also D̲h̲u 'l-Kifl; al-Fayyūm; Hūd; Idrīs; Yād̲j̲ūd̲j̲ wa-Mād̲j̲ūd̲j̲; *and* →
PROPHETHOOD
biblical toponyms   Ṣihyawn
   see also D̲j̲ūdī
translations
   into Arabic   Fāris al-S̲h̲idyāḳ; Saʿadyā Ben Yōsēf; al-Yāzid̲j̲ī.1; [in Suppl.] al-
      Bustānī.2
      see also ʿArabiyya.A.ii.1; Judaeo-Arabic.iii.B; Tawrāt
   into Persian   Abu 'l-Faḍl ʿAllāmī
      see also Judaeo-Persian.i.2

BIBLIOGRAPHY   **Bibliography**; Fahrasa
   see also Ibn K̲h̲ayr al-Is̲h̲bīlī; Ibn al-Nadīm; Kātib Čelebi; al-Ruʿaynī; al-
   Ṭihrānī

BOSNIA   → (former) YUGOSLAVIA

BOTANY   Adwiya; al-ʿAs̲h̲s̲h̲āb; Nabāt
   and → AGRICULTURE; FLORA; MEDICINE; PHARMACOLOGY
botanists   Abū ʿUbayd al-Bakrī; al-Dīnawarī, Abū Ḥanīfa; Ibn al-Bayṭār; al-
   Tig̲h̲narī; [in Suppl.] al-G̲h̲āfiḳī; Ibn al-Rūmiyya
   see also Abu 'l-K̲h̲ayr al-Is̲h̲bīlī; Filāḥa; Nīḳūlāʾūs; al-Suwaydī

BUDDHISM   Bak̲h̲s̲h̲ī; Budd; **Sumaniyya**
   see also Bāmiyān; al-Barāmika.1; Bilawhar wa-Yūdāsaf; Tañri

BULGARIA   **Bulgaria**; Pomaks
   see also Küčük Ḳaynard̲j̲a; Muhād̲j̲ir.2; Muslimūn.1.B.5
physical geography
   waters   Merič
toponyms   Burgas; Deli-Orman; Dobrud̲j̲a; Filibe; Hezārg̲h̲rad; Küstendil; New-
   rokop; Nīkbūlī; ʿOt̲h̲mān Pazar; Plewna; Rusčuk; Selwi; S̲h̲umnu; Ṣofya;
   Tatar Pazarcik; T̊rnowa; Warna; Widin; Zis̲h̲towa

BURMA   Arakan; **Burma**; Mergui; Rangoon; Zerbadis

BYZANTINE EMPIRE   Biṭrīḳ; Ḳayṣar; **Rūm**
   see also Anadolu.iii.1 and 2; Hiba.i; Iznīḳ; Ḳalāwd̲h̲iya; Ḳubrus; (al-)
   Ḳusṭanṭīniyya; al-Maṣṣīṣa; Muʾta; Nauplion.1; Saracens; Umur Pas̲h̲a;
   Wenedik; al-Ẓāhir li-Iʿzāz Dīn Allāh; *and* → GREECE; PALESTINE; SYRIA;
   TURKEY, *in particular the section Toponyms*
allies   D̲j̲arād̲j̲ima; D̲j̲arrāḥids; G̲h̲assān; al-Ḥārit̲h̲ b. D̲j̲abala; Kinda.1; Salīḥ; [in

Suppl.] Djabala b. al-Ḥārith
and → Tribes
military Alay; Lamas-ṣū; Malāzgird.2; Naft.2; Tourkopo(u)loi; [in Suppl.] Dhāt al-Ṣawārī
see also al-ʿAwāṣim; Cilicia; Ṣāʾifa.1; Sayf al-Dawla; al-Thughūr.1
battles Yarmūk.2

C

Caliphate Ahl al-Ḥall wa ʾl-ʿAḳd; Bayʿa; Ḥādjib.i; Ḥarb.ii; Hiba.i; Imāma; Ḳaḍīb; Kātib.i; **Khalīfa**; Libās.i; Madjlis.1; Marāsim.1; Mawākib.1; Shūrā.1; Walī al-ʿAhd; Wazīr
see also Amīr al-Muʾminīn; Ghulām.i; Khilʿa.ii; Laḳab.2; Māl al-Bayʿa; *and* → Court Ceremony
ʿAbbāsids (750-1258) **ʿAbbāsids**; Baghdād; Dīwān.i; Ḥādjib.i; Khalīfa.i.B; Marāsim.1; Mawākib.1; Muṣādara.2; Musawwida; Naḳīb.1; Naḳīb al-Ashrāf.1; Sāmarrāʾ; Wazīr.I.1
see also al-Abnāʾ.III; ʿAlī b. ʿAbd Allāh b. al-ʿAbbās; ʿAlids; Architecture.I.3; Ḍarība; Hāshimiyya; al-Hāshimiyya; Laḳab.2; Libās.i.4; Riḍā.2; al-Shuʿūbiyya; Sikka.2; Walī al-ʿAhd; *and* → Dynasties.persia
caliphs Abu ʾl-ʿAbbās al-Saffāḥ; al-Amīn; al-Hādī ila ʾl-Ḥaḳḳ; Hārūn al-Rashīd; al-Ḳādir bi ʾllāh; al-Ḳāhir bi ʾllāh; al-Ḳāʾim bi-amr Allāh; al-Mahdī; al-Maʾmūn; al-Manṣūr; al-Muhtadī; al-Muḳtadī; al-Muḳtadir; al-Muḳtafī bi-llāh; al-Muḳtafī li-Amr Allāh; al-Muntaṣir; al-Mustaḍīʾ; al-Mustaʿīn (I); al-Mustaʿīn (II); al-Mustakfī; al-Mustandjid (I); al-Mustandjid (II); al-Mustanṣir (I); al-Mustanṣir (II); al-Mustarshid; al-Mustaʿṣim bi ʾllāh; al-Mustaẓhir bi ʾllāh; al-Muʿtaḍid bi ʾllāh; al-Muʿtamid ʿalā ʾllāh; al-Muʿtaṣim bi ʾllāh; al-Mutawakkil ʿalā ʾllāh; al-Muʿtazz bi ʾllāh; al-Muṭīʿ li ʾllāh; al-Muttaḳī li ʾllāh; al-Nāṣir li-Dīn Allāh, Abu ʾl-ʿAbbās; al-Rāḍī bi ʾllāh; al-Rāshid; al-Ṭāʾiʿ li-Amr Allāh; al-Wāthiḳ bi ʾllāh; al-Ẓāhir bi-Amr Allāh
see also ʿAbd Allāh b. ʿAlī; Būrān; al-Khayzurān bint ʿAṭāʾ al-Djurashiyya; Muḥammad b. ʿAlī b. ʿAbd Allāh; al-Muwaffaḳ; al-Ruṣāfa.2
viziers Abū ʿAbd Allāh Yaʿḳūb; Abū Salāma al-Khallāl; Abū ʿUbayd Allāh; ʿAḍud al-Dīn; ʿAlī b. ʿĪsā; al-Barāmika.3; al-Barīdī; al-Djardjarāʾī.1-3; al-Faḍl b. Marwān; al-Faḍl b. al-Rabīʿ; al-Faḍl b. Sahl b. Zadhānfarūkh; al-Fayḍ b. Abī Ṣāliḥ; Ḥamīd; Hibat Allāh b. Muḥammad; Ibn al-Alḳamī; Ibn al-Baladī; Ibn al-Furāt; Ibn Hubayra; Ibn Khāḳan.2 and 3; Ibn Makhlad; Ibn Muḳla; Ibn al-Muslima; Ibn al-Zayyāt; al-Iskāfī, Abu ʾl-Faḍl; al-Iskāfī, Abū Isḥāḳ; Ismāʿīl b. Bulbul; al-Khaṣībī; al-Rabīʿ b.

Yūnus; Rabīb al-Dawla; al-Rū<u>dh</u>rāwarī; Wahb, Banū; al-Zaynabī
see also al-<u>Dj</u>ah<u>sh</u>iyārī; Hilāl al-Ṣābiʾ; <u>Kh</u>ātam; Wazīr.I.1
secretaries Aḥmad b. Abī <u>Kh</u>ālid al-Aḥwal; Aḥmad b. Yūsuf; ʿAmr b. Masʿada; al-Ḥasan b. Sahl; Ibn al-<u>Dj</u>arrāḥ; Ibn <u>Kh</u>āḳan.1 and 4; Ibn al-Mā<u>sh</u>iṭa; al-Mūriyānī
see also Wahb, Banū
historians of al-<u>Dj</u>ah<u>sh</u>iyārī; Ibn Abi 'l-Dam; Ibn Abī Ṭāhir Ṭayfūr; Ibn al-<u>Dj</u>awzī; Ibn al-Naṭṭāḥ; Ibn al-Sāʿī; Ibn al-Ṭiḳṭaḳā; al-Madāʾinī; Ṣābiʾ.(3).4; ʿUbayd Allāh b. Aḥmad b. Abī Ṭāhir; al-Yaʿḳūbī
see also al-Zubayr b. Bakkār
other personages al-ʿAbbās b. ʿAmr al-<u>Gh</u>anawī; al-ʿAbbās b. al-Maʾmūn; al-ʿAbbās b. Muḥammad; ʿAbd Allāh b. ʿAlī; ʿAbd al-<u>Dj</u>abbār b. ʿAbd al-Raḥmān; ʿAbd al-Malik b. Ṣāliḥ; Abū ʿAwn; Abū Muslim; ʿAlī al-Riḍā; Ba<u>dj</u>kam; Badr al-<u>Kh</u>ar<u>sh</u>anī; Bu<u>gh</u>ā al-Kabīr; Bu<u>gh</u>ā al-<u>Sh</u>arābī; Dulafids; al-Fatḥ b. <u>Kh</u>āḳān; Har<u>th</u>ama b. Aʿyan; al-Ḥasan b. Zayd b. al-Ḥasan; Ḥātim b. Har<u>th</u>ama; Ḥumayd b. ʿAbd al-Ḥamīd; Ibn Abi 'l-<u>Sh</u>awārib; Ibn Buhlūl; Ibn al-<u>Dj</u>aṣṣāṣ.II; Ibn Ḥamdūn; Ibn Māhān; Ibn al-Mudabbir; Ibn al-Muʿtazz; Ibn Rāʾiḳ; Ibn <u>Th</u>awāba; Ibrāhīm b. ʿAbd Allāh; ʿĪsā b. Mūsā; ʿĪsā b. al-<u>Sh</u>ay<u>kh</u>; Ḳaḥṭaba; al-Ḳāsim b. ʿĪsā; Maʿn b. Zāʾida; al-Mubarḳaʿ; Muhallabids; Muḥammad b. ʿAbd Allāh (al-Nafs al-Zakiyya); Muḥammad b. Ṭu<u>gh</u><u>dj</u> al-I<u>kh</u><u>sh</u>īd; Muḥammad b. Yāḳūt; Muʾnis al-Faḥl; Muʾnis al-Muẓaffar; al-Muwaffaḳ; Naṣr b. <u>Sh</u>aba<u>th</u>; al-Nāṭiḳ bi 'l-Ḥaḳḳ; al-Nū<u>sh</u>arī; Rāfiʿ b. Har<u>th</u>ama; Rāfiʿ b. al-Lay<u>th</u> b. Naṣr b. Sayyār; al-Rāwandiyya; Rawḥ b. Ḥātim; Sā<u>dj</u>ids; Ṣāliḥ b. ʿAlī; al-Sara<u>kh</u>sī, Abu 'l-ʿAbbās; al-Sarī; <u>Sh</u>abīb b. <u>Sh</u>ayba; Sulaymān b. ʿAlī b. ʿAbd Allāh; Sunbā<u>dh</u>; al-<u>Th</u>a<u>gh</u>rī; ʿU<u>dj</u>ayf b. ʿAnbasa; Ustā<u>dh</u>sīs; al-Walīd b. Ṭarīf; al-Wā<u>th</u>iḳī; Yaḥyā b. ʿAbd Allāh; Yaḥyā b. Ak<u>th</u>am; Yūsuf al-Barm; Zawāḳīl; Ziyād b. Ṣāliḥ al-<u>Kh</u>uzāʿī; Zubayda bt. <u>Dj</u>aʿfar; [in Suppl.] Abū Manṣūr b. Yūsuf; Aytā<u>kh</u> al-Turkī; Badr al-Muʿtaḍidī; al-Dāma<u>gh</u>ānī, Abū ʿAbd Allāh; al-Dāma<u>gh</u>ānī, Abu 'l-Ḥasan; al-<u>Gh</u>iṭrīf b. ʿAṭāʾ; Ibn Dirham
Fāṭimids (909-1171) Dīwān.i and ii.(2); **Fāṭimids**; Ḥā<u>dj</u>ib.iv; Ḥi<u>dj</u>āb.II; al-Ḳāhira; <u>Kh</u>alīfa.i.D; Libās.i.5; Marāsim.1; Mawākib.1; Wazīr.I.2
see also Laḳab.2; Ṣāḥib al-Bāb; Sitr; Wāsiṭa; al-Wazīr al-Ṣa<u>gh</u>īr; Zimām
caliphs Abū ʿAbd Allāh al-<u>Sh</u>īʿī; al-ʿĀḍid li-Dīn Allāh; al-Āmir; al-ʿAzīz bi 'llāh; al-Ḥāfiẓ; al-Ḥākim bi-Amr Allāh; al-Ḳāʾim; al-Mahdī ʿUbayd Allāh; al-Manṣūr bi 'llāh; al-Muʿizz li-Dīn Allāh; al-Mustaʿlī bi 'llāh; al-Mustanṣir (bi 'llāh); al-Ẓāfir bi-Aʿdāʾ Allāh; al-Ẓāhir li-Iʿzāz Dīn Allāh
see also al-Walīd b. Hi<u>sh</u>ām
viziers ʿAbbās b. Abi 'l-Futūḥ; al-ʿĀdil b. al-Salār; al-Afḍal b. Badr al-<u>Dj</u>amālī; al-Afḍal (Kutayfāt); Badr al-<u>Dj</u>amālī; Bahrām; al-Baṭāʾiḥī; Ḍir<u>gh</u>ām; <u>Dj</u>abr Ibn al-Ḳāsim; al-<u>Dj</u>ar<u>dj</u>arāʾī.4; Ibn Killis; Ibn Maṣāl;

Ruzzīk b. Ṭalāʾiʿ; S̲h̲āwar; S̲h̲īrkūh; Ṭalāʾiʿ b. Ruzzīk; Yānis; al-Yāzurī; [in Suppl.] Ibn K̲h̲alaf.2
  see also Wazīr.I.2
secretaries Ibn Mammātī; Ibn al-Ṣayrafī; [in Suppl.] Ibn K̲h̲alaf, Abu 'l-Ḥasan
historians of Ibn al-Ṭuwayr; al-Maḳrīzī; al-Musabbiḥī
  see also Djawd̲h̲ar
other personages Abū Yazīd al-Nukkārī; Bard̲j̲awān; D̲j̲awd̲h̲ar; Djawhar al-Ṣiḳillī; K̲h̲alaf b. Mulāʿib al-As̲h̲habī; al-Kirmānī; Nizār b. al-Mustanṣir; al-Nuʿmān; Sitt al-Mulk; Tamīm b. al-Muʿizz li-Dīn Allāh
  see also al-Farg̲h̲ānī; Ẓāfir al-Ḥaddād
Rightly-Guided Caliphs (632-661) K̲h̲alīfa.i.A; S̲h̲ūrā.1
caliphs Abū Bakr; ʿAlī b. Abī Ṭālib; ʿUmar (I) b. al-K̲h̲aṭṭāb; ʿUt̲h̲mān b. ʿAffān
  see also Ḥarūrāʾ; Ibn Muld̲j̲am; K̲h̲alīfa.i.A; al-Saḳīfa; al-Ṣiddīḳ; Taḥkīm; ʿUt̲h̲māniyya; Wufūd; *and* → MILITARY.BATTLES.633-660
other personages Abān b. ʿUt̲h̲mān; ʿAbd Allāh b. al-ʿAbbās; ʿAbd Allāh b. ʿĀmir; ʿAbd Allāh b. Saʿd; ʿAbd Allāh b. Salām; ʿAbd Allāh b. Wahb; ʿAbd al-Raḥmān b. ʿAwf; ʿAbd al-Raḥmān b. Samura; Abu 'l-Aswad al-Duʾalī; Abū Ayyūb al-Anṣārī; Abu 'l-Dunyā; Abū ʿUbayda al-D̲j̲arrāḥ; al-Aḥnaf b. Ḳays; al-Aḳraʿ b. Ḥābis; ʿAmr b. al-ʿĀṣ; al-As̲h̲ʿarī, Abū Mūsā; al-As̲h̲ʿath; al-As̲h̲tar; al-Bāhilī; Ḥabīb b. Maslama; al-Ḳaʿḳāʿ b. ʿAmr; K̲h̲ālid b. al-Walīd; Muḥammad b. Abī Bakr; al-Mut̲h̲annā b. Ḥārit̲h̲a; Saʿīd b. al-ʿĀṣ; Sulaymān b. Ṣurad; Usāma b. Zayd; Yazīd b. Abī Sufyān; Zayd b. T̲h̲ābit; al-Zibriḳān b. Badr
  and → MUḤAMMAD, THE PROPHET.COMPANIONS OF THE PROPHET *and* FAMILY OF THE PROPHET
Umayyads (661-750) Dimas̲h̲ḳ; Dīwān.i; Ḥād̲j̲ib.i; K̲h̲alīfa.i.A; Mawlā.2.b; **Umayyads**; [in Suppl.] Bādiya
  see also Architecture.I.2; Ḳays ʿAylān; Libās.i.4; Marwānids; Sufyānids; Umayya b. ʿAbd S̲h̲ams; Umayyads.In Spain; ʿUt̲h̲māniyya.4; Wufūd; *and* → DYNASTIES.SPAIN AND NORTH AFRICA.UMAYYADS
caliphs ʿAbd al-Malik b. Marwān; His̲h̲ām; Marwān I b. al-Ḥakam; Marwān II; Muʿāwiya I; Muʿāwiya II; Sulaymān b. ʿAbd al-Malik; ʿUmar (II) b. ʿAbd al-ʿAzīz; al-Walīd; Yazīd (I) b. Muʿāwiya; Yazīd (II) b. ʿAbd al-Malik; Yazīd (III) b. al-Walīd
  see also Būṣīr; al-Ruṣāfa.3; al-S̲h̲ām.2(a); Taḥkīm
historians of ʿAwāna b. al-Ḥakam al-Kalbī; al-Azdī
  see also al-Yaʿḳūbī
secretaries ʿAbd al-Ḥamīd; Yazīd b. Abī Muslim; Ziyād b. Abīhi
other personages ʿAbbād b. Ziyād; al-ʿAbbās b. al-Walīd; ʿAbd Allāh b. ʿAbd al-Malik; ʿAbd Allāh b. Hammām; ʿAbd Allāh b. Ḥanẓala; ʿAbd Allāh b. K̲h̲āzim; ʿAbd Allāh b. Muṭīʿ; ʿAbd Allāh b. al-Zubayr; ʿAbd al-ʿAzīz b.

al-Ḥadjdjādj; ʿAbd al-ʿAzīz b. Marwān; ʿAbd al-ʿAzīz b. al-Walīd; ʿAbd al-Raḥmān b. Khālid; ʿAmr b. Saʿīd; Asad b. ʿAbd Allāh; al-Aṣamm.1; Baldj b. Bishr; Bishr b. Marwān; Bishr b. al-Walīd; Bukayr b. Māhān; Bukayr b. Wishāḥ; Busr; al-Ḍaḥḥāḳ b. Ḳays al-Fihrī; al-Djarrāḥ b. ʿAbd Allāh; al-Djunayd b. ʿAbd Allāh; al-Ḥadjdjādj b. Yūsuf; Ḥanẓala b. Ṣafwān b. Zuhayr; al-Ḥārith b. Suraydj; Ḥassān b. Mālik; Ḥassān b. al-Nuʿmān al-Ghassānī; al-Ḥurr b. Yazīd; al-Ḥusayn b. Numayr; Ibn al-Ashʿath; Ibn al-Ḥaḍramī; Ibn Hubayra; Khālid b. ʿAbd Allāh al-Ḳasrī; Khālid b. Yazīd b. Muʿāwiya; Kulthūm b. ʿIyāḍ al-Ḳushayrī; Ḳurra b. Sharīk; Ḳutayba b. Muslim; Maʿn b. Zāʾida; Masāmiʿa; Maslama b. ʿAbd al-Malik b. Marwān; Maymūn b. Mihrān; Muʿāwiya b. Hishām; al-Mughīra b. Shuʿba; Muhallabids; Muḥammad b. al-Ḳāsim; Muslim b. ʿUḳba; Naṣr b. Sayyār; al-Nuʿmān b. Bashīr; Rawḥ b. Zinbāʿ; Salm b. Ziyād b. Abīhi; Shabīb b. Yazīd; Sulaymān b. Kathīr; Ṭalḥat al-Ṭalaḥāt; Tawwābūn; al-Thaḳafī, Yūsuf b. ʿUmar; ʿUbayd Allāh b. Abī Bakra; ʿUbayd Allāh b. Ḥabḥāb; ʿUbayd Allāh b. ʿUmar; ʿUbayd Allāh b. Ziyād; ʿUḳba b. Nāfiʿ; Zayd b. ʿAlī b. al-Ḥusayn; Ziyād b. Abīhi; [in Suppl.] ʿAdī b. Arṭāt

see also al-Baṭṭāl; Iyās b. Muʿāwiya

treatises on al-Ḳalḳashandī.1

CARTOGRAPHY Kharīṭa

and → GEOGRAPHY; NAVIGATION

cartographers al-Falakī; Ibn Sarābiyūn; Meḥmed Reʾīs; Pīrī Reʾīs

CAUCASUS Ādharbaydjān.ii; Armīniya; Dāghistān; **al-Ḳabḳ**; al-Kurdj

see also Djarīda.iv; Ḳarā Bāgh; Muhādjir.2; Shīrwān Shāh

mysticism Ṭarīḳa.II.5; Walī.4

physical geography

mountains al-Ḳabḳ

waters Alindjaḳ; Gökče-tengiz; Ḳarā Deniz; Ḳi̊zi̊l-üzen; Ḳuban; Kur; al-Rass; Safīd Rūd; Terek

population Abkhāz.2; Alān; Andi; Arči; Avars; Balkar; Čečens; Čerkes; Darghin; Dido; Ingush; Kabards; Ḳapuča; Ḳaračay; Ḳarata; Ḳaytaḳ; Khaputs; Khemshin; Khinalug; Khunzal; Khvarshi̊; Ḳri̊z; Ḳubači; Kwanadi; Laḳ; Laz; Lezgh; Noghay; Ossetians; Rūs; Rutul; Tsakhur; Ubykh; [in Suppl.] Demography.VI

see also Ḳumuḳ

resistance to Russian conquest Ḥamza Beg; Shāmil; Ushurma, Manṣūr

see also Ḥizb.iv

toponyms

ancient Alindjaḳ; Arrān; Bādjarwān.1; Balandjar; Dwin; Saray; Shammākha;

Shimshāṭ; Shīrwān; Shīz
present-day Akhiskha; Astrakhān; Bāb al-Abwāb; Bākū; Bardhaʿa; Batumi; Derbend; Gandja; Ḳubba; Lankoran; Makhač-ḳalʿe; Nakhčiwān; Shakkī; Ṭabarsarān; Tālish; Tiflīs; [in Suppl.] Djulfā.I

CENTRAL ASIA Badakhshān; Čaghāniyān; Khʷārazm; **Mā warāʾ al-Nahr**; Mogholistān
see also Hayāṭila; Ismāʿīl b. Aḥmad; Ḳarā Khiṭāy; Ḳazaḳ; Nīzak, Ṭarkhān; Tīmūrids; Waḳf.V; [in Suppl.] Atalïḳ; Djulfā.II; *and* → DYNASTIES.MONGOLS; MONGOLIA; ONOMASTICS
for former republics of the USSR → *the section Toponyms below*
architecture → ARCHITECTURE.REGIONS
belles-lettres Tādjīkī.2; *and* → LITERATURE.DRAMA *and* POETRY.TURKISH.IN EASTERN TURKISH
former Soviet Union al-ʿArab.iii.Appendix; Basmačis; Djarīda.iv; Fiṭrat; Ḥizb.v; Khodjaev; Ṣadr al-Dīn ʿAynī; [in Suppl.] Demography.VI
and → *the section Toponyms below*
historians of ʿAbd al-Karīm Bukhārī
see also Ḥaydar b. ʿAlī
mysticism → MYSTICISM; SAINTHOOD
physical geography
deserts Ḳaraḳum; Ḳïzïl-ḳum
mountains Ala Dagh; Altai; Balkhān; Pamirs
see also Čopan-ata
waters Aḳ Ṣu; Amū Daryā; Aral; Baḥr al-Khazar; Balkhash; Čaghān-rūd; Ču; Ili; İssïk-kul; Ḳarā-köl; Murghāb; Sïr Daryā; Ṭarāz; Turgay; Wakhsh; Zarafshān
see also Su
population Balūč; Čāwdors (*and* [in Suppl.] Čawdor); Emreli; Gagauz; Ḳaraḳalpaḳ; Khaladj; Ḳungrāt; Ḳurama; Özbeg; Tarančis; Türkmen.3; Yaghma; [in Suppl.] Demography.VI
see also Altaians; al-ʿArab.iii.Appendix; Ghalča; Ghuzz; Ḳarluḳ; Ḳazaḳ; Ḳipčaḳ; Ḳïrgïz; Ḳumān; Kumīdjīs; Ḳun; Sārt; Tādjīk; [in Suppl.] Ersarï
toponyms
ancient Abaskūn; Abīward; Akhsīkath; Ardjīsh; Balāsāghūn; Banākat; Fārāb; Firabr; Gurgandj; Kāth; Ḳayalïḳ; Marw al-Rudh; Marw al-Shāhidjān; Mashhad-i Miṣryān; Nakhshab; Pishpek; Sayrām; Shūmān; Sïghnāḳ; al-Ṣughd; Sūyāb; Ṭarāz; Utrār; Yeti Su; Zamakhshar; Zamm; [in Suppl.] Dandānḳān; Djand; Īlāḳ
present-day
districts Atek; Ḳaratigin; Shughnān; Wakhsh
see also Ākhāl Tekke

regions Farghānā; Khwārazm; Khuttalān; Labāb; Mangishlak; Usrūshana; Wakhān; [in Suppl.] Dasht-i Ḳipčaḳ
republics Tādjīkistān; Turkistān.1; Turkmenistan; Uzbekistan.2
towns Aḳ Masdjid.2; Alma Ata; Āmul.2; Andidjān; ʿAshḳābād; Awliyā Ata; Bayram ʿAlī; Bukhārā; Čimkent; Djalālābād; Ghudjduwān; Hazārasp; Ḥiṣār; Kash; Khīwa; Khoḳand; Khudjand(a); Kish; Ḳubādhiyān; Marghīnān; Mayhana; Ordūbād; Özkend; Pandjdih; Samarḳand; Tashkent; Tirmidh; Toḳmaḳ; Turgay; Turkistān.3; Ürgenč

CHAD Abeshr; Bagirmi; Borkou; Kanem; Kanuri; Wadāī; Zaghāwa; [in Suppl.] **Čad**
and → AFRICA.CENTRAL AFRICA

CHARMS Afsūn; Ḥidjāb.IV; Kabid.4; Māshāʾ Allāh; Tamīma; Tilsam; [in Suppl.] Budūḥ
see also Kahrubā; Ḳarwasha; *and* → MAGIC

CHILDHOOD → LIFE STAGES

CHINA Djarīda.v; Masdjid.V; **al-Ṣīn**
see also Bahādur; Khoḳand; Ṣīnī; Ṭibb.2; ʿUlamāʾ.6; Ziyād b. Ṣāliḥ al-Khuzāʿī
dynasties Ḳarā Khiṭāy
see also Faghfūr; Gūrkhān; Yaʿḳūb Beg
mysticism **Taṣawwuf**.8
see also al-Ṣīn.4; Ma Hua-lung; Ma Ming-hsin; T'ien Wu; Walī.8
personages ʿUlamāʾ.6
see also Ṭibb.2; *for leaders in uprisings,* → *the section Uprisings below*
literary figures Liu Chih; Ma Huan; Wang Tai-yu
officials P'u Shou-keng
warlords Wu Ma
physical geography
waters Aḳ Ṣu; Ili; Tarim
population Salar; Tarančis; Tungans; Yunnan.2
toponyms
ancient Bishbaliḳ; Khansā; Shūl.1
present-day Aḳ Ṣu; Alti Shahr; Kansu; Kāshghar; Khānbaliḳ; Khānfū; Khotan; Ḳuldja; Ning-hsia; Shansi; Shen-si; Sinkiang; Szechuan; Tubbat; Turfan; Yārkand; Yunnan
see also Sandābil; Ṣīn (Čīn) Kalān; Turkistān.1; Zaytūn
treatises on ʿAlī Akbar Khiṭāʾī
uprisings Panthay

see also Tunganistan
leaders Ma Chung-ying; Ma Hua-lung; Ma Ming-hsin; Pai Yen-hu; T'ien Wu; Tu Wen-hsiu; Yulbārs Khān

CHRISTIANITY Ahl al-Kitāb; Dayr; Dayṣāniyya; ʿĪsā; Kanīsa; Maryam; **Naṣārā**; Rāhib; al-Ṣalīb; Tathlīth
see also Dhimma; Djizya; al-Ḥākim bi-Amr Allāh; Ifrandj; Karshūnī; Ḳūmis; Lāhūt and Nāsūt.2; Maʿalthāyā; [in Suppl.] Dāwiyya and Isbitāriyya; Fidāʾ; *and* → BIBLE; CRUSADE(R)S; EUROPE; LANGUAGES.AFRO-ASIATIC.ARABIC.CHRISTIAN ARABIC; NUBIA
apologetics Ibn Zurʿa; al-Kindī, ʿAbd al-Masīḥ
churches **Kanīsa**; Sihyawn
see also Masdjid.I.B.3
communities Anadolu.iii.4; al-Andalus.iv; Istanbul.vii.b; Mozarab; al-Shām.2(a) (271b-2a); Ṭūr ʿAbdīn.3
see also Fener
denominations Ḳibṭ; Nasṭūriyyūn; Yaʿḳūbiyyūn
and → JUDAISM.JEWISH SECTS
Catholics Bashīr Shihāb II; Isḥāḳ, Adīb; Ṣābundjī; Ṣāyigh, Fatḥ Allāh; Shaykhū, Luwīs; Zākhir; [in Suppl.] Buṭrus Karāma
Copts Ibn al-ʿAssāl; Ibn Mammātī; Ibn al-Muḳaffaʿ; **Ḳibṭ**; al-Makīn b. al-ʿAmīd; Māriya; al-Mufaḍḍal b. Abi 'l-Faḍāʾil; [in Suppl.] Ibn Kabar; Ibn al-Rāhib
see also Sullam; Taʾrīkh.I.1.vi; Ziyāra.3; *and* → EGYPT.TOPONYMS; NUBIA
Greek orthodox Gagauz
see also Paṭrīk; Zākhir
Jacobites al-Akhṭal; Ibn al-ʿIbrī; Ibn Zurʿa; al-Ḳuṭāmī; Yaḥyā b. ʿAdī; Yaḥyā al-Naḥwī; **Yaʿḳūbiyyūn**
see also al-Kindī, ʿAbd al-Masīḥ; Paṭrīk; Ṭūr ʿAbdīn.3
Maronites Farḥāt; Isṭifān al-Duwayhī; al-Rayḥānī; Salīm al-Naḳḳāsh; Ṭanyūs, Shāhīn; al-Yāzidjī; Yūsuf Karam; [in Suppl.] Abū Shabaka; al-Bustānī
see also Bsharrā; Durūz.ii; Paṭrīk; *and* → LEBANON
Melkites Abū Ḳurra; al-Antāḳī; Mīkhāʾīl al-Ṣabbāgh; al-Muḳawḳis; Saʿīd b. al-Biṭrīḳ; al-Turk, Niḳūlā; Yaḥyā b. al-Biṭrīḳ; [in Suppl.] Ibn al-Ḳuff
see also Mashāḳa; Paṭrīk
Monophysites → *the sections Copts, Jacobites and Nestorians under this entry*
Nestorians Bukhtīshūʿ; Ibn Buṭlān; Ibn al-Ṭayyib; al-Kindī, ʿAbd al-Masīḥ; Mattā b. Yūnus; **Nasṭūriyyūn**; Sābūr b. Sahl; Yūḥannā b. Sarābiyūn
see also al-Ṭabarī, ʿAlī b. Rabban; Ṭūr ʿAbdīn.3; Urmiya.3
Protestants Fāris al-Shidyāḳ; Mashāḳa; Ṣarrūf; Ṣāyigh, Tawfīḳ; [in Suppl.]

al-Bustānī.2
see also Nimr
unspecified Baḥdal; Ibn al-Tilmīdh; al-Masīḥī; Petrus Alfonsi; Ukaydir b. ʿAbd al-Malik; [in Suppl.] Ḥubaysh b. al-Ḥasan al-Dimashḳī; Ibn al-Ṣuḳāʿī
monasteries **Dayr**; Dayr al-Djāthalīḳ; Dayr Kaʿb; Dayr Ḳunnā; Dayr Murrān; Dayr Samʿān; al-Ṭūr.1
see also Khānḳāh; Rāhib; Ṭūr ʿAbdīn.3
writings on al-Shābushtī
persecutions Ghiyār; al-Ḥākim bi-Amr Allāh; Shiʿār.4; Zunnār
polemics Ahl al-Kitāb; Taḥrīf
anti-Jewish Petrus Alfonsi
Christian-Muslim al-Suʿūdī, Abu 'l-Faḍl; al-Ṭabarī, ʿAlī b. Rabban
see also Zaynab bt. Djaḥsh
pre-Islamic Abraha; ʿAdī b. Zayd; ʿAmr b. ʿAdī; ʿAmr b. Hind; Baḥīrā; Bahrām
see also Ghassān; Lakhmids
saints Djirdjīs; Djuraydj
20th-century al-Khūrī; Ṣarrūf; Shaykhū, Luwīs; [in Suppl.] Abū Shabaka; Abyaḍ
see also al-Maʿlūf

CIRCUMCISION Khafḍ; **Khitān**
see also ʿAbdī; ʿAlī; Kurds.iv.A.i; Mawākib.4.11; Wehbī Sayyidī

CLOTHING Banīḳa; Djallāb; Farw; Ḳumāsh; **Libās**; Sirwāl
see also Ghiyār; Iḥrām; Khayyāṭ; Khilʿa; Kurds.iv.C.1; Shiʿār.4; Ṭirāz; Zeybek; Zunnār; *and* → MYSTICISM.DRESS
accessories Mandīl; Mirwaḥa
see also Shadd
headwear Ḳawuḳlu; Tādj; Tulband
see also Sharīf.(5)
veils Ḥidjāb.I; Lithām
materials Farw; Ḥarīr; Kattān; Khaysh; Ḳuṭn; Ṣūf; Tāfta
see also Fanak; Ḳalamkārī; Ḳumāsh; Lubūd; Mukhattam; *and* → ART.TEXTILES

COLOUR **Lawn**; Musawwida
and → DYEING
colours Asfar
see also Sharīf.(5)

COMMONWEALTH OF INDEPENDENT STATES → CAUCASUS; CENTRAL ASIA; COMMUNISM; EUROPE.EASTERN EUROPE

COMMUNICATIONS Barīd; Ḥamām; Manār
see also Anadolu.iii.(5); *and* → TRANSPORT

COMMUNISM Ḥizb.i; **S̲h̲uyūʿiyya**
see also Lāhūtī

CONGO **Congo**; al-Murd̲j̲ibī

COSMETICS Ḥinnāʾ; al-Kuḥl; al-Was̲h̲m
see also K̲h̲iḍāb

COSMOGRAPHY ʿAd̲j̲āʾib; ʿĀlam; Falak; Ḳāf; Samāʾ.1
see also D̲j̲ug̲h̲rāfiyā; al-K̲h̲aḍir; K̲h̲arīṭa; al-Kura; Makka.4; *and* → ASTROLOGY; ASTRONOMY; GEOGRAPHY
treatises on al-Dimas̲h̲ḳī; al-Ḳazwīnī, Zakariyyāʾ; al-K̲h̲araḳī
see also Kitāb al-D̲j̲ilwa

COURT CEREMONY **Marāsim**; Mawākib
see also Hiba; K̲h̲ilʿa; Miẓalla; Naḳḳāra-k̲h̲āna; Nit̲h̲ār; Sitr; Yādgār; *and* → MONARCHY.ROYAL INSIGNIA

CREATION **Ibdāʿ**; **K̲h̲alḳ**
see also Ḥudūt̲h̲ al-ʿĀlam; Insān; Takwīn; Tawallud; Ṭīn.1

CRETE **Iḳrīṭis̲h̲**
see also Abū Ḥafṣ ʿUmar al-Ballūṭī; Wenedik
toponyms
towns Ḳandiya

CROATIA → (former) YUGOSLAVIA

CRUSADE(R)S **Crusades**; Tourkopo(u)loi; [in Suppl.] Dāwiyya and Isbitāriyya
see also al-ʿĀdil.1; al-Afḍal b. Badr al-D̲j̲amālī; (Sīrat) ʿAntar; Ayyūbids; Balak; Baybars I; Fāṭimids.5; Ifrand̲j̲; Ḳalāwūn; Ḳïlïd̲j̲ Arslan I; Nūr al-Dīn Maḥmūd b. Zankī; Ṣalāḥ al-Dīn; al-S̲h̲ām.2(a); Ṭug̲h̲tigin; Wenedik; *and* → *the section Toponyms under* PALESTINE *and* SYRIA
battles al-Manṣūra; Mard̲j̲ al-Ṣuffar; Nīkbūlī
castles al-Dārūm; Ḥārim; Ḥiṣn al-Akrād; Ḳalʿat al-S̲h̲aḳīf; Ṣāfīt̲h̲a
conquests ʿAkkā; Anadolu.iii.1; ʿĀsḳalān; Ayla; G̲h̲azza; Ḥayfā; Ḳayṣariyya; al-K̲h̲alīl; Ḳubrus.2; al-Ḳuds.10; Ludd; Maʿarrat al-Nuʿmān
historians of Ibn al-Ḳalānisī
see also al-Nuwayrī, Muḥammad

CRYPTOGRAPHY **Muʿammā**; Ramz.2
see also Kitābāt.5; al-Sīm

CUISINE **Maṭbakh**; **Ṭabkh**
drinks Čay; Ḳahwa; Khamr; Kumis; **Mashrūbāt**; Nabīdh; Sherbet
see also Naḥl; Thallādj; Turundjān; Yoghurt; [in Suppl.] Čāy-khāna
food **Ghidhāʾ**; Kabid.5; Khubz; Kuskusū; Mishmish; Nakhl; Nārandj; al-Ruzz; al-Samn; Sawīḳ; Shaʿīr; Sikbādj; Sukkar; **Ṭaʿām**; Tīn; Tuffāḥ; Yoghurt; Zabīb; Zayt; Zaytūn [in Suppl.] Basbās; Djawz; Ḥays; Hindibāʾ
see also Filāḥa; Ḳamḥ; Maḍīra; Milḥ; Naḥl; Pist; Simsim; Ṭīn.3; [in Suppl.] Ibn Shaḳrūn al-Miknāsī
fruit Mishmish; Nakhl; Nārandj; Tīn; Tuffāḥ
see also [in Suppl.] Ḥays
dried fruit Tammām; Zabīb
grains Ḳamḥ; Kuskusū; al-Ruzz; Shaʿīr
see also Filāḥa; Khubz; Sawīḳ
herbs Shibithth; Turundjān; [in Suppl.] Basbās
see also Shīḥ; Timsāḥ
meat Kabid.5
stews Sikbādj
oils al-Samn; Zayt
spices Kammūn; Ḳaranful; [in Suppl.] **Afāwīh**; Dār Ṣīnī
see also Kārimī; Ḳūṣ; Milḥ; Zaʿfarān.1
professions Baḳḳāl; Ṭabbākh; Ṭaḥḥān; Tammār
prohibitions Ghidhāʾ.iii and iv.7; Ḳahwa; Khamr; Mashrūbāt; Mayta; Nabīdh
see also Dhabīḥa.1; Ḥayawān.4; Nadjis; *and → individual articles under* ANIMALS
table manners **Ṭaʿām**

CUSTOM **ʿĀda**; Adab; ʿUrf
see also Abd al-Raḥmān al-Fāsī; ʿĀshūrāʾ.II; Hiba; Ḥidjāb.I; Īdjāra; Khilʿa; Mandīl; ʿUrs.2; *and →* LAW.CUSTOMARY LAW
tribal customs ʿAbābda; al-Dhunūb, Dafn; Khāwa; Muwāraba; Thaʾr; al-Washm; [in Suppl.] ʿĀr
see also Īdjāra; Taḥannuth; Zmāla.2

CYPRUS **Ḳubrus**; Madjlis.4.A.xxiv
see also Wenedik
toponyms
towns Lefḳosha; Maghōsha

(former) CZECHOSLOVAKIA [in Suppl.] **Čeh**

D

DEATH Djanāza; Ḥināṭa; Intiḥār; Ḳabr; Maḳbara; **Mawt**; Niyāḥa; [in Suppl.] Ghassāl
see also Ghā'ib; Ghusl; Ḳatl; Marthiya; Shahīd; Takbīr; Tasnīm.2; *and* → ARCHITECTURE.MONUMENTS.TOMBS; ESCHATOLOGY

DESERTS al-Aḥḳāf; Biyābānak; al-Dahnā'; Ḳaraḳum; Ḳi̊zi̊l-ḳum; Nafūd; al-Naḳb; al-Rubʿ al-Khālī; Sāḥil; al-Ṣaḥrā'; Sīnā'; al-Tīh
see also (Djazīrat) al-ʿArab.ii; Badw.II; Ḥarra; Khabrā'; Reg; Samūm; *and* → NOMADISM

DICTIONARY **Ḳāmūs**
see also Fāris al-Shidyāḳ; Sullam; *and* → LEXICOGRAPHY

DIPLOMACY Imtiyāzāt; Mübādele; Tardjumān
see also Amān; Bālyōs; Berātli̊; Daftar; Hiba; Inshā'; Kātib; Ḳawwās; Mandates
diplomatic accounts Aḥmad Rasmī; Ibn Faḍlān; Meḥmed Yirmisekiz; Wāṣif; [in Suppl.] al-Ghazzāl; Ibn ʿUthmān al-Miknāsī
see also Ṣubḥī Meḥmed
diplomats Consul; Elči; Safīr.2
see also Ẓahīr

DIVINATION **Kihāna**
see also Djafr; Ibn Barradjān; Malāḥim; Nudjūm (Aḥkām al-); Shāma; *and* → ASTROLOGY; DREAMS
diviners ʿArrāf; Kāhin
practices Fa'l; Firāsa; Ghurāb; Ḥisāb al-Djummal; Ḥurūf; Ikhtilādj; Istiḳsām; ʿIyāfa; al-Kaff; Katif; Khaṭṭ; Khawāṣṣ al-Ḳur'ān; Ḳiyāfa; Ḳurʿa; Mā'.1; Riyāfa; Wadaʿ.3; Zā'irdja
see also Būḳalā; Ikhtiyārāt; Mir'āt
treatises on Fāl-nāma; Ibn al-Bannā' al-Marrākushī; Malḥama; [in Suppl.] Ibn ʿAzzūz
see also Djafr; Nudjūm (Aḥkām al-)

DIVORCE Barā'a.I; Faskh; Suknā; al-Suraydjiyya; **Ṭalāḳ**
see also ʿAbd.3; ʿĀda; Ghā'ib; Ḥaḍāna; Ibn Suraydj; ʿIdda; ʿIwaḍ; Ḳasam; Liʿān; al-Mar'a.2; Rapak; *and* → MARRIAGE

DJIBOUTI, REPUBLIC OF **Djibūtī**; Tadjurra
and → AFRICA.EAST AFRICA

DOCUMENTS ʿAlāma; **Diplomatic**; Farmān; Inshāʾ; Kātib; Manshūr; Papyrus; **Sidjill**; Tawḳīʿ.1; Waḳf.I.2.d; Wathīḳa; Ẓahīr; [in Suppl.] Dabīr
see also Barāʾa.I; Ḳaṭʿ; Sharṭ.1; Tughra; ʿUnwān; Yarlïgh; *and* → ADMINISTRATION.RECORDS; WRITING
Ottoman ʿArḍ Ḥāl; Berāt; **Diplomatic**.iv; Farmān.ii; Irāde; Khaṭṭ-ï Humāyūn and Khaṭṭ-ï Sherīf; **Sidjill**.3; Telkhīṣ
See also Tughra.2.(b); *and* → OTTOMAN EMPIRE.ADMINISTRATION

DREAMS **Ru'yā**
see also Istikhāra; Nubuwwa
for dream interpretation, see individual articles on animals, in particular Ayyil; Baghl; Ḍabb; Fīl; Ghurāb; Saraṭān.5; Thaʿlab; ʿUḳāb; Waṭwāṭ; Yarbūʿ
writings on al-Dīnawarī, Abū Saʿīd; Ibn Ghannām; Ibn Shāhīn al-Ẓāhirī; Ibn Sīrīn; al-Wahrānī

DRUGS **Adwiya**; [in Suppl.] Anzarūt
see also Kahrubā; al-Kuḥl; Ṭibb; *and* → MEDICINE; PHARMACOLOGY
narcotics Afyūn; Bandj; Ḥashīsh; Ḳāt; Shahdānadj
see also Filāḥa.iii
tobacco Bahāʾī Meḥmed Efendi; **Tutun**

DRUZES al-Darazī; **Durūz**; Ḥamza b. ʿAlī; al-Muḳtanā; Shakīb Arslān; al-Tanūkhī, Djamāl al-Dīn; [in Suppl.] Binn
see also Ḥadd; Maḥkama.4.ii, iii and v; Maʿn; [in Suppl.] Dawr; Ḥinn; *and* → LEBANON
historians of Ṣāliḥ b. Yaḥyā

DYEING ʿAfṣ; Ḥinnāʾ; Ḳalamkārī; **Khiḍāb**; Nīl; Wars; Zaʿfarān
see also Shaʿr.1
dyer **Ṣabbāgh**

DYNASTIES **Dawla**; Ḥādjib; Mushīr; Sulṭān
see also Čāshna-gīr; Khādim al-Ḥaramayn; Laḳab; Libās.i; Malik; Marāsim; Mashwara; Mawākib; Pādishāh; Parda-dār; Tawḳīʿ.1; Walī al-ʿAhd; Ẓulm; *and* → ADMINISTRATION; ONOMASTICS.TITLES
Afghanistan and India ʿĀdil-Shāhs; Arghūn; Bahmanīs; Barīd Shāhīs; Dihlī Sultanate; Fārūḳids; Ghaznawids; Ghūrids; Hindū-shāhīs; ʿImād Shāhī; Kart; Khaldjīs; Ḳuṭb Shāhī; Lōdīs; Mughals; Niẓām Shāhīs; Sayyids; Sharḳīs; Sūrs; Tughluḳids; [in Suppl.] Bānīdjūrids
see also Afghānistān.v.2 and 3; Awadh; Dāwūdpōtrās; Dīwān.v; Hind.iv; Khʷādja-i Djahān; Lashkar; Marāsim.5; Mawākib.5; Nithār; Rānā Sāngā; Sammā; Tīpū Sulṭān; Zunbīl; *and* → ARCHITECTURE.REGIONS; MILITARY.

INDO-MUSLIM; ONOMASTICS.TITLES.INDO-MUSLIM

ʿĀdil-Shāhs (1490-1686) **ʿĀdil-Shāhs**; Bīdjāpūr; Hind.vii.ix
see also Tālīkōta
rulers Muḥammad b. Ibrāhīm II
historians of Shīrāzī, Rafīʿ al-Dīn

Awadh Nawwābs (1722-1856) **Awadh**
rulers Burhān al-Mulk; Ghāzi 'l-Dīn Ḥaydar; Saʿādat ʿAlī Khān; Ṣafdar Djang; Shudjāʿ al-Dawla
viziers Mahdī ʿAlī Khān

Bahmanids (1347-1527) **Bahmanīs**; Hind.vii.vii
see also Bīdar; Gulbargā; Pēshwā
rulers Humāyūn Shāh Bahmanī; Maḥmūd Shihāb al-Dīn; Muḥammad I; Muḥammad II; Muḥammad III
other personages Khalīl Allāh; Maḥmūd Gāwān

Bārakzays (1819-1973) Afghānistān.v.3.B
kings ʿAbd al-Raḥmān Khān; Dūst Muḥammad; Ḥabīb Allāh Khān; Shīr ʿAlī; [in Suppl] Amān Allāh

Bengal Nawwābs
rulers ʿAlī Werdī Khān; Djaʿfar; Sirādj al-Dawla
see also Murshidābād

Bengal Sultans (1336-1576)
sultans Dāwūd Khān Kararānī; Fakhr al-Dīn Mubārakshāh; Ḥusayn Shāh; Maḥmūd; Rādjā Ganesh; Rukn al-Dīn Bārbak Shāh; Sikandar Shāh
historians of [in Suppl.] ʿAbbās Sarwānī

Dihlī Sultans (1206-1555) Ḍarība.6.a; **Dihlī Sultanate**; Dīwān.v; Khaldjīs; Lōdīs; Nāʾib.1; Naḳīb.2; Sayyids; Sūrs; Tughluḳids
see also Burdj.III.2; Ulugh Khān
sultans Fīrūz Shāh Tughluḳ; Ghiyāth al-Dīn Tughluḳ I; Ghiyāth al-Dīn Tughluḳ Shāh II; Iltutmish; Kayḳubād; Khiḍr Khān; Ḳuṭb al-Dīn Aybak; Maḥmūd; Ibrāhīm Lōdī; Mubārak Shāh; Muḥammad b. Tughluḳ; Muḥammad Shāh I Khaldjī; Raḍiyya; Shir Shāh Sūr; [in Suppl.] Balban; Dawlat Khān Lōdī
viziers Kāfūr (*and* Malik Kāfūr); Khān-i Djahān Maḳbūl; Miʾān Bhuʾā
historians of Baranī; al-Djuzdjānī; Niẓāmī (*and* [in Suppl.] Ḥasan Niẓāmī); Shams al-Dīn-i Sirādj ʿAfīf
other personages Mallū Iḳbāl Khān; [in Suppl.] ʿAbd al-Wahhāb Bukhārī; ʿAyn al-Mulk Multānī; Daryā Khān Noḥānī; Ikhtisān
see also ʿAlī Mardān; Hūlāgū; Khaldjīs; Sammā

Durrānīs (1747-1842) Afghānistān.v.3
kings Aḥmad Shāh Durrānī
historians of ʿAbd al-Karīm Munshī

other personages Kāmrān S͟hāh Durrānī
Fārūḳids (1370-1601) **Fārūḳids**
rulers Mīrān Muḥammad S͟hāh I
G͟haznawids (977-1186) ʿAmīd; Dīwān.v; **G͟haznawids**
see also Ḥiṣār.iii
rulers Alp Takīn; Bahrām S͟hāh; Ismāʿīl b. Sebüktigin; Maḥmūd b. Sebüktigin; Masʿūd b. Maḥmūd; Mawdūd b. Masʿūd; Muḥammad b. Maḥmūd b. Sebüktigin; Sebüktigin
viziers Aḥmad b. Muḥammad; Altūntās͟h; al-Faḍl b. Aḥmad al-Isfarāʾinī; Ḥasanak; Maymandī
historians of Bayhaḳī; al-ʿUtbī.3
see also al-Ḳās͟hānī; S͟habānkāraʾī; [in Suppl.] Fak͟hr-i Mudabbir
other personages Muḥammad Bak͟htiyār K͟haldjī; S͟hāh Malik
G͟hūrids (ca. 1000-1215) **G͟hūrids**
rulers Djahān-sūz; Muḥammad b. Sām; Sayf al-Dīn
see also Niẓāmī
governors Tādj al-Dīn Yildiz
Gudjarāt Sultans (1391-1583) Gudjarāt.c
see also Ulug͟h K͟hān
sultans Bahādur S͟hāh Gudjarātī; Maḥmūd
historians of [in Suppl.] Ḥādjdjī al-Dabīr
other personages Malik Ayāz
Kālpī Sultans Kalpī
sultans Maḥmūd K͟hān
Kas͟hmīr Sultans (1346-1589) Kas͟hmīr.i.4
sultans Sikandar (But-S͟hikan); Zayn al-ʿĀbidīn; [in Suppl.] Čaks
see also [in Suppl.] Gul K͟hātūn
historians of [in Suppl.] Ḥaydar Malik
other personages [in Suppl.] Bayḥaḳī Sayyids
Langāh dynasty of Multān (1437-1526) Multān
sultans Ḥusayn S͟hāh Langāh I; Ḥusayn S͟hāh Langāh II
Madura Sultans
sultans Djalāl al-Dīn Aḥsan
Mālwā Sultans (1401-1531) Mālwā
sultans Dilāwar K͟hān; Hūs͟hang S͟hāh G͟hūrī; Maḥmūd
see also Bāz Bahādur
viziers Mēdinī Rāʾī
other personages Malik Mug͟hīt͟h
Mug͟hals (1526-1858) Ḍarība.6.b and c; Dīwān.v; Manṣab; **Mug͟hals**; [in Suppl.] Ilāhī Era
see also Fawdjdār; Kōtwāl; Maṭbak͟h.4; Nit͟hār; Ṣadr.5; Ṣūba; Ṣūbadār; Ṣūfiyāna; Ṣulḥ-i kull; Suwār; Tak͟ht-i Ṭāwūs; Zamīndār; [in Suppl.] Dāg͟h

u taṣḥīḥa; ʿIbādat K̲h̲āna

emperors　Aḥmad S̲h̲āh.I; Akbar; Awrangzīb; Bābur; Bahādur S̲h̲āh I; Bahādur S̲h̲āh II; D̲j̲ahāndār S̲h̲āh; D̲j̲ahāngīr; Farruk̲h̲-siyar; Humāyūn; Muḥammad S̲h̲āh; S̲h̲āh ʿĀlam II; S̲h̲āh D̲j̲ahān

　　see also Dars̲h̲an; Mumtāz Maḥall; Nūr D̲j̲ahān; Tād̲j̲ Maḥall; Tūzūk

viziers　Iʿtimād al-Dawla

secretaries　Abu ʾl-Faḍl ʿAllāmī; Muḥammad Kāẓim

historians of　ʿAbd al-Ḥamīd Lāhawrī; Abu ʾl Faḍl ʿAllāmī; Bak̲h̲tāwar K̲h̲ān; D̲j̲awhar; G̲h̲ulām Ḥusayn K̲h̲ān Ṭabāṭabāʾī; ʿInāyat Allāh K̲h̲ān; Īsar-dās; K̲h̲ʷāfī K̲h̲ān; Muḥammad Kāẓim; Muḥammad S̲h̲arīf; Mustaʿidd K̲h̲ān; Muʿtamad K̲h̲ān; Niʿmat Allāh b. Ḥabīb Allāh Harawī; Nūr al-Ḥaḳḳ al-Dihlawī; [in Suppl.] ʿĀḳil K̲h̲ān Rāzī

　　see also Aẓfarī; Badāʾūnī; Maʾāt̲h̲ir al-Umarāʾ

other personages　ʿAbd al-Raḥīm K̲h̲ān; ʿAlī Werdī K̲h̲ān; Āṣaf K̲h̲ān; Bak̲h̲tāwar K̲h̲ān; Bayram K̲h̲ān; Burhān al-Mulk; Dāniyāl; G̲h̲ulām Ḳādir Rohilla; Hindāl; Iʿtibār K̲h̲ān; Iʿtiḳād K̲h̲ān; ʿIwaḍ Wad̲j̲īh; Kāmrān; K̲h̲ān D̲j̲ahān Lōdī; K̲h̲usraw Sulṭān; Mahābat K̲h̲ān; Mak̲h̲dūm al-Mulk (*and* [in Suppl.] ʿAbd Allāh Sulṭānpūrī); Mān Singh; Mīr D̲j̲umla; Mīrzā ʿAskarī; Mīrzā ʿAzīz "Kōka"; Murād; Murād Bak̲h̲s̲h̲; Murs̲h̲id Ḳulī K̲h̲ān; Niẓām al-Mulk; S̲h̲afīʿā Yazdī; S̲h̲āh Manṣūr S̲h̲īrāzī; S̲h̲arīf Āmulī; al-Siyālkūtī; Tīpū Sulṭān; Tōdar Mal; Yūsuf K̲h̲ān Riḍwī; Yūsufī; [in Suppl.] Akbar b. Awrangzīb; ʿĀḳil K̲h̲ān Rāzī; G̲h̲āzī K̲h̲ān; Gūran; ʿInāyat K̲h̲ān (2x)

　　see also Bāra Sayyids (*and* [in Suppl.] Bārha Sayyids); Marāt̲h̲ās

Niẓām S̲h̲āhids (1491-1633)　**Niẓām S̲h̲āhīs**

　　see also Aḥmadnagar; Tālīkōtā

rulers　Ḥusayn Niẓām S̲h̲āh; Malik Aḥmad Baḥrī

other personages　Malik ʿAmbar

S̲h̲arḳī Sultans of D̲j̲awnpūr (1394-1479)　**S̲h̲arḳīs**

sultans　Ḥusayn S̲h̲āh; Ibrāhīm S̲h̲āh S̲h̲arḳī; Maḥmūd S̲h̲āh S̲h̲arḳī; Malik Sarwar

Africa　Fund̲j̲; Gwandu; S̲h̲īrāzī

　　see also Bū Saʿīd; Dār Fūr; Kilwa; Songhay; Wadāī.1; Zag̲h̲āwa.(a)

Anatolia and the Turks　Artuḳids; Aydi̊n-og̲h̲lu; Dānis̲h̲mendids; D̲h̲u ʾl-Ḳadr; Eretna; Germiyān-og̲h̲ullari̊; Ḥamīd Og̲h̲ullari̊; Īnāl; Isfendiyār Og̲h̲lu; Ḳarāmān-og̲h̲ullari̊; Ḳarasi̊; Mentes̲h̲e-og̲h̲ullari̊; ʿOt̲h̲mānli̊; Saltuḳ Og̲h̲ullari̊; Ṣarūk̲h̲ān; S̲h̲āh-i Arman; Teke-og̲h̲ullari̊

　　see also Būrids; Derebey; Mangi̊ts; Mengüček; Ramaḍān Og̲h̲ullari̊; *and* → ONOMASTICS.TITLES

Artuḳids (1102-1408)　**Artuḳids**

rulers　Īlg̲h̲āzī; Nūr al-Dīn Muḥammad; Timurtās̲h̲ b. Il-G̲h̲āzī

Aydi̊n-og̲h̲lu (1308-1425)　**Aydi̊n-og̲h̲lu**

amīrs D̲junayd

Ottomans (1281-1924) **ʿOt̲h̲mānli̊**

see also ʿOt̲h̲mān I; *and* → DOCUMENTS.OTTOMAN; MILITARY.OTTOMAN; OTTOMAN EMPIRE; TURKEY.OTTOMAN PERIOD

sultans ʿAbd al-ʿAzīz; ʿAbd al-Ḥamīd I; ʿAbd al-Ḥamīd II; ʿAbd al-Mad̲j̲īd I; ʿAbd al-Mad̲j̲īd II; Aḥmad I; Aḥmad II; Aḥmad III; Bāyazīd I; Bāyazīd II; Ibrāhīm; Maḥmūd; Meḥemmed I; Meḥemmed II; Meḥemmed III; Meḥemmed IV; Meḥemmed V Res̲h̲ād; Meḥemmed VI Waḥīd al-Dīn; Murād I; Murād II; Murād III; Murād IV; Murād V; Muṣṭafā I; Muṣṭafā II; Muṣṭafā III; Muṣṭafā IV; Ork̲h̲an; ʿOt̲h̲mān I; ʿOt̲h̲mān II; ʿOt̲h̲mān III; Selīm I; Selīm II; Selīm III; Süleymān; Süleymān II

see also Bāb-i Humāyūn; D̲jem; Ertog̲h̲rul; K̲h̲ādim al-Ḥaramayn; K̲h̲alīfa.i.E; K̲h̲urrem; Kösem Wālide; Mas̲h̲wara; Muhr.1; Muṣṭafā.1 and 2; Müteferriḳa; Nīlūfer K̲h̲ātūn; Nūr Bānū; Rikāb; Ṣafiyye Wālide Sulṭān; S̲h̲ehzāde; Ṣolaḳ; Ṭopḳapi̊ Sarāyi̊; Ṭurk̲h̲ān Sulṭān; Wālide Sulṭān; Yeñi Čeri.3

grand viziers **Ṣadr-ı Aʿẓam**

see also Bāb-i ʿĀlī; Ba_vekil; Ḳapi̊; ʿOt̲h̲mān-zāde; Telk̲h̲īṣd̲j̲i; Wazīr.III

14th century ʿAlī Pas̲h̲a Čandārli̊-zāde; D̲j̲andarli̊

15th century Aḥmad Pas̲h̲a Gedik; Dāwūd Pas̲h̲a, Ḳod̲j̲a; D̲j̲andarli̊; K̲h̲alīl Pas̲h̲a D̲j̲andarli̊; Maḥmūd Pas̲h̲a; Meḥmed Pas̲h̲a, Ḳaramānī; Meḥmed Pas̲h̲a, Rūm; Sinān Pas̲h̲a, K̲h̲od̲j̲a.1; Zag̲h̲anos Pas̲h̲a

16th century Aḥmad Pas̲h̲a, Ḳara; ʿAlī Pas̲h̲a K̲h̲ādim; ʿAlī Pas̲h̲a Semiz; Ayās Pas̲h̲a; Čig̲h̲āla-zāde Sinān Pās̲h̲ā; Derwīs̲h̲ Pas̲h̲a; Ferhād Pas̲h̲a; Hersek-zāde; Ibrāhīm Pas̲h̲a; Ibrāhīm Pas̲h̲a, Dāmād; K̲h̲ādi̊m Ḥasan Pas̲h̲a Ṣoḳolli̊; K̲h̲ādi̊m Süleymān Pas̲h̲a; Lala Meḥmed Pas̲h̲a (*and* Meḥmed Pas̲h̲a, Lālā, S̲h̲āhīnog̲h̲lu); Luṭfī Pas̲h̲a; Meḥmed Pas̲h̲a, Lālā, Melek-Nihād; Mesīḥ Meḥmed Pas̲h̲a; Mesīḥ Pas̲h̲a; ʿOt̲h̲mān Pas̲h̲a; Pīrī Meḥmed Pas̲h̲a; Rüstem Pas̲h̲a; Sinān Pas̲h̲a, K̲h̲ādi̊m; Sinān Pas̲h̲a, K̲h̲od̲j̲a.2; Siyāwus̲h̲ Pas̲h̲a.1; Soḳollu Meḥmed Pas̲h̲a

17th century ʿAlī Pas̲h̲a ʿArabad̲j̲i̊; ʿAlī Pas̲h̲a Güzeld̲j̲e; ʿAlī Pas̲h̲a Sürmeli; Dāwūd Pas̲h̲a, Ḳara; Derwīs̲h̲ Meḥmed Pas̲h̲a; Dilāwar Pas̲h̲a; Ḥāfiẓ Aḥmed Pas̲h̲a; Ḥusayn Pas̲h̲a; Ibrāhīm Pas̲h̲a, Kara; Ips̲h̲ir Muṣṭafā Pas̲h̲a; Ismāʿīl Pas̲h̲a, Nis̲h̲ānd̲j̲i̊; Ḳarā Muṣṭafā Pas̲h̲a; Kemānkes̲h̲; K̲h̲alīl Pas̲h̲a Ḳayṣariyyeli; K̲h̲osrew Pas̲h̲a, Bosniak; Köprülü.I-III; Meḥmed Pas̲h̲a, Čerkes; Meḥmed Pas̲h̲a, Elmās; Meḥmed Pas̲h̲a, Gürd̲j̲ü, K̲h̲ādi̊m; Meḥmed Pas̲h̲a, Gürd̲j̲ü II; Meḥmed Pas̲h̲a, Öküz; Meḥmed Pas̲h̲a, Sulṭān-zāde; Meḥmed Pas̲h̲a, Tabani̊-yassi̊; Murād Pas̲h̲a, Ḳuyud̲j̲u; Naṣūḥ Pas̲h̲a; Red̲j̲eb Pas̲h̲a; Siyāwus̲h̲

Pasha.2; Süleymān Pasha, Malaṭyalî; Yemishdji Ḥasan Pasha
18th century ʿAbd Allāh Pasha; ʿAlī Pasha Čorlulu; ʿAlī Pasha Dāmād; ʿAlī Pasha Ḥakīm-oghlu; Derwīsh Meḥmed Pasha; Ḥamza Ḥāmid Pasha; Ḥamza Pasha; (Dāmād) Ḥasan Pasha; (Seyyid) Ḥasan Pasha; (Sherīf) Ḥasan Pasha; Ibrāhīm Pasha, Nevshehirli; Kaḥyā Ḥasan Pasha; Khalīl Pasha Ḥādjdjī Arnawud; Köprülü.V; Meḥmed Pasha, Balṭadjî; Meḥmed Pasha, ʿIwaḍ; Meḥmed Pasha, Melek; Meḥmed Pasha, Muḥsin-zāde; Meḥmed Pasha Rāmī (*and* Rāmī Meḥmed Pasha); Meḥmed Pasha, Tiryāḳī; Meḥmed Pasha, Yegen, Gümrükčü; Meḥmed Pasha, Yegen, Ḥādjdjī; Rāghib Pasha; Saʿīd Efendi; Ṭopal ʿOthmān Pasha.1
19th century and on Aḥmad Wafīḳ Pasha; ʿAlī Pasha Muḥammad Amīn; Dāmād Ferīd Pasha; Derwīsh Meḥmed Pasha; Djawād Pasha; Fuʾād Pasha; Ḥusayn ʿAwnī Pasha; Ḥusayn Ḥilmī Pasha; Ibrāhīm Edhem Pasha; Ibrāhīm Ḥaḳḳī Pasha; ʿIzzet Pasha; Kečiboynuzu; Khayr al-Dīn Pasha; Khosrew Pasha, Meḥmed; Küčük Saʿīd Pasha; Maḥmūd Nedīm Pasha; Maḥmūd Shewḳat Pasha; Meḥmed Saʿīd Ghālib Pasha; Midḥat Pasha; Muṣṭafā Pasha, Bayraḳdār; Reshīd Pasha, Muṣṭafā; Ṭalʿat Bey; [in Suppl.] Esʿad Pasha
grand muftis **Shaykh al-Islām**.2
see also Bāb-i Mashīkhat; Fatwā.ii
15th century Fenārī-zāde; Gūrānī; Khosrew
16th century Abu ʾl-Suʿūd; Bostānzāde.2; Čiwi-zāde; Djamālī; Kemāl Pasha-zāde; Khōdja Efendi
17th century Bahāʾī Meḥmed Efendi; Esʿad Efendi, Meḥmed; Ḳarā-Čelebi-zāde.4; Ṣunʿ Allāh
18th century Čelebi-zāde; Dürrīzāde.1-4; Esʿad Efendi, Meḥmed (2x); Ḥayātī-zāde.2; Meḥmed Ṣāliḥ Efendi; Pīrī-zāde
19th century ʿĀrif Ḥikmet Bey; Dürrīzāde.5; Esʿad Efendi, Aḥmed; Ḥasan Fehmī Efendi
20th century Djamāl al-Dīn Efendi; Dürrīzāde,ʿAbd Allāh; Muṣṭafā Khayrī Efendi
high admirals ʿAlī Pasha Güzeldje; Čighāla-zāde Sinān Pasha; Djaʿfar Beg; Djezāʾirli Ghāzī Ḥasan Pasha; Ḥasan Pasha; Ḥusayn Pasha; Kenʿān Pasha; Khalīl Pasha Ḳayṣariyyeli; Khayr al-Dīn Pasha; Piyāle Pasha; ʿUlūdj ʿAlī; Zaghanos Pasha
see also Raʾīs.3
historians of ʿAbdī; ʿAbdī Efendi; ʿAbdī Pasha; Aḥmad Djewdet Pasha; Aḥmad Rasmī; ʿAlī; ʿAlī Amīrī; ʿĀshîḳ-pasha-zāde; ʿĀṣim; ʿAṭāʾ Bey; al-Bakrī.1; Bidlīsī; Bihishtī; Čelebi-zāde; Česhmīzāde; Djalālzāde Muṣṭafā Čelebi; Djalālzāde Ṣāliḥ Čelebi; Enwerī; Esʿad Efendi, Meḥmed; Ḥasan Bey-zāde; ʿIzzī; Ḳarā-čelebi-zāde.4; Kātib Čelebi;

Kemāl, Meḥmed Nāmïḳ; Kemāl Pasha-zāde; Khayr Allāh Efendi; Luḳmān b. Sayyid Ḥusayn; Luṭfī Efendi; Maṭrāḳčï; Meḥmed Ḥākim Efendi; Meḥmed Khalīfe b. Ḥüseyn; Meḥmed Pasha, Ḳaramānī; Meḥmed Zaʿīm; Muḥyi 'l-Dīn Meḥmed; Naʿīmā; ʿOthmān-zāde; Pečewī; Ramaḍān-zāde; Rāshid, Meḥmed; Rūḥī; Selānīkī; Shefīḳ Meḥmed Efendi; Shemʿdānī-zāde; Sheref, ʿAbd al-Raḥmān; Silāḥdār, Fïndïḳlïlï Meḥmed Agha; Ṣolaḳ-zāde; Ṣubḥī Meḥmed; Taʿlīḳī-zāde; Ṭashköprüzāde.2 and 3; Thüreyyā; Ṭūrsūn Beg; Urudj; ʿUshshāḳī-zāde, Ibrāhīm; Wāṣif; Wedjīhī; Yakhshī Faḳīh
see also Ḥadīdī; Shāhnāmedji; Waḳaʿ-nüwīs
other personages
see also Shehzāde; Yazïdjï
13th century Sawdjï.1
14th century ʿAlāʾ al-Dīn Beg; Badr al-Dīn b. Ḳāḍī Samāwnā; Ḳāsim.1; Sawdjï.3; Shāhīn, Lala; Süleymān Pasha
see also Ṭorghud
15th century Aḥmad Pasha Khāʾin; Ewrenos; Ewrenos Oghullarï; Fenārī-zāde; Ibn ʿArabshāh; Ḳāsim.2 and 3; Ḳāsim Pasha, Djazarī; Mūsā Čelebi; Muṣṭafā.1 and 2; Suleymān Čelebi; Tīmūrtāsh Oghullarï; Turakhān Beg
16th century Bostānzāde; Čiwi-zāde; Derwīsh Pasha; Djaʿfar Čelebi; Djalālzāde Muṣṭafā Čelebi; Ferīdūn Beg; Hāmōn; Ḳāsim.4; Ḳāsim Agha; Ḳāsim Pasha; Kemāl Reʾīs; Khosrew Pasha; Ḳorḳud b. Bāyazīd; Maḥmūd Pasha; Maḥmūd Tardjumān; Meḥmed Pasha, Bïyïḳlï; Muṣṭafā.3; Muṣṭafā Pasha, Ḳara Shāhīn; Muṣṭafā Pasha, Lala; Muṣṭafā Pasha al-Nashshār; Özdemir Pasha; Pertew Pasha.I; Pīrī Reʾīs; Ramaḍān-zāde; Rïḍwān Pasha; Ṣarï Kürz; Selmān Reʾīs; Shāh Sulṭān; Shāhīn, Āl; Sīdī ʿAlī Reʾīs; Sinān; Ṭashköprüzāde.1; Ṭorghud Reʾīs; ʿUshshāḳī-zāde.1; Üweys
17th century Ābāza; Ḥaydar-oghlu, Meḥmed; Ḥusayn Pasha; Ḳāsim.5; Ḳāṭïrdjï-oghlï Meḥmed Pasha; Maʿn-zāda; Meḥmed Khalīfe b. Ḥüseyn; ʿOthmān Pasha, Yegen; Shāhīn, Āl; Ṭiflī; ʿUshshāḳī-zāde.1; Warwarī ʿAlī Pasha; [in Suppl.] Aḥmad Pasha Küčük; Cōbān-oghullarï
18th century Ābāza; Aḥmad Pasha; Aḥmad Pasha Bonneval; Aḥmad Rasmī; Djānīkli Ḥādjdji ʿAlī Pasha; Meḥmed Ḥākim Efendi; Meḥmed Yirmisekiz; Paswan-oghlu; Patrona Khalīl; Ṣarï Meḥmed Pasha; ʿUshshāḳī-zāde.1
19th century Aḥmad Djewdet Pasha; ʿAlī Pasha Tepedelenli; Ayyūb Ṣabrī Pasha; Bahdjat Muṣṭafā Efendi; Dāwūd Pasha (2x); Djawād Pasha; Fāḍil Pasha; Ḥālet Efendi; Ḥusayn Pasha; Ibrāhīm Derwīsh Pasha; Kabakčï-oghlu Muṣṭafā; Ḳōzān-oghullarï; Muṣṭafā

Pasha, Bushatli̊; Pertew Pasha.II; Riḍwān Begović; Ṣādi̊ḳ Rifʿat Pasha; Shebṣefa Ḳadi̊n; Ṭopal ʿOthmān Pasha.2; [in Suppl.] Camondo

20th century ʿAbd al-Ḥaḳḳ Ḥāmid; Djāwīd; Djemāl Pasha; Enwer Pasha; Fehīm Pasha; Ḥasan Fehmī; ʿIzzet Pasha; Kāẓi̊m Ḳadrī; Kāẓi̊m Karabekir; Mukhtār Pasha; Münīf Pasha

Saldjūḳs of Rūm (1077-1307) **Saldjūḳids**

rulers Kaykāʾūs; Kaykhusraw; Kayḳubād; Ḳi̊li̊dj Arslan I; Ḳi̊li̊dj Arslan II; Ḳi̊li̊dj Arslan III; Ḳi̊li̊dj Arslan IV; Malik-Shāh.4; Sulaymān b. Ḳutulmi̊sh; Ṭoghri̊l Shāh

historians of Ibn Bībī

other personages Ashraf Oghullari̊; Muʿīn al-Dīn Sulaymān Parwāna; Saʿd al-Dīn Köpek

Arabian Peninsula Bū Saʿīd; Hamdānids; Hāshimids (2x); āl-Khalīfa; Mahdids; Nadjāḥids; Rashīd, Āl; Rasūlids; Ṣabāḥ, Āl; Ṣulayḥids; Suʿūd, Āl; Ṭāhirids.3; al-Ukhayḍir, Banū; ʿUṣfūrids; ʿUyūnids; Wāḥidī; Yaʿrubids; Yuʿfirids; Ziyādids; [in Suppl.] Djabrids

Āl Saʿūd (1746-) **Suʿūd, Āl**

rulers [in Suppl.] ʿAbd al-ʿAzīz; Fayṣal b. ʿAbd al-ʿAzīz

see also Muḥammad b. Suʿūd

Bū Saʿīd (1741-) **Bū Saʿīd**

sultans Barghash; Saʿīd b. Sulṭān

Carmathians (894-end 11th century) **Ḳarmaṭī**

rulers al-Djannābī, Abū Saʿīd; al-Djannābī, Abū Ṭāhir

Hāshimids (1908-1925) **Hāshimids**

rulers Ḥusayn (b. ʿAlī)

see also ʿAbd Allāh b. al-Ḥusayn; Fayṣal I; Fayṣal II

other personages Zayd b. al-Ḥusayn b. ʿAlī

Rasūlids (1229-1454) **Rasūlids**

see also Zabīd

historians of al-Khazradjī

other personages [in Suppl.] Ibn Ḥātim

see also al-Sharīf Abū Muḥammad Idrīs

Ṭāhirids (1454-1517) **Ṭāhirids**.3

rulers ʿĀmir I; ʿĀmir II

Zaydīs (860-) Rassids

imāms Ḥasan al Uṭrūsh; al-Mahdī li-Dīn Allāh Aḥmad; al-Manṣūr bi ’llāh, ʿAbd Allāh; al-Manṣūr bi ’llāh, al-Ḳāsim b. ʿAlī; al-Manṣūr bi ’llāh, al-Ḳāsim b. Muḥammad; al-Muʾayyad bi ’llāh Muḥammad; Muḥammad al-Murtaḍā li-Dīn Allāh; al-Mutawakkil ʿalā ’llāh, Ismāʿīl; al-Mutawakkil ʿalā ’llāh, Sharaf al-Dīn; al-Nāṣir li-Dīn Allāh, Aḥmad; al-Rassī; Yaḥyā b. Ḥamza al-ʿAlawī; Yaḥyā b. Muḥammad;

[in Suppl.] al-Ḥādī ila ʾl-Ḥaḳḳ
see also Imāma; al-Yaman.3.a
other personages al-Muṭahhar; al-Nāṣir li-Dīn Allāh; al-Sharīf Abū Muḥammad Idrīs; al-Thāʾir fi ʾllāh

Zurayʿids (1080-1173) **Zurayʿids**
viziers Bilāl b. Djarīr al-Muḥammadī

Egypt and the Fertile Crescent ʿAbbāsids; ʿAnnāzids; Ayyūbids; Bābān; Būrids; Fāṭimids; Ḥamdānids; Ḥasanwayh; Mamlūks; Marwānids; Mazyad; Mirdās; Ṭūlūnids; ʿUḳaylids; Umayyads; Zangids
see also ʿAmmār; Begteginids; Djalīlī; Ṣadaḳa, Banū; *and* → EGYPT. MODERN PERIOD.MUḤAMMAD ʿALĪ'S LINE; ONOMASTICS.TITLES.ARABIC

ʿAbbāsids (749-1258) → CALIPHATE

Ayyūbids (1169-end 15th century) **Ayyūbids**
see also Rank
rulers al-ʿĀdil; al-Afḍal; Bahrām Shāh; al-Kāmil; al-Muʿaẓẓam; al-Nāṣir; Ṣalāḥ al-Dīn; (al-Malik) al-Ṣāliḥ ʿImād al-Dīn; (al-Malik) al-Ṣāliḥ Nadjm al-Dīn Ayyūb; Tūrānshāh b. Ayyūb; al-Ẓāhir Ghāzī
see also Dīwān.ii.(3)
viziers Ibn al-ʿAdīm; Ibn al-Athīr.3; Ibn Maṭrūḥ
see also Wazīr.I.3
secretaries ʿImād al-Dīn; al-Ḳāḍī al-Fāḍil
historians of Abu ʾl-Fidā; Abū Shāma; Ibn Shaddād; ʿImād al-Dīn; al-Maḳrīzī; al-Manṣūr, al-Malik
other personages Abu ʾl-Fidā; Aybak; Ibn al-ʿAssāl; Ḳarāḳūsh, Bahāʾ al-Dīn; Ḳarāḳūsh, Sharaf al-Dīn; al-Muẓaffar, al-Malik

Būrids (1104-54) **Būrids**; Dimashḳ
rulers Ṭughtigin

Fāṭimids (909-1171) → CALIPHATE

Ḥamdānids (905-1004) **Ḥamdānids**
rulers Nāṣir al-Dawla; Sayf al-Dawla; [in Suppl.] Abū Taghlib
other personages Ḥusayn b. Ḥamdān; Luʾluʾ

Ikhshīdids (935-969)
rulers Kāfūr
viziers Ibn al-Furāt.5
other personages al-Ṣayrafī

Mamluks (1250-1517) Dhu ʾl-Faḳāriyya; Dīwān.ii.(4); Ḥādjib.iv; Hiba.ii; Khādim al-Ḥaramayn; Khaznadār; **Mamlūks**; Mashwara; Nāʾib.1; Ustādār
see also Ḥarfūsh; Ḳumāsh; Mamlūk; Manshūr; Rank; Zaʿīm; *and* → MILITARY.MAMLUK
sultans Barḳūḳ; Barsbāy; Baybars I; Baybars II; Čaḳmaḳ; Faradj; Ḥasan; Īnāl al-Adjrūd; Ḳāʾit Bāy; Ḳalāwūn; Ḳānṣawh al-Ghawrī;

Khalīl; Khushkadam; Ḳuṭuz; Lādjīn; al-Muʾayyad Shaykh; al-Nāṣir; (al-Malik) al-Ṣāliḥ; Shaʿbān; Shadjar al-Durr; Ṭūmān Bāy

administrators Faḍl Allāh; Ibn ʿAbd al-Ẓāhir; Ibn Faḍl al-ʿUmarī; Ibn Ghurāb; Ibn Ḥidjdja; Ibn al-Sadīd (Ibn al-Muzawwiḳ); Ibn al-Sadīd, Karīm al-Dīn; al-Ḳalḳashandī.1; [in Suppl.] Ibn al-Ṣuḳāʿ

historians of Abu 'l-Maḥāsin b. Taghrībirdī; Baybars al-Manṣūrī; Ibn ʿAbd al-Ẓāhir; Ibn Duḳmāḳ; Ibn Ḥabīb, Badr al-Dīn; Ibn Iyās; Ibn Shāhīn al-Ẓāhirī; al-Maḳrīzī; al-Mufaḍḍal b. Abi 'l-Faḍāʾil; al-Nuwayrī, Shihāb al-Dīn; al-Ṣafadī, al-Ḥasan; Shāfiʿ b. ʿAlī; al-Shudjāʿī

other personages Abu 'l-Fidā; al-ʿAynī; Ibn Djamāʿa; Ibn al-Mundhir; Tankiz

Marwānids (983-1085) **Marwānids**

rulers Naṣr al-Dawla

Mazyadids (ca. 961-1150) **Mazyad**; Ṣadaḳa, Banū

rulers Ṣadaḳa b. Manṣūr

Mirdāsids (1023-1079) **Mirdās**

see also Asad al-Dawla

Ṭūlūnids (868-905) **Ṭūlūnids**

rulers Aḥmad b. Ṭūlūn; Khumārawayh

see also Ibn al-Mudabbir.1

historians of al-Balawī; Ibn al-Dāya

other personages [in Suppl.] al-ʿAbbās b. Aḥmad b. Tūlūn

ʿUḳaylids (ca. 990-1169) **ʿUḳaylids**

rulers Muslim b. Ḳuraysh

Umayyads (661-750) → CALIPHATE

Zangids (1127-1222) **Zangids**

rulers Masʿūd b. Mawdūd b. Zangī; Mawdūd b. ʿImād al-Dīn Zankī; Nūr al-Dīn Arslān Shāh; Nūr al-Dīn Maḥmūd b. Zankī; Zangī

viziers al-Djawād al-Iṣfahānī

see also Begteginids; Karīm Khān Zand; Luʾluʾ, Badr al-Dīn

historians of Ibn al-Athīr.2

other personages Shīrkūh

Mongols Batuʾids; Čaghatay Khānate; Čingizids; Djānids; Girāy; Īlkhāns; Ḳarā Khiṭāy; **Mongols**; Shībānids

see also Čūbānids; Ḳāzān; Ordu.2; Soyūrghāl; Tīmūrids; [in Suppl.] Āgahī; Dīwān-begi; Djamāl Ḳarshī; *and* → LAW.MONGOL; MONGOLIA.MONGOLS; ONOMASTICS.TITLES.MONGOLIAN

Batuʾids (1236-1502) **Batuʾids**

see also Saray

rulers Batu; Berke; Mangū-tīmūr; Toḳtamīsh

other personages Masʿūd Beg

Čaghatayids (1227-1370) **Čaghatay Khānate**
rulers Burāḳ Khān; Čaghatay Khān; Tughluḳ Temür
historians of Ḥaydar Mīrzā
Djānids (1598-1785) **Djānids**
rulers Nadhr Muḥammad
see also Bukhārā
Girāy Khāns (ca. 1426-1792) **Girāy**
rulers Dawlat Giray; Ghāzī Girāy I; Ghāzī Girāy II; Ghāzī Girāy III; Ḥādjdjī Girāy; Islām Girāy; Ḳaplan Girāy I; Ḳaplan Girāy II; Meḥmed Girāy I; Mengli Girāy I; Ṣāḥib Girāy Khān I; Selīm Girāy I
see also Ḳalghay; Meḥmed Baghčesarāyī; Meḥmed Girāy; Thābit
Great Khāns (1206-1634) Čingizids
rulers Čingiz Khān; Ḳubilay; Möngke; Ögedey
other personages Ḳaydu; Maḥmūd Yalawač; Ṭārābī, Maḥmūd; Toluy; Töregene Khātūn
Ilkhānids (1256-1353) **Īlkhāns**
see also Ṣadr.2; Tūmān
rulers Baydu; Gaykhātū; Ghāzān; Hūlāgū; Öldjeytü; Tegüder; Togha Temür
viziers Rashīd al-Dīn Ṭabīb; Saʿd al-Dawla
historians of Djuwaynī, ʿAlāʾ al-Dīn; Ḥamd Allāh al-Mustawfī al-Ḳazwīnī; Rashīd al-Dīn Ṭabīb; Waṣṣāf
other personages Djuwaynī, ʿAlāʾ al-Dīn; Ḳutlugh-Shāh Noyan
Shaybānids (1500-1598) **Shībānids**
rulers ʿAbd Allāh b. Iskandar; Abu ʾl-Khayr; Shībānī Khān
historians of Abu ʾl-Ghāzī Bahādur Khān; [in Suppl.] Ḥāfiẓ Tanīsh

Persia Afrāsiyābids; Aḥmadīlīs; Aḳ Ḳoyunlu; Bādūsbānids; Bāwand; Buwayhids; Djalāyir; Dulafids; Faḍlawayh; Farīghūnids; Ḥasanwayh; Hazāraspids; Ildeñizids; Ilek-Khāns; Ilyāsids; Īndjū; Ḳādjār; Kākūyids; Ḳarā-ḳoyunlu; Ḳārinids; Kāwūs; Khwārazm-shāhs; Ḳutlugh-khānids; Lur-i Buzurg; Lur-i Kūčik; Mangîts; Marʿashīs; Muḥtādjids; Musāfirids; Mushaʿshaʿ; Muẓaffarids; Rawwādids; Ṣafawids; Ṣaffārids; Saldjūḳids; Salghurids; Sāmānids; Sarbadārids; Sāsānids; Shaddādids; Shīrwān Shāh; Ṭāhirids.1; Tīmūrids; Zand; Ziyārids
see also Ardalān; Atabak; ʿAwfī; Čāshna-gīr; Daylam; Dīwān.iv; Djalāyir; Ghulām.ii; Ḥādjib.iii; Ḥarb.v; al-Ḥasan b. Zayd b. Muḥammad; Hiba.iv; Ḥiṣār.iii; Īlkhāns; Iran.v; Kayānids; Marāsim.3; Mawākib.3; Pīshdādids; Shāhī; Waḳf.III; Wazīr.II; *and* → LEGENDS.LEGENDARY DYNASTIES; ONOMASTICS.TITLES.PERSIAN
Afshārids (1736-1795) **Afshār**
rulers Nādir Shāh Afshār
see also Takht-i Ṭāwūs

historians of ʿAbd al-Karīm Kashmīrī; Mahdī Khān Astarābādī

Aḳ Ḳoyunlus (1378-1508) **Aḳ Ḳoyunlu**

rulers Uzun Ḥasan

Buwayhids (932-1062) **Buwayhids**

rulers Abū Kālīdjār; ʿAḍud al-Dawla; Bakhtiyār; Djalāl al-Dawla; Fakhr al-Dawla; ʿImād al-Dawla; Khusraw Fīrūz (*and* al-Malik al-Raḥīm); Madjd al-Dawla; Muʾayyid al-Dawla; Muʿizz al-Dawla; Rukn al-Dawla; Ṣamṣām al-Dawla; Shams al-Dawla; Sharaf al-Dawla; Sulṭān al-Dawla; [in Suppl.] Bahāʾ al-Dawla wa-Ḍiyāʾ al-Milla

viziers al-ʿAbbās b. al-Ḥusayn; Ibn ʿAbbād; Ibn al-ʿAmīd; Ibn Baḳiyya; Ibn Mākūlā.1 and 2; al-Muhallabī, Abū Muḥammad; Sābūr b. Ardashīr; [in Suppl.] ʿAbd al-ʿAzīz b. Yūsuf; Ibn Khalaf.1; Ibn Saʿdān

secretaries Hilāl al-Ṣābiʾ (*and* Ṣābiʾ.(3).9); Ibn Hindū; Ṣābiʾ.(3).7

historians of Ṣābiʾ.(3).7

other personages al-Basāsīrī; Fasandjus; Ḥasan b. Ustādh-hurmuz; Ibn Ḥādjib al-Nuʿmān; ʿImrān b. Shāhīn; al-Malik al-ʿAzīz; [in Suppl.] Ibrāhīm Shīrāzī

Dābūyids (660-760)

rulers Dābūya

Djalāyirids (1340-1432) **Djalāyir**

rulers Uways

other personages Salmān-i Sāwadjī

Ildeñizids (1137-1225) **Ildeñizids**

rulers Ildeñiz; Özbeg b. Muḥammad Pahlawān; Pahlawān

Ilek-Khāns (992-1211) **Ilek-Khāns**

see also Yaghma

Ḳādjārs (1779-1924) **Ḳādjār**; Mushīr al-Dawla

see also Ḳāʾim-maḳām-i Farāhānī; Madjlis al-Shūrā; *and* → IRAN. MODERN PERIOD

rulers Āghā Muḥammad Shāh; Fatḥ ʿAlī Shāh; Muḥammad ʿAlī Shāh Ḳādjār; Muḥammad Shāh; Muẓaffar al-Dīn Shāh Ḳādjār; Nāṣir al-Dīn Shāh

see also Takht-i Ṭāwūs

other personages ʿAbbās Mīrzā; [in Suppl.] Amīr Niẓām; Ḥādjdjī Ibrāhīm Khān Kalāntar

Khanate of Khīwa Khīwa

rulers Abu ʾl-Ghāzī Bahādur Khān

historians Muʾnis; [in Suppl.] Āgahī

Khʷārazm-Shāhs (ca. 995-1231) **Khʷārazm-shāhs**

rulers Atsïz b. Anūshtigin; Djalāl al-Dīn Khʷārazm-shāh; Maʾmūn b. Muḥammad; Tekish

historians of Djuwaynī; al-Nasawī
other personages Burāḳ Ḥādjib; Terken Khātūn
Muẓaffarids (1314-1393) **Muẓaffarids**
rulers Shāh-i Shudjāʿ
historians of Muʿīn al-Dīn Yazdī
Pahlawīs (1926-1979) **Pahlawī**
and → IRAN.MODERN PERIOD
rulers Muḥammad Riḍā Shāh Pahlawī; Riḍā Shāh
Sādjids (ca. 856- ca. 930) **Sādjids**
rulers Abu ʾl-Sādj; Muḥammad b. Abi ʾl-Sādj; Yūsuf b. Abi ʾl-Sādj Dīwdād
Ṣafawids (1501-1732) Bārūd.v; Īshīk-āḳāsī; Iʿtimād al-Dawla; Ḳūrčī; Libās.iii; **Ṣafawids**
see also Ḥaydar; Ḳîzîl-bāsh; Nuḳṭawiyya; Ṣadr.4; Ṣadr al-Dīn Ardabīlī; Ṣadr al-Dīn Mūsā; Ṣafī al-Dīn Ardabīlī; Soyūrghāl; Takkalū; Tiyūl
rulers ʿAbbās I; Ḥusayn (*and* Sulṭān Ḥusayn); Ismāʿīl I; Ismāʿīl II; Sulaymān (Shāh); Ṭahmāsp
historians of Ḥasan-i Rūmlū; Iskandar Beg; Ḳummī; Ṭāhir Waḥīd
see also [in Suppl.] Ibn al-Bazzāz al-Ardabīlī
other personages Alḳāṣ Mīrzā; Ḥamza Mīrzā; al-Karakī; Madjlisī
Ṣaffārids (867-ca. 1495) **Ṣaffārids**
rulers ʿAmr b. al-Layth; Yaʿḳūb b. al-Layth
Saldjūḳs (1038-1194) Amīr Dād; Arslan b. Saldjūḳ; Atabak; **Saldjūḳids**
see also Sarāparda; *and* → DYNASTIES.ANATOLIA AND THE TURKS.SALDJŪḲS OF RŪM
rulers Alp Arslan; Bahrām Shāh; Barkyārūḳ; Maḥmūd b. Muḥammad b. Malik-Shāh; Malik-Shāh.1-3; Masʿūd b. Muḥammad b. Malik-Shāh; Muḥammad b. Maḥmūd b. Muḥammad b. Malik-Shāh; Muḥammad b. Malik-Shāh; Riḍwān; Sandjar; Ṭoghrîl (II); Ṭoghrîl (III); Tutush (I) b. Alp Arslan
see also Čaghrî-beg; Silāḥdār; Ṭoghrîl; Ṭoghrîl (I) Beg
viziers Anūshirwān b. Khālid; Djahīr; al-Kundurī; Madjd al-Mulk al-Balāsānī; al-Maybudī.3; Niẓām al-Mulk; Rabīb al-Dawla; [in Suppl.] Ibn Dārust
historians of al-Bundārī; ʿImād al-Dīn; Nīshāpūrī; Rāwandī; [in Suppl.] al-Ḥusaynī
other personages Āḳ Sunḳur al-Bursuḳī; Arslan-Arghūn; Ayāz; al-Basāsīrī; Būrī-bars; Bursuḳ; Büz-abeh; Ḳāwurd; Khalaf b. Mulāʿib al-Ashhabī; Khāṣṣ Beg; Kurbuḳa; Niẓāmiyya; Terken Khātūn; al-Ṭughrāʾī; [in Suppl.] Ekinči
Salghurids (1148-1270) **Salghurids**
rulers Saʿd (I) b. Zangī

Sāmānids (819-1005) **Sāmānids**
rulers Ismāʿīl b. Aḥmad; Ismāʿīl b. Nūḥ; Manṣūr b. Nūḥ; Naṣr b. Aḥmad b. Ismāʿīl; Nūḥ (I); Nūḥ (II)
viziers Balʿamī; al-Muṣʿabī; al-ʿUtbī.1 and 2; [in Suppl.] al-Djayhānī
historians of Narshakhī
see also al-Sallāmī
other personages Arslan b. Saldjūḳ; Sīmdjūrids; [in Suppl.] al-Djayhānī

Ṭāhirids (821-873) **Ṭāhirids**.1
rulers ʿAbd Allāh b. Ṭāhir; Muḥammad b. Ṭāhir; Ṭāhir b. al-Ḥusayn
historians of Ibn al-Daybaʿ
other personages Muḥammad b. ʿAbd Allāh (b. Ṭāhir)

Tīmūrids (1370-1506) **Tīmūrids**
see also Ṣadr.3; Soyūrghāl; Tūzūk
rulers Abū Saʿīd b. Tīmūr; Bāyḳarā; Bāysonghor; Ḥusayn; Shāh Rukh; Tīmūr Lang; Ulugh Beg
see also Khān-zāda Bēgum
historians of Ibn ʿArabshāh; Khʷāfī Khān; Shāmī, Niẓām al-Dīn; Sharaf al-Dīn ʿAlī Yazdī
other personages Mīr ʿAlī Shīr Nawāʾī; Mīrānshāh b. Tīmūr; ʿUmar-Shaykh Mīrzā

Zands (1750-1794) **Zand**
rulers Karīm Khān Zand; Luṭf ʿAlī Khān
see also Lak

Ziyārids (931-ca. 1090) **Ziyārids**
rulers Ḳābūs b. Wushmagīr b. Ziyār; Kay Kāʾūs b. Iskandar; Mardāwīdj; Wushmgīr b. Ziyār

Spain and North Africa ʿAbbādids; ʿAbd al-Wādids; Afṭasids; Aghlabids; ʿAlawīs; ʿĀmirids; ʿAmmār; Dhu ʾl-Nūnids; Djahwarids; Ḥafṣids; Ḥammādids; Ḥammūdids; Hūdids; Ḥusaynids; Idrīsids; (Banū) Khurāsān; Marīnids; Midrār; al-Murābiṭūn; al-Muwaḥḥidūn; Naṣrids; Razīn, Banū; Rustamids; Saʿdids; Ṭāhirids.2; Tudjīb; Umayyads.In Spain; Waṭṭāsids; Zīrids
see also ʿAlāma; Dīwān.iii; Ḥādjib.ii and v; Hiba.iii; Ḥiṣār.ii; al-Ḥulal al-Mawshiyya; Ḳaramānlī; Khalīfa.i.C and D; Laḳab.3; Marāsim.2; Mawākib.2; Parias; Shurafāʾ.1.III; Ṭawīl, Banu; Wazīr.I.4; Ẓahīr; *and* → ANDALUSIA.CONQUEST OF *and* GOVERNORS UNTIL UMAYYAD CONQUEST; CALIPHATE.FĀṬIMIDS

ʿAbbādids (1023-1091) **ʿAbbādids**; Ishbīliya
rulers al-Muʿtaḍid bi ʾllāh; al-Muʿtamid ibn ʿAbbād
see also al-Rundī
viziers Ibn ʿAmmār, Abū Bakr

ʿAbd al-Wādids (1236-1550) **ʿAbd al-Wādids**
rulers Abū Ḥammū I; Abū Ḥammū II; Abū Tāshufīn I; Abū Tāshufīn II; Abū Zayyān I; Abū Zayyān II; Abū Zayyān III; Yaghmurāsan
historians of Ibn Khaldūn, Abū Zakariyyāʾ; al-Tanasī

Afṭasids (1022-1094) **Afṭasids**
rulers al-Mutawakkil ʿalā ʾllāh, Ibn al-Afṭas
viziers Ibn Ḳuzmān.II
secretaries Ibn ʿAbdūn; Ibn Ḳabṭūrnu

Aghlabids (800-909) al-ʿAbbāsiyya; **Aghlabids**; Raḳḳāda
rulers Ibrāhīm I; Ibrāhīm II

ʿAlawids (1631-) **ʿAlawīs**; Ḳāʾid; Mawlāy; Shurafāʾ.1.III
rulers ʿAbd Allāh b. Ismāʿīl; ʿAbd al-ʿAzīz b. al-Ḥasan; ʿAbd al-Raḥmān b. Hishām; Ḥafīẓ (ʿAbd al-); (Mawlāy) al-Ḥasan; Mawlāy Ismāʿīl; Muḥammad III b. ʿAbd Allāh; Muḥammad IV b. ʿAbd al-Raḥmān; Muḥammad b. Yūsuf (Muḥammad V); al-Rashīd (Mawlāy); Sulaymān (Mawlāy)
viziers Akanṣūs; Ibn Idrīs (I); [in Suppl.] Bā Ḥmād; Ibn ʿUthmān al-Miknāsī
historians of Akanṣūs; Ibn Zaydān; al-Kardūdī; al-Zayyānī
other personages Aḥmad al-Nāṣirī al-Salāwī (*and* al-Nāṣir al-Salāwī); Ibn Idrīs (II); Khunātha

Almohads (1130-1269) Hargha; al-ʿIḳāb; Mizwār; **al-Muwaḥḥidūn**
see also Tinmal; Ẓahīr
rulers ʿAbd al-Muʾmin; Abū Yaʿḳūb Yūsuf; Abū Yūsuf Yaʿḳūb al-Manṣūr; Ibn Tūmart; al-Maʾmūn; al-Nāṣir
historians of ʿAbd al-Wāḥid al-Marrākushī; al-Baydhaḳ; Ibn Ṣāḥib al-Ṣalāt
see also al-Ḥulal al-Mawshiyya
other personages [in Suppl.] Ibn al-Ḳaṭṭān
see also Abū Ḥafṣ ʿUmar al-Hintātī; Ibn Mardanīsh

Almoravids (1056-1147) Amīr al-Muslimīn; **al-Murābiṭūn**
see also al-Zallāḳa
rulers ʿAlī b. Yūsuf b. Tāshufīn; al-Lamtūnī; Tāshufīn b. ʿAlī; Yūsuf b. Tāshufīn
secretaries Ibn ʿAbdūn
historians of Ibn al-Ṣayrafī
see also al-Ḥulal al-Mawshiyya
other personages Ibn Bādjdja; Ibn Ḳasī

ʿĀmirids (1021-1096) **ʿĀmirids**
rulers ʿAbd al-Malik b. Abī ʿĀmir; al-Muẓaffar
viziers Ibn al-Ḳaṭṭāʿ
other personages ʿAbd al-Raḥmān b. Abī ʿĀmir

Djahwarids (1030-1070) **Djahwarids**
other personages (al-)Ḥakam ibn ʿUk(k)āsha; Ibn ʿAbdūs
Ḥafṣids (1228-1574) **Ḥafṣids**
secretaries Ḥāzim
historians of al-Ḥādjdj Ḥammūda
other personages Ibn ʿArafa
Ḥammādids (972-1152) **Ḥammādids**
rulers Bādīs; al-Manṣūr; al-Nāṣir
see also Ḳalʿat Banī Ḥammād
Ḥammūdids (1010-1057) **Ḥammūdids**
viziers Ibn Dhakwān
Hūdids (1039-1142) **Hūdids**
rulers al-Muʾtamin
Ḥusaynids (1705-1957) **Ḥusaynids**
rulers Aḥmad Bey; al-Ḥusayn (b. ʿAlī); Muḥammad Bey; Muḥammad al-Ṣādiḳ Bey
ministers Khayr al-Dīn Pasha; Muṣṭafā Khaznadār
Idrīsids (789-926) **Idrīsids**
rulers Idrīs I; Idrīs II
Marīnids (1196-1465) **Marīnids**
rulers Abu ʾl-Ḥasan; Abū ʿInān Fāris
Naṣrids (1230-1492) **Naṣrids**
viziers Ibn al-Khaṭīb
other personages [in Suppl.] Ibn al-Sarrādj
Rustamids (777-909) **Rustamids**
historians of Ibn al-Ṣaghīr
Saʿdids (1511-1659) **Saʿdids**; Shurafāʾ.1.III
rulers ʿAbd Allāh al-Ghālib; Aḥmad al-Manṣūr; Mawlāy Maḥammad al-Shaykh
see also Mawlāy
viziers Ibn ʿĪsā
historians of ʿAbd al-ʿAzīz b. Muḥammad; al-Ifrānī
other personages al-Tamgrūtī; [in Suppl.] Abū Maḥallī
Ṭāhirids (11th-12th centuries) **Ṭāhirids**.2
Tudjībids (1019-1039) **Tudjīb**
rulers Maʿn b. Muḥammad; al-Muʿtaṣim
ʿUbaydids
historians of Ibn Ḥamādu
Umayyads (756-1031) **Umayyads.In Spain**
amīrs and caliphs ʿAbd Allāh b. Muḥammad; ʿAbd al-Raḥmān; al-Ḥakam I; al-Ḥakam II; Hishām I; Hishām II; Hishām III; al-Mahdī; al-Mundhir b. Muḥammad

see also Madīnat al-Zahrāʾ; Muʿāwiya b. Hishām; Rabaḍ; al-Ruṣāfa.4; al-Walīd b. Hishām; [in Suppl.] Bubashtru

viziers Ibn ʿAlḳama.2; Ibn Shuhayd

see also Wazīr.I.4

secretaries ʿArīb b. Saʿd al-Kātib al-Ḳurṭubī; Ibn Burd.I

other personages ʿAbd al-Raḥmān b. Marwān; Ghālib b. ʿAbd al-Raḥmān; Ḥabīb b. ʿAbd al-Malik; Ḥasdāy b. Shaprūṭ; Ibn ʿAlḳama.1; Ibn Dhakwān; Ibn al-Ḥannāṭ; Ibn Ḳasī; Ibn al-Ḳiṭṭ; al-Manṣūr; Rabīʿ b. Zayd; Ṣaḳāliba.3; Ṣubḥ; ʿUmar b. Ḥafṣūn; Ziryāb

Zīrids (972-1152) **Zīrids**.1

rulers Buluggīn b. Zīrī; al-Muʿizz b. Bādīs; Tamīm b. al-Muʿizz

historians of Umayya, Abu ʾl-Ṣalt

other personages Ibn Abi ʾl-Ridjāl

see also Ḳurhub

Zīrids of Granada (1012-1090) **Zīrids**.2

rulers ʿAbd Allāh b. Buluggīn; Zāwī b. Zīrī

E

EARTHQUAKES **Zalzala**

for accounts of earthquakes, see also Aghri̊ Dagh; Amasya; Anṭākiya; ʿAshḳābād; Čanki̊ri̊; Cilicia; Daybul; Djidjelli; Erzindjan; Ḥarra; Ḥulwān; Istanbul.VI.f; Ḳalhāt; Kāṅgṙā; Ḳazwīn; Kilāt; Nīshāpūr; al-Ramla

ECONOMICS Bayʿ; Kasb; Māl, Tadbīr.1; Taʾmīm

see also Muḍāraba; Taʿāwun; Tidjāra.3

EDUCATION **Maʿārif**; **Tadrīs**; Tarbiya

see also ʿArabiyya.B.IV; Idjāza

educational reform → REFORM

institutions of learning Dār al-Ḥadīth; Djāmiʿa; Köy Enstitüleri; Kuttāb; Madrasa; Maktab; Pesantren

see also Kulliyya; Ṣadr.(c); Samāʿ.2; Shaykh; Ustādh; *and* → EDUCATION. LIBRARIES

individual establishments al-Azhar; Bayt al-Ḥikma; Dār al-Ḥikma; Dār al-ʿUlūm; Ghalaṭa-sarāyi̊; Ḥarbiye; al-Ḳarawiyyīn.ii; al-Khaldūniyya; Makhredj; Mulkiyya; al-Ṣādiḳiyya; Zaytūna; [in Suppl.] Institut des hautes études marocaines; Institut des hautes études de Tunis

see also Aligarh; Deoband; Filāḥa.iii; al-Ḳāhira; Lakhnaw; al-Madīna.ii; Makka.3; Muṣṭafā ʿAbd al-Rāziḳ; al-Mustanṣir (I); Nadwat al-ʿUlamāʾ; [in Suppl.] ʿAbd al-Bārī; ʿAbd al-Wahhāb; Farangī Maḥall

learned societies and academies Andjuman; Djamʿiyya; Djemʿiyyet-i ʿIlmiyye-i ʿOthmāniyye; Institut d'Égypte; Khalḳevi; Madjmaʿ ʿIlmī
libraries Dār al-ʿIlm; **Maktaba**
see also ʿAlī Pasha Mubārak; Khāzin; al-Madīna.ii
collections ʿAlī Amīrī (*and* [in Suppl.] ʿAlī Emīrī); Esʿad Efendi, Meḥmed; Khudā Bakhsh; al-Ṭūr.1; [in Suppl.] ʿAbd al-Wahhāb
see also Geniza; *and* → BIBLIOGRAPHY
librarians Ibn al-Fuwaṭī; Ibn Ḥadjar al-ʿAsḳalānī; Ibn al-Sāʿī; al-Kattānī
treatises on
medieval al-Zarnūdjī
modern-day Ergin, Osman

EGYPT al-Azhar; al-Ḳāhira; Ḳibṭ; **Miṣr**; Nūba; al-Ṣaʿīd
see also al-ʿArab.iv; al-Fusṭāṭ; *and* → CHRISTIANITY.DENOMINATIONS. COPTS; DYNASTIES.EGYPT AND THE FERTILE CRESCENT; MUSIC.REGIONAL; NUBIA
administration Dār al-Maḥfūẓāt al-ʿUmūmiyya; Dīwān.ii; Ḳabāla; Kharādj.I; Rawk
see also Miṣr.D.1.b; Waḳf.II.1; *and* → CALIPHATE.ʿABBĀSIDS *and* FĀṬIMIDS; DYNASTIES.EGYPT AND THE FERTILE CRESCENT.MAMLUKS; OTTOMAN EMPIRE.ADMINISTRATION
architecture → ARCHITECTURE.REGIONS
before Islam Firʿawn; Manf; Miṣr.D.1; Nūba.2; Saḳḳāra; [in Suppl.] Abū Sinbil
see also al-Uḳṣur
dynasties ʿAbbāsids; Ayyūbids; Fāṭimids; Mamlūks; Muḥammad ʿAlī Pasha; Ṭūlūnids
and → DYNASTIES.EGYPT AND THE FERTILE CRESCENT
historians of Abu 'l-Maḥāsin b. Taghrābirdī; ʿAlī Pasha Mubārak; al-Bakrī.2; al-Balawī; al-Damurdāshī; al-Djabartī; Ibn ʿAbd al-Ḥakam.4; Ibn Duḳmāk; Ibn Iyās; Ibn Muyassar; al-Kindī, Abū ʿUmar Muḥammad; al-Maḳrīzī; al-Nuwayrī, Muḥammad; Rifāʿa Bey al-Ṭahṭāwī; al-Ṣafadī, al-Ḥasan; Salīm al-Naḳḳāsh; al-Suyūṭī; al-Waṣīfī; Zaydān, Djurdjī
and → DYNASTIES.EGYPT AND THE FERTILE CRESCENT
modern period Ḍarība.4; Djarīda.i.A; Djāmiʿa; Dustūr.iii; Ḥizb.i; Ḥukūma.iii; al-Ikhwān al-Muslimūn; Iltizām; Imtiyāzāt.iv; Institut d'Égypte; Maʿārif.1.ii; Madjlis.4.A.xvi; Madjmaʿ ʿIlmī.i.2.b; Maḥkama.4.i; Miṣr.D.7; Salafiyya.2(a); al-Takfīr wa 'l-Hidjra; Wafd
see also Baladiyya.2; al-Bannāʾ; Madjlis al-Shūrā; Waṭaniyya
belletrists
poets al-Bārūdī; Fikrī; Ḥāfiẓ Ibrāhīm; Ismāʿīl Ṣabrī; Ismāʿīl Ṣabrī Pasha; al-Manfalūṭī; al-Māzinī; Nādjī; Nadjīb al-Ḥaddād; Nadjīb Muḥammad Surūr; Ṣalāḥ ʿAbd al-Ṣabūr; al-Sharḳāwī; Shawḳī; Shukrī; Ṭāhā, ʿAlī Maḥmūd; [in Suppl.] Abū Shādī; al-ʿAḳḳād

writers of prose Aḥmad Amīn; Ḥāfiẓ Ibrāhīm; Maḥmūd Taymūr; al-Manfalūṭī; al-Māzinī; Muḥammad Husayn Haykal; al-Muwayliḥī; Salāma Mūsā; al-Sharḳāwī; Ṭāhā Ḥusayn; Tawfīḳ al-Ḥakīm; Yaḥyā Ḥaḳḳī; [in Suppl.] Abū Shādī; al-ʿAḳḳād
see also Faraḥ Anṭūn; Mayy Ziyāda; *and* → LITERATURE.DRAMA.ARABIC *and* HISTORICAL.ARABIC; PRESS

influential persons Djamāl al-Dīn al-Afghānī; al-Marṣafī; Muḥammad ʿAbduh; Muṣṭafā Kāmil Pasha; al-Muwayliḥī.1; Rifāʿa Bey al-Ṭahṭāwī; Salāma Mūsā; al-Sanhūrī, ʿAbd al-Razzāḳ; Sayyid Ḳuṭb; Shākir, Aḥmad Muḥammad; Shaltūt, Maḥmūd; al-Subkiyyūn; Ṭāhā Ḥusayn; Umm Kulthūm; [in Suppl.] Abu ʾl-ʿAzāʾim; al-ʿAdawī; al-Bakrī; al-Biblāwī; Djawharī, Ṭanṭāwī; al-ʿIdwī al-Ḥamzāwī; ʿIllaysh
see also Rashīd Riḍā; *and* → *the section Statesmen below*

Muḥammad ʿAlī's line ʿAbbās Ḥilmī I; ʿAbbās Ḥilmī II; Fuʾād al-Awwal; Ḥusayn Kāmil; Ibrāhīm Pasha; Ismāʿīl Pasha; Muḥammad ʿAlī Pasha; Saʿīd Pasha; Tawfīḳ Pasha; [in Suppl.] Bakhīt al-Muṭīʿī al-Ḥanafī; Fārūḳ
see also ʿAzīz Miṣr; Khidīw; ʿUmar Makram; [in Suppl.] Dāʾira Saniyya; Ibʿādiyya

statesmen ʿAlī Pasha Mubārak; al-Bārūdī; Fikrī; Ismāʿīl Ṣabrī Pasha; Ismāʿīl Ṣidḳī; Luṭfī al-Sayyid; Muḥammad Farīd Bey; Muḥammad Nadjīb; al-Naḥḥās; Nūbār Pasha; Saʿd Zaghlūl; al-Sādāt; Sharīf Pasha; ʿUrābī Pasha; Yakan, ʿAdlī; [in Suppl.] ʿAbd al-Nāṣir
see also Muṣṭafā Kāmil Pasha

mystic orders Taṣawwuf.4
see also Zār.2; *and* → MYSTICISM

Ottoman period (1517-1798) Dhu ʾl-Faḳāriyya; Ḳāsimiyya; Ḳāzdughliyya; Miṣr.D.6; Muḥammad ʿAlī Pasha; Shaykh al-Balad
see also Ḥurriyya.ii

beys ʿAlī Bey; Muḥammad Abu ʾl-Dhahab (*and* [in Suppl.] Abu ʾl-Dhahab)

physical geography

mountains al-Ṭūr.1

oases al-Wāḥāt

waters Burullus; al-Nīl; Timsāḥ, Lake
see also Miḳyās; Rawḍa; al-Suways

population ʿAbābda; Ḳibṭ
see also [in Suppl.] Demography.IV; *and* → CHRISTIANITY.DENOMINATIONS.COPTS

toponyms

ancient Adfū; Bābalyūn; al-Bahnasā; Burullus; Dabīḳ; al-Ḳulzum; Manf; Shaṭā; Tinnīs
see also al-Sharḳiyya

present-day
regions Buḥayra; al-Fayyūm; al-Gharbiyya; Girgā; al-Sharḳiyya; Sīnāʾ
see also al-Ṣaʿīd
towns ʿAbbāsa; Abūḳīr; Akhmīm; al-ʿAllāḳī; al-ʿArīsh; Asyūṭ; Aṭfīḥ; ʿAyn Shams; Banhā; Banī Suwayf; Bilbays; Būlāḳ; Būṣīr; Dahshūr; Daḳahliyya; Damanhūr; Dimyāṭ; al-Farāfra; al-Fusṭāṭ; Girgā; Ḥulwān; al-Iskandariyya; Ismāʿīliyya; Isna; al-Ḳāhira; Ḳalyūb; Ḳanṭara.3; Ḳifṭ; Ḳunā; Ḳūṣ; Ḳuṣayr; al-Maḥalla al-Kubrā; al-Manṣūra; Manūf; Port Saʿīd; Rafaḥ; Rashīd; Saḳḳāra; Samannūd; Sīwa.1; al-Suways; al-Tall al-Kabīr; Ṭanṭā; al-Uḳṣur; al-Ushmūnayn; Uswān; al-Zaḳāzīḳ; [in Suppl.] Abū Zaʿbal
see also al-Muḳaṭṭam; Rawḍa

EMANCIPATION Ḥurriyya
for manumission, → SLAVERY; *for women*, → WOMEN

EMIGRATION Djāliya; **Hidjra**
see also al-Mahdjar; Muhādjir; al-Muhādjirūn; Pārsīs; Ṣiḥāfa.3; *and* → NEW WORLD

EPIGRAPHY **Kitābāt**
see also Eldem, Khalīl Edhem; Ḥisāb al-Djummal; Khaṭṭ; Musnad.1; Ṭirāz.3
sites of inscriptions Lībiyā.2; Liḥyān; Orkhon; al-Sawdāʾ; Ṣiḳilliya.4; Ṣirwāḥ.1; Ẓafār
see also Ḥaḍramawt; Sabaʾ; Ṣafaitic; Thamudic

ESCHATOLOGY ʿAdhāb al-Ḳabr; Ākhira; al-Aʿrāf; Barzakh; Baʿth; Djahannam; Djanna; Djazāʾ; Dunyā; Ḥawḍ; Ḥisāb; Isrāfīl; ʿIzrāʿīl; Ḳiyāma; Maʿād; al-Mahdī; Mawḳif.2; Munkar wa-Nakīr; Sāʿa.3; Zaḳḳūm
see also Ḳayyim; Shafāʿa; Shaḳāwa; Yawm; al-Zabāniyya; *and* → DEATH; PARADISE
hereafter Adjr.1; **Ākhira**
see also Dunyā
signs ʿAṣā; Dābba; al-Dadjdjāl; Yādjūdj wa-Mādjūdj
see also Baʿth; Sāʿa.3

ETERNITY **Abad**; Ḳidam

ETHICS Adab; **Akhlāḳ**; Ḥisba
see also Ḥurriyya; al-Maḥāsin wa ʾl-Masāwī; Miskawayh; Taḥsīn wa-Taḳbīḥ; Tanẓīm al-Nasl; Ẓarīf; *and* → VIRTUES

ETHIOPIA   Adal; Aḥmad Grāñ; Awfāt; Bāli; Dawāro; Ḏjabart; Ḏjimmā; **Ḥabaṣẖ**;
   Ḥabaṣẖat; al-Naḏjāṣẖī
   see also Ḥabeṣẖ; Kūṣẖ; Ṣẖaykẖ Ḥusayn; Zār.1; *and* → AFRICA.EAST AFRICA;
   LANGUAGES.AFRO-ASIATIC; YEMEN.TOPONYMS
   historians of ʿArabfaḳih
   population   ʿĀmir; Diglal; Ḏjabart; Galla; Māryā; Oromo; Raṣẖāʾida
   toponyms   Assab; Dahlak; Dire Dawa; Eritrea; Harar; Maṣawwaʿ; Ogādēn

ETHNICITY   Magẖāriba; Maṣẖāriḳa; Sārt
   see also Fatā; Ibn Gẖarsiya; Ismāʿīl b. Yasār; Mawlā; Saracens

ETIQUETTE   **Adab**
   see also Āʾīn; Hiba; *and* → CUISINE.TABLE MANNERS; LITERATURE.ETIQUETTE-
   LITERATURE

EUNUCH   **Kẖāṣī**
   see also Kẖādim; Mamlūk.3; Ustāḏẖ.1

EUROPE
   for imitation of, see Tafarnuḏj
Eastern Europe   Arnawutluḳ; Balkan; Bulgaria; Iḳrīṭiṣẖ; Itil; Ḳubrus; Leh;
   Yugoslavia; [in Suppl.] Čeh
      see also Bulgẖār; Ḥizb.v; Ibrāhīm b. Yaʿḳūb; Muhāḏjir.2; Muslimūn.1;
      Rūmeli; al-Ṣaḳāliba
      for individual countries, → ALBANIA; BULGARIA; CRETE; CYPRUS; (former)
      CZECHOSLOVAKIA; GREECE; HUNGARY; POLAND; (former) YUGOSLAVIA; *the*
      section Russia below; and → BALKANS
   waters   Ṭuna; Wardar; Yayîḳ
   Russia   Buḏjāḳ; Ḳîrîm
      see also Bulgẖār; Ḏjadīd; Ḥizb.v; Ḳayyūm Nāṣirī; al-Ṭanṭāwī
      dynasties   Girāy
      population   Baṣẖdjirt; Besermyans; Beskesek-abaza; Bukẖārlîk; Burṭās;
         Čeremiss; Čulîm; Čuwaṣẖ; Gagauz; Ḳarapapakẖ; Lipḳa; Rūs; Teptyar
         see also Ḳangẖli; Kẖazar; Kimäk; Pečenegs; al-Ṣaḳāliba
      toponyms
         ancient   Atil; Saḳsīn
         present-day   Aḳ Kirmān; Aḳ Masḏjid.1; Azaḳ; Bāgẖče Sarāy; Ismāʿīl;
         Ḳamāniča; Ḳaraṣū-bāzār; Ḳāsimov; Ḳāzān; Kefe; Kerč; Kẖotin;
         Ḳîlburun; Sugẖdāḳ; Tümen
         see also Yeñi Ḳalʿe
Western Europe   al-Baṣẖkuniṣẖ; Ifrandj; Īṭaliya; Malta; Nemče; Sardāniya
      see also Ibn Idrīs (II); Ibrāhīm b. Yaʿḳūb; al-Maḏjūs; Muslimūn.2

for individual countries, → Austria; France; Italy; Portugal; Spain
waters Ṭuna

Evil Eye **ʿAyn**, Tamīma
see also Karkaddan; *and* → Charms; Islam.popular beliefs

F

Faith ʿAḳīda; **Īmān**
and → Islam; Religion

Falconry **Bayzara**; Čakïrdjï-bashï; Doghandjï
see also Ṭoghrïl

Fasting ʿĀshūrāʾ; Ramaḍān; **Ṣawm**
see also ʿĪd al-Fiṭr; Ṣūfiyāna
prayer during Ramaḍān **Tarāwīḥ**

Fāṭimids → Caliphate

Festival **ʿĪd**; Kandūrī; Mawlid; Mawsim; Shenlik
see also Maṭbakh.2
festivals ʿAnṣāra; ʿĀshūrāʾ.II; Bārā Wafāt; ʿĪd al-Aḍhā; ʿĪd al-Fiṭr; Khiḍr-ilyās; Mihragān; Nawrūz; Sulṭān al-Ṭalaba (*and* Ṭalaba)
see also Ghadīr Khumm; Kurds.iv.C.3; Lālish; Lĕbaran; Raʾs al-ʿĀm; Walī.9
literature on Wehbī Sayyidī

Finance Ribā
and → Administration.financial; Law.law of obligations; Payments; Taxation
accounting Muḥāsaba.2; Mustawfī
see also Daftar; *and* → Administration.financial
banking Ḳirāḍ; Muḍāraba; Ribā; Suftadja
see also Djahbadh; Sharika
commerce Bayʿ; Imtiyāzāt; Kasb; Ḳirāḍ; Shirāʾ; **Tidjāra**
see also Inshāʾ; Sūḳ; *and* → Industry; Law.law of obligations
functions Dallāl; Malik al-Tudjdjār; Shāh Bandar; Tādjir
see also Tardjumān
trade Ḳahwa; Kārimī; Ḳuṭn; Lubān; Ṭīn.3
see also Kalah; Kārwān; Ḳaysariyya; Kirmān; Mīnāʾ; Ṣafawids.II;

Szechuan; Ta<u>sh</u>āza; Tammār; ʿUḳāẓ; Wenedik

institutions

Arabic Bayt al-Māl; Ma<u>kh</u>zan

Turkish <u>Kh</u>azīne; Māliyya

partnerships Mufāwaḍa; Mu<u>sh</u>āraka; <u>Sh</u>arika

terms ʿĀriyya; Bayʿ; Ḍamān; <u>Gh</u>ārim; Ḥawāla; Hiba; Kafāla; Ḳirāḍ; Muḍāraba; Mufāwaḍa; Muḳāṭaʿa; Mu<u>kh</u>āṭara; Mu<u>sh</u>āraka; Ribā; Sufta<u>dj</u>a; [in Suppl.] Dayn

and → LAW.LAW OF OBLIGATIONS

FLORA (<u>Dj</u>azīrat) al-ʿArab.v; Būstān; Filāḥa; Hind.i.k

and → ARCHITECTURE.MONUMENTS.GARDENS; BOTANY; LITERATURE.POETRY.NATURE

flowers Nar<u>dj</u>is; <u>Sh</u>aḳīḳat al-Nuʿmān; Sūsan; Ward; [in Suppl.] Bābūna<u>dj</u>; <u>Dj</u>ullanār

see also Filāḥa.iv; Lāle Devri; Lālezarī; Nawriyya; *and* → ARCHITECTURE.MONUMENTS.GARDENS; LITERATURE.POETRY.NATURE

plants A<u>dh</u>argūn; Afsantīn; Afyūn; Ḥalfāʾ; Ḥinnāʾ; Kammūn; Ḳaranful; Karm; Ḳaṣab; Naʿām; **Nabāt**; Ṣabr; <u>Sh</u>ibi<u>th</u><u>th</u>; <u>Sh</u>īḥ; <u>Sh</u>ukāʿā; Sidr; Simsim; Sirā<u>dj</u> al-Ḳuṭrub (*and* Yabrūḥ); Sūs; Turun<u>dj</u>ān; Wars; Yāsamīn; Zaʿfarān; [in Suppl.] Aḳūnīṭun; Ās; Bābūna<u>dj</u>; Basbās; <u>Dj</u>āwars; Fū<u>dh</u>an<u>dj</u>; Hindibāʾ; Iklīl al-Malik

see also Maryam; Naḥl; Namir and Nimr; Nasr; Ṣam<u>gh</u>; Sinnawr; Sirwāl; Timsāḥ; *and* → DRUGS.NARCOTICS

trees Abanūs; ʿAfṣ; Argan; Baḳḳam; Bān; Na<u>kh</u>l; Sā<u>dj</u>; Ṣandal; Sidr; Tīn; Tūt; ʿUnnāba; Zaytūn.2; [in Suppl.] <u>Dj</u>awz; <u>Dj</u>ullanār

see also ʿAyn <u>Sh</u>ams; <u>Gh</u>āba; Kāfūr; Kahrubā; Ḳaṭrān; Lubān; Ṣam<u>gh</u>; <u>Th</u>aʿlab; [in Suppl.] Halīla<u>dj</u>

woods Abanūs; Baḳḳam; **<u>Kh</u>a<u>sh</u>ab;** Ṣandal; ʿŪd.I

see also Lamu; *and* → *the section Trees above*; NAVIGATION.SHIPS *and* SHIPYARDS

FRANCE Arbūna; Fraxinetum

see also Balāṭ al-<u>Sh</u>uhadāʾ; Muslimūn.2; Rifāʿa Bey al-Ṭahṭāwī; Ṣāyi<u>gh</u>, Fatḥ Allāh; al-<u>Sh</u>ām.2(b)

FRANKS **Ifran<u>dj</u>**

and → CRUSADE(R)S

FURNISHINGS Mafrū<u>sh</u>āt; Sirā<u>dj</u>; [in Suppl.] **A<u>th</u>ā<u>th</u>**

G

GAMBLING **Ḳimār**; al-Maysir
and → ANIMALS.SPORT; RECREATION.GAMES

GENEALOGY **Ḥasab wa-Nasab; Nasab**; S̲h̲arīf; S̲h̲urafāʾ
see also ʿIrḳ; Naḳīb al-As̲h̲rāf; S̲h̲araf; *and* → LITERATURE.GENEALOGICAL;
ONOMASTICS

GEOGRAPHY **Djug̲h̲rāfiyā**; Iḳlīm; Istiwāʾ; K̲h̲arīṭa; al-Ḳubba; Tak̲h̲ṭīṭ al-Ḥudūd
see also Mag̲h̲rib; Makka.4; Mas̲h̲riḳ
for the geography of individual areas, see Adamawa; Ād̲h̲arbaydjān.i; Afg̲h̲āni-
stān.i; Aḳ Ṣu; Algeria.i; Anadolu.ii; al-Andalus.ii and iii.2; (Djazīrat) al-
ʿArab.ii; Armīniya; Arnawutluḳ.3; ʿAsīr; Baḥr; Djazīra; Filāḥa; Ḥammāda;
Indonesia; ʿIrāḳ; Iran; Lībiyā; al-Mag̲h̲rib; Māzandarān.2; Mūrītāniyā.1;
Nadjd.1; Niger.1; Pākistān; Senegal.1; al-S̲h̲ām.1; Sīstān.2; Somali.2;
Tunisia.I.a; ʿUmān.1; al-Yaman.2; Zāb.1
administrative Kūra; Mamlaka; Mik̲h̲lāf; Rustāḳ.1; S̲h̲ahr; Ṣūba; Ṭassūdj; Ustān
see also Djund; Iḳlīm; Wālī
geographers Abu ʾl-Fidā; Abū ʿUbayd al-Bakrī; ʿĀs̲h̲iḳ; al-Balk̲h̲ī, Abū Zayd;
al-Dimas̲h̲ḳī; Ibn ʿAbd al-Munʿim al-Ḥimyarī; Ibn al-Faḳīh; Ibn G̲h̲ālib; Ibn
Ḥawḳal; Ibn K̲h̲urradād̲h̲bih; Ibn Mādjid; Ibn Rusta; Ibn Sarābiyūn; al-
Idrīsī; al-Iṣṭak̲h̲rī; al-Ḳazwīnī; al-Masʿūdī; al-Muhallabī, Abu ʾl-Ḥusayn; al-
Muḳaddasī; al-ʿUd̲h̲rī; al-Warrāḳ, Muḥammad; Yāḳūt al-Rūmī; al-Zuhrī,
Muḥammad
see also Baṭlamiyūs; Istibṣār; Ḳāsim b. Aṣbag̲h̲; al-Masālik wa ʾl-Mamālik;
al-Sarak̲h̲sī, Abu ʾl-ʿAbbās; [in Suppl.] al-Djayhānī; Ḥudūd al-ʿĀlam
literature Djug̲h̲rāfiyā.IV.c and V; Ṣurat al-Arḍ
see also Tūrān; *and* → LITERATURE.TRAVEL-LITERATURE
physical geography
deserts → DESERTS
mountains → MOUNTAINS
oases **Wāḥa**
salt flats **Sabk̲h̲a**
see also Azalay; Milḥ; S̲h̲aṭṭ; *for regional salt-flats,* → ALGERIA; OMAN
springs ʿAyn Dilfa; ʿAyn Mūsā; al-Ḥamma; Ḥasan Abdāl
see also Ḳaplîdja
volcanoes *see* ʿAdan; Ag̲h̲rî Dag̲h̲; Damāwand; Ḥarra; Lad̲j̲āʾ; al-Ṣafā.2; [in
Suppl.] Djabal Says
wadis **Wādī**
waters
lakes Baikal; Bak̲h̲tigān; Balk̲h̲as̲h̲; Burullus; Gökče-tengiz; Hāmūn;

al-Ḥūla; İssi̊k-kul; Ḳarā-köl; Timsāḥ, Lake; Tuz Gölü; Urmiya.1; al-ʿUtayba; Wān.1; Zirih
see also Buḥayra; al-Ḳulzum; *and* → Oceans and Seas
oceans and seas → Oceans and Seas
rivers → Rivers
straits Bāb al-Mandab; Bog͟haz-iči; Čanaḳ-ḳalʿe Bog͟hazi̊
terms Ḥarra; K͟habrāʾ; Nahr; Reg; Rīf; Sabk͟ha; S͟haṭṭ
see also Ṣanf; Sarḥadd; Wālī
urban Ḳarya; Ḳaṣaba; K͟hiṭṭa; Maḥalle; Medina; Rabaḍ; S͟hahr; S͟hahristān
see also Fener; Ḥayy; K͟hiṭaṭ; Mallāḥ; *and* → Architecture.urban; Sedentarism; *and in particular the larger cities in the section Toponyms under each country*

Gifts **Hiba**; Ṣila.3
see also Bak͟hs͟hīs͟h; Nit͟hār; Pīs͟hkas͟h; Ras͟hwa; *and* → Payments

Greece Yūnān
see also Muhād͟jir.2; Muslimūn.1.B.3; Pomaks
Greek authors in Arabic translation → Literature.translations; Philosophy.philosophers
toponyms
districts Karli̊-īli
islands Čoka Adasi̊; Eğriboz; Körfüz; Levkas; Limni; Midilli; Naḳs͟he; On Iki Ada; Para; Rodos; Ṣaḳi̊z; Santurin Adasi̊; Semedirek; S͟heytānli̊ḳ ; S͟hire; Sisām; Tas͟hoz; Zaklise
see also D͟jazāʾir-i Baḥr-i Safīd
regions Mora, Tesalya
towns Atīna; Aynabak͟hti̊; Baliabadra; Dede Ag͟hač; Dimetoḳa; Karaferye; Ḳawāla; Kerbenes͟h; Kesriye; Ḳordos; Ḳoron; Livadya; Meneks͟he; Modon; Nauplion; Navarino; Olendirek; Preveze; Selānīk; Siroz; Tirḥāla; Wodina; Yanya; Yeñi S͟hehir
see also [in Suppl.] Gümüld͟jine

Guilds **Ṣinf**
Arabic Amīn; ʿArīf; Futuwwa.ii and iii; Ḥammāl; Ḥarfūs͟h; K͟hātam; K͟hayyāṭ; Ṣinf.1
see also S͟hadd; S͟hayk͟h; Sirwāl
Persian Ṣinf.2
see also Ustād͟h.2
Turkish Ak͟hī; Ak͟hī Baba; Anadolu.iii.6; Ḥarīr.ii; Ketk͟hudā.ii; Ṣinf.3; [in Suppl.] Ik͟htiyāriyya; Inḥiṣār
see also Ak͟hī Ewrān; ʿĀlima; Čāʾūs͟h; Kannās; Mawākib.4.4; Muhr.1

Guinea Fūta Djallon; **Guinea**; Konakry
see also Sūdān (Bilād al-).2

Gypsies **Čingāne**; **Lūlī**; Nūrī
see also al-Zuṭṭ

H

Hadith → Literature.tradition-literature

Hagiography **Manāḳib**
see also Walī; *and* → Sainthood
hagiographers Aflākī; ʿAṭāʾī; al-Bādisī.2; "Djamālī"; Ḥasan Dihlawī; Ibn ʿAskar; Ibn Maryam; al-Ifrānī; al-Ḳādirī al-Ḥasanī, Abū ʿAbd Allāh; al-Sharrāṭ; al-Sulamī, Abū ʿAbd al-Raḥmān
see also Aḥmad Bābā; Bāḳi̊khānli̊; al-Kattānī; Sinān Pasha, Khodja.1

Hell Aṣḥāb al-Ukhdūd; **Djahannam**; Saʿīr; Saḳar; Ṣirāṭ; Zaḳḳūm
see also al-Aʿrāf; Shayṭān.1; al-Waʿd wa 'l-Waʿīd; al-Zabāniyya

Hephthalites Hayāṭila; Nīzak, Ṭarkhān

Heraldry al-Asad; Rank

Heresy Bidʿa; Dahriyya; Dīn-i Ilāhī; Ghulāt; Ḳābiḍ; Kāfir; Khūbmesīḥīs; Mulḥid; Zindīḳ
see also al-Ṣalīb; Takfīr; Tanāsukh; *and* → Religion.dualism *and* pantheism
heretics Abū ʿĪsā al-Warrāḳ; Abu 'l-Khaṭṭāb al-Asadī; Bashshār b. Burd; Bishr b. Ghiyāth al-Marīsī; Ibn Dirham; Ibn al-Rawandī; Mollā Ḳābiḍ; Muḥammad b. ʿAlī al-Shalmaghānī
see also Thābit Ḳuṭna; Wāliba b. al-Ḥubāb; *and* → Sects
refutations of Ibn al-Djawzī, ʿAbd al-Raḥmān; [in Suppl.] Afḍal al-Dīn Turka

History → Literature.historical
for the chronological history of dynastic events, → Caliphate; Dynasties; *for the history of early Islam,* → Caliphate.rightly-guided caliphs; Law. early religious law; Military.battles.622-632 *and* 633-660; Muḥammad, the Prophet; *for the history of regions, towns and other topographical sites,* → *the section Toponyms under individual countries*; *for the history of ideas,* → *e.g.* Astronomy; Law; Linguistics; Mathematics; Philosophy; Theology

Hostelry **Funduḳ**; **Khān**; Manzil
see also Ribāṭ.1.b

Humour al-Djidd wa 'l-Hazl; Nādira
see also Hidjā'.ii; Mudjūn
comic figures Djuḥā; Ibn al-Djaṣṣāṣ.II; Naṣr al-Dīn Khodja
humourists Ashʿab; al-Ghāḍirī; Ibn Abī ʿAtīḳ; Ibn Dāniyāl; Ḳaṣāb, Teodor; Sīfawayh al-Ḳāṣṣ; [in Suppl.] Abu 'l-ʿAnbas al-Ṣaymarī

Hungary Budīn; Eğri; Esztergom; Istolnī (Istōnī) Belghrād; **Madjar**; Mohács; Pécs; Pest; Sigetwār; Szeged; Székesfehérvár
see also Bashdjirt; Kanizsa; Maḥmūd Tardjumān; Mezökeresztes; Muslimūn.1.B.1; Ofen

Hunting **Ṣayd**
see also Kurds.iv.C.5; Samak; Shikārī; Zaghardjî Bashî; *and* → Animals; Falconry
poetry **Ṭardiyya**
see also Radjaz
treatises on Kushādjim; [in Suppl.] Ibn Manglī
see also al-Shamardal
wild animals Fahd; Khinzīr; Mahāt; Naʿām; Namir and Nimr; Salūḳī; [in Suppl.] Ḍabuʿ

Hydrology Bi'r; Ḳanāt; Mā'; Ma'ṣir; Ṭāḥūn
see also Filāḥa; Ḳanṭara.5 and 6; Madjrīṭ; al-Mīzān.2; Sāʿa.1; *and* → Architecture.monuments.dams; Geography.waters

I

Idolatry Shirk; **Wathaniyya**
idols Nuṣub; **Ṣanam**; Ṭāghūt.1; al-Uḳayṣir
see also Shaman; Zūn; *and* → Pre-Islam.in arabian peninsula

Illness Madjnūn; Malāryā; Ramad; Saraṭān.7; [in Suppl.] Djudhām
see also Kalb; Ḳuṭrub; Summ; *and* → Plague
treatises on Ḥayātī-zāde; Ibn Buṭlān; Ibn Djazla
and → Medicine

India **Hind**; Hindī
see also ʿĀda.iii; Balharā; Imām-bārā; Maṭbaʿa.4; Sikkat al-Ḥadīd.1; *and* →

LITERATURE; MILITARY; MUSIC

administration Baladiyya.5; Ḍarība.6; Dīwān.v; Djizya.iii; Ḥisba.iv; Kātib.iii; Kharādj.IV; Pargana; Safīr.3; Taḥṣīl; Zamīndār
see also Kitābāt.10; Mā'.9; Waḳf.VI; *and* → MILITARY.INDO-MUSLIM

agriculture Filāḥa.v

architecture → ARCHITECTURE.REGIONS

belles-lettres → LITERATURE.IN OTHER LANGUAGES *and* POETRY.INDO-PERSIAN

dynasties ʿĀdil-Shāhs; Bahmanīs; Barīd Shāhīs; Dihlī Sultanate; Farūḳids; Ghaznavids; Ghūrids; Hindū-Shāhīs; ʿImād Shāhī; Khaldjīs; Ḳuṭb Shāhīs; Lodīs; Mughals; Niẓām Shāhīs; Sayyids; Sharḳīs; Tughluḳids
see also Awadh; Dār al-Ḍarb; Rānā Sāngā; Tīpū Sulṭān; Vidjayanagara; *and* → DYNASTIES.AFGHANISTAN AND INDIA

education Dār al-ʿUlūm.c and d; Djāmiʿa; Madjmaʿ ʿIlmī.iv; Madrasa.II; Nadwat al-ʿUlamā'; [in Suppl.] Farangī Maḥall
see also Aḥmad Khān; Deoband; Maḥmūdābād Family

historians of Ghulām Ḥusayn Khān Ṭabāṭabā'ī; Niẓām al-Dīn Aḥmad b. al-Harawī; Sudjān Rāy Bhandārī
see also Djaʿfar Sharīf; al-Maʿbarī; Mīr Muḥammad Maʿṣūm; *and* → DYNASTIES.AFGHANISTAN AND INDIA; LITERATURE.HISTORICAL

languages Gudjarātī; Hindī; Hindustānī.i and ii; Lahndā; Marāṭhī; Pandjābī.1; Sind.3.a; Urdū.1
see also Kitābāt.10; *and* → LANGUAGES.INDO-IRANIAN

modern period Djamʿiyya.v; Hindustānī.iii; Ḥizb. vi; Indian National Congress; Iṣlāḥ.iv; Kashmīr.ii; Ḳawmiyya.vi; Khāksār; Khilāfa; Madjlis.4.C; al-Mar'a.5; Nikāḥ.II.3; [in Suppl.] Djarīda.vii
see also Mahsūd; Mappila; Tablīghī Djamāʿat; [in Suppl.] Faḳīr of Ipi; *and* → INDIA.EDUCATION

resistance against the British Yāghistān

Indian Mutiny Aẓim Allāh Khān; Bakht Khān; Imdād Allāh; Kānpur

Khilāfat movement **Khilāfa**; Muḥammad ʿAlī; Mushīr Ḥusayn Ḳidwā'ī; Shawkat ʿAlī; [in Suppl.] ʿAbd al-Bārī; Ḥasrat Mohānī
see also Amīr ʿAlī

statesmen Nawwāb Sayyid Ṣiddīḳ Ḥasan Khān; Sālār Djang; [in Suppl.] Āzād, Abu 'l-Kalām
see also Maḥmūdābād Family

mysticism → MYSTICISM.MYSTICS; SAINTHOOD

physical geography

waters Djamnā; Gangā
see also Nahr.2

population Bhaṭṭi; Bohorās; Dāwūdpōtrās; Djāṭ; Gakkhaṛ; Gandāpur; Güdjar; Ḥabshī; Hind.ii; Khaṭak; Khokars; Lambadis; Mappila; Mēd; Memon; Mē'ō; Naitias; Pārsīs; Rādjpūts; Rohillas; Shikārī; Sidi; [in Suppl.]

Demography.VII
see also Khōdja; Marāṭhās; al-Zuṭṭ
Tamils Ceylon; Labbai; Marakkayar; Rawther
religion Ahl-i Ḥadīth; Barāhima; Djayn; Hindū; Ibāḥatiya; Mahdawīs; Pandj Pīr; Sikhs; Tablīghī Djamāʿat
see also Khʷādja Khiḍr; Pārsīs; Taʿziya; Yūsuf Kāndhalawī Dihlawī; Zakariyyā Kāndhalawī Sahāranpūrī; [in Suppl.] Andjuman-i Khuddām-i Kaʿba; *and* → MYSTICISM; SAINTHOOD; THEOLOGY
reform Aḥmad Brēlwī; al-Dihlawī, Shāh Walī Allāh; Ismāʿīl Shahīd; Karāmat ʿAlī; Nānak; Tītū Mīr
toponyms
ancient Arūr; Čāmpānēr; Čhat; Djāba; Djandjīra; Fatḥpūr-sikrī; Hampī; Ḥusaynābād; Kūlam; Lakhnawtī; al-Manṣūra; Mēwāṙ; Nandurbār; Nārnawl; Pānḍuʾā; Shikārpūr.2; Sidhpūr; Sindābūr; Sindān; Sūmanāt; Telingāna; Tonk; Tribenī; Wayhind
present-day
and → ASIA.SOUTH
regions Assam; Bihār; Bombay State; Dakhan; Djaypur; Doʾāb; Gudjarāt; Hariyānā; Ḥaydarābād.b; Kāmrūp; Kashmīr; Khāndēsh; Ḳūhistān.4; Ladākh; Lūdhiāna; Maʿbar; Mahisur; Malabar; Mēwāt; Muẓaffarpur; Nāgpur; Palamāw; Pālānpur; Pandjāb; Rādhanpūr; Rāmpur; Rohilkhand; Sundarban; Tirhut; Urīśā; [in Suppl.] Djammū
see also Alwār; Banganapalle; Bāonī; Berār; Djōdhpur; Hunza and Nagir; Udaypūr
towns Adjmēr; Āgra; Aḥmadābād; Aḥmadnagar; Aligarh; Allāhābād; Ambāla; Amritsar; Anhalwāra; Arcot; Awadh; Awrangābād; Awrangābād Sayyid; Aʿẓamgarh; Badāʾūn; Bālā-ghāt; Bāndā; Bānkīpūr; Banūr; Bareilly; Barōda; Benares; Bharatpūr; Bharoč; Bhattinda; Bhōpāl; Bīdar; Bīdjāpūr; Bidjnawr; Bilgrām; Bombay City; Bulandshahr; Burhānpūr; Buxar; Calcutta; Čandērī; Dawlatābād; Deoband; Dhār; Dhārwār; Dihlī; Diū; Djālor; Djawnpur; Djūnāgaṙh; Djunnar; Dwārkā; Farīdkōṫ; Farrukhābād; Fayḍābād; Fīrūzpūr; Gulbargā; Gwāliyār; Hānsī; Ḥaydarābād.a; Ḥiṣār Fīrūza; Īdar; Islāmābād; Iṫāwā; Kalpī; Kalyāni; Kanawdj; Kāṅgṙā; Kannanūr; Kānpur; Karnāl; Karnāṫak; Katahr; Khambāyat; Khayrābād; Khuldābād; Kōṙā; Koyl; Lakhnaw; Lalitpur; Lūdhiāna; Madras; Mahīm; Māhīm; Māhūr; Mālda; Mālwā; Mānḍū; Manēr; Mangrōl; Mathurā; Mīraṫh; Mīrzāpur; Multān; Mungīr; Murādābad; Murshidābād; Muẓaffarpur; Nadjībābād; Nagar; Nāgawr; Nāgpur; Naldrug; Nāndeṙ; Pānīpat; Parendā; Pāṫan; Paṫnā; Pūna; Rādjmahāl; Rāyčūr; Sahāranpūr; Sahsarām; Sārangpur; Sardhanā; Sarkhēdj; Shakarkhelda; Shikārpūr.3; Shōlāpur; Sirhind; Srīnagar; Śrīanga-

paťťanam; Sūrat; Tālīkōťā; Thālnēr; Thānā; Ťhānesar; Ťhaťťā; Udgīr; Udjdjayn; Warangal; [in Suppl.] Amrōhā; Eličpur; Ghāzīpur

INDONESIA Baladiyya.7; Djāmiʿa; Dustūr.xi; Ḥizb.vii; Ḥukūma.vi; **Indonesia**; Maḥkama.6; Malays; Masjumi; [in Suppl.] Ḍarība.7; Hoesein Djajadiningrat
see also ʿĀda.iv; Nikāḥ.II.4; Pasisir; Prang Sabīl
architecture → ARCHITECTURE.REGIONS
education Pesantren
literature Indonesia.vi; Ḳiṣṣa.6; Miʿrādj.4; Shāʿir.7; Taʾrīkh.II.7
see also Kitābāt.8; Malays; *and* → LITERATURE.POETRY.MYSTICAL
Muslim movements Padri; Sarekat Islam
see also Sulawesi
mysticism→ MYSTICISM.MYSTICS
population Malays; Minangkabau; [in Suppl.] Demography.VIII
see also Sayābidja
religion → MYSTICISM.MYSTICS; SAINTHOOD
festivals Kandūrī; Lĕbaran
toponyms Ambon; Atjèh; Banda Islands; Bandjarmasin; Bangka; Batjan; Billiton; Borneo (*and* [in Suppl.]); Djakarta; Kubu; Kutai; Lombok; Madura; Makassar; Palembang; Pasè; Pasir; Pontianak; Riau; Sambas; Sulawesi (*and* Celebes); Sumatra; Sunda Islands; Surakarta; Ternate; Tidore
see also Zābadj

INDUSTRY Ḥarīr; Kattān; Ḳuṭn; Lubūd; Milḥ
see also Bursa; al-Iskandariyya; Ḳayṣariyya; Zonguldak

INHERITANCE ʿĀda.iii; Akdariyya; ʿAwl; **Farāʾiḍ**; **Mīrāth**; al-Sahm.2; Waṣiyya; Yatīm.2
see also Ḳassām; Khāl; Makhredj; Mukhallefāt; Tanāsukh
works on al-Sadjāwandī, Sirādj al-Dīn; al-Tilimsānī.2; al-ʿUkbarī

INVENTIONS ʿAbbās b. Firnās; Ibn Mādjid; Mūsā (Banū); Sāʿa.1

IRAN al-Furs; **Iran**; Kurds; Lur
see also al-ʿArab.iii; Ḥarb.v; Kitābāt.9; Libās.iii; Zūrkhāna; *and* → DYNASTIES.PERSIA; SHIITES; ZOROASTRIANS
administration Ḍarība.5; Diplomatic.iii; Dīwān.iv; Ghulām.ii; Imtiyāzāt.iii; Kātib.ii; Khāliṣa; Kharādj.II; Maḥkama.3; Parwānačī
see also Kalāntar; Waḳf.III; *and* → IRAN.MODERN PERIOD
agriculture Filāḥa.iii
architecture → ARCHITECTURE.REGIONS

before Islam Anūs͟harwān; Ardas͟hīr; Bahrām; Dārā; Dārābd͟jird; Dihḳan; D͟jams͟hīd; Farīdūn; al-Ḥaḍr; Hayāṭila; Hurmuz; al-Hurmuzān; Ḳārinids; Kayānids; Kay Kāʾūs; Kay K͟husraw; K͟hurs͟hīd; Kisrā; Marzpān; Mazdak; Mulūk al-Ṭawāʾif.1; Parwīz, K͟husraw (II); Pīs͟hdādids; Sāsānids; S͟hāpūr; Ṭahmūrat͟h; Yazdad͟jird III; [in Suppl.] Farruk͟hān

see also Afrāsiyāb; Buzurgmihr; Hamad͟hān; Ik͟hs͟hīd; Iran.iv; Ispahbad͟h; Ḳaṣr-i S͟hīrīn; Ḳūmis; al-Madāʾin; al-Rayy; Rustam b. Farruk͟h Hurmuzd; Sarpul-i D͟huhāb; Tansar; [in Suppl.] Dabīr; *and* → ZOROASTRIANS

dynasties → DYNASTIES.PERSIA

historians of Ḥamza al-Iṣfahānī; Ibn Manda; al-Māfarrūk͟hī; al-Rāfiʿī; Ẓahīr al-Dīn Marʿas͟hī

and → DYNASTIES.PERSIA

language → LANGUAGES.INDO-IRANIAN

literature → LITERATURE

modern period Baladiyya.4; D͟jāmiʿa; D͟jamʿiyya.iii; D͟jarīda.ii; Dustūr.iv; Ḥizb.iii; Ḥukūma.ii; Iran.v.b; Iṣlāḥ.ii; Ḳawmiyya.iii; Maʿārif.3; Mad͟jlis.4.A.iii; Mad͟jmaʿ ʿIlmī.ii; al-Marʾa.3; S͟huyūʿiyya.2; Taḳrīb; [in Suppl.] Demography.III

see also K͟hazʿal K͟hān; Mad͟jlis al-S͟hūrā; Maḥkama.3; [in Suppl.] Amīr Niẓām; *and* → DYNASTIES.PERSIA.ḲĀD͟JĀRS *and* PAHLAWĪS; SHIITES

activists Fidāʾiyyān-i Islām; Kās͟hānī, Āyātullāh; K͟hʷānsārī, Sayyid Muḥammad; K͟hiyābānī, S͟hayk͟h Muḥammad; K͟hurāsānī; Kūčak K͟hān D͟jangalī; Lāhūtī; Maḥallātī; Ṣamṣām al-Salṭana; Ṭālaḳānī; [in Suppl.] Āḳā Nad͟jafī; Ḥaydar K͟hān ʿAmū Ug͟hlī

see also D͟jangalī; Kurds.iii. C; Yazdī; Zayn al-ʿĀbidīn Marāg͟haʾī; [in Suppl.] Āzādī; Farāmūs͟h-k͟hāna

influential persons Kasrawī Tabrīzī; Malkom K͟hān; Muṭahharī; Nāʾīnī; Nūrī, S͟hayk͟h Faḍl Allāh; S͟harīʿatī, ʿAlī; Ṭihrānī; [in Suppl.] Āḳā K͟hān Kirmānī

statesmen Muṣaddiḳ; Ṭabāṭabāʾī; Taḳīzāda; Wut͟hūḳ al-Dawla; [in Suppl.] Amīr Kabīr

physical geography

deserts Biyābānak

mountains Ala Dag͟h; Alburz; Alwand Kūh; Bīsutūn; Damāwand; Hamrīn; Hawrāmān; Zagros

see also Sarḥadd

waters Atrek; Bak͟htigān, Hāmūn; Kark͟ha; Kārūn; Mānd; Ruknābād; Safīd Rūd; S͟hāh Rūd.1; S͟hāpūr; S͟haṭṭ al-ʿArab; Urmiya.1; Zāyanda-Rūd; Zirih

see also Baḥr Fāris

population Bak͟htiyārī; Bāzūkiyyūn; Bilbās; D͟jāf; Eymir.3; Göklän; Gūrān; (Banū) Kaʿb; Ḳarā Gözlu; Ḳās͟hḳāy; Kurds; Lām; Lur; S͟habānkāra; S͟hāhsewan; S͟hakāk; S͟haḳāḳī; Sind͟jābī; Türkmen.3

see also Daylam; Dulafids; Eymir.2; Fīrūzānids; Iran.ii; Ḳufṣ; Shūlistān; Tat.1; [in Suppl.] Demography.III

religion Iran.vi; Ṣafawids.IV

and → MYSTICISM.MYSTICS; SAINTHOOD; SHIITES

toponyms

ancient Abarshahr; Ardalān; Arradjān; ʿAskar Mukram; Bādj; Bākusāyā; Bayhaḳ; Dārābdjird; Daskara; Dawraḳ; Dihistān; Dīnawar; al-Djazīra; Djibāl; Djīruft; Gurgān; Ḥafrak; Ḥulwān; Īdhadj; Iṣṭakhr; (al-)Karadj; Khargird.2; Ḳūmis; Ḳurḳūb; Mihragān.iv.1; Narmāshīr; Nasā; Nawbandadjān; al-Rayy; Rūdhbār.2; Rūdhrāwar; Ṣaymara; Shāpūr; Shūlistān; al-Sīradjān; Sīrāf; Sīsar; Suhraward; al-Sūs; Ṭālaḳān.2; Ṭārum; Tawwadj; Tūn; Ṭurshīz; Ṭūs; Tūsān; Urm; Ustuwā; Zarang; [in Suppl.] Arghiyān; Ghubayrā

present-day

islands al-Fārisiyya; Ṭunb

provinces Ādharbaydjān; Balūčistān; Fārs; Gīlān; Hamadhān; Iṣfahān; Khurāsān; Khūzistān; Kirmān; Kirmānshāh; Kurdistān; Māzandarān; Yazd

see also Astarābādh.2; Rūyān; Ṭabaristān

regions Bākharz; Hawrāmān; Ḳūhistān.1; Makrān; Sarḥadd; Sīstān; [in Suppl.] Bashkard

see also Gulistān

towns and districts Ābādah; Abarḳūh; ʿAbbādān; ʿAbbāsābād; Abhar; al-Ahwāz; Āmul.1; Ardakān; Ardistān; Asadābādh; Ashraf; Astarābādh.1; Āwa; Bam; Bampūr; Bandar ʿAbbās; Bandar Pahlawī; Bārfurūsh; Barūdjird; Barzand; Bīrdjand; Bisṭām; Būshahr; Dāmghān; Dizfūl; Djannāba; Djuwayn.1 and 2; Faraḥābād; Faryāb; Fasā; Fīrūzābād; Fūman; Gulpāyagān; Gunbadh-i Ḳābūs; Hurmuz; Iṣfahān; Isfarāyīn; Kāshān; Ḳaṣr-i Shīrīn; Kāzarūn; Ḳazwīn; Khʷāf; Khalkhāl; Khʷār; Khārag; Khargird.1; Khōī; Khurramābād; Khurramshahr; Kinkiwar; Ḳishm; Ḳūčān; Ḳūhistān.2; Ḳuhrūd; Ḳum; Lāhīdjān; Lār (2x); Linga; Luristān; Mahābād; Mākū; Marāgha; Marand; Mashhad; Miyāna; Narāḳ; Naṭanz; Nayrīz; Nihāwand; Nīshāpūr; Rafsandjān; Rām-hurmuz; Rasht; Rūdhbār.3; Sabzawār.1; Ṣaḥna; Ṣāʾīn Ḳalʿa; Saḳḳiz; Salmās; Sanandadj; Sarakhs; Sārī; Sar-pul-i Dhuhāb; Sarwistān; Sāwa; Shāh Rūd.3; Shīrāz; Shushtar; Simnān; al-Sīradjān; Ṣōmāy; Suldūz; Sulṭānābād; Sulṭāniyya; Sunḳur; al-Sūs; Ṭabas; Tabrīz; Ṭārum; Tihrān; Turbat-i [Shaykh-i] Djām; Türkmen Čay (i̊); Urmiya.2; Ushnū; Warāmīn; Yazd; Zāhidān; Zandjān; Zāwa; Zawāra; Zawzan; [in Suppl.] Bashkard; Biyār; Djārdjarm; Djulfa.II; Hawsam

see also Shahr; Shahristān; Tūn; *and* → KURDS.TOPONYMS

IRAQ **ʿIrāḳ**; Kurds
see also al-ʿArabiyya; Djalīlī; Lakhmids; Sawād; Shahāridja; *and* → CALIPHATE.ʿABBĀSIDS; DYNASTIES.EGYPT AND THE FERTILE CRESCENT

architecture → ARCHITECTURE.REGIONS

before Islam → PRE-ISLAM.IN FERTILE CRESCENT

historians of al-Azdī; Baḥshal; Ibn Abī Ṭāhir Ṭayfūr; Ibn al-Bannāʾ; Ibn al-Dubaythī; al-Khaṭīb al-Baghdādī; ʿUbayd Allāh b. Aḥmad b. Abī Ṭāhir
see also Ibn al-Nadjdjār; *and* → CALIPHATE.ʿABBĀSIDS; DYNASTIES.EGYPT AND THE FERTILE CRESCENT

modern period Djarīda.i.A; Djāmiʿa; Dustūr.vi; Ḥizb.i; Ḥukūma.iii; Kurds.iii.C; Madjlis.4.A.iv; Madjmaʿ ʿIlmī.i.2.c; Maḥkama.4.iv; Mandates
see also Bābān; Kūt al-ʿAmāra; al-Mawṣil.2

bellettrists

poets al-Akhras; al-Fārūḳī; al-Kāẓimī, ʿAbd al-Muḥsin; Maʿrūf al-Ruṣāfī; Shāʾūl; al-Zahāwī, Djamīl Ṣidḳī

writers of prose Shāʾūl

monarchy Fayṣal I; Fayṣal II; Ghazī
see also Hāshimids

opposition leaders Ḳāsim ʿAbd al-Karīm; Muṣṭafā Barzānī

politicians al-Shahrastānī, Sayyid Muḥammad; Shīnā

prime ministers Nūrī al-Saʿīd; Rashīd ʿAlī al-Gaylānī

physical geography

mountains Sindjār

waters Abu ʾl-Khaṣīb; al-ʿAḍaym; Didjla; Diyālā; al-Furāt; Khābūr; al-Khāzir; Shaṭṭ al-ʿArab; al-Zāb

population Bādjalān; Bilbās; Djubūr; Dulaym; Lām; al-Manāṣir; Türkmen.3
see also Shammar; [in Suppl.] Demography.III; *and* → KURDS

toponyms

ancient Abarḳubādh; ʿAḳarḳūf; ʿAlth; al-Anbār; Bābil; Badjimzā; Bādjisrā; Bādūrayā; Bākhamrā; Baradān; Barāthā; Bawāzīdj; Bihḳubādh; Birs; Dayr ʿAbd al-Raḥmān; Dayr al-ʿĀḳūl; Dayr al-Aʿwar; Dayr al-Djamādjim; Diyār Rabīʿa; Djabbul; al-Djazīra; Fallūdja; Ḥadītha.I; Ḥarbāʾ; Ḥarūrāʾ; Ḥawīza; al-Ḳādisiyya; Kalwādhā; Kaskar; Ḳaṣr ibn Hubayra; Khāniḳīn; al-Khawarnaḳ; Kūthā; Ḳuṭrabbul; al-Madāʾin; Niffar; Nimrūd; Nīnawā; al-Nukhayla; al-Ruṣāfa.1; Sāmarrāʾ; al-Ṭaff; al-Ubulla; al-Warkāʾ; Wāsiṭ
see also al-Karkh; Nuṣratābād; Senkere

present-day

regions Bahdīnān; al-Baṭīḥa; Maysān
see also Lālish

towns Altin̊ Köprü; ʿAmādiya; ʿAmāra; ʿĀna; ʿAyn al-Tamr; Badra; Baghdād; Baʿḳūba; Balāwāt; Bārzān; al-Baṣra; Daḳūḳāʾ; Daltāwa;

Dīwāniyya; al-Fallūdja; Ḥadītha.II; al-Ḥilla; Hīt; Irbil; Karbalāʾ; Kāẓimayn; Kirkūk; al-Kūfa; Kūt al-ʿAmāra; Maʿalthāyā; al-Mawṣil; al-Nadjaf; al-Nāṣiriyya; Nuṣratābād; Rawāndiz; Sāmarrāʾ; al-Samāwa.2; Senkere; Shahrazūr; Sindjār; Sūḳ al-Shuyūkh; Sulaymāniyya; Takrīt; Zākhū; [in Suppl.] Athūr
see also Djalūlāʾ; *and* → Kurds.toponyms

Irrigation Band; Ḳanāt; Māʾ; Nāʿūra
see also Filāḥa; Kārūn; al-Nahrawān; *and* → Rivers
water **Māʾ**
see also Ḥawḍ; Sabīl.2; Saḳḳāʾ; *and* → Architecture.monuments; Hydrology; Navigation; Oceans and Seas; Rivers

Islam ʿAḳīda; Dīn; Djamāʿa; ʿIbādāt; **Islām**; Masdjid; Muḥammad; Murtadd; Muslim; Rukn.1; Shīʿa; Taḳiyya; Tawḥīd; Umma
see also Iṣlāḥ; Iʿtikāf; Nubuwwa; Rahbāniyya; Shirk; Tawakkul; *and* → Ablution; Alms; Fasting; Koran; Pilgrimage; Prayer; Theology
conversion to Islām.ii
early converts to → Muhammad.companions of
European converts Pickthall
five pillars of Islam Ḥadjdj; Ṣalāt; Ṣawm; Shahāda; Zakāt
see also ʿIbādāt; al-Ḳurṭubī, Yaḥyā; Rukn.1; ʿUmra
formulas Allāhumma; Basmala; Ḥamdala; In Shāʾ Allāh; Māshāʾ Allāh; Salām; Subḥān; Taʿawwudh; Tahlīl.2; Takbīr; Talbiya; Tashahhud; Taṣliya
see also Tashrīḳ; [in Suppl.] Abbreviations
popular beliefs ʿAyn; Dīw; Djinn; Ghūl; Muḥammad.2; Zār; [in Suppl.] ʿĀʾisha Ḳandīsha; Ḥinn
see also ʿAnḳāʾ; Shafāʿa.2; *and* → Law.customary law
preaching Ḳāṣṣ; Wāʿiẓ
proselytisism Daʿwa; Tablīghī Djamāʿat

Israel → Palestine/Israel

Italy **Īṭaliya**; Ḳawṣara; Ḳillawriya; Rūmiya; Sardāniya; Ṣiḳilliya; Wenedik
and → Sicily

Ivory Coast **Côte d'Ivoire**; Kong

J

Jacobites → Christianity.denominations

JEWELRY [in Suppl.] **Djawhar**
see also Khātam
pearls and precious stones ʿAḳīḳ; al-Durr; Kūh-i Nūr; Luʾluʾ; Mardjān; Yāḳūt; Zumurrud
see also Dhahab; Fiḍḍa; Ḥadjar; Kahrubā; Maʿdin.2.3

JORDAN Dustūr.x; Ḥukūma.iii; Madjlis.4.A.vii; Maḥkama.4.vi; Mandates; **al-Urdunn**.2
see also Taḳī al-Dīn al-Nabhānī
physical geography
mountains al-Djibāl; al-Ṭūr.5
waters al-Urdunn.1; Yarmūk.1
population al-Ḥuwayṭāt; al-Manāṣir
see also [in Suppl.] Demography.III
statesmen ʿAbd Allāh b. al-Ḥusayn; Waṣfī al-Tall
see also Hāshimids
toponyms
ancient Adhrūḥ; Ayla; al-Balḳāʾ; Djarash; al-Djarbāʾ; al-Djibāl; Faḥl; al-Ḥumayma; al-Muwaḳḳar; Umm al-Raṣāṣ; Umm al-Walīd
present-day ʿAdjlūn; al-ʿAḳaba; ʿAmmān; Bayt Rās; al-Ghawr.1; Irbid.I; Maʿān; al-Salṭ; al-Shawbak; al-Zarḳāʾ

JUDAISM Ahl al-Kitāb; Banū Isrāʾīl; Tawrāt; Yahūd
see also Filasṭīn; Hūd; Nasīʾ; al-Sāmira; *and* → BIBLE; PALESTINE/ISRAEL
communities al-Andalus.iv; al-Fāsiyyūn; Iran.ii and vi; Iṣfahān.1; al-Iskandariyya; Istanbul.vii.b; al-Ḳuds; Lār.2; Mallāḥ; Marrākush; Ṣufrūy
influences in Islam ʿĀshūrāʾ.I
see also Ḳibla; Muḥammad.i.I.C.2
Jewish personages in Muslim world ʿAbd Allāh b. Salām; Abū ʿĪsā al-Iṣfahānī; Abū Naḍḍāra; Dhū Nuwās; Hāmōn; Ḥasdāy b. Shaprūṭ; Ibn Abi ʾl-Bayān; Ibn Djāmiʿ; Ibn Djanāḥ; Ibn Gabirol; Ibn Kammūna; Ibn Maymūn; Ibn Yaʿīsh; Ibrāhīm b. Yaʿḳūb; Isḥāḳ b. Sulaymān al-Isrāʾīlī; Kaʿb b. al-Ashraf; al-Kōhēn al-ʿAṭṭār; Māsardjawayh; Māshāʾ Allāh; Mūsā b. ʿAzra; al-Rādhāniyya; Saʿadyā Ben Yōsēf; Saʿd al-Dawla; al-Samawʾal b. ʿĀdiyā; Shabbatay Ṣebī; Shāʾūl; Shīnā; Yaʿḳūb Pasha; [in Suppl.] Camondo; Ibn Biklārish
see also Abu ʾl-Barakāt; Kaʿb al-Aḥbār; Ḳaynuḳāʿ; Ḳurayẓa; ʿUzayr
Jewish sects ʿĀnāniyya; al-ʿĪsāwiyya; Karaites
Judaeo-Christian sects Ṣābiʾa.1
see also Naṣārā
Judaeo-Muslim sects Shabbatay Ṣebī

Jewish-Muslim relations
persecution Dhimma; Djizya; Ghiyār; al-Ḥākim bi-Amr Allāh; al-Maghīlī; Shiʿār.4; Zunnār
polemics Abū Isḥāḳ al-Ilbīrī; Ibn Ḥazm, Abū Muḥammad; al-Suʿūdī, Abu 'l-Faḍl; ʿUzayr
see also Ahl al-Kitāb; Taḥrīf; Yahūd
with Muḥammad Fadak; Ḳaynuḳāʿ; Khaybar; Ḳurayẓa; al-Madīna.i.1; Naḍīr
see also Muḥammad.1.I.C
language and literature Judaeo-Arabic; Judaeo-Berber; Judaeo-Persian; Ḳiṣṣa.8; Risāla.1.VII
see also Geniza; Mukhtaṣar; Musammaṭ; Muwashshaḥ; Yūsuf and Zulaykhā.1; *and* → LEXICOGRAPHY; LITERATURE.IN OTHER LANGUAGES

K

KENYA Gede; **Kenya**; Kilifi; Lamu; Malindi; Manda; Mazrūʿī; Mombasa; Pate; Siu
see also Nabhān; [in Suppl.] Djarīda.viii; *and* → AFRICA.EAST AFRICA
Swahili literature Ḳiṣṣa.7; Madīḥ.5; Marthiya.5; Mathal.5; [in Suppl.] Ḥamāsa.vi
see also Miʿrādj.3
poets Shaaban Robert
song Siti Binti Saad

KORAN Allāh.i; Āya; Fāṣila; Iʿdjāz; Ḳirāʾa; **al-Ḳurʾān**; Muḳaṭṭaʿāt; Muṣḥaf; Naskh; Sūra; Tafsīr; Umm al-Kitāb
see also ʿArabiyya.A.ii; Basmala; Faḍīla; Hamza; Indjīl; Iṣlāḥ.i.B.1; Khalḳ.II; Khawāṣṣ al-Ḳurʾān; ʿUmūm wa-Khuṣūṣ; Zayd b. Thābit
commentaries Mukhtaṣar; Sharḥ.III; **Tafsīr**; Taʾwīl
see also al-Ẓāhir wa 'l-Bāṭin
in Arabic ʿAbd al-Razzāḳ al-Ḳāshānī; Abu 'l-Faḍl ʿAllāmī; Abū Ḥayyān al-Gharnāṭī; Abu 'l-Layth al-Samarḳandī; Abu 'l-Suʿūd; Abū ʿUbayda; al-ʿAskarī.ii; al-Baghawī; Baḳī b. Makhlad; al-Bayḍāwī; al-Bulḳīnī.4; al-Dāmād; al-Dārimī; Djīwan; Fakhr al-Dīn al-Rāzī; Fayḍī; Ghulām Ḥusayn Khān Ṭabāṭabāʾī; Gīsū Darāz; Gūrānī; Ibn Abi 'l-Ridjāl; Ibn ʿAdjība; Ibn Barradjān; Ibn Kathīr, ʿImād al-Dīn; Ismāʿīl Ḥaḳḳi; al-Kalbī.I; Kalīm Allāh al-Djahānābādī; Kemāl Pasha-zāde; al-Ḳurṭubī, Abū ʿAbd Allāh; al-Ḳushayrī.1; al-Maḥallī; al-Māturīdī; Mudjāhid b. Djabr al-Makkī; Mudjīr al-Dīn al-ʿUlaymī; Muḥsin-i Fayḍ-i Kāshānī; Muḳātil b. Sulaymān; al-Nīsābūrī; al-Rāghib al-Iṣfahānī; al-Rummānī; Sahl al-Tustarī; al-Shaḥḥām; al-Shahrastānī, Abu 'l-Fatḥ; al-Sharīf al-Raḍī; al-Suhrawardī, Shihāb al-Dīn Abū Ḥafṣ; al-Sulamī, Abū ʿAbd al-

Raḥmān; al-Suyūṭī; al-Ṭabarī, Abū Dja'far; al-Ṭabrisī, Amīn al-Dīn; al-Tha'ālibī, 'Abd al-Raḥmān; al-Tha'labī, Aḥmad b. Muḥammad; al-Wāḥidī; al-Yadālī; [in Suppl.] 'Abd al-Wahhāb Bukhārī; Abu 'l-Fatḥ al-Daylamī; al-Aṣamm

see also 'Abd Allāh b. al-'Abbās; Abū Nu'aym al-Mulā'ī; Aḥmadiyya; al-'Alamī; al-Dihlawī, Shāh Walī Allāh; Djafr; Djilwatiyya; Ḥādjdjī Pasha; Hind.v.e; Ibn Mas'ūd; Ḳuṭb al-Dīn Shīrāzī; al-Manār; al-Suddī; Sufyān b. 'Uyayna; al-Sulamī, 'Izz al-Dīn; Thānesarī.3; al-Ṭūfī; Warḳā' b. 'Umar

late 19th and 20th centuries al-Ālūsī.2; Aṭfiyāsh; Mawdūdī; Muḥammad b. Aḥmad al-Iskandarānī; Muḥammad Abū Zayd; Muḥammad Farīd Wadjdī; Sayyid Ḳuṭb; Shaltūt, Maḥmūd; [in Suppl.] Djawharī, Ṭanṭāwī

in Persian Abu 'l-Futūḥ al-Rāzī; al-Dawlatābādī; Djāmī; Kāshifī; al-Maybudī.1; Muṣannifak; al-Taftāzānī

in Turkish Aḳ Ḥiṣārī.b

in Urdu Ashraf 'Alī

createdness of Miḥna

see also Djahmiyya; al-Zuhrī, Hārūn

readers 'Abd Allāh b. Abī Isḥāḳ; Abū 'Amr b. al-'Alā'; al-A'mash; 'Āṣim; al-Dānī; Ḥamza b. Ḥabīb; Ibn 'Āmir; Ibn Kathīr; 'Īsā b. 'Umar; al-Kisā'ī; Nāfi' al-Laythī; al-Sadjāwandī, Abū 'Abd Allāh

see also Abu 'l-'Āliya al-Riyāḥī; al-Dāraḳuṭnī; Ḥafṣ b. Sulaymān; Ibn al-Djazarī; Ibn al-Faḥḥām; Ibn Mudjāhid; Ibn Shanabūdh; al-Ḳasṭallānī; Makkī; al-Malaṭī; Mudjāhid b. Djabr al-Makkī; [in Suppl.] Ibn Miḳsam

transmitters al-Yazīdī.1

reading Adā'; Ḥarf; Ḳaṭ'; Khatma; **Ḳirā'a**; **Tadjwīd**

see also al-Shāṭibī, Abu 'l-Ḳāsim; al-Sidjistānī; Ta'awwudh; Tahadjdjud; Waṣl; Yaḥyā b. Ādam

recensions 'Abd Allāh b. al-Zubayr; 'Abd al-Malik b. Marwān; Abu 'l-Dardā'; 'Ā'isha bint Abī Bakr; al-Ash'arī, Abū Mūsā; 'Āṣim; al-Dimyāṭī; al-Ḥadjdjādj b. Yūsuf; Ibn Mas'ūd; Nāfi' al-Laythī; Ubayy b. Ka'b

see also Abu 'l-Aswad al-Du'alī; 'Arabiyya.ii.1 and 2; al-Ḥuṣrī.II; Warsh; Zayd b. Thābit

stories 'Ād; Ādam; Aṣḥāb al-Kahf; Ayyūb; Bilḳīs; Dāwūd; Djālūt; Fir'awn; Ḥābīl wa Ḳābīl; Ḥawwā'; Ibrāhīm; 'Īsā; al-Iskandar; al-Khaḍir; Lūṭ; Maryam; Mūsā; Nūḥ; Sulaymān b. Dāwūd; Yūnus; Yūsuf; Zakariyyā'

see also Ḳiṣaṣ al-Anbiyā'; Shayṭān.2; al-Tha'labī, Aḥmad b. Muḥammad; Yāfith; *and* → BIBLE.BIBLICAL PERSONAGES

suras al-Aḥḳāf; Aṣḥāb al-Kahf; Fātiḥa; al-Fīl; Ghāshiya; Kawthar; Luḳmān; al-Mu'awwidhatān[1]; al-Muddaththir and al-Muzzammil; al-Musabbiḥāt; Sadjda; al-Ṣāffāt; Ṭā-Hā

see also Ḥayawān.3; **Sūra**

terms Adjr.1; Aḥkām; ʿĀlam; Amr; al-Aʿrāf; ʿAṣā; Aṣḥāb al-Kahf; Aṣḥāb al-Rass; Aṣḥāb al-Ukhdūd; Āya; Baḥīra; al-Baḥrayn; Baʿl; Barāʾa; Baraka; Barzakh; Birr; Dābba; Daʿwa; Dharra; Dīn; Djahannam; Djāhiliyya; Djanna; Djinn; Dunyā; Faḳīr; Farāʾiḍ; Fitna; Fiṭra; Furḳān; al-Ghayb; Ḥadd; Ḥaḳḳ; Ḥanīf; Hātif; Ḥawārī; Ḥayāt; Ḥidjāb; Ḥisāb; Ḥizb; Ḥudjdja; Ḥūr; Iblīs; Īlāf; Ilhām; ʿIlliyyūn; Kaffāra; Kāfir; Kalima; Ḳarīn; Ḳarya; Ḳawm; Ḳayyim; Khalḳ; Khaṭīʾa; Ḳiyāma; Kursī; Ḳuwwa.2; Lawḥ; Madjnūn; Maḳām Ibrāhīm; Milla; Millet; Miskīn; Mīthāḳ; al-Munāfiḳūn.1; Nadhīr; Nafs.I; Nār; Raḥma; Rizḳ; Rudjūʿ; Rukn; Ṣabr; Ṣadr; al-Ṣāffāt; Ṣaḥīfa; Sakīna; Salām; al-Ṣāliḥūn; Shaḳāwa; Shakk.1; Shirk; al-Ṣiddīḳ; Sidjdjīl; Sidjdjīn; Sidrat al-Muntahā; Sirādj;; Ṣirāṭ; Subḥān; Sulṭān; Takhyīl.3; Umm al-Kitāb; Umm al-Ḳurā; Umma.1; Ummī.1; Waḥy; Yatīm.1; al-Zabāniyya; Zabūr; Ẓulm; [in Suppl.] Asāṭīr al-Awwalīn
see also Ḥikāya.I; Sabab.1; Samāʾ.1
translations Ḳurʾān.9
see also Aljamía
into English Aḥmadiyya; Pickthall
into Malay ʿAbd al-Raʾūf al-Sinkilī
into Persian al-Dihlawī, Shāh Walī Allāh
see also Khaṭṭ.ii
into Swahili Kenya (891a)
into Urdu ʿAbd al-Ḳādir Dihlawī; Djawān; Rafīʿ al-Dīn

KURDS **Kurds**
see also Kitāb al-Djilwa; *and* → IRAN; IRAQ; TURKEY
dynasties ʿAnnāzids; Bābān; Faḍlawayh; Ḥasanwayh; Marwānids; Rawwādids; Shaddādids
see also Kurds.iii.B
Kurdish national movement Badrkhānī; Ḳāḍī Muḥammad; Kurds.iii.C; Muṣṭafā Barzānī
see also Bārzān; Mahābād
languages Kurds.v; Ṭūr ʿAbdīn.4.iii
sects Ṣārliyya; Shabak; Yazīdī
toponyms Ardalān; Bahdīnān; Barādūst; Bārzān; Djawānrūd; Hakkārī.2; Rawāndiz; Saḳḳiz; Sanandadj; Sāwdj-Bulāḳ; Shahrazūr; Shamdīnān; Ṣōmāy; Sulaymāniyya; Zākhū
see also Kirkūk; Kurds.ii; Orāmār; Shabānkāra; Sīsar
tribes Djāf; Hakkārī.1; Hamawand; Kurds.iii.B and iv.A.2; Lak.1; Shabānkāra; Shakāk; Shaḳāḳī; Sindjābī
see also Zāzā

KUWAIT Djarīda.i.A; Dustūr.xvi; **al-Kuwayt**; Madjlis.4.A.ix; Maḥkama.4.ix;

Ṣabāḥ, Āl
see also (Djazīrat) al-ʿArab; al-ʿArabiyya; Djāmiʿa; ʿUtūb
toponyms al-Dibdiba; [in Suppl.] Aḥmadī
see also Ḳarya al-ʿUlyā

L

LAMENTATION Bakkāʾ; **Niyāḥa**; Rawḍa-khʷānī

LAND → PROPERTY; TAXATION
in the sense of agriculture, see Filāḥa; *in the sense of cooperative ownership, see* Taʿāwun; *in the sense of surveying, see* Misāḥa; Rawk

LANGUAGES **Lugha**
and → LINGUISTICS
Afro-Asiatic Ḥām; Sām.2
see also Karshūnī; Maʿlūlā.2; Sullam
Arabic **Arabiyya**.A
see also Ibn Makkī; Ḳarwasha; Khaṭṭ; Madjmaʿ ʿIlmī.i; al-Sīm; Taʿrīb; [in Suppl.] Ḥaḍramawt.iii; *and* → ALPHABET
Arabic dialects Algeria.v; Aljamía; al-Andalus.x; Arabiyya.A.iii; ʿIrāḳ.iv; Judaeo-Arabic.i and ii; Lībiya.2; al-Maghrib.VII; Mahrī; Malta.2; Mūrītāniyā.6; al-Ṣaʿīd.2; al-Shām.3; Shāwiya.3; Shuwa; Siʿird; Sūdān.2; Sūdān (Bilād al-).3; Tunisia.IV; Ṭūr ʿAbdīn.4.i; ʿUmān.4; al-Yaman.5
see also Ibn al-Birr; Takrīt; al-Ṭanṭāwī; ʿUtūb; Zawdj.2; *and* → LITERATURE.POETRY.VERNACULAR
Christian Arabic Karshūnī; Shaykhū, Luwīs
see also ʿArabiyya.A.ii.1; Ṭūr ʿAbdīn.4
Judaeo-Arabic → JUDAISM.LANGUAGE AND LITERATURE; LITERATURE.IN OTHER LANGUAGES
Bantu Swahili; Yao
Berber **Berbers**.V; Judaeo-Berber; Mūrītāniyā.6; Sīwa.2; Taḳbaylit; Tamazight; Tarifiyt; Tashelḥīt; Ṭawāriḳ.2
see also Mzāb; Tifinagh
Berber words in Arabic Āfrāg; Agadir; Āgdāl; Aménokal; Amghar; Argan; Ayt; Imzad
see also Ḳallala; Rīf.I.2(a); Tīṭ
Chadic Hausa.ii
see also Wadāī.2
Cushitic Kūsh; Somali.5

Ethiopian-Semitic Eritrea.iv; Ḥabash.iv
Hebrew Ibn Djanāḥ
Neo-Aramaic Ṭūr ʿAbdīn.4.ii
North Arabian Liḥyān; Ṣafaitic; Thamudic
and → EPIGRAPHY
South Arabian Sabaʾ
see also Ḥaḍramawt (*and* [in Suppl.] Ḥaḍramawt.iii); al-Ḥarāsīs; al-Sawdāʾ; Zabūr; *and* → EPIGRAPHY
Modern South Arabian Mahrī; Shiḥrī; Suḳuṭra.3
see also al-Baṭāḥira; al-Ḥarāsīs; [in Suppl.] Ḥaḍramawt.iii
Teda-Daza Kanuri; Tubu.3
Austronesian Atjèh; Indonesia.iii; Malays
Ibero-Caucasian Andi; Beskesek-abaza; Čerkes; Dāghistān; Darghin; al-Ḳabḳ; Ḳayyūm Nāṣirī
see also al-Kurdj; Tsakhur
Indo-European Arnawutluḳ.1
see also al-Ḳabḳ
Indo-Iranian
Indian Afghānistān.iii; Bengali.i; Ceylon; Chitral.II; Dardic and Kāfir Languages; Gudjarātī; Hind.iii; Hindī; Hindustānī; Kashmīrī; Lahndā; Maldives.2; Marāṫhī; Pandjābī.1; Sind.3.a; Urdū.1
see also Madjmaʿ ʿIlmī.iv; Sidi; [in Suppl.] Burushaski
Iranian Afghān.ii; Afghānistān.iii; Balūčistān.B; Darī; Gūrān; Hind.iii; ʿIrāḳ.iv.b; Judaeo-Persian.ii; Kurds.v; Lur; Tādjīkī.1; Tālish.2; Tat.2; Ṭūr ʿAbdīn.4.iii; Zāzā
see also Dāghistān; al-Ḳabḳ; Khwārazm; Madjmaʿ ʿIlmī.ii; Ossetians; Shughnān; al-Ṣughd
Persian dialects Simnān.3
(Niger-)Kordofanian Nūba.3
Nilo-Saharan Nūba.3; Songhay.1; Sūdān.2; Wadāī.2
Turkic Ādharī; Balkar; Bulghār; Gagauz; Khaladj.2; Turks.II
see also Afghānistān.iii; Dāghistān; al-Ḳabḳ; Khazar; Madjmaʿ ʿIlmī.iii; Sārt

LAW ʿĀda; Dustūr; **Fiḳh**; ʿIbādāt; Idjmāʿ; **Ḳānūn**.i and iii; Ḳiyās; Maḥkama; **Sharīʿa**; Tashrīʿ; ʿUrf; Uṣūl al-Fiḳh
see also Aṣḥāb al-Raʾy; Ḥuḳūḳ; Siyāsa.3; *and* → DIVORCE; INHERITANCE; MARRIAGE
for questions of law, see ʿAbd.3; Djāsūs; Filāḥa.i.4; Ḥarb.i; Ḥarīr; In Shāʾ Allāh; Intiḥār; Ḳabr; Kāfir; Khāliṣa; Khiṭba; Māʾ; al-Marʾa; Murtadd; Raḍāʿ; Rāḳid; Rashwa; Safar.1; Shaʿr.2; Ṣūra; al-Suraydjiyya; ʿUrs.1.c; Waḳf.I.3; Wilāya.1
Anglo-Mohammedan law ʿĀda.iii; Amīr ʿAlī; Munṣif
see also Ḥanafiyya

commercial law → FINANCE

customary law **ʿĀda**; Dakhīl; Ḳānūn.iv; Ṭāghūt.2; Thaʾr; **ʿUrf**; [in Suppl.] Djirga
see also Baranta; Berbers.IV; al-Māmī; al-Marʾa.2; Mushāʿ

early religious law Abū Ḥanīfa; Abū Yūsuf; al-Ashʿarī, Abū Burda; ʿAṭāʾ b. Abī Rabāḥ; al-Awzāʿī; Ibn Abī Laylā.II; Ibn Shubruma; al-Layth b. Saʿd; Mālik b. Anas; Maymūn b. Mihrān; al-Nakhaʿī, Ibrāhīm; al-Shaʿbī; al-Shāfiʿī; Shurayḥ; Sufyān al-Thawrī; Yaḥyā b. Ādam; [in Suppl.] Fuḳahāʾ al-Madīna al-Sabʿa; Ibn Abi ʾl-Zinād

genres Fatwā; Ikhtilāf; Uṣūl al-Fiḳh
see also Sharṭ

Ibāḍī law ʿAbd al-ʿAzīz b. al-Ḥādjdj Ibrāhīm; Abū Ghānim al-Khurāsānī; Abū Muḥammad b. Baraka (*and* Ibn Baraka); Abū Zakariyyāʾ al-Djanāwunī; Ibn Djaʿfar
see also al-Djayṭālī; Maḥkama.4.ix (Oman)

in South-east Asia Penghulu; Rapak; Sharīʿa (In South-East Asia); ʿUlamāʾ.5

inheritance → INHERITANCE

jurisprudence Fatwā; **Fiḳh**; Īdjāb; Idjmāʿ; Idjtihād; Ikhtilāf; Istiḥsān; Ḳiyās; Maṣlaḥa; Nāzila; Taḳlīd
see also Sadd al-Dharāʾiʿ

jurist **Faḳīh**; Mardjaʿ-i Taḳlīd; Mudjtahid; ʿUlamāʾ
see also Sharḥ.III

Ḥanafī Abū Ḥanīfa al-Nuʿmān; Abu ʾl-Layth al-Samarḳandī; Abu ʾl-Suʿūd; al-ʿAmīdī; al-Bihārī; al-Djaṣṣāṣ; al-Ḥalabī; Ḥamza al-Ḥarrānī; Ibn ʿĀbidīn; Ibn Buhlūl; Ibn Ghānim; Ibn Ḳuṭlūbughā; Ibn Nudjaym; Ibn al-Shiḥna; Ḳāḍī Khān; al-Kāsānī; Ḳasṭallānī; al-Ḳudūrī, Abu ʾl-Ḥusayn Aḥmad; al-Marghīnānī; al-Nasafī.4; al-Sadjāwandī, Sirādj al-Dīn; al-Sarakhsī, Muḥammad b. Aḥmad; al-Shaybānī, Abū ʿAbd Allāh; al-Shiblī, Abū Ḥafs; al-Ṭaḥāwī; al-Ūshī; Wānḳulī; [in Suppl.] Abū ʿAbd Allāh al-Baṣrī; Abu ʾl-Barakāt; al-Dāmaghānī, Abū ʿAbd Allāh Muḥammad b. ʿAlī; al-Dāmaghānī, Abu ʾl-Ḥasan ʿAlī b. Muḥammad
see also ʿAbd al-Ḳādir al-Ḳurashī; al-Fatāwā al-ʿĀlamgīriyya; Ibn Duḳmāḳ; al-Ṣayrafī; al-Taftāzānī; Ẓāhir

Ḥanbalī Aḥmad b. Ḥanbal; al-Bahūtī; al-Barbahārī; Ghulām al-Khallāl; Ibn ʿAḳīl; Ibn al-Bannāʾ; Ibn Baṭṭa al-ʿUkbarī; Ibn al-Djawzī; Ibn al-Farrāʾ; Ibn Ḥāmid; Ibn Ḳayyim al-Djawziyya; Ibn Ḳudāma al-Maḳdisī; Ibn Mufliḥ; Ibn Radjab; Ibn Taymiyya; al-Kalwadhānī; al-Khallāl; al-Khiraḳī; al-Marwazī; al-Ṭūfī; al-ʿUkbarī; al-Yūnīnī; Yūsuf b. ʿAbd al-Hādī
see also ʿUthmān b. Marzūḳ; *and* → THEOLOGY

Mālikī Aḥmad Bābā; Asad b. al-Furāt; al-Bādjī; al-Bāḳillānī; Bannānī; al-Burzulī; al-Dānī; al-Fāsī; Ibn ʿAbd al-Ḥakam; Ibn Abī Zamanayn; Ibn Abī Zayd al-Ḳayrawānī; Ibn ʿAmmār, Abu ʾl-ʿAbbās; Ibn ʿArafa; Ibn

ʿĀṣim; Ibn al-Faraḍī; Ibn Farḥūn; Ibn Ḥabīb, Abū Marwān; Ibn al-Ḥādjdj; Ibn al-Ḥādjib; Ibn al-Ḳāsim; Ibn Maḍāʾ; Ibn Rushayd; Ibn Sūda; al-Ibshīhī(1); ʿĪsā b. Dīnār; ʿIyāḍ b. Mūsā; al-Ḳābisī; al-Ḳalaṣādī; al-Kardūdī; Ḳaṣṣāra; Khalīl b. Isḥāḳ; al-Khushanī; al-Ḳurṭubī, Abū ʿAbd Allāh; al-Ḳurṭubī, Yaḥyā; Mālik b. Anas; al-Manūfī.4 and 5; al-Māzarī; Muḥammad b. Saḥnūn; Saḥnūn; Sālim b. Muḥammad; al-Sanhūrī, Abu 'l-Ḥasan; Shabṭūn; al-Shāṭibī, Abū Isḥāḳ; Shihāb al-Dīn al-Ḳarāfī; al-Ṭulayṭulī; al-Ṭurṭushī; al-ʿUtbī, Abū ʿAbd Allāh; al-Wansharīsī; Yaḥyā b. Yaḥyā al-Laythī; al-Zaḳḳāḳ; al-Zuhrī, Hārūn; al-Zurḳānī; [in Suppl.] Abū ʿImrān al-Fāsī; al-Azdī; Ibn Daḳīḳ al-ʿĪd; Ibn Dirham; Ibn Rushd
see also Ibn ʿAbd al-Barr; al-Ḳaṣṣār; Laḳīṭ; al-Sharīf al-Tilimsānī; al-Tilimsānī.1; *and* → ANDALUSIA.JURISTS

Shāfiʿī al-ʿAbbādī; Abū Shudjāʿ; Bādjūrī; al-Baghawī; al-Bulḳīnī; Daḥlān; al-Djanadī; al-Djīzī; al-Djuwaynī; Ibn Abī ʿAṣrūn; Ibn Abi 'l-Dam; Ibn ʿAḳīl; Ibn ʿAsākir; Ibn Djamāʿa; Ibn Ḥabīb, Badr al-Dīn; Ibn Ḥadjar al-Haytamī; Ibn Ḳāḍī Shuhba.1; Ibn Ḳāsim al-Ghazzī; Ibn al-Ṣalāḥ; Ibn Suraydj; al-Ḳalḳashandī; al-Ḳalyūbī; al-Ḳazwīnī, Abū Ḥātim; al-Ḳazwīnī, Djalāl al-Dīn; al-Ḳazwīnī, Nadjm al-Dīn; al-Kiyā al-Harrāsī; Makhrama; al-Māwardī; al-Mutawallī; al-Muzanī; al-Nawawī; al-Rāfiʿī; al-Ramlī; al-Shāfiʿī; al-Shahrazūrī; al-Shīrāzī, Abū Isḥāḳ; al-Subkī; al-Sulamī, ʿIzz al-Dīn; al-Ṣuʿlūkī; al-Ṭabarī, Abū 'l-Ṭayyib; al-Ṭabarī, Aḥmad b. ʿAbd Allāh; Zakariyyāʾ al-Anṣārī; [in Suppl.] Abū Zurʿa; Ibn Daḳīḳ al-ʿĪd
see also Abū Thawr; Dāwūd b. Khalaf; al-Isfarāyīnī; al-Ṭabarī, Abū Djaʿfar; al-Taftāzānī; al-Ziyādī

Shiite → SHIITES

Ẓāhirī Dāwūd b. Khalaf; al-Ḥumaydī; Ibn Dāwūd; Ibn Ḥazm, Abū Muḥammad; (al-)Mundhir b. Saʿīd
see also Ṣāʿid al-Andalusī; [in Suppl.] Ibn al-Rūmiyya

law of obligations ʿAḳd; ʿĀriyya; Bayʿ; Ḍamān; Dhimma; Fāsid wa Bāṭil; Faskh; Hiba; Īdjāb; Īdjār; Inkār; ʿIwaḍ; Kafāla; Khiyār; Ḳirāḍ; Muʿāmalāt; Muʿāwaḍa.3; Muḍāraba; Mufāwaḍa; Mughārasa; Mushāraka; Rahn; Ṣulḥ; Wadīʿa; Wakāla; [in Suppl.] Dayn; Ghārūḳa
see also ʿAmal.4; Djāʾiz; Ghasb; Ḳabḍ.i; Ḳasam; Maḍmūn; Suftadja; Wathīḳa; Yamīn; [in Suppl.] Ikrāh

contract of hire and lease Adjr; **Īdjār**; Kirāʾ; Musāḳāt; Muzāraʿa; [in Suppl.] Ḥikr; Inzāl

contract of sale Barāʾa.I; **Bayʿ**; Iḳāla; ʿIwaḍ; Muʿāwaḍa.1; Muwāḍaʿa.1; Salam; Shirāʾ; Tadlīs.1; Taghrīr; [in Suppl.] Darak
see also Ḍarūra; Ildjāʾ; Mukhāṭara; Ṣafḳa; Salaf; Sawm; Tidjāra

law of personal status Ḥaḍāna; Hiba; ʿIdda; Mahr; Mīrāth; Nikāḥ; Riḍāʿ; Ṭalāḳ; Waḳf; Yatīm *see also* Wilāya.1; *and* → DIVORCE; INHERITANCE; MARRIAGE

law of procedure   ʿAdl; Amīn; Bayyina; Daʿwā; G̲h̲āʾib; Ḥakam; Iḳrār; Ḳaḍāʾ; Maẓālim; S̲h̲āhid; Sid̲j̲ill.2

Mongol   Ṣadr.2; Yarg̲h̲u; Yāsā

offices   Faḳīh; Ḥakam; Ḳāḍī; Ḳāḍī ʿAskar; Ḳassām; Mard̲j̲aʿ-i Taḳlīd; Nāʾib.1; S̲h̲ayk̲h̲ al-Islām

    see also Amīn; Fatwā; K̲h̲alīfa.ii; Maḥkama; S̲h̲urṭa

Ottoman   Bāb-i Mas̲h̲īk̲h̲at; D̲j̲azāʾ.ii; D̲j̲urm; Fatwā.ii; ʿIlmiyye; Ḳānūn.iii; Ḳānūnnāme; Ḳassām; Maḥkama.2; Mak̲h̲red̲j̲; Med̲j̲elle; Med̲j̲lis-i Wālā; Mewlewiyyet; Nark̲h̲; S̲h̲ayk̲h̲ al-Islām.2; Sid̲j̲ill.3

    see also Ḥanafiyya; al-Ḥaramayn; ʿUlamāʾ.3; *and* → DYNASTIES.ANATOLIA AND THE TURKS.OTTOMANS.GRAND MUFTIS

penal law   ʿĀḳila; Diya; Ḥadd; Ḳad̲h̲f; Ḳatl; K̲h̲aṭaʾ; Ḳiṣāṣ.5; Ṣalb; Sariḳa; Taʿzīr; ʿUḳūba

    see also D̲j̲azāʾ.ii; Muḥṣan; al-Ṣalīb; S̲h̲ubha; Sid̲j̲n; Ṭarrār; T̲h̲aʾr; ʿUrf.2.II; Zinā; [in Suppl.] Ikrāh

reform   → REFORM

schools   Ḥanābila; Ḥanafiyya; Mālikiyya; al-S̲h̲āfiʿiyya; al-Ẓāhiriyya

    see also Ibn Abī Laylā; Sufyān al-T̲h̲awrī; al-Ṭabarī, Abū D̲j̲aʿfar; Wahhābiyya

terms   Adāʾ; Ad̲j̲r.2; ʿAdl; Aḥkām; Ahl al-Ḥall wa ʾl-ʿAḳd; ʿAḳd; Akdariyya; ʿAḳīḳa; ʿĀḳila; ʿAmal.3 and 4; Amān; ʿĀmil; Amīn; ʿĀriyya; ʿArs̲h̲; ʿAwl; ʿAzīma.1; Baʾl.2.b; Bālig̲h̲; Barāʾa.I; Bayʿ; Bayʿa; Bayyina; Burhān; Ḍamān; Dār al-ʿAhd; Dār al-Ḥarb; Dār al-Islām; Dār al-Ṣulḥ; Ḍarūra; Daʿwā; Dhabīḥa; Dhimma; Diya; D̲j̲āʾiz; D̲j̲anāba; D̲j̲azāʾ.ii; D̲j̲ihād; D̲j̲izya; D̲j̲urm; Faḳīh; Farāʾiḍ; Farḍ; Fāsid wa-Bāṭil; Fāsiḳ; Fask̲h̲; Fatwā; Fayʾ; Fiḳh; G̲h̲āʾib; G̲h̲anīma; G̲h̲ārim; G̲h̲aṣb; G̲h̲usl; Ḥaḍāna; Ḥadat̲h̲; Ḥadd; Ḥad̲j̲r; Hady; Ḥakam; Ḥaḳḳ; Ḥawāla; Ḥayḍ; Hiba; Ḥiyal.4; Ḥuḳūḳ; Ḥulūl; ʿIbādāt; Ibāḥa.I; ʿIdda; Id̲h̲n; Īd̲j̲āb; Īd̲j̲ār; Id̲j̲māʿ; Id̲j̲tihād; Iḥrām; Iḥyāʾ; Iḳāla; Ik̲h̲tilāf; Iḳrār; Ild̲j̲āʾ; Inkār; Inṣāf; Istibrāʾ; Istiḥsān; Istiʾnāf; Istiṣḥāb; ʿIwaḍ; Ḳabāla; Ḳabḍ.i; Ḳaḍāʾ; Ḳad̲h̲f; Kafāʾa; Kafāla; Ḳānūn; Ḳānūnnāme; Ḳasam; Ḳatl; K̲h̲aṭaʾ; K̲h̲iyār; Kirāʾ; Ḳirāḍ; Ḳiṣāṣ; Ḳiyās; Liʿān; Liṣṣ; Luḳaṭa; Maḍmūn; Mafsūl; Mahr; Maṣlaḥa; Mawāt; Mawlā.5; Maẓālim; Milk; Muʿāmalāt; Muʿāwaḍa; Muḍāraba; Mud̲j̲tahid; Mufāwaḍa; Mug̲h̲ārasa; Muḥṣan; Muk̲h̲āṭara; Munāṣafa; Musāḳāt; Mus̲h̲āraka; Mutʿa; Muṭlaḳ; Muwāḍaʿa.1; Muzāraʿa; Nad̲j̲is; Nāfila; Naṣṣ; Nāzila; Niyya; Rahn; Ribā; Ruk̲h̲ṣa.1; Sabab.2; Ṣadaḳa; Sadd al-D̲h̲arāʾīʿ; Ṣafḳa; Ṣaḥīḥ.2; al-Sahm.2; Salaf; Salam; Sariḳa; Sawm; S̲h̲āhid; S̲h̲ak̲h̲ṣ; S̲h̲akk.1; S̲h̲arika; S̲h̲arṭ.1; S̲h̲irāʾ; S̲h̲ubha; S̲h̲ufʿa; Sid̲j̲n; Suftad̲j̲a; Suknā; Sukūt; Ṣulḥ; Sunna.2; Tadlīs.1; Tag̲h̲rīr; Ṭahāra; Taḳlīd; Taklīf; Ṭalāḳ; Talfīḳ; Tas̲h̲rīʿ; Tasʿīr; Taʿzīr; Umm al-Walad; ʿUmūm wa-K̲h̲uṣūṣ; ʿUrf; Uṣūl al-Fiḳh; Wadīʿa; Wakāla; Waḳf; Waṣf.2; Waṣiyya; Wat̲h̲īḳa; Wilāya.1; Wuḍūʾ;

Yamīn; Ẓāhir; Zaʿīm; Zakāt; Zinā; [in Suppl.] ʿAḳār; Darak; Dayn; Djabr; Ghārūḳa; Ḥikr; Ikrāh; Inzāl

see also Bayt al-Māl; Hudna; Ṣaghīr; Shukr.2; Shūrā.2; Siyāsa.3; Taḥkīm

LEBANON Djarīda.i.A; Djāmiʿa; Dustūr.ix; Ḥizb.i; Ḥukūma.iii; **Lubnān**; Madjlis.4.A.vi; Maḥkama.4.iii; Mandates; Mutawālī; Ṭāʾifiyya

see also Baladiyya.2; Djāliya; Ḳays ʿAylān; al-Maʿlūf; Ṭanyūs, Shāhīn; Türkmen.3; Yūsuf Karam; Zaʿīm; [in Suppl.] Aḥmad Pasha Küčük; al-Bustānī; Demography.III; *and* → DRUZES

belletrists

poets Fāris al-Shidyāḳ; Khalīl Muṭrān; al-Maʿlūf; Ṭuʿma, Ilyās; al-Yāzidjī; [in Suppl.] Abū Māḍī; al-Bustānī.4 and 8

see also al-Bustānī.7; Nuʿayma, Mīkhāʾīl; al-Rayḥānī

writers of prose al-Maʿlūf; Nuʿayma, Mīkhāʾīl; al-Yāzidjī; [in Suppl.] al-Bustānī.6

see also Faraḥ Anṭūn; Mayy Ziyāda

governors Bashīr Shihāb II; Dāwūd Pasha; Djānbulāt; Fakhr al-Dīn; Ḥarfūsh; Shihāb

see also Maʿn; Maʿn-zāda

historians of Iskandar Agha

religious leaders Sharaf al-Dīn; Yūsuf Karam

see also Mutawālī

toponyms

ancient ʿAyn al-Djarr

present-day

regions al-Biḳāʿ; al-Shūf

towns Baʿlabakk; Batrūn; Bayrūt; Bsharrā; Bteddīn; Djubayl; Karak Nūḥ; Ṣaydā; Ṣūr; Ṭarābulus al-Shām

LEGENDS Ḥikāya

and → BIBLE.BIBLICAL PERSONAGES; ESCHATOLOGY; KORAN.STORIES

legendary beings ʿAnḳāʾ; al-Burāḳ; Dīw; al-Djassāsa; Djinn; Ghūl; Hātif; ʿIfrīt; Ḳuṭrub; Parī; Sīmurgh; ʿŪdj; Zuhāk

see also al-Rukhkh

legendary dynasties Kayānids; Pīshdādids

see also Firdawsī; Ḥamāsa.ii

legendary locations Damāwand; Djūdī; Ergenekon; Ḥūsh; Ḳïzïl-elma; Sāwa.3; Wabār

see also Tūrān; Wāḳwāḳ

legendary people Abū Righāl; Abū Safyān; Abū Zayd; ʿAdnān; Afrāsiyāb; Ahl al-Ṣuffa; Amīna; Āṣaf b. Barakhyā; Asḥāb al-Kahf; Barṣīṣā; al-Basūs; Bilḳīs; al-Dadjdjāl; Djamshīd; Ḥabīb al-Nadjdjār; Ḥanẓala b. Ṣafwān; Hind

bint al-Khuss; Hirmis; Hūshang; Ibn Buḳayla; al-Kāhina; Ḳaḥṭān; Kāwah; al-Khaḍir; Luḳmān; Masʿūd; Naṣr al-Dīn Khodja; Sām; Saṭīḥ b. Rabīʿa; Shiḳḳ; Siyāwush; Sulaymān b. Dāwūd; Ṭahmūrath; Yādjūdj wa-Mādjūdj; [in Suppl.] al-Djarādatān[i]
see also Akhī Ewrān; ʿAmr b. ʿAdī; ʿAmr b. Luḥayy; Aṣḥāb al-Rass; Ḳuss b. Sāʿida; Muʿammar; Ṣarı̊ Ṣalṭūḳ Dede; Ṭursun Faḳīh; Zarḳāʾ al-Yamāma; Zuhayr b. Djanāb; *and* → KORAN.STORIES

legendary stories ʿAbd Allāh b. Djudʿān; Aktham b. Ṣayfī; Almās; al-Baṭṭāl; Buhlūl; Damāwand; Djirdjīs; Djūdī; al-Durr; Fāṭima; al-Ghazāl; al-Ḥaḍr; Ḥāʾiṭ al-ʿAdjūz; Haram; Hārūt wa-Mārūt; Hudhud; Isrāʾīliyyāt; Khālid b. Yazīd b. Muʿāwiya; Ḳiṣaṣ al-Anbiyāʾ; Nūḥ
see also Wāḳwāḳ

LEXICOGRAPHY **Ḳāmūs**; Laḥn al-ʿĀmma
see also Sharḥ.I; Sullam; *and* → LINGUISTICS

lexicographers
for Andalusian lexicographers, → ANDALUSIA
Arabic Abū Zayd al-Anṣārī; al-Azharī; al-Djawālīḳī; al-Djawharī; Farḥāt; al-Fīrūzābādī; Ibn al-Birr; Ibn Durayd; Ibn Fāris; Ibn Makkī; Ibn Manẓūr; Ibn Sīda; Ibn al-Sikkīt; al-Ḳazzāz; al-Khalīl b. Aḥmad; Muḥammad Murtaḍā; Nashwān b. Saʿīd; al-Ṣaghānī, Raḍiyy al-Dīn; al-Shaybānī, Abū ʿAmr (*and* [in Suppl.] Abū ʿAmr al-Shaybānī); al-Tahānawī; Tammām b. Ghālib; al-Yāzidjī.2 and 3; al-Zamakhsharī; al-Zubaydī; [in Suppl.] Abū Isḥāḳ al-Fārisī; al-Bustānī.1 and 2; al-Fārābī
see also Abū Ḥātim al-Rāzī; Akhtarī; al-Rāghib al-Iṣfahānī; al-Tanūkhī, Djamāl al-Dīn; al-Thaʿālibī, Abū Manṣūr ʿAbd al-Malik; [in Suppl.] Ibn Kabar
Hebrew Ibn Djanāḥ
see also Judaeo-Arabic.iii.B
Persian ʿAbd al-Rashīd al-Tattawī; Aḥmad Wafīḳ Pasha; Burhān; Surūrī Kāshānī; Taḳī Awḥadī; [in Suppl.] Dehkhudā
see also Ārzū Khān; Mahdī Khān Astarābādī; Riḍā Ḳulī Khān; al-Tahānawī
Turkish Akhtarī; al-Kāshgharī; Kāẓim Ḳadrī; Niʿmat Allāh b. Aḥmad; Sāmī
see also Esʿad Efendi, Meḥmed; Luṭfī Efendi; Riyāḍī; Shināsī; Wānḳulı̊

terms Farḍ.b

LIBYA Djāmiʿa; Djarīda.i.B; Dustūr.xii; **Lībiyā**; Madjlis.4.A.xviii
see also ʿArabiyya.A.iii.3; al-Bārūnī; Ḳaramānlī; Khalīfa b. ʿAskar; Sanūsiyya; *and* → DYNASTIES.SPAIN AND NORTH AFRICA

population → AFRICA.NORTH AFRICA; BERBERS

toponyms
ancient Ṣabra; Surt; Zawīla
present-day
oases Awdjila; Baḥriyya; al-Djaghbūb; Djawf Kufra; al-Djufra; Ghadamès; Kufra
regions Barḳa; al-Djufra; Fazzān
see also Nafūsa
towns Adjdābiya; Benghāzī; Darna; Djādū; Murzuḳ; Ṭarābulus al-Gharb
see also Ghāt

LIFE STAGES **Ḥayāt**
childbirth ʿAḳīḳa; Āl; Liʿān; al-Marʾa.2.c; Mawākib.4.2
see also Raḍāʿ; Waʾd al-Banāt
pregnancy Rāḳid; Waḥam
birth control **Tanẓīm al-Nasl**
suckling Raḍāʿ
treatises on ʿArīb b. Saʿd al-Kātib al-Ḳurṭubī
childhood Bāligh; **Ṣaghīr**; Yatīm
see also Ḥaḍāna; al-Shayb wa ʾl-Shabāb; *and* → CIRCUMCISION; EDUCATION; MARRIAGE
old age **Muʿammar**
see also al-Shayb wa ʾl-Shabāb; Shaykh; *and* → DEATH

LINGUISTICS **Lugha**; Naḥw; Taṣrīf; Uṣūl
see also Balāgha; Bayān; Laḥn al-ʿĀmma; Sharḥ.I; *and* → LANGUAGES; LEXICOGRAPHY
grammarians/philologists
biographies of al-Zubaydī
8th century ʿAbd Allāh b. Abī Isḥāḳ; Abū ʿAmr al-ʿAlāʾ; al-Akhfash.I; ʿĪsā b. ʿUmar; al-Khalīl b. Aḥmad; Ḳuṭrub; al-Mufaḍḍal al-Ḍabbī; Sībawayhi; al-Shaybānī, Abū ʿAmr (*and* [in Suppl.] Abū ʿAmr al-Shaybānī); Yūnus b. Ḥabīb
see also [in Suppl.] Abu ʾl-Bayḍāʾ al-Riyāḥī
9th century Abū Ḥātim al-Sidjistānī; Abū ʿUbayd al-Ḳāsim b. Sallām; Abū ʿUbayda; Abū Zayd al-Anṣārī; al-Akhfash.II; al-Aṣmaʿī; al-Bāhilī, Abū Naṣr; Djūdī al-Mawrūrī; al-Farrāʾ; Ibn al-Aʿrābī, Muḥammad; Ibn Sallām al-Djumaḥī; Ibn al-Sikkīt; al-Kisāʾī, Abu ʾl-Ḥasan; al-Layth b. al-Muẓaffar; al-Māzinī, Abū ʿUthmān; al-Mubarrad; Muḥammad b. Ḥabīb; al-Ruʾāsī; al-Yazīdī.2; [in Suppl.] Abu ʾl-ʿAmaythal
10th century al-Akhfash.III; al-Anbārī, Abū Bakr; al-Anbārī, Abū Muḥammad; al-ʿAskarī.i; Djaḥẓa; al-Fārisī; Ghulām Thaʿlab; Ḥamza al-Iṣfahānī;

Ibn al-ʿArīf, al-Ḥusayn; Ibn Djinnī; Ibn Durayd; Ibn Durustawayh; Ibn Kaysān; Ibn Khālawayh; Ibn al-Khayyāṭ, Abū Bakr; Ibn al-Ḳūṭiyya; Ibn al-Naḥḥās; Ibn al-Sarrādj; al-Ḳālī; Ḳudāma; Nifṭawayh; al-Rummānī; al-Sīrāfī; al-Ṭayālisī, Djaʿfar; Thaʿlab; al-Zadjdjādj; al-Zadjdjādjī; al-Zubaydī; [in Suppl.] Abū Isḥāḳ al-Fārisī; Abū Riyāsh al-Ḳaysī; Abu 'l-Ṭayyib al-Lughawī; al-Ḥātimī; Ibn Kaysān; Ibn Miḳsam

11th century al-Adjdābī; al-ʿAskarī. ii; Ibn al-Birr; Ibn Fāris; Ibn al-Ḥādjdj; Ibn al-Iflīlī; Ibn Makkī; Ibn Sīda; al-Ḳazzāz; al-Marzūḳī; al-Rabaḥī; al-Rabaʿī; al-Shantamarī; Ṭāhir b. Aḥmad b. Bābashādh; al-Wāḥidī; [in Suppl.] Abū Usāma al-Harawī; al-Djurdjānī

12th century al-Anbārī, Abu 'l-Barakāt; al-Baṭalyawsī; al-Djawālīḳī; al-Djazūlī, Abū Mūsā; al-Ḥarīrī; Ibn Barrī, Abū Muḥammad; Ibn Maḍāʾ; Ibn al-Shadjarī al-Baghdādī; al-Maydānī; al-Tibrīzī; al-Zamakhsharī; [in Suppl.] Abu 'l-Barakāt; Ibn Hishām al-Lakhmī

13th century al-Astarābādhī, Raḍī al-Dīn; Ibn al-Adjdābī; Ibn al-Athīr.1; Ibn al-Ḥādjdj; Ibn al-Ḥādjib; Ibn Mālik; Ibn Muʿṭī; al-Muṭarrizī; al-Shalawbīn; al-Sharīshī; al-ʿUkbarī; [in Suppl.] al-Balaṭī, Abu 'l-Fatḥ ʿUthmān; Ibn al-Adjdābī

14th century Abū Ḥayyān al-Gharnāṭī; al-Astarābādhī, Rukn al-Dīn; Fakhrī; Ibn Ādjurrūm; Ibn ʿAḳīl, ʿAbd Allāh; Ibn Barrī, Abu 'l-Ḥasan; Ibn Hishām, Djamāl al-Dīn; Ibn Khātima; Ibn al-Ṣāʾigh; al-Sharīf al-Gharnatī; Yaḥyā b. Ḥamza al-ʿAlawī

15th century al-Azharī, Khālid; Ibn ʿĀṣim; al-Sanhūrī, Abu 'l-Ḥasan; al-Suyūṭī

17th century ʿAbd al-Ḳādir al-Baghdādī

18th century Farḥāt

19th century Fāris al-Shidyāḳ; Ibn al-Ḥādjdj; al-Nabarāwī; al-Yāzidjī.1

see also Fuʾād Pasha

20th century [in Suppl.] Arat

phonetics Ḥurūf al-Hidjāʾ.II; Makhāridj al-Ḥurūf; Mushtarik; Ṣawtiyya; Tafkhīm

see also Hāwī; Ḥurūf al-Hidjāʾ; Imāla; Uṣūl

for Arabic and Persian dialects, → LANGUAGES; *for the letters of the alphabet,* → ALPHABET

terms Aḍdād; Āla.i.; ʿĀmil; ʿAṭf; Dakhīl; Djāmʿ; Fard.c; Fiʿl; Gharīb; Ḥaraka wa-Sukūn.ii; Ḥarf; Hāwī; Ḥikāya.I; Ḥukm.II; Ḥulūl; Ibdāl; Iḍāfa; Idghām; Iḍmār; ʿIlla.i; Imāla; Iʿrāb; Ishtiḳāḳ; Ism; Istifhām; Istithnāʾ; Kasra; Ḳaṭʿ; Khabar; Ḳiyās.2; Māḍī; Maʿnā.1; Muʿarrab; Mubālagha.a; Mubtadaʾ.1; Muḍāriʿ; Mudhakkar; Muḍmar; Musnad.2; Muṭlaḳ; Muwallad.2; Muzdawidj; Nafy; Naṣb; Naʿt; Nisba.1; Rafʿ.1; Sabab.4; Ṣaḥīḥ.3; Sālim.2; Ṣarf; Sharṭ.3; Ṣifa.1; Ṣila.1; Taʿaddī; Tafḍīl; Tafkhīm; Taḳdīr.1; Tamthīl.1; Tanwīn; Taʿrīb; Taʿrīf.2; Taṣrīf; Waḍʿ al-Lugha; Waḥda.1; Waṣl; Wazn.2; Ẓarf; [in Suppl.] Ḥāl *see also* Basīṭ wa-Murakkab; Ghalaṭāt-i Meshhūre; Ḥurūf al-Hidjāʾ; Taʿlīḳ

LITERATURE **Adab**; ʿArabiyya.B; ʿIrāḳ.v; Iran.vii; ʿOthmānli̊.III; Tunisia.V; Turks.III; Urdū.2
autobiographical Nuʿayma, Mīkhāʾīl; Sālim; Shāʾūl; Zaydān, Djurdjī
see also Shaybānī; Tardjama.1; Tūzūk
biographical Faḍīla; **Manāḳib**; Mathālib; **Ṭabaḳāt**; Tadhkira.2 and 3; Tardjama.1; Tūzūk
see also ʿIlm al-Ridjāl; Maʾāthir al-Umarāʾ; Mughals.10; Shurafāʾ.2; Ṣila.2.II.c; *and* → HAGIOGRAPHY; LITERATURE.HISTORICAL *and* POETRY; MEDICINE.PHYSICIANS.BIOGRAPHIES OF; MUḤAMMAD, THE PROPHET
criticism Ibn al-Athīr.3; Ibn Rashīḳ; Ḳudāma; [in Suppl.] al-Djurdjānī; al-Ḥātimī
modern Kemāl, Meḥmed Nāmi̊ḳ; Köprülü; Kurd ʿAlī; al-Māzinī; Olghun, Meḥmed Ṭāhir; [in Suppl.] Alangu; Atač
terms Mubālagha.b; Waḥshī
drama **Masraḥ**; Taʿziya
Arabic Khayāl al-Ẓill; Masraḥ.1 and 2
see also ʿArabiyya.B.V
playwrights Abū Naḍḍāra; Faraḥ Anṭūn; Ibn Dāniyāl; al-Ḳusanṭīnī; al-Maʿlūf; Nadjīb al-Ḥaddād; Nadjīb Muḥammad Surūr; al-Naḳḳāsh; Ṣalāḥ ʿAbd al-Ṣabūr; Salīm al-Naḳḳāsh; al-Sharḳāwī; Shawḳī; al-Yāzidjī.3; [in Suppl.] al-Bustānī.1
see also Isḥāḳ, Adīb; Ismāʿīl Ṣabrī; Khalīl Muṭrān; Shumayyil, Shiblī; Ṭuʿma, Ilyās
Central Asian Masraḥ.5
Persian Masraḥ.4; Taʿziya
playwrights Muḥammad Djaʿfar Ḳaradja-dāghī; [in Suppl.] Amīrī
Turkish Ḳaragöz; Ḳawuḳlu; Masraḥ.3; Orta Oyunu
playwrights ʿAbd al-Ḥaḳḳ Ḥāmid; Aḥmad Wafīḳ Pasha; Ākhund-zāda; Djewdet; Karay, Refīḳ Khālid; Ḳaṣāb, Teodor; Kemāl, Meḥmed Nāmi̊ḳ; Khayr Allāh Efendi; Manāṣti̊rli̊ Meḥmed Rifʿat; Meḥmed Raʾūf; Mīzāndji̊ Meḥmed Murād; Muḥibb Aḥmed "Diranas"; Muṣāḥib-zāde Djelāl; Oktay Rifat; Shināsī; [in Suppl.] Alus; Bashḳut; Čamli̊bel; Ḥasan Bedr al-Dīn
see also Djanāb Shihāb al-Dīn; Ebüzziya Tevfik; Ekrem Bey; Kaygi̊li̊, ʿOthmān Djemāl; Khālide Edīb; Muʿallim Nādjī
Urdu Masraḥ.6
playwrights Amānat; [in Suppl.] Āghā Ḥashar Kashmīrī
epistolary **Inshāʾ**; Kātib; **Risāla**
see also Ṣadr.(b)
letter-writers ʿAbd al-Ḥamīd; Aḥmad Sirhindī; ʿAmr b. Masʿada; al-Babbaghāʾ; Ghālib; Ḥāletī; al-Hamadhānī; Harkarn; Ibn ʿAmīra; Ibn al-

Athīr.3; Ibn Idrīs.I; Ibn Ḳalāḳis; Ibn al-Khaṣīb; Ibn al-Ṣayrafī; al-Ḳabtawrī; al-Ḳāḍī al-Fāḍil; Kānī; Khalīfa Shāh Muḥammad; Khwāndamīr; al-Khwārazmī; al-Maʿarrī; Makhdūm al-Mulk Manīrī; Meḥmed Pasha Rāmī (*and* Rāmī Meḥmed Pasha); Muḥammad b. Hindū-Shāh; Oḳčuzāde; Rashīd al-Dīn (Waṭwāṭ); Saʿīd b. Ḥumayd; al-Shaybānī, Ibrāhīm; Ṭāhir b. Muḥammad; Ṭāhir Waḥīd; al-ʿUtbī, Abū ʿAbd al-Raḥmān; al-Wahrānī; Yūsufī; [in Suppl.] ʿAbd al-ʿAzīz b. Yūsuf; Amīr Niẓām; Ibn Khalaf

see also Aljamía; al-Djunayd; Ibn al-ʿAmīd.1; Ibn al-Khaṭīb; Mughals.10; Sudjān Rāy Bhandārī; al-Washshāʾ

etiquette-literature **Adab**; al-Maḥāsin wa ʾl-Masāwī

see also al-Djidd wa ʾl-Hazl; Djins; Ḥiyal; Iyās b. Muʿāwiya; Kalīla wa-Dimna; Kātib; Marzban-nāma; Nadīm; Sulūk.1; Ṭufaylī; Ẓarīf

authors Abū Ḥayyān al-Tawḥīdī; al-Bayhaḳī; Djāḥiẓ; al-Ghuzūlī; Hilāl al-Ṣābiʾ; al-Ḥuṣrī.I; Ibn ʿAbd Rabbih; Ibn Abi ʾl-Dunyā; Ibn al-Muḳaffaʿ; al-Ḳalyūbī; al-Ḳāshānī; al-Kisrawī; al-Marzubānī; Merdjümek; al-Nīsābūrī; al-Rāghib al-Iṣfahānī; al-Shimshāṭī; al-Ṣūlī; al-Tanūkhī, al-Muḥassin; al-Washshāʾ

see also al-Djahshiyārī; al-Ḳalḳashandī.1; Shabīb b. Shayba; al-Zarnūdjī

genealogical Mathālib

see also Ṭabaḳāt

genealogists al-Abīwardī; al-Djawwānī; al-Hamdānī; al-Kalbī.II; al-Ḳalḳashandī.1; Ḳāsim b. Aṣbagh; al-Marwazī; Muṣʿab; al-Rushāṭī; al-Zubayr b. Bakkār; [in Suppl.] Fakhr-i Mudabbir

see also Ibn Daʾb; al-Ḳādirī al-Ḥasanī; al-Khwārazmī; Mihmindār

genres

for the genres of non-literary disciplines, → ASTRONOMY; LAW; THEOLOGY; *etc.*

poetry Ghazal; Ḥamāsa; Hidjāʾ; Ḳaṣīda; Khamriyya; Madīḥ; Marthiya; Mathnawī; Mufākhara; Munṣifa; Musammaṭ; Muwashshaḥ; Nawriyya; Shahrangīz; Sharḳī; Ṣuʿlūḳ.II.4 and III.2; Tadhkira.2 and 3; Ṭardiyya; Tardjīʿ-band; Waṣf.1; Zadjal; Zahriyyāt; Zuhdiyya

see also ʿArabiyya.B; Iran.vii; Rabīʿiyyāt; Sāḳī.2; Shawāhid; Takhmīs; Wā-sōkht

prose Adab; Adjāʾib; Awāʾil; Badīʿ; Bilmedje; Djafr; Faḍīla; Fahrasa; Ḥikāya; Ilāhī; Inshāʾ; Isrāʾīliyyāt; Kān wa-Kān; Khiṭaṭ; Ḳiṣṣa; al-Ḳūmā; Laḥn al-ʿĀmma; Lughz; al-Maghāzī; al-Maḥāsin wa ʾl-Masāwī; Maḳāla; Maḳāma; Malḥūn; Manāḳib; Masāʾil wa-Adjwiba; al-Masālik wa ʾl-Mamālik; Masraḥ; Mathālib; Mawsūʿa; Muḳaddima; Mukhtaṣar; Munāẓara; Nādira; Naḳāʾiḍ; Naṣīḥat al-Mulūk; Riḥla; Risāla; Sharḥ; Ṣila.2; Sīra; Sunan; Ṭabaḳāt; Tadhkira.1; Tafsīr; Tardjama; Uḳṣūṣa; [in Suppl.] Arbaʿūn Ḥadīth; Ḥabsiyya

see also Alf Layla wa-Layla (363b); ʿArabiyya.B; Bibliography;

D̲j̲ug̲h̲rāfiyā; Fatḥnāme; Ḥayawān; Ḥiyal; Iran.vii; Malāḥim; Mat̲h̲al; S̲h̲āhnāmed̲j̲i; Zuhd; *and* → CHRISTIANITY.MONASTERIES.WRITINGS ON; LITERATURE.TRADITION-LITERATURE; PILGRIMAGE

historical Isrāʾīliyyāt; al-Mag̲h̲āzī; Tard̲j̲ama.1; **Taʾrīk̲h̲**.II

see also Fatḥnāme; Ṣaḥāba; Ṣila.2.II; *and* → *the sections Biographical, Mag̲h̲āzī-literature and Tradition-literature under this entry*

Andalusian → ANDALUSIA

Arabic Taʾrīk̲h̲.II.1

on countries/cities → *individual countries*

on dynasties/caliphs → *individual dynasties under* DYNASTIES

universal histories Abu ʾl-Fidā; Abū Mik̲h̲naf; Akanṣūs; al-Antāḳī; ʿArīb b. Saʿd al-Kātib al-Ḳurṭubī; al-ʿAynī; al-Bakrī.1 and 2; al-Balād̲h̲urī; Baybars al-Manṣūrī; al-Birzālī; Daḥlān; al-D̲h̲ahabī; al-Diyārbakrī; al-D̲j̲annābī; al-D̲j̲azarī; al-Farg̲h̲ānī; Ḥamza al-Iṣfahānī; Ḥasan-i Rūmlū; al-Hayt̲h̲am b. ʿAdī; Ibn Abī S̲h̲ayba; Ibn Abī Ṭayyiʾ; Ibn Aʿt̲h̲am al-Kūfī; Ibn al-At̲h̲īr.2; Ibn al-Dawādārī; Ibn al-D̲j̲awzī (Sibṭ); Ibn al-Furāt; Ibn Kat̲h̲īr; Ibn K̲h̲aldūn; Ibn K̲h̲ayyāṭ al-ʿUṣfurī; Ibn al-Sāʿī; al-Kalbī.II; Kātib Čelebi; al-Kutubī; al-Makīn b. al-ʿAmīd; al-Masʿūdī; Miskawayh; Müned̲j̲d̲j̲im Bas̲h̲î; al-Muṭahhar b. Ṭāhir al-Maḳdisī; al-Nuwayrī, S̲h̲ihāb al-Dīn; Saʿīd b. al-Biṭrīḳ; al-Ṭabarī, Abū D̲j̲aʿfar; al-T̲h̲aʿālibī, Abū Manṣūr (*and* al-T̲h̲aʿālibī, Abū Manṣūr ʿAbd al-Malik); al-T̲h̲aḳafī, Ibrāhīm; Wat̲h̲īma b. Mūsā; al-Yaʿḳūbī; al-Yūnīnī

see also Ak̲h̲bār Mad̲j̲mūʿa

8th-century authors Abū Mik̲h̲naf; ʿAwāna b. al-Ḥakam al-Kalbī; Sayf b. ʿUmar

9th-century authors al-Balād̲h̲urī; al-Fāḳihī; al-Farg̲h̲ānī; al-Hayt̲h̲am b. ʿAdī; Ibn ʿAbd al-Ḥakam.4; Ibn Abī S̲h̲ayba; Ibn Abī Ṭāhir Ṭayfūr; Ibn Aʿt̲h̲am al-Kūfī; Ibn K̲h̲ayyāṭ al-ʿUṣfurī; Ibn al-Naṭṭāḥ; al-Kalbī.II; al-Madāʾinī; Naṣr b. Muzāḥim; al-Wāḳidī; Wat̲h̲īma b. Mūsā; al-Yaʿḳūbī; al-Ziyādī

10th-century authors ʿArīb b. Saʿd al-Kātib al-Ḳurṭubī; al-Azdī; Baḥs̲h̲al; al-Balawī; al-D̲j̲ahs̲h̲iyārī; Ḥamza al-Iṣfahānī; Ibn al-Dāya; Ibn al-Ḳūṭiyya; Ibn Manda; Ibn al-Ṣag̲h̲īr; al-Kindī, Abū ʿUmar Muḥammad; al-Masʿūdī; al-Muṭahhar b. Ṭāhir al-Maḳdisī; Saʿīd b. al-Biṭrīḳ; al-Ṭabarī, Abū D̲j̲aʿfar; Wakīʿ; al-Waṣīfī

11th-century authors al-Antāḳī, Abu ʾl-Farad̲j̲; Ibn al-Bannāʾ; Ibn Burd.I; Ibn Ḥayyān; Ibn al-Raḳīḳ; al-Māfarrūk̲h̲ī; al-T̲h̲aʿālibī, Abū Manṣūr

12th-century authors al-ʿAẓīmī; Ibn al-D̲j̲awzī; Ibn G̲h̲ālib; Ibn al-Ḳalānisī; Ibn Ṣāḥib al-Ṣalāt; Ibn al-Ṣayrafī, Abū Bakr; Ibn S̲h̲addād, Abū Muḥammad; ʿImād al-Dīn; S̲h̲īrawayh; ʿUmāra al-Yamanī *see also* al-Bayd̲h̲ak; Ibn Manda

13th-century authors   ʿAbd al-Wāḥid al-Marrākus̲h̲ī; Abū S̲h̲āma; al-Bundārī; al-D̲janadī; Ibn Abi ʾl-Dam; Ibn Abī Ṭayyiʾ; Ibn al-ʿAdīm; Ibn al-At̲h̲īr.2; Ibn al-D̲jawzī (Sibṭ); Ibn Ḥamādu; Ibn al-Mud̲jāwir; Ibn Muyassar; Ibn al-Nad̲jd̲jār; Ibn al-Sāʿī; Ibn Saʿīd al-Mag̲h̲ribī; Ibn S̲h̲addād, ʿIzz al-Dīn; Ibn S̲h̲addād, Bahāʾ al-Dīn; Ibn al-Ṭuwayr; al-Makīn b. al-ʿAmīd; al-Manṣūr, al-Malik; al-Rāfiʿī; [in Suppl.] Ibn ʿAskar; Ibn Ḥātim

14th-century authors   Abu ʾl-Fidā; Baybars al-Manṣūrī; al-Birzālī; al-D̲h̲ahabī; al-D̲jazarī; Ibn Abī Zarʿ; Ibn al-Dawādārī; Ibn Dukmāk; Ibn al-Furāt, Nāṣir al-Dīn; Ibn Ḥabīb, Badr al-Dīn; Ibn ʿId̲h̲ārī; Ibn Kat̲h̲īr, ʿImād al-Dīn; Ibn K̲h̲aldūn; Ibn al-K̲h̲aṭīb; Ibn al-Ṭiḳṭaḳā; al-K̲h̲azrad̲jī, Muwaffaḳ al-Dīn; al-Kutubī; al-Mufaḍḍal b. Abi ʾl-Faḍāʾil; al-Nuwayrī, S̲h̲ihāb al-Dīn; al-Ṣafadī, Ṣalāḥ al-Dīn; S̲h̲āfiʿ b. ʿAlī; al-Wādīʾās̲h̲ī; al-Yūnīnī

15th-century authors   Abu ʾl-Maḥāsin b. Tag̲h̲rībirdī; ʿArabfaḳih; al-ʿAynī; al-Fāsī; Ibn ʿArabs̲h̲āh; Ibn S̲h̲āhīn al-Ẓāhirī; al-Maḳrīzī; al-Sak̲h̲āwī

16th-century authors   al-Diyārbakrī; al-D̲jannābī, Abū Muḥammad; Ḥasan-i Rūmlū; Ibn al-Daybaʿ; Ibn Iyās; Mud̲jīr al-Dīn al-ʿUlaymī; al-Suyūṭī

17th-century authors   ʿAbd al-ʿAzīz b. Muḥammad; al-Bakrī (b. Abi ʾl-Surūr); Ibn Abī Dīnār; Kātib Čelebi; al-Maḳḳarī; al-Mawzaʿī

18th-century authors   al-Damurdās̲h̲ī; al-Ḥād̲jd̲j Ḥammūda; al-Ifrānī; Müned̲jd̲jim Bas̲h̲i̊

19th-century authors   Aḥmad al-Nāṣirī al-Salāwī (*and* al-Nāṣir al-Salāwī); Akansūs; ʿAlī Pas̲h̲a Mubārak; Daḥlān; al-D̲jabartī; G̲h̲ulām Ḥusayn K̲h̲ān Ṭabāṭabāʾī; Ibn Abi ʾl-Ḍiyāf; al-Turk, Niḳūlā; al-Zayyānī

see also al-Kardūdī

20th-century authors   Ibn Zaydān; Kurd ʿAlī

Indo-Persian   Mug̲h̲als.10; Taʾrīk̲h̲.II.4

on countries/cities   → INDIA

on dynasties/caliphs   → *individual dynasties under* DYNASTIES.AFGHANISTAN AND INDIA

13th and 14th-century authors   Baranī; al-D̲juzd̲jānī; S̲h̲ams al-Dīn-i Sirād̲j ʿAfīf

15th and 16th-century authors   Abu ʾl-Faḍl ʿAllāmī; D̲jawhar; Gulbadan Bēgam; Niẓām al-Dīn Aḥmad b. al-Harawī; [in Suppl.] ʿAbbās Sarwānī

17th-century authors   ʿAbd al-Ḥamīd Lāhawrī; Bak̲h̲tāwar K̲h̲ān; Firis̲h̲ta; Ināyat Allāh Kanbū; Mīr Muḥammad Maʿṣūm; Niʿmat Allāh

b. Ḥabīb Allāh Harawī; Nūr al-Ḥaḳḳ al-Dihlawī; Shīrāzī, Rafīʿ al-Dīn; [in Suppl.] ʿĀḳil Khān Rāzī; Ḥādjdjī al-Dabīr; Ḥaydar Malik
see also Badāʾūnī
18th-century authors ʿAbd al-Karīm Kashmīrī; Ḳāniʿ; Khwāfī Khān; Niʿmat Khān
19th-century authors ʿAbd al-Karīm Munshī; Ghulām Ḥusayn Khān Ṭabāṭabāʾī; Ghulām Ḥusayn "Salīm"
see also Aẓfarī
Persian Taʾrīkh.II.2; [in Suppl.] Čač-nāma
on Iran → IRAN
on dynasties/caliphs → *individual dynasties under* DYNASTIES.PERSIA
universal histories Mīrkhwānd; Niẓām-shāhī; Sipihr
10th-century authors Balʿamī.2
11th-century authors Bayhaḳī; Gardīzī
12th-century authors Anūshirwān b. Khālid; al-Bayhaḳī, Ẓahīr al-Dīn; [in Suppl.] Ibn al-Balkhī
13th-century authors Djuwaynī, ʿAlāʾ al-Dīn; Ibn Bībī; Ibn-i Isfandiyār; [in Suppl.] Ḥasan Niẓāmī; al-Ḥusaynī
14th-century authors Banākitī; Ḥamd Allāh al-Mustawfī al-Ḳazwīnī; Shabānkāraʾī; Waṣṣāf; [in Suppl.] al-Aḳsarāyī
15th-century authors ʿAbd al-Razzāḳ al-Samarḳandī; Ḥāfiẓ-i Abrū; Ẓahīr al-Dīn Marʿashī
16th-century authors Bidlīsī, Sharaf al-Dīn; Djamāl al-Ḥusaynī; Ghaffārī; Ḥaydar Mīrzā; Khwāndamīr; Ḳum(m)ī; al-Lārī; Shāmī, Niẓām al-Dīn; [in Suppl.] Ḥāfiẓ Tanīsh
see also ʿAlī b. Shams al-Dīn
17th-century authors ʿAbd al-Fattāh Fūmanī; Ḥaydar b. ʿAlī; Iskandar Beg; Rāzī, Amīn Aḥmad; Ṭāhir Waḥīd
18th-century authors Mahdī Khān Astarābādī
see also Īsar-dās
19th and 20th-century authors ʿAbd al-Karīm Bukhārī; [in Suppl.] Fasāʾī
Turkish Shāhnāmedji; Taʾrīkh.II.3; Waḳaʿ-nüwīs
on the Ottoman Empire → DYNASTIES.ANATOLIA AND THE TURKS. OTTOMANS.HISTORIANS OF
universal histories Shāriḥ ül-Menār-zāde
see also Neshrī
15th-century authors ʿĀshiḳ-pasha-zāde; Meḥmed Pasha, Ḳaramānī; Yakhshī Faḳīh
16th-century authors ʿĀlī; Bihishtī; Djalālzāde Muṣṭafā Čelebi; Djalālzāde Ṣāliḥ Čelebi; Kemāl Pasha-zāde; Luḳmān b. Sayyid Ḥusayn; Maṭrāḳčī; Meḥmed Zaʿīm; Neshrī; Selānīkī; Seyfī
see also Ḥadīdī; Medjdī

17th-century authors ʿAbdī; ʿAbdī Pasha; Ḥasan Bey-zāde; Ḥibrī; Ḳarā-čelebi-zāde.4; Kātib Čelebi; Meḥmed Khalīfe b. Hüseyn; Shāriḥ ül-Menār-zāde; Ṭashköprüzāde.2; Wedjīhī
18th-century authors ʿAbdī Efendi; Aḥmad Rasmī; Čelebi-zāde; Česhmīzāde; Enwerī; ʿIzzī; Münedjdjim Bashi̊; ʿOthmān-zāde; ʿUshshāḳī-zāde, Ibrāhīm
19th-century authors Aḥmad Djewdet Pasha; ʿĀṣim; ʿAṭāʾ Bey, Ṭayyārzāda; Esʿad Efendi, Meḥmed; Kemāl, Meḥmed Nāmi̊ḳ; Khayr Allāh Efendi; Wāṣif
20th-century authors Aḥmad Rafīk; ʿAlī Amīrī; (Meḥmed) ʿAṭāʾ Beg; Luṭfī Efendi; Mīzāndji̊ Meḥmed Murād; Shems al-Dīn Günaltay; Sheref, ʿAbd al-Raḥmān; Thüreyyā
see also Ḥilmī
in Eastern Turkish Abu ʾl-Ghāzī Bahādur Khān; Bāḳi̊khānli̊; Muʾnis; [in Suppl.] Āgahī
hunting → HUNTING.POETRY
in other languages Afghān.iii; Aljamía; Bengali.ii; Berbers.VI; Beskesek-abaza; Bosna.3; Hausa.iii; Hindī; Indonesia.vi; Judaeo-Arabic.iii; Judaeo-Persian.i; Kano; Ḳiṣṣa.8; Lahndā.2; Laḳ; Masraḥ.6; Pandjābī.2; Shiʿr.7; Sind.3.b; Somali.6; Tādjīkī.2; Tashelḥīt.3
for Swahili, → KENYA; *for Malaysian,* → MALAYSIA; *and* → LITERATURE.POETRY.MYSTICAL *and* TRANSLATIONS
Bengali authors Nadhr al-Islām; Nūr Ḳuṭb al-ʿĀlam
Hindi authors Malik Muḥammad Djāyasī; Nihāl Čand Lāhawrī; Prēm Čand; Sudjān Rāy Bhandārī
see also ʿAbd al-Raḥīm Khān; Inshāʾ; Lallūdjī Lāl
Judaeo-Arabic authors Mūsā b. ʿAzra; al-Samawʾal b. ʿĀdiyā
and → JUDAISM.LANGUAGE AND LITERATURE
Judaeo-Persian authors Shāhīn-i Shīrāzī
and → JUDAISM.LANGUAGE AND LITERATURE
Pashto authors Khushḥāl Khān Khaṭak
Tatar authors Ghafūrī, Medjīd
maghāzī-literature Abū Maʿshar al-Sindī; Ibn ʿĀʾidh; al-Kalāʿī; **al-Maghāzī**; Mūsā b. ʿUḳba
see also al-Baṭṭāl; Sīra
personages in literature Abū Ḍamḍam; Abu ʾl-Ḳāsim; Abū Zayd; Ali Baba; Ayāz; Aywaz.2; al-Basūs; al-Baṭṭāl; Bekrī Muṣṭafā Agha; Buzurgmihr; Dhu ʾl-Himma; Djamshīd; Djuḥā; al-Ghāḍirī; Ḥamza b. ʿAbd al-Muṭṭalib; Ḥātim al-Ṭāʾī; Ḥayy b. Yaḳẓān; Köroghlu; Manas; Naṣr al-Dīn Khodja; Rustam; Sām; Ṣari̊ Ṣalṭūḳ Dede; Shahrazād; al-Sīd; Sindbād; Siyāwush
see also Ṭufaylī; Yūsuf and Zulaykhā
picaresque Maḳāma; Mukaddī

pilgrimage-literature → PILGRIMAGE
poetry ʿArūḍ; Ḥamāsa; Ḳāfiya; Lughz; Maʿnā.3; Mukhtārāt; Muzdawidj; Shāʿir; **Shiʿr**, Wazn.2
see also Rāwī; Sharḥ.II; Takhalluṣ.1; Taʾrīkh.III; *for poetical genres,* → LITERATURE.GENRES.POETRY; *and* → METRICS
Andalusian ʿArabiyya.B.Appendix; Khamriyya.vi; Muwashshaḥ; Nawriyya; Shāʿir.1.D; Zadjal; Zahriyyāt.1
anthologies al-Fatḥ b. Khāḳān; al-Fihrī; Ibn Bassām; Ibn Diḥya; Ibn Faradj al-Djayyānī; al-Shaḳundī
8th-century poets Ghirbīb b. ʿAbd Allāh
9th-century poets ʿAbbās b. Firnās; ʿAbbās b. Nāṣih; al-Ghazāl
see also Ibn ʿAlḳama.2
10th-century poets Ibn ʿAbd Rabbih; Ibn Abī Zamanayn; Ibn Faradj al-Djayyānī; Ibn Ḳuzmān.I; Muḳaddam b. Muʿāfā; al-Ramādī; al-Sharīf al-Ṭalīḳ
11th-century poets Abū Isḥāḳ al-Ilbīrī; Ibn al-Abbār; Ibn ʿAbd al-Ṣamad; Ibn ʿAmmār; Ibn Burd.II; Ibn Darrādj al-Ḳasṭallī; Ibn Gharsiya; Ibn al-Ḥaddād; Ibn al-Ḥannāṭ; Ibn al-Labbāna; Ibn Māʾ al-Samāʾ; Ibn al-Shahīd; Ibn Shuhayd; Ibn Zaydūn; al-Muʿtamid ibn ʿAbbād; Wallāda
see also Ṣāʿid al-Baghdādī; al-Waḳḳashī
12th-century poets al-Aʿmā al-Tuṭīlī; Ḥafṣa bint al-Ḥādjdj; Ibn ʿAbdūn; Ibn Baḳī; Ibn Ḳabṭūrnu; Ibn Khafādja; Ibn Ḳuzmān.II and V; Ibn al-Ṣayrafī; al-Ḳurṭubī; al-Ruṣāfī; Ṣafwān b. Idrīs
see also Mūsā b. ʿAzra
13th-century poets Ḥāzim; Ibn al-Abbār; Ibn ʿAmīra; Ibn Sahl; Ibn Saʿīd al-Maghribī; al-Ḳabtawrī; al-Shushtarī
14th-century poets Ibn al-Ḥādjdj; Ibn Khātima; Ibn Luyūn; Ibn al-Murābiʿ; al-Sharīf al-Gharnāṭī
Arabic ʿAtāba; Ghazal.i; Ḥamāsa.i; Hidjāʾ; Kān wa-Kān; Ḳaṣīda.1; al-Ḳūmā; Madīḥ.1; Maḳṣūra; Malḥūn; Marthiya.1; Mawāliyā; Mawlidiyya; Mukhtārāt.1; Musammaṭ.1; Muwashshaḥ; Naḳāʾiḍ; Nasīb; Rubāʿī.3; Shāʿir.1; **Shiʿr**.1; Takhmīs; Ṭardiyya; Ṭayf al-Khayāl; ʿUdhrī; Zahriyyāt.1; Zuhdiyya
see also ʿArabiyya.B.II; ʿIlm al-Djamāl; Ḳalb.II; Mawlid; Muwallad.2; Ṣuʿlūk; *and* → LITERATURE.POETRY.ANDALUSIAN *and* POETRY.MYSTICAL
anthologies al-Muʿallaḳāt; al-Mufaḍḍaliyyāt; **Mukhtārāt**.1
anthologists Abu ʾl-Faradj al-Iṣbahānī; Abū Tammām; al-ʿAlamī; al-Bākharzī; al-Buḥturī; Diʿbil; al-Hamdānī; Ḥammād al-Rāwiya; Ibn Abī Ṭāhir Ṭayfūr; Ibn Dāwūd; Ibn al-Ḳutayba; Ibn al-Muʿtazz; Ibn al-Ṣayrafī; ʿImād al-Dīn; al-Nawādjī; al-Sarī al-Raffāʾ; al-Shayzarī; al-Shimshāṭī; al-Thaʿālibī, Abū Manṣūr ʿAbd al-Malik; [in Suppl.] Abū

Zayd al-Ḳurashī; al-Bustānī.3
see also al-Ṭayālisī, Djaʿfar
works Bānat Suʿād; Burda.2; Madjnūn Laylā.1; al-Muʿallaḳāt
pre-Islamic poets ʿAbīd b. al-Abraṣ; Abū Dhuʾayb al-Hudhalī; Abū Duʾād al-Iyādī; Abū Kabīr al-Hudhalī; ʿAdī b. Zayd; al-Afwah al-Awdī; al-Aghlab al-ʿIdjlī; ʿAlḳama; ʿĀmir b. al-Ṭufayl; ʿAmr b. al-Ahtam; ʿAmr b. Ḳamīʾa; ʿAmr b. Kulthūm; ʿAntara; al-Aʿshā; al-Aswad b. Yaʿfur; Aws b. Ḥadjar; Bishr b. Abī Khāzim; Bisṭām b. Ḳays; Durayd b. al-Ṣimma; al-Ḥādira; al-Ḥārith b. Ḥilliza; Ḥassān b. Thābit; Ḥātim al-Ṭāʾī; Ibn al-Iṭnāba al-Khazradjī; Imruʾ al-Ḳays b. Ḥudjr; Ḳays b. al-Khaṭīm; al-Khansāʾ; Laḳīṭ al-Iyādī; Laḳīṭ b. Zurāra; al-Munakhkhal al-Yashkurī; Muraḳḳish; al-Mutalammis; al-Nābigha al-Dhubyānī; Salāma b. Djandal; al-Samawʾal b. ʿĀdiyā; al-Shanfarā; Taʾabbaṭa Sharran; Ṭarafa; Ṭufayl b. ʿAwf; Uḥayḥa b. al-Djulāḥ; Umayya b. ʿAbi ʾl-Ṣalt; ʿUrwa b. al-Ward; Zuhayr
see also ʿArabiyya.B.I; Ghazal; Hudhayl; al-Muʿallaḳāt; al-Mufaḍḍaliyyāt; Mufākhara.2; Nasīb.2.a; Shāʿir.1A; al-Shantamarī; Ṣuʿlūk.II.4
mukhaḍramūn poets (6th-7th centuries) al-ʿAbbās b. Mirdās; ʿAbd Allāh b. Rawāḥa; Abū Khirāsh; Abū Miḥdjān; ʿAmr b. Maʿdīkarib; Ḍirār b. al-Khaṭṭāb; Ḥassān b. Thābit; al-Ḥuṭayʾa; Ibn (al-)Aḥmar; Kaʿb b. Mālik; Kaʿb b. Zuhayr; Khidāsh b. Zuhayr al-Aṣghar; Labīd b. Rabīʿa; Maʿn b. Aws al-Muzanī; **Mukhaḍram**; Mutammim b. Nuwayra; al-Nābigha al-Djaʿdī; al-Namir b. Tawlab al-ʿUklī; al-Shammākh b. Ḍirār; Suḥaym; [in Suppl.] Abu ʾl-Ṭamaḥān al-Ḳaynī; Ibn Muḳbil
see also Hudhayl; Nasīb.2.b
7th and 8th-century poets al-ʿAbbās b. al-Aḥnaf; ʿAbd Allāh b. Hammān; Abū ʿAṭāʾ al-Sindī; Abū Dahbal al-Djumaḥī; Abū Dulāma; Abu ʾl-Nadjm al-ʿIdjlī; Abū Ṣakhr al-Hudhalī; Abu ʾl-Shamaḳmaḳ; Adī b. al-Riḳāʿ; al-ʿAdjdjādj; al-Aḥwaṣ; al-Akhṭal; al-ʿArdjī; Aʿshā Hamdān; al-Ashdjaʿ b. ʿAmr al-Sulamī; Ayman b. Khuraym; al-Baʿīth; Bashshār b. Burd; Dhu ʾl-Rumma; Djamīl; Djarīr; Dukayn al-Rādjiz; al-Farazdaḳ; al-Ḥakam b. ʿAbdal; al-Ḥakam b. Ḳanbar; Ḥammād ʿAdjrad; Ḥamza b. Bīḍ; Ḥāritha b. Badr al-Ghudānī; al-Ḥuḍayn; Ḥumayd b. Thawr; Ḥumayd al-Arḳaṭ; Ibn Abī ʿUyayna; Ibn al-Dumayna; Ibn Harma; Ibn Ḳays al-Ruḳayyāt; Ibn Ladjaʾ; Ibn al-Mawlā; Ibn Mayyāda; Ibn Mufarrigh; Ibn Muṭayr; Ibn Sayḥān; ʿImrān b. Ḥiṭṭān; ʿInān; Ismāʿīl b. Yasār; Kaʿb b. Djuʿayl al-Taghlabī; Ḳaṭarī b. al-Fudjāʾa; al-Kumayt b. Zayd al-Asadī; al-Ḳuṭāmī; Kuthayyir b. ʿAbd al-Raḥmān; Laylā al-Akhyaliyya; Manṣūr al-Namarī; Marwān b. Abī Ḥafṣa and Marwān b. Abi ʾl-Djanūb; Miskīn al-Dārimī; Mūsā Shahawātin; Musāwir al-Warrāḳ; Muṭīʿ b. Iyās; Nubāta b. ʿAbd Allāh;

Nuṣayb; Nuṣayb b. Rabāḥ; al-Rāʿī; Ruʾba b. al-ʿAd̲j̲d̲j̲ād̲j̲; Ṣafī al-Dīn al-Ḥillī; Ṣafwān al-Anṣārī; Saḥbān Wāʾil; Ṣāliḥ b. ʿAbd al-Ḳuddūs; Salm al-K̲h̲āsir; al-Sayyid al-Ḥimyarī; al-S̲h̲amardal; Sudayf b. Maymūn; Sufyān al-ʿAbdī; Sulaymān b. Yaḥyā; Surāḳa b. Mirdās al-Aṣg̲h̲ar; Ṭahmān b. ʿAmr al-Kilābī; Tawba b. al-Ḥumayyir; T̲h̲ābit Ḳuṭna; al-Ṭirimmāḥ; al-Uḳays̲h̲ir; ʿUmar b. Abī Rabīʿa; ʿUrwa b. Ḥizām; ʿUrwa b. Ud̲h̲ayna; Waḍḍāḥ al-Yaman; Wāliba b. al-Ḥubāb; al-Walīd.2; al-Walīd b. Ṭarīf; al-Walīd b. ʿUḳba; Yazīd Ibn Ḍabba; al-Zafayān; al-Zibriḳān b. Badr; Ziyād al-Aʿd̲j̲am; [in Suppl.] ʿAbd al-Raḥmān b. Ḥassān; Abū ʿAmr al-S̲h̲aybānī (*and* al-S̲h̲aybānī, Abū ʿAmr); Abū Ḥayyā al-Numayrī; Abū Ḥuzāba; Abū Nuk̲h̲ayla; Bakr b. al-Naṭṭāḥ

see also Nasīb.2.c and d; Ṣuʿlūk.III.2

9th and 10th-century poets   Abān b. ʿAbd al-Ḥamīd; ʿAbd Allāh b. Ṭāhir; Abu ʾl-ʿAtāhiya; Abu ʾl-ʿAynāʾ; Abū Dulaf; Abu ʾl-Farad̲j̲ al-Iṣbahānī; Abū Firās; Abū Nuwās; Abu ʾl-S̲h̲īṣ; Abū Tammām; Abū Yaʿḳūb al-K̲h̲uraymī; al-ʿAkawwak; ʿAlī b. al-D̲j̲ahm; al-ʿAttābī; al-Babbag̲h̲āʾ; al-Baṣīr; al-Buḥturī; al-Bustī; Diʿbil; Dīk al-D̲j̲inn; al-Ḥimṣī; al-D̲j̲ammāz; al-Hamdānī; (al-)Ḥusayn b. al-Ḍaḥḥāk; Ibn al-ʿAllāf; Ibn Bassām; Ibn al-Ḥad̲j̲d̲j̲ād̲j̲; Ibn Kunāsa; Ibn Lankak; Ibn al-Muʿad̲h̲d̲h̲al; Ibn Munād̲h̲ir; Ibn al-Muʿtazz; Ibn al-Rūmī; al-Ḳāsim b. ʿĪsā; K̲h̲ālid b. Yazīd al-Kātib al-Tamīmī; al-K̲h̲ālidiyyāni; al-K̲h̲aṭṭābī; al-K̲h̲ubzaʾaruzzī; al-Kisrawī; Kus̲h̲ād̲j̲im; al-Maʾmūnī; Muḥammad b. ʿAbd al-Raḥmān al-ʿAṭawī; Muḥammad b. Ḥāzim al-Bāhilī; Muḥammad b. Umayya; Muḥammad b. Yasīr al-Riyās̲h̲ī; al-Muṣʿabī; Muslim b. al-Walīd; al-Mutanabbī; Naṣr b. Nuṣayr; Sahl b. Hārūn b. Rāhawayh; Saʿīd b. Ḥumayd; al-Ṣanawbarī; al-Sarī al-Raffāʾ; al-S̲h̲ims̲h̲āṭī; Ṭāhir b. Muḥammad; Tamīm b. al-Muʿizz li-Dīn Allāh; ʿUlayya; al-ʿUtbī, Abū ʿAbd al-Raḥmān; al-Warrāḳ, Maḥmūd; al-Waʾwāʾ al-Dimas̲h̲ḳī; Yamūt b. al-Muzarraʿ; [in Suppl.] Abu ʾl-ʿAmayt̲h̲al; Abu ʾl-Asad al-Ḥimmānī; Abu ʾl-Ḥasan al-Mag̲h̲ribī; Abū Hiffān; Abu ʾl-ʿIbar; Abū Riyās̲h̲ al-Ḳaysī; Abū Saʿd al-Mak̲h̲zūmī; Abū S̲h̲urāʿa; ʿAlī b. Muḥammad al-Tūnisī al-Iyādī; Faḍl al-S̲h̲āʿira; al-Fazārī; al-Ḥamdawī

see also al-Hamad̲h̲ānī; Ibn Abī Zamanayn; Nasīb.2.d; S̲h̲ahīd; al-Ṣūlī; al-Ṭufaylī; al-Yazīdī.2

11th-13th-century poets   al-Abīwardī; ʿAmīd al-Dīn al-Abzārī; al-Arrad̲j̲ānī; al-Badīʿ al-Asṭurlābī; Bahāʾ al-Dīn Zuhayr; al-Bāk̲h̲arzī; Ḥayṣa Bayṣa; al-Ḥuṣrī.II; Ibn Abi ʾl-Ḥadīd; Ibn Abī Ḥaṣīna; Ibn al-ʿAfīf al-Tilimsānī; Ibn al-Habbāriyya; Ibn Ḥamdīs; Ibn Ḥayyūs; Ibn Hindū; Ibn al-Ḳaṭṭān; Ibn al-Ḳaysarānī.2; Ibn K̲h̲amīs; Ibn Maṭrūḥ; Ibn al-Nabīh; Ibn Ras̲h̲īḳ; Ibn Sanāʾ al-Mulk; Ibn al-S̲h̲ad̲j̲arī al-

Baghdādī; Ibn Sharaf al-Ḳayrawānī; Ibn Shibl; Ibn al-Taʿāwīdhī; al-Kammūnī; Ḳurhub; al-Maʿarrī; al-Marwazī; Mihyār; Muḥammad b. ʿAlī b. ʿUmar; al-Rūdhrāwarī; al-Ṣaghānī, ʿAbd al-Muʾmin; Ṣāʿid al-Baghdādī; al-Sharīf al-ʿAḳīlī; al-Sharīf al-Raḍī; Shumaym; al-Tallaʿfarī; Tamīm b. al-Muʿizz; al-Ṭarābulusī al-Raffāʾ; al-Tihāmī; al-Tilimsānī.3; al-Ṭughrāʾī; ʿUmāra al-Yamanī; al-Wāsānī; Ẓāfir al-Ḥaddād; [in Suppl.] Abu ʾl-Ḥasan al-Anṣārī; al-Balaṭī, Abu ʾl-Fatḥ ʿUthmān; al-Būṣīrī; al-Ghazzī

see also al-Khazradjī; Nasīb.2.d; al-Wāthiḳī; Yāḳūt al-Rūmī

14th-18th-century poets ʿAbd al-ʿAzīz b. Muḥammad; ʿAbd al-Ghanī; al-Bakrī; al-Būrīnī; Farḥāt; Ibn Abī Ḥadjala; Ibn ʿAmmār; Ibn Ḥidjdja; Ibn Nubāta; Ibn al-Ṣāʾigh; Ibn al-Wannān; al-Ṣanʿānī, Ḍiyāʾ al-Dīn; Suʿūdī; al-Warghī; al-Yadālī; al-Yūsī

see also Khiḍr Beg; al-Shirbīnī; al-Wādīʾāshī

19th and 20th-century poets al-Akhras; al-Bārūdī; Fāris al-Shidyāḳ; al-Fārūḳī; Fikrī; Ḥāfiẓ Ibrāhīm; Ibn Idrīs (I); Ismāʿīl Ṣabrī; Ismāʿīl Ṣabrī Pasha; Ḳaddūr al-ʿAlamī; al-Kāẓimī, ʿAbd al-Muḥsin; Khalīl Muṭrān; al-Khūrī; al-Maʿlūf; al-Manfalūṭī; Mardam.2; Maʿrūf al-Ruṣāfī; al-Māzinī; Nādjī; Nadjīb al-Ḥaddād; Nadjīb Muḥammad Surūr; Saʿīd Abū Bakr; Ṣalāḥ ʿAbd al-Ṣabūr; Ṣāyigh, Tawfīḳ; al-Shābbī; al-Sharḳāwī; Shāʾūl; Shawḳī; Shukrī; Ṭāhā, ʿAlī Maḥmūd; Ṭuʿma, Ilyās; al-Tūnisī, Maḥmūd Bayram; al-Turk, Niḳūlā; Yakan, Muḥammad Walī al-Dīn; al-Yāzidjī.1-4; al-Zahāwī, Djamīl Ṣidḳī; [in Suppl.] Abū Māḍī; Abū Shādī; al-ʿAḳḳād; al-Bustānī; Buṭrus Karāma; Ibn ʿAmr al-Ribāṭī; Ibn al-Ḥādjdj

see also Shāʿir.1.C; Shiʿr.1.b

transmission of **Rāwī**

transmitters Ḥammād al-Rāwiya; Ibn Daʾb; Ibn Kunāsa; Khalaf b. Ḥayyān al-Aḥmar; Khālid b. Ṣafwān b. al-Ahtam; al-Kisrawī; al-Mufaḍḍal al-Ḍabbī; Muḥammad b. al-Ḥasan b. Dīnār; al-Sharḳī b. al-Ḳuṭāmī; al-Sukkarī; al-Ṣūlī; [in Suppl.] Abū ʿAmr al-Shaybānī (*and* al-Shaybānī, Abū ʿAmr)

and → LINGUISTICS.GRAMMARIANS.8TH *and* 9TH CENTURY

bacchic → WINE

Indo-Persian Mughals.10; Sabk-i Hindī; Shāʿir.4

see also Pandjābī.2; *and* → LITERATURE.POETRY.MYSTICAL *and* PERSIAN

11th-century poets Masʿūd-i Saʿd-i Salmān; [in Suppl.] Abu ʾl-Faradj b. Masʿūd Rūnī

14th-century poets Amīr Khusraw; Ḥasan Dihlawī; [in Suppl.] Ḥamīd Ḳalandar

16th-century poets Fayḍī; Thanāʾī

see also ʿAbd al-Raḥīm Khān

17th-century poets G̲h̲anī; G̲h̲anīmat; Idrākī Bēglārī; Ḳudsī, Muḥammad D̲j̲ān; Malik Ḳummi; Munīr Lāhawrī; Nāṣir ʿAlī Sirhindī; Naẓīrī;
Salīm, Muḥammad Ḳulī; S̲h̲aydā, Mullā; Ṭālib Āmulī; Tug̲h̲rā, Mullā;
[in Suppl.] G̲h̲anīmat Kund̲j̲āhī

18th-century poets Ārzū K̲h̲ān; As̲h̲raf ʿAlī K̲h̲ān; Bīdil; Dard; Ḥazīn;
Ḳāniʿ; Mak̲h̲fī; Wafā.1
see also Taḥsīn

19th-century poets Aẓfarī; G̲h̲ālib; Rangīn; [in Suppl.] Adīb Pīs̲h̲āwarī
see also Afsūs

love **G̲h̲azal**; **Nasīb**; Raḳīb; S̲h̲ahrangīz; Turks.III.4; ʿUd̲h̲rī
see also al-Marzubānī; Nard̲j̲is; S̲h̲awḳ.1(a); S̲h̲awḳ, Taṣadduḳ Ḥusayn;
and → Love

Arabic poets al-ʿAbbās b. al-Aḥnaf; Abū D̲h̲uʾayb al-Hud̲h̲alī; Abū
Nuwās; al-Aḥwaṣ; al-ʿArd̲j̲ī; Bas̲h̲s̲h̲ār b. Burd; D̲j̲amīl al-ʿUd̲h̲rī; Ibn
Dāwūd; Ibn al-Dumayna; Ibn Mayyāda; Ibn al-Nabīh; Ibn Sahl; Ibn
Zaydūn; Imruʾ al-Ḳays; Kut̲h̲ayyir b. ʿAbd al-Raḥmān; Laylā al-
Ak̲h̲yaliyya; Manṣūr al-Namarī; Murakkis̲h̲.1; Nād̲j̲ī; Nuṣayb b.
Rabāḥ; al-Ramādī; Saʿīd b. Ḥumayd; Suḥaym; ʿUmar b. Abī Rabīʿa;
ʿUrwa b. Ḥizām; ʿUrwa b. Ud̲h̲ayna; al-Walīd.2
see also ʿInān; Mad̲j̲nūn Laylā.1; *and* → Love.erotic

Persian poets Ḥāfiẓ; Muḥtas̲h̲am-i Kās̲h̲ānī; Saʿdī; Ṣāʾib; S̲h̲ahriyār;
Zulālī-yi K̲h̲ʷānsārī
see also Farhād wa-S̲h̲īrīn; Mad̲j̲nūn Laylā.2; S̲h̲ahīd; Wāmiḳ wa
ʿAd̲h̲rāʾ; Wīs u Rāmīn

Turkish poets
see also Farhād wa-S̲h̲īrīn; Mad̲j̲nūn Laylā.3

Urdu poets Dāg̲h̲; Mīr Muḥammad Taḳī; S̲h̲awḳ
see also Mad̲j̲nūn Laylā.4; *and* → Love.erotic

mystical

Arabic ʿAbd al-G̲h̲anī; al-Bakrī, Muḥammad; al-Bakrī, Muṣṭafā; al-
Dimyāṭī; al-Ḥallād̲j̲; Ibn ʿAd̲j̲ība; Ibn ʿAlīwa; Ibn al-ʿArabī; al-
Mad̲j̲d̲h̲ūb; Mak̲h̲rama.3; al-S̲h̲us̲h̲tarī
see also ʿAbd al-Ḳādir al-D̲j̲īlānī; Abū Madyan; al-Ḳādirī al-Ḥasanī;
al-Yāfiʿī; [in Suppl.] al-Hilālī

Central Asian Aḥmad Yasawī

Indian Bāḳī bi ʾllāh; Bīdil; Dard; "D̲j̲amālī"; Hānsawī; Ḥusaynī Sādāt
Amīr; Imdād Allāh; Malik Muḥammad D̲j̲āyasī; [in Suppl.] Ḥamīd
Ḳalandar
see also Bhitāʾī; Pand̲j̲ābī.2; S̲h̲āʿir.4

Indonesian Ḥamza Fanṣūrī

Persian Aḥmad-i D̲j̲ām; ʿAṭṭār; Bābā-Ṭāhir; D̲j̲alāl al-Dīn Rūmī; Faḍl
Allāh Ḥurūfī; G̲h̲ud̲j̲duwānī; Humām al-Dīn b. ʿAlāʾ Tabrīzī; ʿIrāḳī;

Kamāl Khudjandī; Ḳāsim-i Anwār; Kirmānī; Lāhidjī; Maḥmūd Shabistarī; Sanā'ī; Shīrīn Maghribī, Muḥammad; Sulṭān Walad; [in Suppl.] ʿĀrif Čelebī; ʿImād al-Dīn ʿAlī, Faḳīh-i Kirmānī
see also Abū Saʿīd b. Abi 'l-Khayr; Kharaḳānī; Shawḳ; [in Suppl.] Aḥmad-i Rūmī
Turkish ʿĀshiḳ Pasha; Faṣīḥ Dede; Gulshanī; Gülshehrī; Hüdā'ī; Münedjdjim Bashi; Nefes; Nesīmī; Refīʿī; Ṣari ʿAbd Allāh Efendī; Sezā'ī, Ḥasan Dede; Sheyyād Ḥamza; Yūnus Emre; [in Suppl.] Eshrefoghlu; Esrār Dede
see also Ḥusām al-Dīn Čelebi; Ismāʿīl al-Anḳarawī; Ismāʿīl Ḥaḳḳī; Ḳayghusuz Abdāl; Khalīlī; Sulṭān Walad; Yazidji-oghlu
nature Ibn Khafādja; Nawriyya; Rabīʿiyyāt; al-Ṣanawbarī; Zahriyyāt
see also al-Walīd.2
Persian Ghazal.ii; Ḥamāsa.ii; Hidjā'.ii; Ḳaṣīda.2; Khamsa; Madīḥ.2; Malik al-Shuʿarā'; Marthiya.2; Mathnawī.2; Mukhtārāt.2; Musammaṭ; Mustazād; Rubāʿī.1; Shahrangīz.1; Shāʿir.2; **Shiʿr**.2; Takhalluṣ.2; Tardjīʿ-band; Zahriyyāt.2; [in Suppl.] Ḥabsiyya
see also Radīf.2; Ṣafawids.III; Sāḳī.2; Shaman; Shaʿr.3; Sharīf; Wāsēkht; Yaghmā Djandaḳī; *and* → LITERATURE.POETRY.INDO-PERSIAN *and* POETRY.MYSTICAL
anthologies **Mukhtārāt**.2; **Tadhkira**.2
anthologists ʿAwfī; Dawlat-Shāh; Luṭf ʿAlī Beg; Taḳī Awḥadī; Taḳī al-Dīn; [in Suppl.] Djādjarmī.2
biographies Dawlat-Shāh; Sām Mīrzā; **Tadhkira**.2; Taḳī al-Dīn; Wafā.4
stories Barzū-nāma; Farhād wa-Shīrīn; Iskandar Nāma.ii; Kalīla wa-Dimna; Madjnūn Laylā.2; Wāmiḳ wa ʿAdhrā'; Wīs u Rāmīn; Yūsuf and Zulaykhā.1
9th-century poets Muḥammad b. Waṣīf
see also Sahl b. Hārūn b. Rāhawayh
10th-century poets Bābā-Ṭāhir; Daḳīḳī; Kisā'ī; al-Muṣʿabī; Rūdakī; Shahīd; [in Suppl.] Abū Shakūr Balkhī
11th-13th-century poets ʿAbd al-Wāsiʿ Djabalī; Anwarī; Asadī; ʿAṭṭār; Azraḳī; Bābā Afḍal; Djalāl al-Dīn Rūmī; Falakī Shirwānī; Farrukhī; Firdawsī; Gurgānī; Humām al-Dīn b. ʿAlā' Tabrīzī; ʿImādī (*and* [in Suppl.]); ʿIrāḳī; Kamāl al-Dīn Ismāʿīl; Ḳaṭrān; Khwādjū; Khāḳānī; Labībī; Lāmiʿī; Mahsatī; Manūčihrī; Muʿizzī; Mukhtārī; Niẓāmī Gandjawī; Pūr-i Bahā'; Ṣābir; Saʿdī; Sanā'ī; Sayyid Ḥasan Ghaznawī; Shufurwa; Sūzanī; ʿUmar Khayyām; ʿUnṣurī; Ẓahīr-i Fāryābī; [in Suppl.] ʿAmʿaḳ; Djādjarmī; Djamāl al-Dīn Iṣfahānī
see also Shams-i Ḳays; Sūdī
14th and 15th-century poets ʿAṣṣār; Awḥadī; Banākitī; Busḥāḳ; Djāmī;

Faḍl Allāh Ḥurūfī; Fattāḥī; Ḥāfiẓ; Ḥāmidī; Ibn-i Yamīn; ʿIṣāmī; Kātibī; Nizārī Ḳuhistānī; Rāmī Tabrīzī; Salmān-i Sāwadjī; Sayfī ʿArūḍī Bukhārī; Sharaf al-Dīn ʿAlī Yazdī; Shīrīn Maghribī, Muḥammad; ʿUbayd-i Zākānī; [in Suppl.] ʿĀrifī; Badr-i Čāčī; ʿImād al-Dīn ʿAlī, Faḳīh-i Kirmānī

see also Djem; Ḥamd Allāh al-Mustawfī al-Ḳazwīnī; Sūdī

16th-century poets Bannāʾī; Baṣīrī; Fighānī; Hātifī; Hilālī; Muḥtasham-i Kāshānī; Mushfiḳī; Nawʿī; Saḥābī Astarābādī; Sām Mīrzā; ʿUrfī Shīrāzī; Waḥshī Bāfḳī

see also Luḳmān b. Sayyid Ḥusayn

17th-century poets Asīr; al-Dāmād; Ḳadrī; Ḳalīm Abū Ṭālib; Kāshif; Lāhīdjī.2; Nāẓim Farrukh Ḥusayn; Ṣāʾib; Saʿīdā Gīlānī; Shawkat Bukhārī; Shifāʾī Iṣfahānī; Ṭāhir Waḥīd; Taḳī Awḥadī; ʿUnwān, Muḥammad Riḍā; Ẓuhūrī Turshīzī; Zulālī-yi Khʷānsārī

see also al-ʿĀmilī; Ghanīmat; Khushḥāl Khān Khaṭak; [in Suppl.] Findiriskī; *and* → LITERATURE.POETRY.INDO-PERSIAN

18th-century poets Hātif; Ḥazīn; Luṭf ʿAlī Beg; Nadjāt; Shihāb Turshīzī; Wafā.2 and 3

see also Āzād Bilgrāmī

19th and 20th-century poets Bahār; Furūgh; Furūghī; Ḳāʾānī; Ḳurrat al-ʿAyn; Lāhūtī; Nafīsī, Saʿīd; Nashāṭ; Nīmā Yūshīdj; Parwīn Iʿtiṣāmī; Pūr-i Dāwūd; Rashīd Yāsimī; Riḍā Ḳulī Khān; Ṣabā; Sabzawārī; Shahriyār; Shaybānī; Shihāb Iṣfahānī; Shūrīda, Muḥammad Taḳī; Sipihrī; Surūsh; Wafā.5-9; Waḳār; Wuthūḳ al-Dawla; Yaghmā Djandaḳī; Yaghmāʾī; Yazdī; [in Suppl.] ʿĀrif, Mīrzā; Ashraf al-Dīn Gīlānī; Dehkhudā

see also Ghālib; Iḳbāl; Ḳāʾim-maḳām-i Farāhānī; Sipihr; Wafā.4

Turkish Ḥamāsa.iii; Hidjāʾ.iii; Ḳaṣīda.3; Khamsa; Ḳoshma; Madīḥ.3; Māni; Marthiya.3; Mathnawī.3; Mukhtārāt.3; Musammaṭ.1; Rabīʿiyyāt; Rubāʿī.2; Shahrangīz.2; Sharḳi; **Shiʿr**.3; Turks.III; [in Suppl.] Ghazal.iii

see also Alpamïsh; ʿĀshiḳ; Ilāhī; Karadja Oghlan; Ozan; Shāhnāmedji; Shāʿir.3; Tardjīʿ-band; Therwet-i Fünūn; *and* → LITERATURE.POETRY.MYSTICAL

anthologies **Mukhtārāt**.3; **Tadhkira**.3

anthologists Żiyā Pasha

biographies ʿĀshïḳ Čelebi; Laṭīfī; Riḍā; Riyāḍī; Sālim; Sehī Bey; **Tadhkira**.3

stories Farhād wa-Shīrīn; Iskandar Nāma.iii; Madjnūn Laylā.3; Yūsuf and Zulaykhā.2

11th and 12th-century poets Aḥmad Yuknakī; Ḥakīm Ata; Ḳutadghu Bilig; Yūsuf Khāṣṣ Ḥādjib

13th and 14th-century poets Aḥmadī; ʿĀshïḳ Pasha; Burhān al-Dīn;

Dehhānī; Gülshehrī; Sheykh-oghlu; Sheyyād Ḥamza; Yūnus Emre

15th-century poets Āhī; Aḥmad Pasha Bursalî; Dāʿī; Firdewsī; Gulshanī; Ḥamdī, Ḥamd Allāh; Ḳāsim Pasha; Ḳayghusuz Abdāl; Khalīlī; Khiḍr Beg; Süleymān Čelebi, Dede; Yazîdjî-oghlu

see also Djem; Ḥāmidī

16th-century poets Āgehī; ʿAzīzī; Bāḳī; Baṣīrī; Bihishtī; Dhātī; Djaʿfar Čelebi; Djalāl Ḥusayn Čelebi; Djalālzāde Muṣṭafā Čelebi; Djalālzāde Ṣāliḥ Čelebi; Faḍli; Faḳīrī; Fawrī; Ferdī; Fighānī; Fuḍūlī; Ghazālī; Gulshanī; Ḥadīdī; Ḳarā-čelebi-zāde; Kemāl Pasha-zāde; Khāḳānī; Khayālī; Ḳorḳud b. Bāyazīd; Lāmiʿī; Laṭīfī; Luḳmān b. Sayyid Ḥusayn; Meʾalī; Medjdī; Mesīḥī; Mihrī Khātūn; Naẓmī, Edirneli; Nedjātī Bey; Newʿī; Rewānī; Sehī Bey; Surūrī.1; Sūzī Čelebi; Tashlîdjalî Yaḥyā; Wālihi

see also Ṭashköprüzāde.1

17th-century poets ʿAṭāʾī; ʿAzmī-zāde; Bahāʾī Meḥmed Efendi; Faṣīḥ Dede; Fehīm, Undjuzāde Muṣṭafā; Ḥāletī; Ḳarā-čelebi-zāde; Ḳul Muṣṭafā; Ḳuloghlu; Nāʾilī; Nāẓîm, Muṣṭafā; Naẓmī, Sheykh Meḥmed; Nefʿī; Niyāzī; ʿÖmer ʿĀshîḳ; Riyāḍī; Ṣarî ʿAbd Allāh Efendī; Ṭiflī; Wedjīhī; Weysī

see also Ṭashköprüzāde.3

18th-century poets Belīgh, Ismāʿīl; Belīgh, Meḥmed Emīn; Čelebi-zāde; Česhmīzāde; Fiṭnat; Gevherī; Ghālib; Ḥāmī-i Āmidī; Ḥashmet; Kānī; Meḥmed Pasha Rāmī (*and* Rāmī Meḥmed Pasha); Nābī; Naḥīfī; Naẓīm; Nedīm; Neshʾet; Newres.1; ʿOthmān-zāde; Rāghib Pasha; Sezāʾī, Ḥasan Dede; Thābit; Wehbī Sayyidī

see also ʿUshshāḳī-zāde, Ibrāhīm

19th-century poets ʿĀrif Hikmet Bey; ʿAynī; Dadaloghlu; Derdli; Dhihnī; Fāḍil Bey; Faṭīn; Fehīm, Süleymān; Ismāʿīl Ṣafā; ʿIzzet Molla; Kemāl, Meḥmed Nāmîḳ; Laylā Khānîm; Menemenli-zāde Meḥmed Ṭāhir; Muʿallim Nādjī; Newres.2; Pertew Pasha.II; Redjāʾī-zāde; Shināsī; Sünbül-zāde Wehbī; Surūrī.2; Wāṣif Enderūnī; Żiyā Pasha

20th-century poets ʿAbd al-Ḥāḳḳ Ḥāmid; Djanāb Shihāb al-Dīn; Djewdet; Ekrem Bey; Hāshim; Kanık; Köprülü (Meḥmed Fuad); Ḳoryürek; Laylā Khānîm; Meḥmed ʿĀkif; Meḥmed Emīn; Muḥibb Aḥmed "Diranas"; Nāẓim Ḥikmet; Oktay Rifat; Orkhan Seyfī; Ortač, Yūsuf Ḍiyā; Sāhir, Djelāl; Tanpinar, Aḥmed Ḥamdī; Tewfīḳ Fikret; Yaḥyā Kemāl; Yücel, Ḥasan ʿAlī; [in Suppl.] ʿĀshîk Weysel; Bölükbashî; Čamlîbel; Eshref; Eyyūboghlu; Gövsa

see also Therwet-i Fünūn; [in Suppl.] Ergun; Fîndîḳoghlu

in Eastern Turkish Ādharī.ii; Bābur; Bāḳîkhānlî; Dhākir; Djambul Djabaev; Ghāzī Girāy II; Ḥamāsa.iv; Hidjāʾ.iii; Iskandar Nāma.iii;

Ismāʿīl I; Ḳayyūm Nāṣirī; Ḳutadg̲h̲u Bilig; Luṭfī; Mīr ʿAlī S̲h̲īr Nawāʾī; Muʾnis; Sakkākī; S̲h̲ahriyār

translations from Western langs. Ismāʿīl Ḥaḳḳi ʿĀlīs̲h̲ān; Kanık; S̲h̲ināsī; Tewfīḳ Fikret

Urdu G̲h̲azal.iv; Ḥamāsa.v; Hid̲j̲āʾ.iv; Ḳaṣīda.4; Madīḥ.4; Mad̲j̲nūn Laylā.4; Mart̲h̲iya.4; Mat̲h̲nawī.4; Muk̲h̲tārāt.4; Musammaṭ.2; Mus̲h̲āʿara; S̲h̲ahrangīz.3; **S̲h̲iʿr**.4; Urdū.2

   see also Tard̲j̲īʿ-band; Wā-sēk̲h̲t

   17th-century poets Nuṣratī

   18th-century poets As̲h̲raf ʿAlī K̲h̲ān; Dard; D̲j̲urʾat; Maẓhar; Sawdā; Sūz; Walī; [in Suppl.] Ḥasan, Mīr G̲h̲ulām

      see also Ārzū K̲h̲ān; Taḥsīn

   19th-century poets Amānat; Anīs; Aẓfarī; Dabīr, Salāmat ʿAlī; Dāg̲h̲; Dhawḳ; G̲h̲ālib; Faḳīr Muḥammad K̲h̲ān; Ḥālī; Ilāhī Bak̲h̲s̲h̲ "Maʿrūf"; Ins̲h̲āʾ; Mīr Muḥammad Taḳī; Muḥsin ʿAlī Muḥsin; Muʾmin; Muṣḥafī; Nāsik̲h̲; Nasīm; Rangīn; S̲h̲awḳ, Taṣadduḳ Ḥusayn; [in Suppl.] Ātis̲h̲

      see also [in Suppl.] Āzād

   20th-century poets Akbar, Ḥusayn Allāhābādī; Āzād; D̲j̲awān; Iḳbāl; Muḥammad ʿAlī; Rās̲h̲id, N.M.; Ruswā; S̲h̲abbīr Ḥasan K̲h̲ān D̲j̲os̲h̲; S̲h̲iblī Nuʿmānī; [in Suppl.] Ḥasrat Mohānī

      see also Āzurda

vernacular Ḥawfī; Malḥūn; Mawāliyā; Nabaṭī; Zad̲j̲al

   see also Būḳalā; al-S̲h̲ām.3

prose Adab; Ḥikāya; Ḳiṣṣa; Maḳāma; Muḳaddima; Naṣīḥat al-Mulūk; Risāla; S̲h̲arḥ; Tafsīr; Uḳṣūṣa

   and → LITERATURE.ETIQUETTE-LITERATURE *and* HISTORICAL; PRESS; *for authors in fields other than belles-lettres, see the respective entries*

Arabic ʿArabiyya.B.V; Ḥikāya.i; Ḳiṣṣa.2; Maḳāla.1; Maḳāma; Nahḍa; Naṣīḥat al-Mulūk.1; Risāla.1; Sad̲j̲ʿ.3; Sīra S̲h̲aʿbiyya; Uḳṣūṣa

   and → LITERATURE.DRAMA; PRESS

   works Alf Layla wa-Layla; ʿAntar; Baybars; Bilawhar wa-Yūdāsaf; Dhu 'l-Himma; Kalīla wa-Dimna; Luḳmān.3; Sayf Ibn Dhī Yazan; Sindbād al-Ḥakīm; ʿUmar al-Nuʿmān

      see also Sindbād; Tawaddud

   9th and 10th-century authors al-D̲j̲āḥiẓ; al-Hamad̲h̲ānī; Ibn al-Muḳaffaʿ; al-T̲h̲aʿlabī, Muḥammad; [in Suppl.] Abu 'l-ʿAnbas al-Ṣaymarī

   11th-13th-century authors al-Ḥarīrī; Ibn Nāḳiyā; al-Ṣaymarī; al-Wahrānī; [in Suppl.] Abu 'l-Muṭahhar al-Azdī; al-D̲j̲azarī

      see also al-S̲h̲arīs̲h̲ī; al-T̲h̲aʿālibī, Abū Manṣūr ʿAbd al-Malik

   14th-18th-century authors Ibn Abī Ḥad̲j̲ala; al-S̲h̲irbīnī; al-Warg̲h̲ī; al-Yūsī

see also al-Ibshīhī
19th and 20th-century authors Aḥmad Amīn; Faraḥ Anṭūn; Ḥāfiẓ Ibrāhīm; Maḥmūd Taymūr; al-Maʿlūf; al-Manfalūṭī; Mayy Ziyāda; al-Māzinī; Muḥammad Ḥusayn Haykal; al-Muwayliḥī; Nuʿayma, Mīkhāʾīl; al-Rayḥānī; Salāma Mūsā; Sayyid Ḳuṭb; al-Sharḳāwī; Shāʾūl; Ṭāhā Ḥusayn; Tawfīḳ al-Ḥakīm; Ṭuʿma, Ilyās; al-Tūnisī, Maḥmūd Bayram; Yaḥyā Ḥaḳḳī; al-Yāzidjī.1; Zaydān, Djurdjī; [in Suppl.] Abū Shādī; al-ʿAḳḳād; al-Bustānī.6
see also Djamīl al-Mudawwar; al-Khālidī; Kurd ʿAlī; Shumayyil, Shiblī
Persian Ḥikāya.ii; Iran.vii; Ḳiṣṣa.4; Maḳāla.2; Naṣīḥat al-Mulūk.2; Risāla.2
see also Ṣafawids.III; *and* → LITERATURE.DRAMA; PRESS
works Bakhtiyār-nāma; Dabistān al-Madhāhib; Ḳahramān-nāma; Kalīla wa-Dimna; Madjnūn Laylā.2; Marzbān-nāma; Wāmiḳ wa ʿAdhrāʾ
see also Niẓām al-Mulk; Niẓāmī ʿArūḍī Samarḳandī
11th and 12th-century authors Ḥamīdī; al-Ḳāshānī; Kay Kāʾūs b. Iskandar; Nāṣir-i Khusraw; Naṣr Allāh b. Muḥammad; Niẓāmī ʿArūḍī Samarḳandī; Rashīd al-Dīn (Waṭwāṭ); al-Samʿānī, Abu ʾl-Ḳāsim
13th-century authors Saʿdī
14th-century authors Nakhshabī
15th-century authors Kāshifī
16th-century authors
see also Shemʿī
17th and 18th-century authors ʿInāyat Allāh Kańbū; Mumtāz
19th and 20th-century authors Bahār; Hidāyat, Ṣādiḳ; Nafīsī, Saʿīd; Shaybānī; Shaykh Mūsā Nathrī; Ṭālibūf; Zayn al-ʿĀbidīn Marāghaʾī; [in Suppl.] Āl-i Aḥmad; Bihrangī; Dehkhudā
see also Furūgh.2
Turkish Ḥikāya.iii; Ḳiṣṣa.3; Maddāḥ; Maḳāla.3; Risāla.3; Turks.III
see also Bilmedje; Therwet-i Fünūn; *and* → LITERATURE.DRAMA; PRESS
works Alpamïsh; Billur Köshk; Dede Ḳorḳut; Ḳahramān-nāma; Oghuz-nāma; Yūsuf and Zulaykhā.2
see also Merdjümek; Ṣarï Ṣalṭūḳ Dede
14th-century authors Sheykh-oghlu
15th-century authors Sheykh-zāde.3
16th-century authors Wāsiʿ ʿAlīsi
see also Shemʿī
17th-century authors Nergisī; Weysī
18th-century authors ʿAlī ʿAzīz, Giridli; Nābī
19th and 20th-century authors Aḥmad Ḥikmet; Aḥmad Midḥat; Aḥmad Rāsim; Djanāb Shihāb al-Dīn; Ebüzziya Tevfik; Ekrem Bey;

Fiṭrat; Hi̊sar; Ḥusayn D̲j̲āhid; Ḥusayn Raḥmī; Karay, Refi̊ḳ K̲h̲ālid; Ḳaṣāb, Teodor; Kaygi̊li̊, ʿOt̲h̲mān D̲j̲emāl; Kemāl; Kemāl, Meḥmed Nāmi̊ḳ; Kemal Tahir; K̲h̲ālid Ḍiyāʾ; K̲h̲ālide Edīb; Laylā K̲h̲āni̊m; Meḥmed Raʾūf; Oktay Rifat; ʿÖmer Seyf ül-Dīn; Ork̲h̲an Kemāl; Res̲h̲ād Nūrī; Sabahattin Ali; Sāmī; Sezāʾī, Sāmī; Tanpinar, Aḥmed Ḥamdī; Yaḥyā Kemāl; Yaʿḳūb Ḳadrī; Żiyā Pas̲h̲a; [in Suppl.] Atač; Atay; Čaylaḳ Tewfīḳ; Esendal; Haliḳarnas Bali̊ḳči̊si̊

see also Aḥmad Iḥsān; Ileri, D̲j̲elāl Nūrī; İnal; Ismāʿīl Ḥaḳḳi ʿĀlīs̲h̲ān; Ḳiṣṣa.3(b); T̲h̲erwet-i Fünūn; [in Suppl.] Eyyūbog̲h̲lu

in Eastern Turkish Bābur; Rabg̲h̲ūzī; [in Suppl.] Āgahī

see also Tīmūrids.2; Turks.III.6

Urdu Ḥikāya.iv; Ḳiṣṣa.5; Urdū.2

and → LITERATURE.DRAMA; PRESS

18th-century authors Taḥsīn

19th and 20th-century authors Amān, Mīr; D̲j̲awān; Faḳīr Muḥammad K̲h̲ān; Iḳbāl; Nad̲h̲īr Aḥmad Dihlawī; Prēm Čand; Ruswā; S̲h̲abbīr Ḥasan K̲h̲ān D̲j̲os̲h̲; S̲h̲iblī Nuʿmānī; Surūr; [in Suppl.] Āzād

proverbs in Mat̲h̲al.4

and → PROVERBS.COLLECTIONS OF

terms ʿArūḍ; ʿAtāba; Badīʿ; Balāg̲h̲a; Bayān; Dak̲h̲īl; Fard.a; Faṣāḥa; Fāṣila; Ibtidāʾ; Id̲j̲āza; Iḍmār; Iḳtibās; Intihāʾ; Irtid̲j̲āl; Istiʿāra; Ḳabḍ.iii; Ḳāfiya; Ḳaṭʿ; Kināya; Luzūm mā lā yalzam; al-Maʿānī wa ʾl-Bayān; Mad̲j̲āz; Maʿnā.3; Muʿāraḍa; Muzāwad̲j̲a; Radīf.2; Rad̲j̲az.4; S̲h̲awāhid; Ṣila.2; Taʿad̲j̲d̲j̲ub; Tad̲j̲nīs; Taḍmīn; Tak̲h̲alluṣ; Tak̲h̲mīs; Tak̲h̲yīl.1; Taʾrīk̲h̲.III; Tas̲h̲bīh; Tawriya; Ṭayf al-K̲h̲ayāl; Waḥs̲h̲ī; Waṣf.1

and → LITERATURE.GENRES; METRICS; RHETORIC

topoi Buk̲h̲l; Bulbul; G̲h̲urāb; Gul; Ḥamām; Ḥayawān.5; Inṣāf; al-Ḳamar.II; Ḳaṭā; Nard̲j̲is; Raḥīl; Sāḳī; S̲h̲amʿa; S̲h̲aʿr.3; al-S̲h̲ayb wa ʾl-S̲h̲abāb

see also G̲h̲azal.ii; ʿIs̲h̲ḳ; K̲h̲amriyya; Rabīʿiyyāt; Zahriyyāt

tradition-literature At̲h̲ar; **Ḥadīt̲h̲**; Ḥadīt̲h̲ Ḳudsī; Hind.v.e; Sunan; Sunna; Uṣūl al-Ḥadīt̲h̲; [in Suppl.] Arbaʿūn Ḥadīt̲h̲

see also Ahl al-Ḥadīt̲h̲; Ḥas̲h̲wiyya; K̲h̲abar; Mustamlī; Nask̲h̲; Riwāya; S̲h̲arḥ.III; ʿUlamāʾ

authoritative collections Abū Dāʾūd al-Sid̲j̲istānī; Aḥmad b. Ḥanbal; Anas b. Mālik; al-Bayhaḳī; al-Buk̲h̲ārī, Muḥammad b. Ismāʿīl; al-Dāraḳuṭnī; al-Dārimī; Ibn Ḥibbān; Ibn Mād̲j̲a; Muslim b. al-Ḥad̲j̲d̲j̲ād̲j̲; al-Nasāʾī; al-Ṭayālisī, Abū Dāwūd; al-Tirmid̲h̲ī, Abū ʿĪsā

see also al-ʿAynī; Ibn Hubayra

terms al-D̲j̲arḥ wa ʾl-Taʿdīl; Fard.d; G̲h̲arīb; Ḥikāya.I; Id̲j̲āza; Isnād; K̲h̲abar al-Wāḥid; Mas̲h̲hūr; Matn; Muʿanʿan; Munkar; Mursal; Muṣannaf; Musnad.3; Mustamlī; Mutawātir.(a); Rafʿ.2; Rid̲j̲āl; Ṣaḥīḥ.1; Ṣāliḥ; Sunan; Tadlīs.2; Tadwīn; Tawātur; T̲h̲iḳa; Umma.2

see also Ḥadīth; Taʿlīḳ
traditionists Rāwī; Ridjāl; Ṣāliḥ; Thiḳa
see also al-Rāmahurmuzī
7th century ʿAbd Allāh b. ʿUmar b. al-Khaṭṭāb; Abū Bakra; Abū Hurayra; al-Aʿmash; Ibn Abī Laylā.I; Ibn Masʿūd; Kaʿb al-Aḥbār; al-Khawlānī, Abū Idrīs; al-Khawlānī, Abū Muslim; [in Suppl.] Djābir b. ʿAbd Allāh
see also ʿĀʾisha bint Abī Bakr; Umm Salama Hind
8th century Abu ʾl-ʿĀliya al-Riyāḥī; Abū Mikhnaf; al-Ashʿarī, Abū Burda; Djābir b. Zayd; al-Fuḍayl b. ʿIyāḍ; Ghundjār; al-Ḥasan b. Ṣāliḥ b. Ḥayy al-Kūfī; al-Ḥasan al-Baṣrī; Ibn Abī Laylā.II; Ibn Daʾb; Ibn Isḥāḳ; Ibn al-Naṭṭāḥ; Ibn Shubruma; Ibn Sīrīn; ʿIkrima; al-Layth b. Saʿd; Maymūn b. Mihrān; Muḳātil b. Sulaymān; Nāfiʿ; al-Nakhaʿī, Ibrāhīm; Saʿīd b. Abī Arūba; al-Shaʿbī; Shuʿba b. al-Ḥadjdjādj; al-Suddī; ʿUrwa b. al-Zubayr; Warḳāʾ b. ʿUmar; Yazīd b. Zurayʿ; al-Zuhrī, Ibn Shihāb; [in Suppl.] Abū ʿAmr al-Shaybānī (*and* al-Shaybānī, Abū ʿAmr); Ibn Djuraydj
9th century Abū Nuʿaym al-Mulāʾī; Baḳī b. Makhlad; Ibn Abī Khaythama; Ibn Abi ʾl-Shawārib; Ibn Abī Shayba; Ibn ʿĀʾisha.IV; Ibn Rāhwayh; Ibn Saʿd; Ibn Sallām al-Djumaḥī; Ibrāhīm al-Ḥarbī; al-Karābīsī.2; al-Marwazī; Muslim b. al-Ḥadjdjādj; Nuʿaym b. Ḥammād; al-Ṣanʿānī, ʿAbd al-Razzāḳ; Sufyān b. ʿUyayna; al-Ṭayālisī, Abū Dāwūd; ʿUmar b. Shabba; Wakīʿ b. al-Djarrāḥ; al-Wāḳidī; Yaḥyā b. Maʿīn; al-Ziyādī; Zuhayr b. Ḥarb; [in Suppl.] Abū ʿĀṣim al-Nabīl; Asad b. Mūsā b. Ibrāhīm
see also Ibn Khayyāṭ al-ʿUṣfurī; Ibn Ḳuṭlūbughā; Yamūt b. al-Muzarraʿ
10th century Abū ʿArūba; al-Anbārī, Abū Bakr; al-Anbārī, Abū Muḥammad; Ghulām Thaʿlab; Ibn al-ʿAllāf; Ḳāsim b. Aṣbagh; al-Khaṭṭābī; al-Saraḳusṭī; al-Sidjistānī; al-Ṭabarānī; [in Suppl.] Ibn ʿUḳda
11th century al-Ḥākim al-Naysābūrī; Ibn ʿAbd al-Barr; Ibn al-Bannāʾ; Ibn Fūrak; Ibn Mākūlā.3; al-Ḳābisī; al-Khaṭīb al-Baghdādī; al-Sahmī; al-ʿUdhrī
12th century al-Baghawī; Ibn al-ʿArabī; Ibn ʿAsākir; Ibn Ḥubaysh; Ibn al-Ḳaysarānī.1; Ibn al-Nadjdjār; al-Lawātī; Razīn b. Muʿāwiya; al-Rushāṭī; al-Ṣadafī; al-Sarrādj, Abū Muḥammad; Shīrawayh; al-Silafī
see also al-Samʿānī, Abū Saʿd
13th century al-Dimyāṭī al-Shāfiʿī; Ibn al-Athīr.1; Ibn Diḥya; Ibn Faraḥ al-Ishbīlī; al-Ṣaghānī, Raḍiyy al-Dīn; al-Ṭabarī, Aḥmad b. ʿAbd Allāh; [in Suppl.] Ibn Daḳīḳ al-ʿĪd

14th century al-Dhahabī; Ibn Kathīr; al-Mizzī; al-Wādī'āshī
15th century Ibn Ḥadjar al-ʿAsḳalānī; al-Ibshīhī.2; al-Ḳasṭallānī; Muʿīn al-Miskīn; al-Suyūṭī
see also Ibn Ḳuṭlūbughā
19th and 20th centuries Shākir, Aḥmad Muḥammad
Shiite ʿAbd Allāh b. Maymūn; Dindān; Djaʿfar al-Ṣādiḳ; Ibn Bābawayh(i); al-Kashshī; al-Kāẓimī, ʿAbd al-Nabī; al-Kulaynī, Abū Djaʿfar Muḥammad; Madjlisī; Muḥammad b. Makkī; Shāh ʿAbd al-ʿAẓīm al-Ḥasanī; [in Suppl.] Akhbāriyya; al-Barḳī; Djābir al-Djuʿfī
see also Asmā'; al-Ṭihrānī

translations
from Greek and Syriac **Tardjama**.2
and → MEDICINE.PHYSICIANS.GREEK; PHILOSOPHY.PHILOSOPHERS.GREEK
from Middle Persian Ibn al-Muḳaffaʿ; Tansar; **Tardjama**.3
from Western languages
into Arabic Muḥammad Bey ʿUthmān Djalāl; Shā'ūl; Shumayyil, Shiblī; **Tardjama**.4; al-Yāzidjī.5
into Persian Muḥammad Ḥasan Khān; Nafīsī, Saʿīd; Sharīʿatī, ʿAlī; **Tardjama**.5
into Turkish Ismāʿīl Ḥaḳḳi ʿĀlīshān; Kanık; Khālide Edīb; Shināsī; **Tardjama**.6; Żiyā Pasha

travel-literature Djughrāfiyā.(d); **Riḥla**
authors ʿAbd al-Ghanī; al-ʿAbdarī; Abū Dulaf; Abū Ṭālib Khān; Aḥmad Iḥsān; ʿAlī Bey al-ʿAbbāsī; ʿAlī Khān; al-ʿAyyāshī; Ewliyā Čelebi; Fāris al-Shidyāḳ; al-Ghassānī; Ghiyāth al-Dīn Naḳḳāsh; Ibn Baṭṭūṭa; Ibn Djubayr; Ibn Idrīs(II); Kurd ʿAlī; Ma Huan; Meḥmed Yirmisekiz; Nāṣir-i Khusraw; Shiblī Nuʿmānī; Sīdī ʿAlī Re'īs; al-Tamgrūtī; Tamīm b. Baḥr al-Muṭṭawwiʿ; al-Tidjānī, Abū Muḥammad; al-Tudjībī; al-Tūnisī, Muḥammad; al-Tūnisī, Shaykh Zayn al-ʿĀbidīn; Yāḳūt al-Rūmī; al-Zayyānī; [in Suppl.] al-Ghazzāl; Ibn Nāṣir.3
see also Hārūn b. Yaḥyā; Ibn Djuzayy; Ibn Rushayd; Ibn Saʿīd al-Maghribī; Ibrāhīm b. Yaʿḳūb; Khayr Allāh Efendi; Leo Africanus; Zayn al-ʿĀbidīn Marāgha'ī; Zayn al-ʿĀbidīn Shīrwānī
narratives [in Suppl.] Akhbār al-Ṣīn wa 'l-Hind

wisdom-literature al-Aḥnaf b. Ḳays; ʿAlī b. Abī Ṭālib; Buzurgmihr; Hūshang; Luḳmān; Sahl b. Hārūn b. Rāhawayh; [in Suppl.] Djāwīdhān Khirad
see also Aktham b. Ṣayfī; Buhlūl; al-Ibshīhī

wondrous literature Abū Ḥāmid al-Gharnāṭī; **ʿAdjā'ib**; Buzurg b. Shahriyār; al-Ḳazwīnī
see also Ibn Sarābiyūn; Ḳiṣaṣ al-Anbiyā'; Sindbād

LOVE **ʿIshḳ**
see also Ishāra; Ḳalb.II; *and* → LITERATURE.POETRY.LOVE
erotic Djins; Ghazal; Nasīb
see also Abū Dahbal al-Djumaḥī; Abū Nuwās; Abū Ṣakhr al-Hudhalī; al-ʿArdjī; Dayr; Dīk al-Djinn al-Ḥimṣī; Djurʿat; Fāḍil Bey; Ḥammād ʿAdjrad; Ibn ʿAbd Rabbih; Ibn Faradj al-Djayyānī; Ibn Ḳays al-Ruḳayyāt; Ibn Maṭrūḥ; Khamriyya; Wāliba b. al-Ḥubāb
mystical ʿĀshiḳ; ʿIshḳ; Shawḳ
and → LITERATURE.POETRY.MYSTICAL; MYSTICISM
platonic Ghazal.i.3; **ʿUdhrī**
see also Djamīl al-ʿUdhrī; Ibn Dāwūd; Kuthayyir b. ʿAbd al-Raḥmān; Laylā al-Akhyaliyya; Muraḳḳish.1; Nuṣayb b. Rabāḥ; al-Ramādī; ʿUmar b. Abī Rabīʿa; ʿUrwa b. Ḥizām; al-Walīd.2
poetry → LITERATURE.POETRY.LOVE
treatises on al-Antāḳī, Dāʾūd; Ibn Ḥazm, Abū Muḥammad; Rafīʿ al-Dīn; al-Tidjānī, Abū Muḥammad
see also Bukhtīshūʿ

M

MACEDONIA → (former) YUGOSLAVIA

MADAGASCAR **Madagascar**; Massalajem
and → AFRICA.EAST AFRICA

MAGIC ʿAzīma.2; Djadwal; Istinzāl; Khāṣṣa; Nīrandj; Ruḳya; **Siḥr**; Sīmiyāʾ; Wafḳ; Yada Tash; [in Suppl.] Budūḥ
see also Djinn.III; Ḥadjar; Ḥurūf; Istikhāra; Istiḳsām; Istisḳāʾ; Kabid.4; al-Ḳamar.II; Ḳatl.ii.2; Khawāṣṣ al-Ḳurʾān; Kihāna; Kitābāt.5; Rūḥāniyya; Sidr; Zār; *and* → CHARMS; DIVINATION
magicians ʿAbd Allāh b. Hilāl; Shaʿbadha
see also Antemuru
treatises on al-Maḳḳarī; al-Zarḳālī; [in Suppl.] Ibn ʿAzzūz; al-Būnī

MALAWI Kota Kota
and → AFRICA.EAST AFRICA

MALAYSIA Malacca; **Malay Peninsula**; Malays; **Malaysia**
see also Baladiyya.6; Djāmiʿa; Indonesia; Kandūrī; Kitābāt.8; Partai Islam se Malaysia (Pas); Rembau
architecture → ARCHITECTURE.REGIONS
literature ʿAbd Allāh b. ʿAbd al-Ḳādir; Dāwūd al-Faṭānī; Ḥikāya.v; Ḳiṣṣa.6;

Malays; Shāʿir.7; Taʾrīkh.II.7
see also Indonesia.vi
states Penang; Perak; Sabah; Sarawak; Terengganu

MALI Adrar.2; Aḥmad al-Shaykh; Aḥmadu Lobbo; Ḥamāliyya; Kaʿti; **Mali**; Mansa Mūsā
see also Mande; Sūdān (Bilād al-).2
historians of al-Saʿdī
toponyms
ancient Tādmakkat
present-day
regions Kaarta
towns Bamako; Dienné; Gao; Segu; Timbuktu

MAMLUKS **Mamlūks**
see also Ḥarfūsh; Manshūr; Mihmindār; Rank; Yāsā.2; *and* → DYNASTIES. EGYPT AND THE FERTILE CRESCENT; MILITARY.MAMLUK

MARONITES → CHRISTIANITY.DENOMINATIONS; LEBANON

MARRIAGE Djilwa; Khiṭba; Mutʿa; **Nikāḥ**; ʿUrs; [in Suppl.] Djabr
see also ʿAbd.3.e; ʿĀda.iii and iv.4; ʿArūs Resmi; Fāsid wa-Bāṭil.III; Ghāʾib; Ḥaḍāna; Kafāʾa; Kurds.iv.A.1; al-Marʾa.2; Mawākib.4.3 and 5; Raḍāʿ; Shawwāl; Suknā; Sukūt; Wilāya.1; *and* → DIVORCE
dowry **Mahr**; Ṣadāḳ

MARTYRDOM Fidāʾī; Maẓlūm; **Shahīd**
see also Ḥabīb al-Nadjdjār; (al-)Ḥusayn b. ʿAlī b. Abī Ṭālib; Khubayb; Madjlis.3; Mashhad; Masʿūd; Ziyāra.5; [in Suppl.] ʿAbd Allāh b. Abī Bakr al-Miyānadjī

MATHEMATICS Algorithmus; al-Djabr wa ʾl-Muḳābala; Ḥisāb al-ʿAḳd; Ḥisāb al-Ghubār; **ʿIlm al-Ḥisāb**; Misāḥa; **al-Riyāḍiyyāt**; [in Suppl.] ʿIlm al-Handasa
and → NUMBER
algebra **al-Djabr wa ʾl-Muḳābala**
geometry **Misāḥa**; [in Suppl.] **ʿIlm al-Handasa**
mathematicians
Greek Uḳlīdis
see also Balīnūs
Islamic Abū Kāmil Shudjāʿ; Abu ʾl-Wafāʾ al-Būzadjānī; ʿAlī al-Ḳūshdjī; al-Bīrūnī; Ibn al-Bannāʾ al-Marrākushī; Ibn al-Haytham; Ibn ʿIrāḳ; Isḥāḳ Efendi; al-Ḳalaṣādī; al-Karābīsī.1; al-Karadjī; al-Kāshī; al-Khʷārazmī;

al-Khāzin; al-Khudjandī; Kushiyār b. Labān; al-Madjrīṭī; al-Mārdīnī; Muḥammad b. ʿĪsā al-Māhānī; Muḥammad b. ʿUmar; al-Shīrāzī, Abu ʾl-Ḥusayn; Thābit b. Ḳurra; al-Ṭūsī, Naṣīr al-Dīn; ʿUmar Khayyām; ʿUṭārid b. Muḥammad
see also Ḳusṭā b. Lūḳā
terms Fard.f; Kasr; Ḳaṭʿ; Ḳuṭr; Māl; Manshūr; Muḳaddam; Muṣādara.1; Muthallath; al-Sahm.1.a; al-Taʿdīl bayn al-Saṭrayn
see also al-Mīzān; [in Suppl.] Halīladj

MAURITANIA Adrar.3; Atar; Ḥawḍ; Māʾ al-ʿAynayn al-Ḳalḳamī; Madjlis.4.A. xxii; **Mūrītāniyā**
see also Dustūr.xv; Lamtūna; al-Māmī; Sūdān (Bilād al-).2
historians of al-Shinḳīṭī; al-Yadālī
toponyms
ancient Awdaghost; Ghāna; Ḳunbi Ṣāliḥ; Shinḳīṭ
present-day Nouakchott; Walāta

MECHANICS Ḥiyal.2; al-Ḳarasṭūn; [in Suppl.] al-Djazarī; **Ḥiyal**
see also Ibn al-Sāʿātī; ʿUmar Khayyām; Urghan; *and* → HYDROLOGY

MEDICINE **Ṭibb**
and → ANATOMY; DRUGS; ILLNESS; PHARMACOLOGY
centres of Bīmāristān; Gondēshāpūr; Ḳalāwūn; [in Suppl.] Abū Zaʿbal
see also Baghdād; Dimashḳ; al-Madīna
dentistry
dental care Miswāk
see also ʿAḳīḳ; Mardjān
treatises on Hāmōn
see also Ibn Abi ʾl-Bayān
diseases → ILLNESS; PLAGUE
medical handbooks/encyclopaedias ʿAlī b. al-ʿAbbās; al-Djurdjānī, Ismāʿīl b. al-Ḥusayn; Ibn al-Nafīs; Ibn Sīnā; al-Masīḥī; Shānī-zāde; al-Ṭabarī, ʿAlī b. Rabban; Yūḥannā b. Sarābiyūn; al-Zahrāwī, Abu ʾl-Ḳāsim
medicines Almās; ʿAnbar; al-Dahnadj; Dhahab; al-Durr; Fiḍḍa; Kāfūr; Ḳaṭrān; al-Ḳily; al-Kuḥl; Lubān; Maghnāṭīs.1; Mardjān; Milḥ.2; Misk; Mūmiyāʾ; Ṣābūn; Ṣamgh; Ṭabāshīr; Zaʿfarān.2; [in Suppl.] Bawraḳ; Halīladj
see also Bāzahr; al-Iksīr; Kabid.3; Ziʾbaḳ; [in Suppl.] Afāwīh; Dam; *for medicinal use of animal parts, food and plants or flowers, see specific articles under* ANIMALS, CUISINE *and* FLORA, *respectively*
obstetrics ʿArīb b. Saʿd al-Kātib al-Ḳurṭubī
and → LIFE STAGES.CHILDBIRTH
ophthalmology ʿAyn; Ramad; Ṭibb

and → ANATOMY.EYE; OPTICS
ophthalmologists ʿAlī b. ʿĪsā; ʿAmmār al-Mawṣilī; al-Ghāfiḳī; Ibn Dāniyāl; Khalīfa b. Abi ʾl-Maḥāsin
see also Ḥunayn b. Isḥāḳ al-ʿIbādī; Ibn al-Nafīs; Ibn Zuhr.V
physicians Djarrāḥ; Ḥāwī; [in Suppl.] Faṣṣād
see also ʿAyn; Constantinus Africanus; Ḥikma; Kabid.3; Masāʾil wa-Adjwiba; *and* → MEDICINE.OPHTHALMOLOGY.OPHTHALMOLOGISTS; PHARMACOLOGY
biographies of Ibn Abī Uṣaybiʿa; Ibn Djuldjul; Ibn al-Ḳāḍī; Isḥāḳ b. Ḥunayn
see also Ibn al-Ḳifṭī
7th century [in Suppl.] Ahrun; al-Ḥārith b. Kalada
and → *the section Physicians.Greek below*
9th century Bukhtīshūʿ; Ḥunayn b. Isḥāḳ al-ʿIbādī; Ibn Māsawayh; Sābūr b. Sahl; Yūḥannā b. Sarābiyūn
see also Māsardjawayh; al-Ṭabarī, ʿAlī
10th century ʿAlī b. al-ʿAbbās; ʿArīb b. Saʿd al-Kātib al-Ḳurṭubī; Ibn Djuldjul; Isḥāḳ b. Ḥunayn; Isḥāḳ b. Sulaymān al-Isrāʾīlī; Ḳusṭā b. Lūḳā; al-Rāzī, Abū Bakr; Ṣābiʾ.(3); Saʿīd al-Dimashḳī; [in Suppl.] Ibn Abi ʾl-Ashʿath
11th century al-Anṭākī, Abu ʾl-Faradj; Ibn Buṭlān; Ibn Djanāḥ; Ibn Djazla; Ibn al-Djazzār; Ibn Riḍwān; Ibn Sīnā; Ibn al-Ṭayyib; Ibn Wāfid; Ibn Zuhr.II; al-Masīḥī; al-Zahrāwī, Abu ʾl-Ḳāsim
12th century Abu ʾl-Barakāt; al-Djurdjānī, Ismāʿīl b. al-Ḥusayn; Ibn Djāmiʿ; Ibn al-Tilmīdh; Ibn Zuhr.III and IV; al-Marwazī, Sharaf al-Zamān; Umayya, Abu ʾl-Ṣalt; [in Suppl.] Ibn Biklārish
see also Ibn Rushd
13th century Ibn Abi ʾl-Bayān; Ibn Abī Uṣaybiʿa; Ibn Hubal; Ibn al-Nafīs; Ibn Ṭumlūs; Saʿd al-Dawla; al-Suwaydī; [in Suppl.] Ibn al-Ḳuff
14th century Ḥādjdjī Pasha; Ibn al-Khaṭīb; Isḥāḳ b. Murād; Ḳuṭb al-Dīn Shīrāzī
15th century Bashīr Čelebi; Yaʿḳūb Pasha
16th century al-Anṭākī, Dāʾūd; Hāmōn; Yūsufī
17th century Ḥayātī-zāde
18th century al-Ṣanʿānī, Ḍiyāʾ al-Dīn; [in Suppl.] Ādarrāḳ; Ibn Shaḳrūn al-Miknāsī
19th century and on Bahdjat Muṣṭafā Efendi; Muḥammad b. Aḥmad al-Iskandarānī; Shānī-zāde; Shumayyil, Shiblī; [in Suppl.] ʿAbd al-Salām b. Muḥammad
Christian Bukhtīshūʿ; Ḥunayn b. Isḥāḳ al-ʿIbādī; Ibn Buṭlān; Ibn Māsawayh; Ibn al-Ṭayyib; Isḥāḳ b. Ḥunayn; Ḳusṭā b. Lūḳā; Ṣābiʾ.(3); Sābūr b. Sahl; al-Ṭabarī, ʿAlī; Yūḥannā b. Sarābiyūn; [in Suppl.] Ahrun; Ḥubaysh b. al-Ḥasan al-Dimashḳī; Ibn al-Ḳuff
Greek Diyusḳuridīs; Djālīnūs; Rūfus al-Afsīsī; [in Suppl.] Ahrun; Buḳrāṭ

see also Ḥunayn b. Isḥāḳ al-ʿIbādī; Ibn Riḍwān; Ibn al-Ṭayyib; Isḥāḳ b. Ḥunayn; Iṣṭifān b. Basīl; Usṭāth; Yaḥyā b. al-Biṭrīḳ; Yūnān; [in Suppl.] Ḥubaysh b. al-Ḥasan al-Dimashḳī; Ibn Abi ʾl-Ashʿath

Jewish Hāmōn; Ibn Abi ʾl-Bayān; Ibn Djāmiʿ; Ibn Djanāḥ; Isḥāḳ b. Sulaymān al-Isrāʾīlī; Māsardjawayh; Saʿd al-Dawla; Yaʿḳūb Pasha; [in Suppl.] Ibn Biklārish

see also Abu ʾl-Barakāt; Ḥayātī-zāde.1; Ibn Maymūn

Ottoman Bahdjat Muṣṭafā Efendi; Bashīr Čelebi; Ḥādjdjī Pasha; Hāmōn; Ḥayātī-zāde; Isḥāḳ b. Murād; Shānī-zāde; Yaʿḳūb Pasha

see also Ḥekīm-bashi̊

surgery al-Zahrāwī, Abu ʾl-Ḳāsim

terms Bīmāristān; Djarrāḥ; Ḥidjāb; Ḳuwwa.5; Sabab.1

see also Ḥāl

veterinary Bayṭār; Ibn Hudhayl; Ibn al-Mundhir

MELKITES → CHRISTIANITY.DENOMINATIONS

MESOPOTAMIA → IRAQ

METALLURGY Ḳalʿī; Khārṣīnī; **Maʿdin**

see also Kalah; al-Mīzān.1; *and* → MINERALOGY.MINES

metals Dhahab; Fiḍḍa; al-Ḥadīd; Nuḥās; Ziʾbaḳ

and → MINERALOGY.MINERALS; PROFESSIONS.CRAFTSMEN AND TRADESMEN.ARTISANS

METAPHYSICS **Mā baʿd al-Ṭabīʿa**

see also ʿAbd al-Laṭīf al-Baghdādī; Māhiyya; Muṭlaḳ

METEOROLOGY al-Āthār al-ʿUlwiyya

see also Anwāʾ; Sadjʿ.2; [in Suppl.] Ibn al-Adjdābī

weather magic Yada Tash

winds **Rīḥ**; Samūm

METRICS **ʿArūḍ**, Wazn.2

and → LITERATURE.POETRY

metres Mudjtathth; Mutadārik; Mutaḳārib; Mutawātir.(b); Radjaz; Ramal.1; Sarīʿ; Ṭawīl; Wāfir

terms Dakhīl; Fard.a; Ḳaṭʿ; Sabab.3; Ṣadr.(a); Sālim.3; Watid; Ziḥāf

treatises on Bābur; al-Djawharī; al-Khalīl b. Aḥmad; al-Khazradjī, Ḍiyāʾ al-Dīn; Mīr ʿAlī Shīr Nawāʾī; Shams-i Ḳays; al-Tibrīzī

MILITARY Baḥriyya; Djaysh; **Ḥarb**; [in Suppl.] Baḥriyya

see also Dār al-Ḥarb; Djihād; Fatḥnāme; Ghazw

architecture Ribāṭ

see also Ṭabaḳa; *and* → ARCHITECTURE.MONUMENTS.STRONGHOLDS

army **Djaysh**; Istiʿrāḍ (ʿArḍ); **Lashkar**; Radīf.3

see also Djāsūs; Ṣaff.2; *and* → MILITARY.MAMLUK *and* OTTOMAN

contingents Bāzinḳir; Djāndār; Djaysh.iii.2; Djund; Ghulām; Gūm; Ḳūrčī; Maḥalla; Mamlūk; Mutaṭawwiʿa; Sipāhī.2; Ṭabūr; Ṭalīʿa; Ṭulb; Tūmān.1

see also Almogávares; Fāris; *and* → MILITARY.OTTOMAN.ARMY CONTINGENTS

band Naḳḳāra-khāna; Ṭabl-khāna

see also Mehter

battles

see also Shiʿār.1; Tugh; *and* → MILITARY.EXPEDITIONS; TREATIES

before 622 Buʿāth; Dhū Ḳār; Djabala; Fidjār; Ḥalīma; Shiʿb Djabala; Ubāgh; [in Suppl.] Dāḥis

see also Ayyām al-ʿArab; Ḥanẓala b. Mālik

622-632 Badr; Biʾr Maʿūna; Buzākha; Ḥunayn; Khandaḳ; Khaybar; Muʾta; Uḥud

see also Mālik b. ʿAwf

633-660 Adjnādayn; ʿAḳrabāʾ; al-Djamal; Djisr; Faḥl; Ḥarūrāʾ; al-Ḳādisiyya.2; Mardj al-Ṣuffar; Ṣiffīn; Yarmūk.2; [in Suppl.] Dhāt al-Ṣawārī

see also ʿAbd Allāh b. Saʿd; ʿĀʾisha bint Abī Bakr; ʿAlī b. Abī Ṭālib; al-Hurmuzān; Musaylima; al-Nahrawān; Rustam b. Farrukh Hurmuzd; Taḥkīm

661-750 ʿAyn al-Warda; Balāṭ al-Shuhadāʾ; Baldj b. Bishr; al-Bishr; Dayr al-Djamādjim; Dayr al-Djāthalīḳ; al-Ḥarra; al-Khāzir; Mardj Rāhiṭ

see also (al-)Ḥusayn b. ʿAlī b. Abī Ṭālib; Kulthūm b. ʿIyāḍ al-Ḳushayrī; (al-)Ḳusṭanṭīniyya

751-1258 al-Arak; Bākhamrā; Dayr al-ʿĀḳūl; Fakhkh; Ḥaydarān; Hazārasp; al-ʿIḳāb; Köse Dāgh; Malāzgird.2; Shant Mānkash; Ṭarāz; Ubbadha; al-Zallāḳa; [in Suppl.] Dandānḳān

see also Ḥadjar al-Nasr; al-Madjūs; al-Manṣūr bi ʾllāh, Ismāʿīl; Mardj Dābiḳ

1258-18th century ʿAyn Djālūt; Čāldirān; Dābiḳ; Djarba; Ḥimṣ; Ḳoṣowa; Mardj Dābiḳ; Mardj Rāhiṭ; Mardj al-Ṣuffar; Mezőkeresztes; Mohács.a and b; Nīkbūlī; Pānīpat; Tālīkōṭā; Tukarōʾī; Wādī ʾl-Khaznadār; Zenta

see also Aynabakhtī; Baḥriyya.iii; Fatḥnāme; Ḥarb; Nahr Abī Fuṭrus; ʿOthmān Pasha; Wenedik.2; Zsitvatorok

after 18th century Abuklea; Atjèh; Česhme; Farwān; Gök Tepe; Isly; Kūt al-ʿAmāra; Maysalūn; Nizīb; Rīf.II; al-Tall al-Kabīr

see also al-ʿAḳaba; Gulistān

bodies ʿAyyār; Dawāʾir; Djaysh.iii.1; Futuwwa; Ghāzī; al-Shākiriyya
see also ʿAlī b. Muḥammad al-Zandjī; al-Ikhwān; Khashabiyya; Sarhang; *and* → MILITARY.ARMY.CONTINGENTS

booty Fayʾ; **Ghanīma**
see also Baranta; Ghazw; Khāliṣa; Pendjik; *and* → MILITARY.PRISONERS

Byzantine → BYZANTINE EMPIRE; *for battles fought between the Arabs and Byzantines,* → BYZANTINE EMPIRE.MILITARY

decorations **Nishān**; **Wisām**

expeditions Ghāzī; **Ṣāʾifa**
see also Ghazw

Indo-Muslim Bārūd.vi; Ghulām.iii; Ḥarb.vi; Ḥiṣār.vi; Lashkar; Sipāhī.3; Suwār
see also Istiʿrāḍ (Arḍ)

Mamluk al-Baḥriyya; Baḥriyya.II; Bārūd.iii; Burdjiyya; Ḥalḳa; Ḥarb.iii; Ḥiṣār.iv; **Mamlūk**; Ṭabaḳa; Wāfidiyya
see also Amīr Ākhūr; al-Amīr al-Kabīr; Atābak al-ʿAsākir; Čerkes.ii; ʿĪsā b. Muhannā; Khāṣṣakiyya; Ḳumāsh; Rikābdār; Silāḥdār; Ṭulb

battles ʿAyn Djālūt; Dābiḳ; Ḥimṣ; Mardj Rāhiṭ; Wādī ʾl-Khaznadār

navy **Baḥriyya**; Dār al-Ṣināʿa; Daryā-begi; Ḳapudan Pasha; Lewend.1; Nassads; Raʾīs.3; Riyāla; Usṭūl; [in Suppl.] **Baḥriyya**
see also ʿAzab; Gelibolu; Kātib Çelebi; [in Suppl.] Dhāt al-Ṣawārī; *and* → NAVIGATION.SHIPS; PIRACY; *for Ottoman maritime topics,* → DYNASTIES.ANATOLIA AND THE TURKS.OTTOMANS.HIGH ADMIRALS; MILITARY.OTTOMAN

offices Amīr; ʿArīf; Atābak al-ʿAsākir; Fawdjdār; Ispahbadh; Ispahsālār; Istiʿrāḍ (ʿArḍ); Ḳāʾid; Manṣab; Sālār; Sardār; Sarhang; Shiḥna; Silāḥdār
see also Amīr al-Umarāʾ; Dārūgha; Ḳāḍī ʿAskar; Ḳūrčī; *and* → MILITARY.OTTOMAN

Ottoman Bāb-i Serʿaskeri; Baḥriyya.iii; Balyemez; Bārūd.iv; Devshirme; Djebeli; Ghulām.iv; Ḥarb.iv; Ḥarbiye; Ḥiṣār.v; Müsellem; Radīf.3; Sandjaḳ; Sipāhī.1; Tersāne; Tugh.2; ʿUlūfe; Yeñi Čeri; [in Suppl.] Djebedji
see also ʿAskarī; Ḍabṭiyya; Gelibolu; Gūm; Ḥareket Ordusu; Istiʿrāḍ (Arḍ); Ḳapïdji; Karakol; Martolos; Mensūkhāt; Mondros; Nefīr; Ordu; Pendjik; Tīmār; Ziʿāmet; *and* → MILITARY.NAVY

army contingents al-Abnāʾ.V; ʿAdjamī Oghlān; Akïndjï; Alay; ʿAzab; Bashï-bozuḳ; Bölük; Deli; Devedji; Djānbāzān; Eshkindji; Ghurabāʾ; Gönüllü; Khāṣṣekī; Khumbaradjï; Lewend; Niẓām-ï Djedīd; Odjaḳ; Orta; Woynuḳ; Yaya; Yeñi Čeri; Yerliyya; Zeybek; [in Suppl.] Djebedji
see also Akhī; Eflāḳ; Martolos; Nefīr; Sipāhī.1

battles Čaldirān; Dābiḳ; Ḳoṣowa; Mezőkeresztes; Mohács.a and b; Nīkbūlī
see also Wenedik

officers Bayraḳdār; Biñbashï; Bölük-bashï; Čāʾūsh; Čorbadjï.1; Ḍābiṭ; Daryā-begi; Ḳapudan Pasha; Mushīr; Rikābdār; Riyāla; Zaghardjï Bashï
see also Sandjaḳ; Silāḥdār

pay ʿAṭāʾ; Inʿām; Māl al-Bayʿa; Rizḳ.3; ʿUlūfe
police Aḥdāth; ʿAsas; Ḍabṭiyya; Karakol; **Shurṭa**
see also Dawāʾir; Futuwwa; Kōtwāl; Martolos; Naḳīb.2
prisoners Lamas-ṣū; Mübādele.ii; [in Suppl.] Fidāʾ
see also Sidjn; *and* → MILITARY.BOOTY
reform → REFORM.MILITARY
tactics Ḥarb; Ḥiṣār; Ḥiyal.1
see also al-ʿAwāṣim; Fīl; al-Thughūr; *and* → ARCHITECTURE.MONUMENTS.STRONGHOLDS
terms Tadjmīr; Zaʿīm
treatises on Ibn Hudhayl; al-Ṭarsūsī; [in Suppl.] Fakhr-i Mudabbir
see also Ḥarb.ii; Ḥiyal.1
weapons ʿAnaza; ʿArrāda; Balyemez; Bārūd; Dūrbāsh; Ḳaws; Mandjanīḳ; Nafṭ.2; Ṭop
see also ʿAlam; Asad Allāh Iṣfahānī; Hilāl.ii; Ḥiṣār; Ḳalʿī; Lamṭ; Marātib

MINERALOGY **Maʿdin**
see also al-Mīzān.1
minerals Abū Ḳalamūn; ʿAḳīḳ; Almās; Bārūd; Billawr; al-Dahnadj; Fīrūzadj; al-Kibrīt; al-Kuḥl; Maghnāṭīs.1; Milḥ; Mūmiyāʾ; Naṭrūn; Yāḳūt; Yashm; [in Suppl.] Bawraḳ
see also al-Andalus.v; Damāwand; Golkonḍā; Ḥadjar; Kirmān; Maʿdin; Malindi; *and* → JEWELRY; METALLURGY
mines al-ʿAllāḳī; Anadolu.iii.6; al-Andalus.v.2; ʿAraba; Armīniya.III; Badakhshān; Billiton; Bilma; Čankiri; al-Djabbūl; Djayzān; al-Durūʿ; Farghānā; Firrīsh; Gümüsh-khāne; Kalah; Ḳarā Ḥiṣār.2 and 3; Ḳayṣariyya; al-Ḳily; Ḳishm; Maʿdin.2; al-Maʿdin; Sofāla; Zonguldak
see also Fāzūghlī; Filasṭīn; Milḥ
treatises on al-Suwaydī; al-Tīfāshī
see also ʿUṭārid b. Muḥammad

MIRACLES **Karāma**; **Muʿdjiza**
see also Āya; Dawsa; Māʾ al-ʿAynayn al-Ḳalḳamī; Miʿrādj; *and* → SAINTHOOD

MONARCHY Malik; Mamlaka
see also Darshan; Naṣīḥat al-Mulūk; Shāh; Tigin; *and* → COURT CEREMONY
royal insignia Miẓalla; Sandjaḳ; Sarāparda; Shamsa; Tādj; Takht-i Ṭāwūs; Tughra
see also Shams.3; Tamgha; Tugh

MONASTICISM **Rahbāniyya**
and → CHRISTIANITY.MONASTERIES

MONGOLIA Ḳaraḳorum; Khalkha; **Mongolia**; Mongols
Mongols Batu᾿ids; Čaghatay Khānate; Čūbānids; Djalāyir; Djānids; Giray; Hayāṭila; Ilkhāns; Kalmuk; Ḳarā Khiṭāy; Ḳūrīltāy; Mangi̊t; **Mongols**
see also Dūghlāt; Ergenekon; Khānbali̊ḳ; Ḳi̊shlaḳ; Ḳūbčūr; Ḳungrāt; Libās.iii; Ötüken; Tīmūrids; Tūmān.1; Ulus; Yaylaḳ; *and* → DYNASTIES.MONGOLS; LAW.MONGOL; TRIBES.CENTRAL ASIA, MONGOLIA AND POINTS FURTHER NORTH
administration Soyūrghāl; Yām; Yarli̊gh; [in Suppl.] Dīwān-begi
and → LAW.MONGOL
battles ʿAyn Djālūt; Ḥimṣ; Mardj Rāhiṭ; Wādī ʼl-Khaznadār
historians of Djuwaynī, ʿAlāʾ al-Dīn; Ḥamd Allāh al-Mustawfī al-Ḳazwīnī; Ḥaydar Mīrzā; Rashīd al-Dīn Ṭabīb; Waṣṣāf
see also Tamīm b. Baḥr al-Muṭṭawwiʿ; *and* → DYNASTIES.MONGOLS; *and the section Historians Of under individual dynasties*
physical geography
waters Orkhon

MONOPHYSITES → CHRISTIANITY.DENOMINATIONS

MOROCCO **al-Maghrib**
see also ʿArabiyya.A.iii.3; Ḥimāya.ii; Mallāḥ; Rīf.II; Sulṭān al-Ṭalaba (*and* Ṭalaba)
architecture → ARCHITECTURE.REGIONS.NORTH AFRICA
dynasties ʿAlawīs; Idrīsids; Marīnids; Saʿdids; Waṭṭāsids
see also Bū Ḥmāra; Ḥasanī; Shurafāʾ.1.III; Ẓahīr; [in Suppl.] Aḥmad al-Hība; *and* → DYNASTIES.SPAIN AND NORTH AFRICA
historians of Aḥmad al-Nāṣirī al-Salāwī (*and* al-Nāṣir al-Salāwī); Akanṣūs; Ibn Abī Zarʿ; Ibn al-Ḳāḍī; al-Zayyānī
see also Ibn al-Raḳīḳ; al-Kattānī; [in Suppl.] ʿAllāl al-Fāsī; *and* → DYNASTIES.SPAIN AND NORTH AFRICA
modern period Baladiyya.3; Djāmiʿa; Djarīda.i.B; Djaysh.iii.2; Dustūr.xvii; Ḥizb.i; Ḥukūma.iv; Maʿārif.2.C; Madjlis.4.A.xxi; Madjmaʿ ʿIlmī.i.2.d; Maḥkama.4.x; Makhzan; [in Suppl.] Institut des hautes études marocaines
belletrists
poets Ibn Idrīs (I); Ḳaddūr al-ʿAlamī; [in Suppl.] Ibn ʿAmr al-Ribāṭī; Ibn al-Ḥādjdj
reform Salafiyya.1(c); Tartīb
scholars al-Tādilī
statesmen [in Suppl.] ʿAllāl al-Fāsī
physical geography al-Maghrib.I
deserts al-Ṣaḥrāʾ
see also Reg

mountains Atlas; Rīf.I.2
plateaux Ḥammāda
population Dukkāla; Glāwā; Ḥarṭānī; Khulṭ; Shāwiya.1; [in Suppl.] Awraba
see also al-Fāsiyyūn; al-Maʿḳil; *and* → Berbers
religion al-Maghrib.VI
mystical orders Darḳāwa; Hansaliyya; Hazmīriyyūn; ʿIsāwā; al-Nāṣiriyya; Shādhiliyya; Wazzāniyya; [in Suppl.] Ḥamādisha
for Djazūliyya, *see* al-Djazūlī, Abū ʿAbd Allāh
see also Sharḳāwa; Ziyāniyya; [in Suppl.] ʿĀʾisha Ḳandīsha; *and* → Mysticism; Sainthood
toponyms
ancient Anfā; Bādis; al-Baṣra; Fāzāz; al-Ḳaṣr al-Ṣaghīr; Nakūr; Shalla; Sidjilmāsa; Tāmasna; Tinmal; Tīṭ; Walīlī
present-day
districts Tafilālt; Tāzarwālt
islands [in Suppl.] al-Ḥusayma
regions Darʿa; Figuig; Gharb; Ḥawz; Ifni; Rīf.I.2; Spartel; al-Sūs al-Aḳṣā; Tādlā; Wādī Nūn
towns Agadir-ighir; Āghmāt; al-ʿArāʾish; Aṣfī; Aṣīla; Azammūr; Damnāt; (al-)Dār al-Bayḍāʾ; al-Djadīda; Dubdū; Faḍāla; Fās; Garsīf; al-Ḳaṣr al-Kabīr; al-Mahdiyya; Marrākush; Mawlāy Idrīs; Melilla; Miknās; Ribāṭ al-Fatḥ; Sabta; Salā; Shafshāwan; Ṣufrūy; al-Suwayra; Tamgrūt; Ṭandja; Tārūdānt; Tāzā; Tīṭṭāwīn; Tīznīt; Wadjda; Wazzān; [in Suppl.] Azrū; Benī Mellāl
see also al-Ḥamrāʾ; Tīṭ

Mountains Adjaʾ and Salmā; Adrar.2; Aghrì Dagh; Aïr; Ala Dagh; Aladja Dagh; Alburz; Altai; Alwand Kūh; ʿAmūr; Atlas; Awrās; Balkhān; Besh-parmaḳ; Bībān; Bingöl Dagh; Bīsutūn; Čopan-ata; Damāwand; Deve Boynu; Djabala; al-Djibāl; Djūdī; Djurdjura; Elma Daghì; Erdjiyas Daghì; Fūta Djallon; Gāwur Daghlarì; Ḥaḍūr; Ḥamrīn; Ḥarāz; Hawrāmān; Hindū Kush; Ḥirāʾ; Ḥiṣn al-Ghurāb; Ḥufāsh; al-Ḳabḳ; Kabylia; Ḳaraḳorum; Ḳāsiyūn; Khumayr; Kūh-i Bābā; al-Lukkām; Nafūsa; Pamirs; Safīd Kūh; al-Sarāt; al-Sharāt; Sindjār; Sulaymān; Tibesti; Toros Dağları; al-Ṭūr; Ulu Dāgh; Wansharīs; Zagros
see also Hind.i.i; Ḳarā Bāgh; Tasili; Thabīr; *and* → *the section Physical Geography under individual countries*

Mozambique Kerimba; Makua; **Mozambique**; Pemba; Sofāla

Muḥammad, the Prophet Hidjra; Ḥirāʾ; al-Ḥudaybiya; Khaybar; Khuzāʿa; Ḳudāʿa; Ḳuraysh; al-Madīna.i.2; Mawlid; Miʿrādj; **Muḥammad**; Ṣaḥāba;

Sunna; Tābiʿūn; Ṭulaḳāʾ; Ummī.2; Wufūd

see also al-Ḳurʾān; Muʾākhāt; al-Muʾallafa Ḳulūbuhum; Nubuwwa; Nūr Muḥammadī; Sayyid; Sharaf; Sharīf; Taḥannuth; Taṣliya; Waḥy; [in Suppl.] Bayʿat al-Riḍwān; *and* → MILITARY.BATTLES.622-632

belongings of Athar; al-Burāḳ; Burda.1; Dhu 'l-Faḳār; Duldul; Emānet-i Muḳaddese; Ḳadam Sharīf; Khirḳa-yi Sherīf; Liḥya-yi Sherīf

biographies of **al-Maghāzī**; **Sīra**

biographers Abd al-Ḥaḳḳ b. Sayf al-Dīn; al-Bakrī, Abu 'l-Ḥasan; Daḥlān; al-Diyārbakrī; al-Djawwānī; al-Ḥalabī, Nūr al-Dīn; Ibn Hishām; Ibn Isḥāḳ; Ibn Sayyid al-Nās; ʿIyāḍ b. Mūsā; Ḳarā-čelebi-zāde.4; al-Ḳasṭallānī; Liu Chih; Mughulṭāy; Muḥammad Ḥusayn Haykal; Muʿīn al-Miskīn; al-Ṭabrisī, Amīn al-Dīn; al-Tanūkhī, Djamāl al-Dīn; Wahb b. Munabbih; Weysī; [in Suppl.] Dinet

see also Hind.v.e; Ibn Saʿd; al-Khargūshī

companions of **Ṣaḥāba**

see also Ahl al-Ṣuffa; al-Salaf wa 'l-Khalaf; Tābiʿūn

individual companions Abū Ayyūb al-Anṣārī; Abū Bakra; Abu 'l-Dardāʾ; Abū Dharr; Abū Hurayra; ʿAdī b. Ḥātim; ʿAmmār b. Yāsir; Anas b. Mālik; al-Arḳam; al-Ashʿarī, Abū Mūsā; ʿAttāb; al-Barāʾ (b. ʿĀzib); al-Barāʾ (b. Maʿrūr); Bashīr b. Saʿd; Bilāl b. Rabāḥ; Bishr b. al-Barāʾ; Burayda b. al-Ḥuṣayb; Diḥya; Djāriya b. Ḳudāma; Ghasīl al-Malāʾika; Hāshim b. ʿUtba; Ḥurḳūṣ b. Zuhayr al-Saʿdī; Ibn Masʿūd; Kaʿb b. Mālik; Khabbāb b. al-Aratt; Khālid b. Saʿīd; Ḳutham b. al-ʿAbbās; Maslama b. Mukhallad; al-Miḳdād b. ʿAmr; Muʿāwiya b. Ḥudaydj; al-Mughīra b. Shuʿba; Muḥammad b. Abī Ḥudhayfa; Muṣʿab b. ʿUmayr; al-Nābigha al-Djaʿdī; al-Nuʿmān b. Bashīr; Saʿd b. Abī Waḳḳāṣ; Ṣafwān b. al-Muʿaṭṭal; Saʿīd b. Zayd; Shaddād b. ʿAmr; Shuraḥbīl b. Ḥasana; Ṭalḥa; Tamīm al-Dārī; ʿUbayd Allāh b. al-ʿAbbās; ʿUbayd Allāh b. ʿUmar; ʿUḳba b. Nāfiʿ; ʿUrwa b. Masʿūd; ʿUtba b. Ghazwān; ʿUthmān b. Maẓʿūn; al-Walīd b. ʿUḳba; Zayd b. Thābit; al-Zibriḳān b. Badr; al-Zubayr b. al-ʿAwwām; Zuhayr b. Ḳays; [in Suppl.] Djābir b. ʿAbd Allāh; Ibn Mītham

see also al-Ḳaʿḳāʿ; Khawlān.2; Ḳuss b. Sāʿida; Rawḥ b. Zinbāʿ; Ubayy b. Kaʿb; Usāma b. Zayd; Uways al-Ḳaranī; ʿUyayna b. Ḥiṣn; Waraḳa b. Nawfal; Zayd b. ʿAmr

family of al-ʿAbbās b. ʿAbd al-Muṭṭalib; ʿAbd Allāh b. ʿAbd al-Muṭṭalib; ʿAbd al-Muṭṭalib b. Hāshim; Abū Lahab; Abū Ṭālib; ʿAḳīl b. Abī Ṭālib; ʿAlī b. Abī Ṭālib; Āmina; Djaʿfar b. Abī Ṭālib; Fāṭima; Ḥalīma bint Abī Dhuʾayb; Ḥamza b. ʿAbd al-Muṭṭalib; (al-)Ḥasan b. ʿAlī b. Abī Ṭālib; al-Ḥasan b. Zayd b. al-Ḥasan; Hāshim b. ʿAbd Manāf; (al-)Ḥusayn b. ʿAlī b. Abī Ṭālib; Ruḳayya; ʿUbayd Allāh b. al-ʿAbbās; Umm Kulthūm; Zayd b. Ḥāritha

see also Ahl al-Bayt; Sharīf; Shurafāʾ; *and* → *the section Wives below*

daughters Fāṭima; Ruḳayya; Umm Kulthūm; Zaynab bt. Muḥammad

wives ʿĀʾisha bint Abī Bakr; Ḥafṣa; Khadīdja; Māriya; Maymūna bint al-Ḥārith; Ṣafiyya; Sawda bt. Zamʿa; Umm Salama Hind; Zaynab bt. Djaḥsh; Zaynab bt. Khuzayma
opponents of Abū Djahl; Kaʿb b. al-Ashraf; Umayya b. Khalaf; ʿUtba b. Rabīʿa; al-Walīd b. al-Mughīra
see also Zuhra

MUSIC Ghināʾ; Ḳayna; Maḳām; Malāhī; **Mūsīḳī**; Ramal.2; Shashmaḳom; [in Suppl.] Īḳāʿ
see also Lamak; al-Rashīdiyya; Samāʿ.1
composers → *the section Musicians below*
instruments Būḳ; Darabukka; Duff; Ghayṭa; Imẓad; Ḳithāra; Miʿzaf; Mizmār; Nefīr; Rabāb; Ṣandj; Sanṭūr; Saz; Ṭabl; Ṭunbūr; ʿŪd.II; Urghan; Zurna
see also Mehter; Mūrisṭus; Naḳḳāra-khāna; Ṭabbāl
military → MILITARY.BAND
musicians
composers
first centuries Ibn Muḥriz; Ibrāhīm al-Mawṣilī; Isḥāḳ b. Ibrāhīm al-Mawṣilī; Maʿbad b. Wahb; Yaḥyā al-Makkī; Yūnus al-Kātib al-Mughannī; Ziryāb; [in Suppl.] ʿAllawayh al-Aʿsar; al-Dalāl; Faḍl al-Shāʿira
see also al-Ḳāsim b. ʿĪsā
13th to 16th centuries Ṣafī al-Dīn al-Urmawī; Tānsin; [in Suppl.] Ḥabba Khātūn
17th and 18th centuries Ismāʿīl Ḥaḳḳi; Ṣolaḳ-zāde
19th and 20th centuries al-Ḳusanṭīnī; Lāhūtī; Laylā Khānîm; Shewḳī Beg; Zekāʾī Dede
flautists [in Suppl.] Barṣawmā al-Zāmir
lute players ʿAzza al-Maylāʾ; Djaḥẓa; Ṣafī al-Dīn al-Urmawī; Sāʾib Khāthir; Zalzal; Ziryāb; [in Suppl.] ʿAllawayh al-Aʿsar
regional
Andalusian al-Ḥāʾik; Umayya, Abu ʾl-Ṣalt
Egyptian Ṭaḳṭūḳa
Indian **Hind**.viii; Khayāl
see also Bāyazīd Anṣārī; Tānsin; [in Suppl.] Ḥabba Khātūn
Kurdish Kurds.iv.C.4
Persian Mihragān.iv.3
see also Lāhūtī; Naḳḳāra-khāna
Turkish Ilāhī; Ḳoshma; Mehter; Sharḳî; Taḳsīm; Turks.IV; Türkü
see also Laylā Khānîm; Māni; Nefīr; Shewḳī Beg; Zekāʾī Dede
song **Ghināʾ**; Khayāl; Nashīd; Nawba; Shashmaḳom; Türkü
see also Abu ʾl-Faradj al-Iṣbahānī; Ḥawfī; Ilāhī; Mawāliyā.3; Shāʿir.1.E

singers ʿĀlima; Ḳayna
see also ʿĀshiḳ; al-Barāmika.5
legendary [in Suppl.] al-Djarādatān[i]
see also [in Suppl.] Ḥabba Khātūn
early Islamic period ʿAzza al-Maylāʾ; Djamīla; al-Gharīḍ; Ḥabāba; Ibn ʿĀʾisha.I; Ibn Misdjaḥ; Ibn Muḥriz; Ibn Suraydj; Maʿbad b. Wahb; Mālik b. Abi ʾl-Samḥ; Nashīṭ; Rāʾiḳa; Sāʾib Khāthir; Ṭuways; [in Suppl.] al-Dalāl
during the ʿAbbāsid caliphate Ibn Bāna; Ibn Djāmiʿ; Ibrāhīm al-Mawṣilī; Isḥāḳ b. Ibrāhīm al-Mawṣilī; Mukhāriḳ; Sallāma al-Zarḳāʾ; Shāriya; ʿUlayya; Yaḥyā al-Makkī; Yūnus al-Kātib al-Mughannī; [in Suppl.] Badhl al-Kubrā
mid-13th to 19th centuries [in Suppl.] Ḥabba Khātūn
20th century Siti Binti Saad; Umm Kulthūm
songwriters → MUSIC.MUSICIANS.COMPOSERS
terms Ṭarab; Taḳsīm; Tik wa-tum; [in Suppl.] Īḳāʿ
see also Ustādh.1; Wadjd
treatises on ʿAbd al-Ḳādir b. Ghaybī; Abu ʾl-Faradj al-Iṣbahānī; al-Ḥāʾik; Ibn Bāna; Ibn Khurradādhbih; Mashāḳa; (Banu ʾl-) Munadjdjim.4; Mūrisṭus; Mushāḳa; Ṣafī al-Dīn al-Urmawī; al-Ṣaydāwī; al-Tādilī; ʿUmar Khayyām; Yūnus al-Kātib al-Mughannī
see also Abu ʾl-Maḥāsin b. Taghrībirdī; İnal; Malāhī

MYSTICISM Allāh.III.4; Darwīsh; Dhikr; Ibāḥa.II; Karāma; Murīd; Murshid; Pīr; Samāʿ.1; Shaykh; Ṭarīḳa; **Taṣawwuf**; Zuhd
see also Sadjdjāda.3; Saʿīd al-Suʿadāʾ; Ṭāʾifa; *and* → DYNASTIES.PERSIA.ṢAFAWIDS
architecture → *the section Monasteries below*
concepts Baḳāʾ wa-Fanāʾ; al-Insān al-Kāmil; Ishrāḳ; Lāhūt and Nāsūt; Tawakkul; Zāʾirdja.2
see also Allāh.III.4; al-Ḥallādj.IV; Ibn al-ʿArabī; al-Niffarī; Uwaysiyya
dervishes **Darwīsh**; Raḳṣ
see also Tādj; [in Suppl.] Buḳʿa; *and* → MYSTICISM.ORDERS
dress Khirḳa; Pālāhang; Shadd.1
early ascetics ʿĀmir b. ʿAbd al-Ḳays al-ʿAnbarī; al-Ḥasan al-Baṣrī; al-Fuḍayl b. ʿIyāḍ; Ibrāhīm b. Adham; Maʿrūf al-Karkhī; Sarī al-Saḳaṭī
see also Bakkāʾ
literature → LITERATURE.POETRY.MYSTICAL
see also Zuhdiyya
monasteries Khānḳāh; Ribāṭ.1.b; Tekke; Zāwiya
mystics Darwīsh
see also Pist; Walī; *and* → HAGIOGRAPHY

African (excluding North Africa) ʿUmar b. Saʿīd al-Fūtī; [in Suppl.] al-Duwayḥī
see also Ṣāliḥiyya; Sūdān (Bilād al-).2; Ṭarīḳa.II.3; Taṣawwuf.9; Walī.9 and 10; Zāwiya.3; Ziyāra.9 and 10

Andalusian Abū Madyan; Ibn al-ʿArabī; Ibn al-ʿArīf, Abu ʾl-ʿAbbās; Ibn ʿĀshir; Ibn Barradjān; Ibn Ḳasī; Ibn Masarra; al-Shushtarī
see also al-Ṭalamankī

Arabic (excluding Andalusian and North African) ʿAbd al-Ghanī; ʿAbd al-Ḳādir al-Djīlānī; ʿAbd al-Karīm al-Djīlī; ʿAdī b. Musāfir; Aḥmad al-Badawī; ʿAydarūs; al-Bakrī, Muḥammad; al-Bakrī, Muṣṭafā; Bishr al-Ḥāfī; al-Bisṭāmī, ʿAbd al-Raḥmān; al-Damīrī; al-Dasūḳī, Ibrāhīm b. ʿAbd al-ʿAzīz; al-Dasūḳī, Ibrāhīm b. Muḥammad; Dhu ʾl-Nūn, Abu ʾl-Fayḍ; al-Dimyāṭī, al-Bannāʾ; al-Dimyāṭī, Nūr al-Dīn; al-Djunayd; al-Ghazālī, Abū Ḥāmid; al-Ghazālī, Aḥmad; al-Ḥallādj; al-Harawī al-Mawṣilī; Ibn ʿAṭāʾ Allāh; al-Ḳazwīnī, Nadjm al-Dīn; al-Kharrāz; al-Kurdī; al-Ḳushashī; Makhrama; al-Manūfī; al-Muḥāsibī; al-Munāwī; al-Niffarī; al-Nūrī; Rābiʿa al-ʿAdawiyya al-Ḳaysiyya; al-Rifāʿī; Sahl al-Tustarī; al-Sarrādj, Abū Naṣr; al-Shaʿrānī; al-Shiblī, Abū Bakr; Sumnūn; ʿUthmān b. Marzūḳ; al-Yāfiʿī; Yūsuf b. ʿĀbid al-Idrīsī; Zakariyyāʾ al-Anṣārī; [in Suppl.] Abu ʾl-ʿAzāʾim; al-ʿAdawī; al-ʿAfīfī; al-Ḥiṣāfī
see also Abū Nuʿaym al-Iṣfahānī; Abū Ṭālib al-Makkī; Bā ʿAlawī; Baḥraḳ; Bakriyya; Bayyūmiyya; Faḍl, Bā; Faḳīh, Bā; Faḳīh, Bal; Hurmuz, Bā; Ḳādiriyya; Marwāniyya; Saʿdiyya; al-Ṣiddīḳī; Yashruṭiyya; [in Suppl.] al-Bakrī; Demirdāshiyya; *and* → MYSTICISM.EARLY ASCETICS

Central Asian Aḥmad Yasawī; Ḥakīm Ata; Naḳshband; al-Tirmidhī, Abū ʿAbd Allāh; Tirmidhī; Zangī Ātā; [in Suppl.] Aḥrār
see also Ḳalandariyya; Pārsāʾiyya; Ṭarīḳa.II.5; Uwaysiyya; Walī.5; Yasawiyya

Chinese → CHINA

Indian Abū ʿAlī Ḳalandar; Aḥmad Sirhindī; Ashraf ʿAlī; Bahāʾ al-Dīn Zakariyyā; Bāḳī bi ʾllāh (*and* [in Suppl.]); al-Banūrī; Budhan; Burhān al-Dīn Gharīb; Burhān al-Dīn Ḳuṭb-i ʿĀlam; Čirāgh-i Dihlī; Čishtī; Djahānārā Bēgam; Djalāl al-Dīn Ḥusayn al-Bukhārī; "Djamālī"; Farīd al-Dīn Masʿūd "Gandj-i-Shakar"; Gīsū Darāz; Hānsawī; Ḥusaynī Sādāt Amīr; Imdād Allāh; Kalīm Allāh al-Djahānābādī; Ḳuṭb al-Dīn Bakhtiyār Kākī; Malik Muḥammad Djāyasī; Miyān Mīr, Miyādjī; Mubārak Ghāzī; Muḥammad Ghawth Gwāliyārī; al-Muttaḳī al-Hindī; Muẓaffar Shams Balkhī; Niẓām al-Dīn Awliyāʾ; Niẓām al-Dīn, Mullā Muḥammad; Nūr Ḳuṭb al-ʿĀlam; Shāh Muḥammad b. ʿAbd Aḥmad; Thānesarī; [in Suppl.] ʿAbd al-Bārī; ʿAbd al-Wahhāb Bukhārī; Bulbul Shāh; Farangī Maḥall; Gadāʾī Kambō; Ḥamīd Ḳalandar; Ḥamīd al-Dīn Ḳāḍī Nāgawrī; Ḥamīd al-Dīn Ṣūfī Nāgawrī Siwālī; Ḥamza Makhdūm *see also* ʿAydarūs; Čis͟htiyya; Dārā S͟hukōh; Dard; D̲j̲īwan; Hind.v; K͟halīl Allāh (*and* K͟halīl Allāh But-s͟hikan); Malang; Mug͟hals.6; Naḳs͟hbandiyya.3; S͟haṭṭāriyya; Suhrawardiyya.2; Ṭarīḳa.II.7; Taṣawwuf.7; Walī.6; Ziyāra.7

Indonesian ʿAbd al-Raʾūf al-Sinkilī; ʿAbd al-Ṣamad al-Palimbānī; Ḥamza Fanṣūrī; S͟hams al-Dīn al-Samaṭrānī

see also Ṭarīḳa.II.8; Walī.7; Ziyāra.8

North African ʿAbd al-Ḳādir al-Fāsī; ʿAbd al-Salām b. Mas͟hīs͟h; Abu ʾl-Maḥāsin al-Fāsī; Abū Muḥammad Ṣāliḥ; Aḥmad b. Idrīs; ʿAlī b. Maymūn; al-ʿAyyās͟hī; al-Daḳḳāḳ; al-D̲j̲azūlī; al-Hās͟himī; Ḥmād u-Mūsā; Ibn ʿAbbād; Ibn ʿAd̲j̲ība; Ibn ʿAlīwa; Ibn ʿArūs; Ibn Ḥirzihim; al-Ḳādirī al-Ḥasanī; al-Kūhin; al-Lamaṭī; Māʾ al-ʿAynayn al-Ḳalḳamī; al-Mad̲j̲d͟hūb; al-Sanūsī, Abū ʿAbd Allāh; al-Sanūsī, Muḥammad b. ʿAlī; al-Sanūsī, S͟hayk͟h Sayyid Aḥmad; al-S͟hād͟hilī; al-Tid̲j̲ānī, Aḥmad; [in Suppl.] al-Asmar; al-Dilāʾ; al-Fāsī; Ibn ʿAzzūz

see also ʿAmmāriyya; ʿArūsiyya; Darḳāwa; Hansaliyya; Hazmīriyyūn; al-Ifrānī; ʿĪsāwā; Madaniyya; al-Nāṣiriyya; Raḥmāniyya; S͟hād͟hiliyya; Tid̲j̲āniyya; Walī.2; Wazzāniyya; Zāwiya.2; Ziyāniyya; [in Suppl.] Ḥamādis͟ha

Persian ʿAbd al-Razzāḳ al-Ḳās͟hānī; Abū Saʿīd b. Abi ʾl-K͟hayr; Abū Yazīd al-Bisṭāmī; Aḥmad-i D̲j̲ām; ʿAlāʾ al-Dawla al-Simnānī; ʿAlī al-Hamadānī; al-Anṣārī al-Harawī; As͟hraf D̲j̲ahāngīr; Bābā-Ṭāhir; D̲j̲alāl al-Dīn Rūmī; Faḍl Allāh Ḥurūfī; G͟hud̲j̲duwānī; Ḥamdūn al-Ḳaṣṣār; Hud̲j̲wīrī; Ibn K͟hafīf; ʿIrāḳī; al-Kalābād͟hī; Kamāl K͟hud̲j̲andī; Ḳāsim-i Anwār; Kāzarūnī; K͟halīl Allāh (*and* K͟halīl Allāh But-s͟hikan); K͟haraḳānī; al-K͟hargūs͟hī; Kirmānī; Kubrā; al-Ḳus͟hayrī.1; Lāhīd̲j̲ī.1; Maḥmūd S͟habistarī; Nad̲j̲m al-Dīn Rāzī Dāya; Naḳs͟hband; Rūzbihān; Saʿd al-Dīn al-Ḥammūʾī; Saʿd al-Dīn Kās͟hg͟harī; Ṣadr al-Dīn Ardabīlī; Ṣadr al-Dīn Mūsā; Ṣafī; Saʿīd al-Dīn Farg͟hānī; Sayf al-Dīn Bāk͟harzī; S͟hams-i Tabrīz(ī); al-Suhrawardī, Abu ʾl-Nad̲j̲īb; al-Suhrawardī, S͟hihāb al-Dīn Abū Ḥafṣ; Sulṭān Walad; Tirmid͟hī; Zayn al-ʿĀbidīn S͟hīrwānī; [in Suppl.] ʿAbd Allāh b. Abī Bakr al-Miyānad̲j̲ī; Abū ʿAlī; Aḥmad-i Rūmī; ʿAyn al-Ḳuḍāt al-Hamad͟hānī; Ibn al-Bazzāz al-Ardabīlī

see also D̲j̲āmī; Mad̲j̲lisī-yi Awwal; Naḳs͟hbandiyya.1; Niʿmat-Allāhiyya; Ṣafawids.I.ii; Taṣawwuf.5;

Turkish Aḳ S͟hams al-Dīn; Altı̊ Parmak; ʿĀs͟hı̊ḳ Pas͟ha; Badr al-Dīn b. Ḳāḍī Samāwnā; Baraḳ Baba; Bīd̲j̲ān; Emīr Sulṭān; Faṣīḥ Dede; Fehmī; Guls͟hanī; Güls͟hehrī; Ḥād̲j̲d̲j̲ī Bayrām Walī; Hüdāʾī; Ḥusām al-Dīn Čelebi; Ismāʿīl al-Anḳarawī; Ismāʿīl Ḥaḳḳi; Ḳayg͟husuz Abdāl; K͟halīlī; Ḳuṭb al-Dīn-zāde; Merkez; Niyāzī; Sezāʾī, Ḥasan Dede; ʿUs͟hs͟hāḳī-zāde.1; [in Suppl.] ʿĀrif Čelebī; Es͟hrefog͟hlu; Esrār Dede *see also* Ashrafiyya; Bakriyya; Bayrāmiyya; Bektāshiyya; Djilwatiyya; Gülbaba; Ilāhī; Khalwatiyya; Mawlawiyya; Naḳshbandiyya.2; Shaʿbāniyya; Shamsiyya; Sunbuliyya; Ṭarīḳa.II.5; Taṣawwuf.6; ʿUshshāḳiyya; Walī.4

orders **Ṭarīḳa**.II

individual orders ʿAmmāriyya; ʿArūsiyya; Ashrafiyya; Bakriyya; Bayrāmiyya; Bayyūmiyya; Bektāshiyya; Čishtiyya; Darḳāwa; Djilwatiyya; Hansaliyya; Hazmīriyyūn; ʿĪsāwā; Ḳādiriyya; Ḳalandariyya; Khalwatiyya; Madaniyya; Marwāniyya; Mawlawiyya; Mīrghaniyya; Murīdiyya; Naḳshbandiyya; al-Nāṣiriyya; Niʿmat-Allāhiyya; Pārsāʾiyya; Raḥmāniyya; Rifāʿiyya; Saʿdiyya; Ṣāliḥiyya; Sanūsiyya; Shaʿbāniyya; Shādhiliyya; Shamsiyya; Shaṭṭāriyya; Suhrawardiyya; Sunbuliyya; Tidjāniyya; ʿUshshāḳiyya; Wazzāniyya; Yasawiyya; Yashruṭiyya; Ziyāniyya; [in Suppl.] Demirdāshiyya; Ḥamādisha

for ʿAdawiyya, *see* ʿAdī b. Musāfir; *for* ʿAfīfiyya, *see* [in Suppl.] al-ʿAfīfī; *for* Aḥmadiyya (Badawiyya), *see* Aḥmad al-Badawī; *for* Dasūḳiyya (Burhāmiyya), *see* al-Dasūḳī, Ibrāhīm b. ʿAbd al-ʿAzīz; *for* al-Djazūliyya, *see* al-Djazūlī; *for* Gulshaniyya, *see* Gulshanī; for Idrīsiyya, *see* Aḥmad b. Idrīs; *for* Kāzarūniyya (Murshidiyya, Isḥāḳiyya), *see* Kāzarūnī; *for* Kubrawiyya, *see* Kubrā; *for* Yāfiʿiyya, *see* al-Yāfiʿī

see also Nūrbakhshiyya; Ṣafawids.I.ii; Uwaysiyya

terms Abdāl; ʿĀshiḳ; Awtād; Baḳāʾ wa-Fanāʾ; Basṭ; Bīsharʿ; Čāʾūsh; Darwīsh; Dawsa; Dede; Dhawḳ; Dhikr; Djilwa; Faḳīr; Fikr; al-Ghayb; Ghayba; Ghufrān; Ḥaḍra; Ḥaḳīḳa.3; Ḥaḳḳ; Ḥāl; Ḥidjāb.III; Ḥuḳūḳ; Ḥulūl; Ḥurriyya; Huwa huwa; Ikhlāṣ; Ilhām; ʿInāya; al-Insān al-Kāmil; Ishān; Ishāra; ʿIshḳ; Ishrāḳ; Ithbāt; Ittiḥād; Ḳabḍ.ii; Kāfir; Ḳalb.I; Kalima; Karāma; Kashf; Khalīfa.iii; Khalwa; Khānḳāh; Khirḳa; al-Ḳuṭb; Lāhūt and Nāsūt; Madjdhūb; Manzil; Maʿrifa; Muḥāsaba.1; Munādjāt; Murīd; Murshid; Nafs; Odjaḳ; Pālāhang; Pīr; Pūst; Pūst-neshīn; Rābiṭa; Ramz.3; Rātib; Ribāṭ; Riḍā.1; Rind; Rūḥāniyya; Rukhṣa.2; Ṣabr; Ṣadr; Shaṭḥ; Shawḳ; Shaykh; Shukr.1; Ṣidḳ; Silsila; Sulṭān.4; Sulūk.2; Tadjallī; Ṭāʾifa; Ṭarīḳa.I; Tekke; Terdjümān; Wadjd; Waḥdat al-Shuhūd; Waraʿ; Waẓīfa.2; Wird; Wudjūd.2; [in Suppl.] Buḳʿa; Ghawth

see also Čelebī; Futuwwa; Gülbaba; Gulbāng; Lawḥ; Lawn; Waṭan

N

NATIONALISM Istiḳlāl; **Ḳawmiyya; Waṭaniyya**

see also Djangalī; Khilāfa; Pāshtūnistān; al-Shuʿūbiyya; ʿUrūba; Waṭan; *and* → PANARABISM; PANISLAMISM; PANTURKISM; POLITICS.MOVEMENTS

NATURAL SCIENCE **al-Āthār al-ʿUlwiyya**; **Ḥikma**; Masāʾil wa-Adjwiba; Ṭabīʿa
see also Nūr.1
natural scientists al-Bīrūnī; al-Dimashḳī; Ibn Bādjdja; Ibn al-Haytham; Ibn Rushd; Ibn Sīnā; Ikhwān al-Ṣafāʾ; al-Ḳazwīnī; al-Marwazī, Sharaf al-Zamān
and → ALCHEMY; ASTRONOMY; BOTANY; METAPHYSICS; ZOOLOGY

NATURE → BOTANY; FLORA; LITERATURE.POETRY.NATURE

NAVIGATION Djughrāfiyā; Iṣbaʿ; Kharīṭa; Maghnāṭīs.2; Manār; **Milāḥa**; Mīnāʾ
see also al-Khashabāt; Rīḥ; al-Ṭāsa
ships Milāḥa (esp. 4); Nassads; **Safīna**; Shīnī; Usṭūl
see also Baḥriyya.2; Kelek; *and* → MILITARY.NAVY
shipyards Dār al-Ṣināʿa; Tersāne
treatises on Ibn Mādjid; Sīdī ʿAlī Reʾīs; Sulaymān al-Mahrī; al-Tādilī
see also Djughrāfiyā.IV.d; Milāḥa.1 and 3

NEPAL **Nepal**

NESTORIANS → CHRISTIANITY.DENOMINATIONS

NEW WORLD Djāliya; Djarīda.i.C.; **al-Mahdjar**
immigrants Djabrān Khalīl Djabrān; al-Maʿlūf; Nuʿayma, Mīkhāʾīl; al-Rayḥānī; [in Suppl.] Abū Māḍī; Abū Shādī
see also Pārsīs; Ṭuʿma, Ilyās

NIGER **Niger**
see also Sūdān (Bilād al-).2
physical geography Niger.1
toponyms Bilma; Djādū; Kawār

NIGERIA Hausa; **Nigeria**; Yoruba
see also Djarīda.vi; Fulbe; al-Kānemī; Kanuri; Nikāḥ.II.6; Sūdān (Bilād al-).2; *and* → AFRICA.CENTRAL AFRICA *and* WEST AFRICA
leaders Muḥammad Bello; ʿUthmān b. Fūdī
see also Gwandu
toponyms
provinces Adamawa; Bornū
towns Ibadan; Kano; Katsina; Kūkawa; Sokoto

NOMADISM **Badw**; Horde; Īlāt; Khāwa; Khayma; Marʿā; Yörük

see also Baḳḳāra; Baranta; Da<u>kh</u>īl; Dawār; Ḥayy; Ḳayn; *and* → BEDOUINS; GYPSIES; TRIBES
nomadic ideology **Taʿarrub**
nomadic possessions <u>Kh</u>ayma; Mifra<u>sh</u>
see also <u>Kh</u>ayl; Zmāla.2
residences Ḳi̊<u>sh</u>laḳ; Yaylaḳ

NUBIA ʿAlwa; Barābra; Dongola; al-Marīs; **Nūba**
see also Baḳṭ; Dār al-Ṣulḥ; Ibn Sulaym al-Aswānī; al-Muḳurra; Sōba; *and* → EGYPT.TOPONYMS; SUDAN.TOPONYMS
languages Nūba.3
peoples Nūba.4

NUMBER Ab<u>dj</u>ad; Ḥisāb al-ʿAḳd; Ḥisāb al-<u>Dj</u>ummal; Ḥurūf; ʿIlm al-Ḥisāb
and → MATHEMATICS
numbers <u>Kh</u>amsa; Sabʿ
see also al-Ṣifr

NUMISMATICS Dār al-Ḍarb; Sikka; Tazyīf; Wazn.1
see also ʿAlī Pa<u>sh</u>a Mubārak; Ismāʿīl <u>Gh</u>ālib; Makāyil; Ni<u>th</u>ār
coinage Aḳče; Bāli<u>sh</u>; Čao; Čeyrek; Dīnār; Dirham.2; Fals; Ḥasanī; Larin; Mohur; Pāʾī; Pāra; Pawlā; Paysā; Riyāl; Rūpiyya; Ṣadīḳī; Ṣāḥib Ḳirān; <u>Sh</u>āhī; Tanga; Ṭarī; Wariḳ
see also <u>Dh</u>ahab; Fidda; Filori; Hilāl.ii; Sana<u>dj</u>āt; Tam<u>gh</u>a; Wadaʿ.1; Yādgār; *and* → DYNASTIES; WEIGHTS AND MEASUREMENTS
for coinage in the name of rulers, see al-Afḍal (Kutayfāt); ʿAlī Bey; <u>Gh</u>āzi ʾl-Dīn Ḥaydar; Ḳaṭarī b. al-Fu<u>dj</u>āʾa; <u>Kh</u>ur<u>sh</u>īd; al-Manṣūr, al-Malik Muḥammad; Muṣṭafā.1; [in Suppl.] Farru<u>kh</u>ān.2; *for coinage under dynasties, see in particular* Artuḳids; Barīd <u>Sh</u>āhīs; <u>Kh</u>ʷārazm-<u>sh</u>āhs; Lōdīs.5; Mu<u>gh</u>als.10; al-Muwaḥḥidūn; ʿO<u>th</u>mānli̊.IX; Rasūlids.2; Ṣafawids.VI; Sal<u>dj</u>ūḳids.VIII; Ṣiḳilliya.3; Ṣulayḥids.2; Tīmūrids.4; Yādgār
shell currency Wadaʿ.1
special issues Yādgār
mint localities Abar<u>sh</u>ahr; al-Abbāsiyya; Andarāb.1; Ānī; Bā<u>gh</u>če Sarāy; Islāmābād; Iṣṭa<u>kh</u>r; al-Kur<u>dj</u>; Māh al-Baṣra; Mawlāy Idrīs; Māzandarān.7; Wāsiṭ.4; [in Suppl.] Biyār; Firrīm
reform ʿAbd al-Malik b. Marwān; [in Suppl.] al-<u>Gh</u>iṭrīf b. ʿAṭāʾ
see also Tūmān.2
terms ʿAdl.2; Salām (*and* Sālim.1); Tūmān.2; Wazn.1

O

OBSCENITY **Mudjūn**; **Sukhf**

OCEANS AND SEAS **Baḥr**; al-Madd wa 'l-Djazr
see also Kharīṭa; *and* → CARTOGRAPHY; NAVIGATION
waters Aral; Baḥr Adriyās; Baḥr Bunṭus; Baḥr Fāris; Baḥr al-Hind; Baḥr al-Khazar; Baḥr al-Ḳulzum; Baḥr Lūṭ; Baḥr Māyuṭis; al-Baḥr al-Muḥīṭ; Baḥr al-Rūm; Baḥr al-Zandj; Marmara Deñizi

OIL **Nafṭ**.3
see also Ta'mīm
oilfields ʿAbbādān; Abḳayḳ; Altın Köprü; al-Baḥrayn; al-Dahnā'; al-Ghawār; al-Ḥasā; al-Ḳaṭīf; Khārag; Khūzistān; Kirkūk; Kirmānshāh; al-Kuwayt; Lībiyā; Nadjd.3; Rām-hurmuz; Ra's (al-)Tannūra; (al-)Ẓahrān; [in Suppl.] Aḥmadī
see also Djannāba; Fārs; al-Khubar; Yanbuʿ

OMAN al-Ibāḍiyya.g; Madjlis.4.A.xiii; Maḥkama.4.ix; Nabhān; **ʿUmān**
see also [in Suppl.] al-Ḥārithī
dynasties Bū Saʿīd; Yaʿrubids
physical geography ʿUmān.1
salt-flats Umm al-Samīm
population ʿAwāmir; al-Baṭāḥira; al-Djanaba; al-Durūʿ; Hinā; al-Ḥubūs; al-ʿIfār; (Banū) Kharūṣ; Mahra; Mazrūʿī; Nabhān; Wahība
and → TRIBES.ARABIAN PENINSULA
toponyms
islands Khūryān-mūryān; Maṣīra
regions al-Bāṭina; Ra's Musandam; al-Rustāḳ; al-Sharḳiyya; Ẓafār; al-Ẓāhira
towns al-Buraymī; Ḥāsik; ʿIbrī; Ḳalhāt; Masḳaṭ; Maṭraḥ; al-Mirbāṭ; Nizwa; al-Rustāḳ; Ṣalāla; Ṣuḥār
see also (Djazīrat) al-ʿArab; Wabār.2; [in Suppl.] Gwādar

ONOMASTICS Bā; Ibn; Ism; Kisrā; Kunya; Laḳab; Nisba.2
see also al-Asmā' al-Ḥusnā; Oghul; Ṣiḳilliya.2
epithets Ata; Baba; Ghufrān; Humāyūn; al-Ṣiddīḳ; Tādj
in form of address Agha; Ākhūnd; Beg; Begum; Čelebī; Efendi; Khwādja; Khātūn; Khudāwand; Shaykh; Ustādh
see also Akhī; Sharīf.(3)
proper names Aḥmad; Dhu 'l-Faḳār; Humā; Marzpān; Meḥemmed; Mihragān.iv.2; Sonḳor; Thaʿlaba; Ṭoghrıl
see also al-Asad; Payghū; Yaylaḳ

titles

African Diglal; Sulṭān.3

Arabic ʿAmīd; Amīr al-Muʾminīn; Amīr al-Muslimīn; Asad al-Dawla; ʿAzīz Miṣr; ʿIzz al-Dawla; ʿIzz al-Dīn; Khādim al-Ḥaramayn; Khidīw; Malik; Mihmindār; Mushīr; Sardār; Sayyid; Shaykh al-Balad; Shaykh al-Islām.1; Sulṭān.1; Tubbaʿ

see also Dawla.2

Central Asian Afshīn; Ikhshīd; Ḳosh-begi; Shār; [in Suppl.] Atalïḳ; Dīwān-begi; İnaḳ

Indo-Muslim Āṣāf-Djāh; Khʷādja-i Djahān; Khān Khānān; Nawwāb; Niẓām; Pēshwā; Ṣāḥib Ḳirān; Sardār; Shār; Ulugh Khān

Mongolian Noyan; Ṣāḥib Ḳirān; Ṭarkhān

Persian Agha Khān; Ispahbadh; Ispahsālār; Iʿtimād al-Dawla; Khʷādja; Marzpān; Mīr; Mīrzā; Mollā; Pādishāh; Ṣadr; Sālār; Sardār; Sarkār Āḳā; Shāh; Tekfur; Ustāndār

South-east Asian Penghulu; Sulṭān.2

Turkish Alp; Beglerbegi; Dāmād; Daryā-begi; Dayï; Gülbaba; Khʷādjegān-i Dīwān-i Humāyūn; Khāḳān; Khān; Khudāwendigār; Mīr-i Mīrān; Mushīr; Pasha; Payghū; Ṣadr-i Aʿẓam; Shaykh al-Islām.2; Ṣu Bashï; Tekfur; Tigin; Yabghu

see also Čorbadjï; Terken Khātūn; Tughra

OPTICS Ḳaws Ḳuzaḥ; **Manāẓir**

see also Mirʾāt; Sarāb

works on Ibn al-Haytham; Kamāl al-Dīn al-Fārisī; Uḳlīdis

see also Ḳuṭb al-Dīn Shīrāzī

OTTOMAN EMPIRE Anadolu.iii.2 and 3; Ertoghrul.1; Istanbul; Lāle Devri; **ʿOthmānlï**; Tanẓīmāt

see also Bāb-i ʿĀlī; Ḥidjāz Railway; Maṭbakh.2; Pasha Ḳapusu; Shenlik; Ṭursun Faḳīh; *and* → DYNASTIES.ANATOLIA AND THE TURKS; EUROPE.EASTERN; LAW.OTTOMAN; MILITARY.OTTOMAN; *and the section Ottoman Period under individual countries*

administration Berātlï; Ḍabṭiyya; Dīwān-i Humāyūn; Eyālet; Imtiyāzāt.ii; Khāṣṣ; Khazīne; Mashwara; Millet.3; Mukhtār; Mülāzemet; Mulāzim; Mulkiyya; Nāḥiye; Nishāndjï; Reʾīs ül-Küttāb; Sandjaḳ; Tīmār; Ulaḳ; Ziʿāmet; [in Suppl.] Dāʾira Saniyya

see also Ḳaḍāʾ; Maʾmūr; Odjaḳ; Waḳf.IV; *and* → DOCUMENTS.OTTOMAN; LAW.OTTOMAN; MILITARY.OTTOMAN

archives and registers Başvekalet Arşivi; Daftar-i Khāḳānī; Ḳānūn.iii; Maṣraf Defteri; Mühimme Defterleri; Sāl-nāme; **Sidjill**.3; Taḥrīr

see also Daftar.III; Ferīdūn Beg; Maḥlūl

financial Arpalïḳ; Ashām; Bayt al-Māl.II; Daftardār; Dār al-Ḍarb; Dirlik; Djayb-i Humāyūn; Duyūn-i ʿUmūmiyye; Irsāliyye; Ḳāʾime; Khazīne; Māliyye; Muḥāsaba.2; Mukhallefāt; Muṣādara.3; Rūznāmedji; Sāliyāne; Siyāḳat; ʿUlūfe
see also Bakhshīsh; Ṣurra
fiscal Ḍarība.3; Djizya.ii; Ḥisba.ii; Kharādj.III; Muḥaṣṣil; Mültezim; ʿOthmānlï.II; Resm; Taḥrīr; Ṭapu; Tekālīf; Tīmār; Ziʿāmet
see also Mutaṣarrif; Shehir Ketkhüdāsï
agriculture Filāḥa.iv; Māʾ.8; Raʿiyya.2
and → AGRICULTURE
architecture → ARCHITECTURE.REGIONS.TURKEY
court ceremony Čāʾūsh; Khirḳa-yi Sherīf; Marāsim.4; Mawākib.4; Mehter; Selāmlïḳ
diplomacy Bālyōs; Consul; Elči; Hiba.v; Penče
see also Berātlï; Imtiyāzāt.ii; Ḳawwās; *and* → DIPLOMACY
education Ghalaṭa-sarāyï; Külliyye; Maʿārif.I.i; Makhredj; Mulkiyya; Ṣaḥn-i Thamān; Ṣofta
see also Ḥarbiye; *and* → EDUCATION; REFORM.EDUCATIONAL
functionaries Āmeddji; Aʿyān; Bazïrgan; Bostāndjï; Bostāndjï-bashï; Čakïrdjï-bashï; Čāshnagīr-bashï; Ḍābiṭ; Ḍabṭiyya; Daftardār; Dilsiz; Doghandjï; Elči; Emīn; Ghulām.iv; Ḥekīm-bashï; Ič-oghlanï; ʿIlmiyye; Ḳāʾim-maḳām; Ḳapu Aghasï; Ḳawwās; Ketkhudā.1; Khaznadār; Khʷādjegān-i Dīwān-i Humāyūn; Maʾmūr; Mewḳūfātčï; Mīr-Ākhūr; Mushīr; Mustashār; Mutaṣarrif; Nishāndjï; Reʾīs ül-Küttāb; Rūznāmedji; Ṣadr-ı Aʿẓam; Shāhnāmedji; Shehir Emāneti; Shehir Ketkhüdāsï; Tardjumān.2; Telkhīṣdji; Ṭulumbadjï; ʿUlamāʾ.3; Waḳaʿ-nüwīs; Wālī; Wazīr.III; Yazïdjï
see also ʿAdjamī oghlān; ʿAsas; Bālā; Balṭadjï; Bālyōs; Bīrūn; Enderūn; al-Ḥaramayn; Khāṣī.III; Khāṣṣ Oda; Khāṣṣekī; Mābeyn; *and* → LAW.OTTOMAN; MILITARY.OTTOMAN
history ʿOthmānlï.I
and → DYNASTIES.ANATOLIA AND THE TURKS.OTTOMANS; LITERATURE.HISTORICAL.TURKISH; TURKEY.OTTOMAN PERIOD; *and the section Toponyms in the countries once falling within the Ottoman Empire*
industry and trade Ḥarīr.ii; Kārwān; Ḳuṭn.2; Milḥ.3; ʿOthmānlï.II; Sūḳ.7
see also Maʿdin.3
law → LAW.OTTOMAN
literature → LITERATURE
military → MILITARY.OTTOMAN
modernisation of Baladiyya.1; Ḥukūma.i; Ḥurriyya.ii; Iṣlāḥ.iii; Ittiḥād we Teraḳḳī Djemʿiyyeti; Madjlis.4.A.i; Madjlis al-Shūrā; Tanẓīmāt
and → TURKEY.OTTOMAN PERIOD
mysticism → MYSTICISM.MYSTICS.TURKISH

reform of **Tanẓīmāt**; Yeñi ʿO<u>th</u>mānlı̊lar

P

PAKISTAN <u>D</u>jinā<u>h</u>; Dustūr.xiv; Ḥizb.vi; Ḥukūma.v; Ma<u>d</u>jlis.4.C; al-Marʾa.5; **Pākistān**; Urdū.1; Ziyāʾ al-Ḥaḳḳ; [in Suppl.] <u>D</u>jarīda.vii
see also Ahl-i Ḥadī<u>th</u>; Dār al-ʿUlūm.c; <u>D</u>jamʿiyya.v; <u>D</u>jūnāgaŕh; Hind.ii and iv; Ka<u>sh</u>mīr.ii; Ḳawmiyya.vi; <u>Kh</u>aybar; Muhā<u>d</u>jir.3; Pa<u>sh</u>tūnistān; Sind.2; *and* → INDIA
architecture → ARCHITECTURE.REGIONS
education <u>D</u>jāmiʿa
language Urdū.1
see also Pākistān; *and* → LANGUAGE.INDO-EUROPEAN.INDO-IRANIAN.INDIAN
literature Urdū.2
and → *the subsection Urdu under* LITERATURE.POETRY *and* PROSE
physical geography
see also Pākistān
mountains Sulaymān
waters Kurram; Mihrān; <u>Zh</u>ōb
population Afrīdī; Dāwūdpōtrās; Mahsūd; Mohmand; Mullagorī; Wazīrīs; Yūsufzay; [in Suppl.] Demography.VII; Gurčānī
see also <u>D</u>jirga
statesmen <u>D</u>jinā<u>h</u>; Liyāḳat ʿAlī <u>Kh</u>ān; Ziyāʾ al-Ḥaḳḳ
see also Mawdūdī
toponyms
ancient Čīnīōt; Daybul; Ḳandābīl; <u>Kh</u>ayrābād.ii; Ṭūrān
present-day
districts Chitral; Ḥāfiẓābād; Hazāra; <u>Kh</u>ārān; <u>Kh</u>ayrpūr; Kilāt.2; Kōhāt; Kwaťťa; Mastū<u>d</u>j; Sībī
regions Balūčistān; Dardistān; Dēra<u>d</u>jāt; Dīr; <u>D</u>jahlāwān; Kaččhī; Las Bēla; Makrān; Pan<u>d</u>jāb; Sind; Swāt; Wazīrīs
towns Amarkot; Bā<u>d</u>jawr; Bahāwalpūr; Bakkār; Bannū; Bhakkar; Gū<u>d</u>jrāńwāla; Gu<u>d</u>jrāt; Ḥasan Abdāl; Ḥaydarābād; Islāmābād; Karāčī; Kilāt.1; Ḳuṣdār; Kwaťťa; Lāhawr; Mastū<u>d</u>j; Pe<u>sh</u>āwar; Rāwalpindi; <u>Sh</u>ikārpūr.1; Sībī; Siyālkūt; Uččh; <u>Zh</u>ōb; [in Suppl.] Gilgit; Gwādar

PALESTINE/ISRAEL <u>D</u>jarīda.i.A; **Filasṭīn**; Ḥizb.i; Ma<u>d</u>jlis.4.A.xxiii; Maḥkama.4.v; Mandates
see also <u>D</u>jarrā<u>h</u>ids; Ḳays ʿAylān; al-<u>Kh</u>ālidī; al-Sāmira; <u>Sh</u>āhīn, Āl; Ya<u>sh</u>ruṭiyya; [in Suppl.] Demography.III; *and* → CRUSADE(R)S

architecture Ḳubbat al-Ṣakhra; al-Ḳuds; al-Masdjid al-Aḳṣā
see also Kawkab al-Hawāʾ
belletrists Ṣāyigh, Tawfīḳ
historians of Mudjīr al-Dīn al-ʿUlaymī
Ottoman period Ẓāhir al-ʿUmar al-Zaydānī
physical geography
deserts al-Naḳb; Sīnāʾ
see also al-Tīh
mountains/hills al-Ṭūr.2, 3 and 4
waters Baḥr Lūṭ; al-Ḥūla; Nahr Abī Fuṭrus; al-Urdunn.1; Yarmūk.1
toponyms
ancient Arsūf; ʿAthlīth; ʿAyn Djālūt; Bayt Djibrīn; al-Dārūm; Irbid.II; Sabasṭiyya.1; Subayta
present-day
regions al-Ghawr.1; Mardj Banī ʿĀmir; al-Naḳb
towns ʿAkkā; ʿAmwās; ʿĀsḳalān; Baysān; Bayt Laḥm; Bīr al-Sabʿ; Ghazza; Ḥayfā; Ḥiṭṭīn; al-Khalīl; al-Ḳuds; Ladjdjūn; Ludd; Nābulus; al-Nāṣira; Rafaḥ; al-Ramla; Rīḥā.1; Ṣafad; Ṭabariyya; Ṭulkarm; Yāfā
see also Ḳayṣariyya; Ṣihyawn
under British mandate Filasṭīn.2; Muḥammad ʿIzzat Darwaza; [in Suppl.] Amīn al-Ḥusaynī
see also Mandates

PANARABISM Ḳawmiyya; **Pan-Arabism**; **ʿUrūba**; [in Suppl.] al-Djāmiʿa al-ʿArabiyya
see also Waṭaniyya
partisans of al-Kawākibī; Nūrī al-Saʿīd; Rashīd Riḍā; al-Zahrāwī, ʿAbd al-Ḥamīd; [in Suppl.] ʿAbd al-Nāṣir
see also al-Kāẓimī, ʿAbd al-Muḥsin

PANISLAMISM Ḳawmiyya; **Pan-Islamism**; **al-Rābiṭa al-Islāmiyya**
see also Dustūr.xviii; Iṣlāḥ.ii; Khilāfa; Muʾtamar; Taḳrīb
partisans of ʿAbd al-Ḥamīd II; Djamāl al-Dīn al-Afghānī; Fiṭrat; Gasprali (Gasprinski), Ismāʿīl; Ḥālī; Kūčak Khān Djangalī; Māʾ al-ʿAynayn al-Ḳalḳamī; Meḥmed ʿĀkif; Rashīd Riḍā; Ṣafar; [in Suppl.] Andjuman-i Khuddām-i Kaʿba; al-Bakrī
see also Djadīd

PANTURKISM Ḳawmiyya.iv; **Pan-Turkism**
partisans of Gasprali (Gasprinski), Ismāʿīl; Gökalp, Ziya; Rịḍā Nūr; Suʿāwī, ʿAlī; Yūsuf Aḳčura
see also Türk Odjaghi̊

PAPYROLOGY Ḳirṭās; Papyrus
see also Diplomatic.i.15; *and* → DOCUMENTS

PARADISE al-ʿAs͟hara al-Mubas͟hs͟hara; Dār al-Salām; **D̲janna**; Ḥūr; Kawt͟har; Riḍwān; Salsabīl; Tasnīm.1
see also al-Aʿrāf

PAYMENTS Ad̲jr.2; ʿAṭāʾ; D̲jāmakiyya; Ḥawāla; Inʿām; Māl al-Bayʿa; Maʿūna; Rizḳ.3; Ṣila.3; Soyūrg͟hāl; Ṣurra; ʿUlūfe
see also Waẓīfa.1
bribery Marāfiḳ; **Ras͟hwa**

PERFUME Bān; Ḥinnāʾ; Kāfūr; Misk
see also al-ʿAṭṭār; Maʿdin.4; ʿŪd.I.1

PERSIA → IRAN

PHARMACOLOGY Adwiya; Aḳrābād͟hīn; **al-Ṣaydana**; Ṭibb
see also Diyusḳuridīs; D̲jālīnūs; Nabāt; *and* → BOTANY; DRUGS; MEDICINE
pharmacologists Ibn al-Bayṭār; Ibn Samad̲jūn; Ibn al-Tilmīd͟h; Ibn Wāfid; al-Kōhēn al-ʿAṭṭār; Sābūr b. Sahl; [in Suppl.] al-G͟hāfiḳī; Ibn Biklāris͟h; Ibn al-Rūmiyya
see also al-ʿAs͟hs͟hāb; al-ʿAṭṭār; al-Bīrūnī; al-Suwaydī; Yaḥyā b. al-Biṭrīḳ

PHILATELY **Posta**
and → TRANSPORT.POSTAL SERVICE

PHILOSOPHY Falāsifa; **Falsafa**; Ḥikma; Mā baʿd al-Ṭabīʿa; Manṭiḳ; Naẓar
see also ʿĀlam.1; Allāh.iii.2; al-Maḳūlāt; Muk͟htaṣar; S͟harḥ.IV
logic **Manṭiḳ**
terms Āla.iii; ʿAraḍ; Dalīl; Faṣl; Fiʿl; Ḥadd; Ḥaḳīḳa.2; Ḥud̲jd̲ja; Ḥukm.I; Huwa huwa.A; Muḳaddam; Natīd̲ja; S͟harṭ.2; Taʿrīf.1
see also Ḳaṭʿ; al-Sūfisṭāʾiyyūn
philosophers **Falāsifa**
Christian Ibn al-Ṭayyib; Ibn Zurʿa; Mattā b. Yūnus; Yaḥyā b. ʿAdī; Yaḥyā al-Naḥwī
Greek Aflāṭūn; Anbaduḳlīs; Arisṭūṭālīs; Balīnūs; Baṭlamiyūs; Buruḳlus; D̲jālīnūs; Fīt͟hāg͟hūras; Furfūriyūs; al-Iskandar al-Afrūdīsī; al-Sūfisṭāʾiyyūn; Suḳrāṭ; T͟hamisṭiyus
see also Ḥunayn b. Isḥāḳ al-ʿIbādī; Īsāg͟hūd̲jī; Isḥāḳ b. Ḥunayn; Lawn; al-Maḳūlāt; Mattā b. Yūnus; Nīḳūlāʾūs; al-S͟hayk͟h al-Yūnānī; Usṭāt͟h; Ut͟hūlūd̲jiyā; Yaḥyā b. al-Biṭrīḳ; Yaḥyā al-Naḥwī; Yūnān

Islamic

biographers of al-Shahrazūrī, Shams al-Dīn

9th century Abu 'l-Hudhayl al-ʿAllāf; al-Kindī, Abū Yūsuf; al-Sarakhsī, Abu 'l-ʿAbbās

see also Dahriyya; Falāsifa; Lawn

10th century Abū Sulaymān al-Manṭiḳī; al-Fārābī; Ibn Masarrā; al-Mawṣilī; al-Rāzī, Abū Bakr; [in Suppl.] al-ʿĀmirī

11th century Abū Ḥayyān al-Tawḥīdī; Bahmanyār; Ibn Ḥazm; Ibn Sīnā; Miskawayh

12th century Abu 'l-Barakāt; al-Baṭalyawsī; Ibn Bādjdja; Ibn Rushd; Ibn Ṭufayl; al-Suhrawardī, Shihāb al-Dīn Yaḥyā; ʿUmar Khayyām

see also al-Ghazālī; Ḥayy b. Yaḳẓān; Ishrāḳiyyūn; al-Shahrastānī, Abu 'l-Fatḥ

13th century al-Abharī; Ibn Sabʿīn; al-Kātibī;; Ṣadr al-Dīn al-Ḳūnawī; al-Shahrazūrī, Shams al-Dīn; al-Ṭūsī, Naṣīr al-Dīn

see also Fakhr al-Dīn al-Rāzī

14th century Djamāl al-Dīn Aḳsarayī

16th century al-Maybudī.2

17th century al-Dāmād; al-Fārūḳī, Mullā; Lāhīdjī.2; [in Suppl.] Findiriskī

19th century Sabzawārī; [in Suppl.] Abu 'l-Ḥasan Djilwa

Jewish Ibn Gabirol; Ibn Kammūna; Isḥāḳ b. Sulaymān al-Isrāʾīlī; Judaeo-Arabic.iii; Saʿadyā Ben Yōsēf

see also Abu 'l-Barakāt

terms Abad; ʿAdam; ʿAḳl; ʿAmal.1 and 2; Anniyya; Awwal; Basīṭ wa-Murakkab; Dhāt; Dhawḳ; Ḍidd; Djawhar; Djins; Djism; Djuzʾ; Fard.g; Ḥadd; Ḥaraka wa-Sukūn.I.1; Hayʾa; Ḥayāt; Hayūlā; Ḥiss; Ḥudūth al-ʿĀlam; Ḥulūl; Huwiyya; Ibdāʿ; Idrāk; Iḥdāth; Ikhtiyār; ʿIlla.ii; ʿInāya; Inṣāf; ʿIshḳ; Ishrāḳ; al-Ḳaḍāʾ wa 'l-Ḳadar.A.3; Kawn wa-Fasād; Ḳidam; Ḳuwwa.4, 6 and 7; Maʿād; Māhiyya; Maḥsūsāt; Malaka; Maʿnā.2; Nafs; Nihāya; Nūr.2; Saʿāda; Sabab.1; Shakhṣ; Shakk.2; Shayʾ; Shubha; Ṭafra; Takhyīl.2; Tawallud; Ṭīna; ʿUnṣur; Waḥda.2; Wahm; Wudjūd.1; al-Ẓāhir wa 'l-Bāṭin; Zamān.1

see also Athar.3; ʿAyn; Dahriyya; Insān; Ḳaṭʿ; Ḳiyāma; Siyāsa.2; Takwīn; *and* → PHILOSOPHY.LOGIC.TERMS

PHYSIOGNOMY Firāsa; Ḳiyāfa; Shāma; [in Suppl.] Aflīmūn

and → ANATOMY

PILGRIMAGE ʿArafa; al-Djamra; **Ḥadjdj**; Hady; Iḥrām; Kaʿba; Minā; Muṭawwif; al-Muzdalifa; Radjm; al-Ṣafā.1; Saʿy; Shiʿār.1; Talbiya; Tarwiya; Tashrīḳ; Ṭawāf; **ʿUmra**; al-Wuḳūf; Zamzam; **Ziyāra**

see also Amīr al-Ḥādjdj; Ḥidjāz Railway; Kārwān; Kāẓimayn; Makka; Thabīr; al-Thaʿlabiyya; [in Suppl.] ʿAtabāt; Darb Zubayda; Fayd; *and* → ISLAM
pilgrimage literature Ziyāra.1.d and e

PIRACY **Ḳurṣān**
see also al-ʿAnnāba; Djarba; Ḥusayn Pasha (Küčük); Lewend
corsairs ʿArūdj; Ḥasan Baba; Ḥusayn Pasha, Mezzomorto; Kemāl Reʾīs; Khayr al-Dīn Pasha; Selmān Reʾīs; Ṭorghud Reʾīs; ʿUlūdj ʿAlī; Umur Pasha

PLAGUE ʿAmwās; **Wabāʾ**
see also Ibn Khaldūn, Walī al-Dīn
treatises on Ibn Khātima; Ibn Riḍwān; al-Masīḥī

POLAND **Leh**
see also Islām Girāy; Ḳamāniča; Köprülü; Lipḳa; Muslimūn.1.A.1; *and* → OTTOMAN EMPIRE

POLITICS Baladiyya; Dawla; Djumhūriyya; Dustūr; Ḥimāya.2; Ḥizb; Ḥukūma; Ḥurriyya.ii; Istiḳlāl; Ḳawmiyya; Madjlis; Makhzan; Mandates; Mashyakha; Medeniyyet; Musāwāt; Muwāṭin; Nāʾib.2; Shūrā.3; Siyāsa; Takhṭīṭ al-Ḥudūd; Tawāzun al-Suluṭāt; Thawra; Waṭaniyya; Ẓulm.2; [in Suppl.] Āzādī; al-Djāmiʿa al-ʿArabiyya
see also Ahl al-Ḥall wa ʾl-ʿAḳd; Imtiyāzāt; Mashwara; Salṭana; *and* → ADMINISTRATION; DIPLOMACY; OTTOMAN EMPIRE
doctrines Ḥizb.i; Ishtirākiyya; Mārk(i)siyya; Shuyūʿiyya; Taʾmīm; [in Suppl.] Hidjra
see also Musāwāt; Muslimūn.4; Radjʿiyya; Tawāzun al-Suluṭāt; *and* → PANARABISM; PANISLAMISM; PANTURKISM
movements Djadīd; Djangalī; Istiḳlāl; Ittiḥād we Teraḳḳī Djemʿiyyeti; Khāksār; Khilāfa; al-Rābiṭa al-Islāmiyya
see also Fiṭrat; Ḥamza Beg; Ḥizb; Ḥurriyya.ii; Kūčak Khān Djangalī; Taṭarruf; Thawra; ʿUrābī Pasha; [in Suppl.] ʿAbd al-Bārī; *and* → PANARABISM; PANISLAMISM; PANTURKISM; REFORM.POLITICO-RELIGIOUS
parties Demokrat Parti; **Ḥizb**; Ḥürriyet we Iʾtilāf Fïrḳasï; Partai Islam se Malaysia (Pas); Shuyūʿiyya.1.2; Teraḳḳī-perver Djumhūriyyet Fïrḳasï; Wafd
see also Andjuman; Djamʿiyya; (Tunalï) Ḥilmī; Ḥizb.i; Ishtirākiyya; Khīyābānī, Shaykh Muḥammad; Leff; Luṭfī al-Sayyid; Mārk(i)siyya; Muṣṭafā Kāmil Pasha; Sarekat Islam; [in Suppl.] ʿAbd al-Nāṣir; *and* → COMMUNISM; REFORM
reform → REFORM
terms Shaʿb.2; Thawra; Zaʿīm; Ẓulm.2

PORTUGAL   **Burtuḳāl**; G̲h̲arb al-Andalus
  see also Ḥabes̲h̲; *and* → ANDALUSIA; SPAIN
toponyms   Bād̲j̲a; Ḳulumriya; al-Maʿdin; Mīrtula; S̲h̲antamariyyat al-G̲h̲arb;
    S̲h̲antarīn; S̲h̲ilb; S̲h̲intara; Uks̲h̲ūnuba; (al-)Us̲h̲būna; Yābura

PRAYER   Ad̲h̲ān; D̲h̲ikr; D̲j̲umʿa; **Duʿāʾ**; Fātiḥa; Iḳāma; K̲h̲aṭīb; K̲h̲uṭba; Ḳibla;
    Ḳunūt; Ḳuʿūd; Maḥyā; Masd̲j̲id; Miḥrāb; Mīḳāt; Muṣallā; Rakʿa; Rātib; **Ṣalāt**;
    Ṣalāt al-K̲h̲awf; Subḥa; Sutra; Tahad̲j̲d̲j̲ud; Tarāwīḥ; Waẓīfa.2; Wird; Witr
    see also Amīn; Dikka; G̲h̲āʾib; Gulbāng; Istiʾnāf; Maḳām Ibrāhīm; al-Masḥ ʿalā
    ʾl-K̲h̲uffayn; Namāzgāh; Takbīr; Tas̲h̲ahhud; *and* → ABLUTION; ARCHITEC-
    TURE.MOSQUES; ISLAM
bowing   Sad̲j̲da
carpet   Sad̲j̲d̲j̲āda
collections of
    shiite   Zayn al-ʿĀbidīn
of petition   Istisḳāʾ; Munās̲h̲ada

PRE-ISLAM   al-ʿArab.i; (D̲j̲azīrat) al-ʿArab.vii; Armīniya.II.1; Badw.III; D̲j̲āhi-
    liyya; G̲h̲assān; Kinda.1 and Appendix; Lak̲h̲mids; Liḥyān; Maʿīn; Makka.1;
    Nabaṭ; Rūm
    see also Ḥayawān.2; Ilāh; al-Kalbī.II; Lībiyā.2; *and* → ASSYRIA; BYZANTINE
    EMPIRE; IDOLATRY; MILITARY.BATTLES; ZOROASTRIANS
customs/institutions   ʿAtīra; Baliyya; G̲h̲idāʾ.i and ii; Ḥad̲j̲d̲j̲.i; Ḥilf; Ḥimā;
    Ḥimāya; Istisḳāʾ; Kāhin; K̲h̲afāra; Mawlā; Nuṣub; Radāʿ.2; Sādin; Ṭawāf;
    ʿUkāẓ; ʿUmra; ʿUrs; Waʾd al-Banāt
    see also Fayʾ; G̲h̲anīma; Īlāf; Karkūr; Nār; Ṣadā; S̲h̲ayba; Taḥannuth; T̲h̲abīr
gods   Dhu ʾl-K̲h̲alaṣa; Dhu ʾl-S̲h̲arā; Hubal; Isāf wa-Nāʾila; Ḳaws Ḳuzaḥ; al-Lāt;
    Manāf; Manāt; Nasr; S̲h̲ams.1; S̲h̲ayʿ al-Ḳawm; Suʿayr; al-Sud̲j̲d̲j̲a; Suwāʿ;
    Ṭāg̲h̲ūt.1; Tañrī; al-Uḳayṣir; al-ʿUzzā
    see also Ag̲h̲āt̲h̲ūd̲h̲īmūn; ʿAmr b. Luḥayy; D̲j̲āhiliyya; Hirmis; Hurmuz;
    Ilāh; Kaʿba.V; al-Ḳamar.II; Mawḳif.3; Rabb; Ṣanam; S̲h̲ayṭān; Zūn
in Arabian peninsula   Abraha; (D̲j̲azīrat) al-ʿArab.i and vi; Bakr b. Wāʾil;
    D̲j̲ad̲h̲īma al-Abras̲h̲; G̲h̲umdān; Ḥabas̲h̲at; Ḥād̲j̲ib b. Zurāra; Ḥaḍramawt;
    Hās̲h̲im b. ʿAbd Manāf; Hind bint al-K̲h̲uss; Ḥums; Ḳatabān; Ḳayl; Ḳuṣayy;
    Ḳuss b. Sāʿida; Mārib; Nuṣub; Sabaʾ; Sad̲j̲ʿ.1; Salḥīn; Taʾrīk̲h̲.I.1.iv; T̲h̲ād̲j̲;
    Tubbaʿ; ʿUkāẓ Yahūd.1; [in Suppl.] Ḥaḍramawt.i
    see also Badw.III; Dār al-Nadwa; Ḥanīf.4; Kinda.Appendix; T̲h̲abīr; Zabūr;
    and → IDOLATRY; LITERATURE.POETRY.ARABIC; MILITARY.BATTLES; OMAN.
    TOPONYMS; SAUDIA ARABIA.TOPONYMS; TRIBES.ARABIAN PENINSULA;
    YEMEN.TOPONYMS
in Egypt   → EGYPT.BEFORE ISLAM
in Fertile Crescent   K̲h̲ursābād; Manbid̲j̲; Maysān; Nabaṭ; al-Zabbāʾ; [in

Suppl.] Athūr
see also Biṭrīḳ.I; Ḥarrān; Shahāridja; Shahrazūr; Tadmur; *and* → Military.battles
Ghassānids Djabala b. al-Ayham; Djilliḳ; **Ghassān**; al-Ḥārith b. Djabala; [in Suppl.] Djabala b. al-Ḥārith
Lakhmids ʿAmr b. ʿAdī; ʿAmr b. Hind; al-Ḥīra; **Lakhmids**; al-Mundhir IV; al-Nuʿmān (III) b. al-Mundhir
in Iran → Iran.before islam
in Turkey Tañri̊; Turks.I.1

Predestination Adjal; Allāh.II.B; Iḍṭirār; Ikhtiyār; Istiṭāʿa; **al-Ḳaḍāʾ wa ʾl-Ḳadar**; Ḳadariyya; Kasb; Ḳisma
see also ʿAbd al-Razzāḳ al-Ḳāshānī; Badāʾ; Dahr; Duʿāʾ.II.b; Ḳaḍāʾ; Shaḳāwa
advocates of Djabriyya; Djahmiyya; al-Karābīsī.2 ; Sulaymān b. Djarīr al-Raḳḳī; Zayd b. ʿAlī b. al-Ḥusayn
opponents of Ghaylān b. Muslim; **Ḳadariyya**; Ḳatāda b. Diʿāma; Maʿbad al-Djuhanī

Press **Djarīda**; Maḳāla; **Maṭbaʿa**; **Ṣiḥāfa**
Arabic ʿArabiyya.B.V.a; Baghdād (906b); Būlāḳ; **Djarīda**.i; Ḳiṣṣa.2; Maḳāla.1; al-Manār; **Maṭbaʿa**.1; al-Rāʾid al-Tūnusī; **Ṣiḥāfa**
see also Nahḍa; Zākhir
journalism Abū Naḍḍāra; al-Bārūnī; Djabrān Khalīl Djabrān; Djamāl al-Dīn al-Afghānī; Djamīl; Fāris al-Shidyāḳ; Ibn Bādīs; Isḥāḳ, Adīb; al-Kawākibī; al-Khaḍir; Khalīl Ghānim; Khalīl Muṭrān; Kurd ʿAlī; Luṭfī al-Sayyid; al-Maʿlūf; Mandūr; al-Manūfī.7; al-Māzinī; Muṣṭafā ʿAbd al-Rāziḳ; al-Muwayliḥī; al-Nadīm, ʿAbd Allāh; Nadjīb al-Ḥaddād; Nimr; Rashīd Riḍā; Ṣafar; Saʿīd Abū Bakr; Salāma Mūsā; Salīm al-Naḳḳāsh; Ṣarrūf; Shāʾūl; Shaykhū, Luwīs; Shīnā; Shumayyil, Shiblī; Ṭāhā Ḥusayn; Yaḥyā Ḥaḳḳī; al-Yāzidjī.2 and 3; Yūsuf, ʿAlī; al-Zahrāwī, ʿAbd al-Ḥamīd; Zaydān, Djurdjī; [in Suppl.] Abū Shādī; al-Bustānī
see also al-Mahdjar
Indian **Maṭbaʿa**.4; [in Suppl.] **Djarīda**.vii
journalism Muḥammad ʿAlī; Ruswā; Shabbīr Ḥasan Khān Djosh; [in Suppl.] Āzād; Ḥasrat Mohānī
see also Nadwat al-ʿUlamāʾ
Persian **Djarīda**.ii; Maḳāla; **Maṭbaʿa**.3
journalism Furūghī.3; Lāhūtī; Malkom Khān; Rashīd Yāsimī; Yaghmāʾī; Yazdī; [in Suppl.] Amīrī
Turkish **Djarīda**.iii; Djemʿiyyet-i ʿIlmiyye-i ʿOthmāniyye; Ibrāhīm Müteferriḳa; Maḳāla; **Maṭbaʿa**.2; Meshʿale; Mīzān
see also Ādharī.ii

journalism Aḥmad Iḥsān; Aḥmad Midḥat; Djewdet; Ebüzziya Tevfik; Gasprali (Gasprinski), Ismāʿīl; Ḥasan Fehmī; (Aḥmed) Ḥilmī; Hi̊sar; Ḥusayn Djāhid; Ileri, Djelāl Nūrī; İnal; Ḳaṣāb, Teodor; al-Kāẓimī, Meḥmed Sālim; Kemāl; Kemāl, Meḥmed Nāmi̊ḳ; Khālid Ḍiyā'; Köprülü (Meḥmed Fuad); Manāṣti̊rli̊ Meḥmed Rifʿat; Meḥmed ʿĀkif; Mīzāndji̊ Meḥmed Murād; Örik, Nahīd Ṣi̊rrī; Orkhan Seyfi; Ortač, Yūsuf Ḍiyā; Ri̊ḍā Nūr; Sāhir, Djelāl; Sāmī; Shināsī; Suʿāwī, ʿAlī; Tewfīḳ Fikret; Yūsuf Aḳčura; Żiyā Pasha; [in Suppl.] Aghaoghlu; Atay; Čaylaḳ Tewfīḳ; Eshref
see also Badrkhānī; Fedjr-i Ātī; Khalīl Ghānim; Saʿīd Efendi

PROFESSIONS al-ʿAṭṭār; Baḳḳāl; Bayṭār; Dallāl; Djānbāz; Djarrāḥ; Ḥammāl; Kannās; Kātib; Ḳayn; Ḳayna; Khayyāṭ; Mukārī; Munādī; Munadjdjim; al-Nassādj; Ṣabbāgh; Ṣā'igh; Saḳḳā'; Sāsān; Shaʿbadha; Shāʿir; Shammāʿ; Ṭabbākh; Ṭabbāl; Tādjir; Ṭaḥḥān; Tardjumān; Ṭarrār; Thallādj; Ṭulumbadji̊; ʿUlamā'; Warrāḳ; [in Suppl.] Dabbāgh; Djammāl; Djazzār; Faṣṣād; Ghassāl; Ḥā'ik; Ḥallāḳ
see also Asad Allāh Iṣfahānī; Aywaz.1; Khādim; Shāwiya; Ṣinf; Ustādh; *and* → LAW.OFFICES; MILITARY.OFFICES

craftsmanship **Ṣināʿa**

craftsmen and tradesmen

artisans Ṣabbāgh; Ṣā'igh; Warrāḳ; [in Suppl.] Ḥā'ik

labourers Ḥammāl; Kannās; Ḳayn; Khayyāṭ; Shammāʿ; Ṭaḥḥān; [in Suppl.] Dabbāgh; Djazzār; Ghassāl; Ḥallāḳ

merchants al-ʿAṭṭār; Baḳḳāl; Mukārī; **Tādjir**; Tammām; Thallādj; [in Suppl.] Djammāl
see also Tidjāra; *and* → FINANCE.COMMERCE.FUNCTIONS

performers Djānbāz; Ḳayna; Shāʿir.1.E; Ṭabbāl
see also al-Sīm

PROPERTY **Māl**; Milk; Taʿāwun; Waḳf; Zamīndār; [in Suppl.] ʿAḳār
see also Munāṣafa; Shufʿa; Soyūrghāl; Tiyūl; *and* → TAXATION.TAXES *and* TITHE-LANDS

PROPHETHOOD **Nubuwwa**; Rasūl; Waḥy
and → MUḤAMMAD, THE PROPHET

prophets Ādam; Alīsaʿ; Ayyūb; Hārūn b. ʿImrān; Ḥizḳīl; Hūd; Ibrāhīm; Idrīs; Ilyās; Irmiyā; ʿĪsā; Isḥāḳ; Ismāʿīl; Lūṭ; Muḥammad; Mūsā; Nūḥ; Ṣāliḥ; Shamwīl; Shaʿyā; Shīth; Shuʿayb; Yaḥyā b. Zakariyyā'; Yaʿḳūb; Yūnus; Yūshaʿ b. Nūn; Yūsuf; Zakariyyā'
see also Fatra; Ḥanẓala b. Ṣafwān; ʿIṣma; Khālid b. Sinān; Luḳmān; Mubtada'.2; Zayd b. ʿAmr; *and* → MUḤAMMAD, THE PROPHET

false prophets Ḥā-Mīm; Musaylima; Sadjāḥ; Ṭulayḥa

lives of al-Kisāʾī; **Ḳiṣaṣ al-Anbiyāʾ**; al-Thaʿlabī, Aḥmad b. Muḥammad; ʿUmāra b. Wathīma; Wahb b. Munabbih; Wathīma b. Mūsā

PROVERBS **Mathal**; Tamthīl.2
see also Iyās b. Muʿāwiya; Nār; *and* → ANIMALS.AND PROVERBS; LITERATURE. PROVERBS IN
collections of Abū ʿUbayd al-Ḳāsim b. Sallām; al-ʿAskarī.ii; Ḥamza al-Iṣfahānī; al-Maydānī; Rashīd al-Dīn (Waṭwāṭ); Shināsī; al-Thaʿālibī, Abū Manṣūr ʿAbd al-Malik; al-Yūsī; al-Zamakhsharī

PUNISHMENT **ʿAdhāb**; **ʿUḳūba**
in law Diya; Djazāʾ.ii; Ḥadd; Ḳatl.ii; Ḳiṣāṣ; Ṣalb; Taʿzīr; **ʿUḳūba**
see also ʿAbd.3.i; Kaffāra; Siyāsa.1; *and* → LAW.PENAL LAW
in theology ʿAdhāb; ʿAdhāb al-Ḳabr; Djazāʾ; Munkar wa-Nakīr
see also Ḳiyāma; Maskh
physical Falaḳa; Ṣalb
see also Radjm

Q

QATAR **Ḳaṭar**; Madjlis.4.A.xi; Maḥkama.4.ix
toponyms al-Dawḥa; Hādjir; al-Zubāra
see also al-ʿUdayd

QURʾĀN → KORAN

R

RAIDS Baranta; Ghanīma; **Ghazw**
and → BEDOUINS; MILITARY.EXPEDITIONS

RECREATION Cinema; Ḳaragöz; Khayāl al-Ẓill; Masraḥ; Orta Oyunu
games Djerīd; Kharbga; Ḳimār; **Laʿib**; al-Maysir; Mukhāradja; Nard; Shaṭrandj
see also Ishāra; Kurds.iv.C.5; Maydān; *and* → ANIMALS.SPORT
sports Čawgān; Pahlawān; Zūrkhāna

REFORM Djamʿiyya; **Iṣlāḥ**
see also Baladiyya; Ḥukūma; al-Manār; *and* → WOMEN.EMANCIPATION
educational Aḥmad Djewdet Pasha; Aḥmad Khān; al-Azhar.IV; Ḥabīb Allāh Khān; Maʿārif; Münīf Pasha; Nadwat al-ʿUlamāʾ; Yücel, Ḥasan ʿAlī; [in Suppl.] al-ʿAdawī
see also al-Marṣafī

financial Muḥaṣṣil
land Taʿāwun
legal Medjelle; Mīrāth.2; Nikāḥ.II; Ṭalāḳ.II; Talfīḳ; Tashrīʿ; Waḳf.II.5
see also Djazāʾ.ii; Imtiyāzāt.iv; Maḥkama
reformers Abu 'l-Suʿūd; Aḥmad Djewdet Pasha; Küčük Saʿīd Pasha; al-Sanhūrī, ʿAbd al-Razzāḳ
see also Ileri, Djelāl Nūrī; Khayr al-Dīn Pasha
military Niẓām-i̊ Djedīd
numismatic → NUMISMATICS
Ottoman Tanẓīmāt
politico-religious Atatürk; Djamāl al-Dīn al-Afghānī; Ileri, Djelāl Nūrī; Ibn Bādīs; (al-)Ibrāhīmī; Ismāʿīl Ṣidḳī; Ḳāsim Amīn; Khayr al-Dīn Pasha; Midḥat Pasha; Muḥammad ʿAbduh; Muḥammad Bayram al-Khāmis; Nurculuk; Padri; Rashīd Riḍā; Shaltūt, Maḥmūd; al-Subkiyyūn; Ṭāhā, Maḥmūd Muḥammad; Taḳī al-Dīn al-Nabhānī; [in Suppl.] ʿAbd al-Nāṣir
see also Baladiyya; Bast; Djamʿiyya; Dustūr; Ḥarbiye; Ibrāhīm Müteferriḳa; al-Ikhwān al-Muslimūn; Iṣlāḥ; Mappila.5.ii; Salafiyya; Shaʿb; al-Shawkānī; Tadjdīd; Taḳrīb; [in Suppl.] Abu 'l-ʿAzāʾim; *and* → POLITICS
militant al-Bannāʾ; Fidāʾiyyān-i Islām; Ḥamāliyya; Ibn Bādīs; al-Ikhwān al-Muslimūn; Mawdūdī; Sayyid Ḳuṭb; al-Takfīr wa 'l-Hidjra; Taṭarruf; **Uṣūliyya**.2; ʿUthmān b. Fūdī
see also Ibn al-Muwaḳḳit; Mudjāhid; [in Suppl.] al-Djanbīhī

RELIGION ʿAḳīda; **Dīn**; al-Milal wa'l-Niḥal; Milla; Millet.1
see also Ḥanīf; Tawḥīd; Umma; *and* → BAHAIS; BUDDHISM; CHRISTIANITY; DRUZES; ISLAM; JUDAISM; ZOROASTRIANS
dualism Dayṣāniyya; Mānī; Mazdak; **Thanawiyya**; Zindīḳ
see also Īrān.vi; Kumūn; al-Naẓẓām
pantheism ʿAmr b. Luḥayy; Djāhiliyya; Hindū; Kaʿba.V
see also Ḥarīriyya; Ḥadjdj.i; Ibn al-ʿArabī; Ibn al-ʿArīf; Kāfiristān; Kamāl Khudjandī; *and* → IDOLATRY; PRE-ISLAM.GODS
popular → ISLAM.POPULAR BELIEFS
religious communities Bābīs; Bahāʾīs; Djayn; Durūz; Hindū; Islām; Madjūs; Naṣārā; Ṣābiʾ; Ṣābiʾa; al-Sāmira; Sikhs; Sumaniyya; Yahūd; Yazīdī; Zindīḳ
see also al-Barāmika.1; Ibāḥatiya; Kitāb al-Djilwa; al-Milal wa'l-Niḥal; Millet; Nānak; al-Shahrastānī, Abu 'l-Fatḥ; *and* → BAHAIS; BUDDHISM; CHRISTIANITY; DRUZES; ISLAM; JUDAISM; SECTS; ZOROASTRIANS

RHETORIC Badīʿ; Balāgha; Bayān; Faṣāḥa; Ḥaḳīḳa.1; Ibtidāʾ; Idjāza; Iḳtibās; Intihāʾ; Istiʿāra; Kināya; al-Maʿānī wa 'l-Bayān; Madjāz; Mubālagha; Muḳābala.3; Muwāraba; Muzāwadja; Muzdawidj; Ramz.1; Taʿadjdjub; Tadjnīs; Taḍmīn; Takhyīl.4; Tamthīl.2; Tarṣīʿ; Tashbīh; Tawriya; Ṭibāḳ

see also Is<u>h</u>āra
treatises on al-ʿAskarī.ii; Ḥāzim; Ibn al-Muʿtazz; al-Ḳazwīnī (<u>Kh</u>aṭīb Dimas<u>h</u>ḳ); al-Rādūyānī; Ra<u>sh</u>īd al-Dīn Waṭwāṭ; al-Sakkākī; al-Si<u>dj</u>ilmāsī; Yaḥyā b. Ḥamza al-ʿAlawī; [in Suppl.] al-<u>Dj</u>ur<u>dj</u>ānī; Ibn Wahb

RHYME **Ḳāfiya**; Luzūm mā lā yalzam
and → LITERATURE.POETRY; METRICS

RITUALS ʿAḳīḳa; ʿAnṣāra; ʿĀ<u>sh</u>ūrāʾ; <u>Kh</u>itān; Rawḍa-<u>kh</u>ʷānī
see also Bakkāʾ; Ḥammām; al-Ma<u>gh</u>rib.VI; Zār; [in Suppl.] Dam; *and* → CUSTOMS; ISLAM.FIVE PILLARS OF ISLAM *and* POPULAR BELIEFS

RIVERS **Nahr**
see also Maʾṣir; *and* → NAVIGATION
waters al-ʿAḍaym; ʿAfrīn; Alin<u>dj</u>aḳ; al-ʿAlḳamī; Amū Daryā; al-ʿĀṣī; Atbara; Atrek; Baḥr al-<u>Gh</u>azāl.1; Baradā; Ča<u>gh</u>ān-rūd; Congo; Čoruh; Ču; Darʿa; Dawʿan; Dehās; Di<u>dj</u>la; Diyālā; <u>Dj</u>amnā; <u>Dj</u>ayḥān; al-Furāt; Gangā; Gediz Čayi̊; Göksu; al-Ḥamma; Harī Rūd; Ibruh; Ili; Isly; Itil; Kābul.1; Kar<u>kh</u>a; Kārūn; <u>Kh</u>ābūr; <u>Kh</u>al<u>kh</u>a; al-<u>Kh</u>āzir; Ḳi̊zi̊l-irmāḳ; Ḳi̊zi̊l-üzen; Ḳuban; Ḳunduz; Kur; Kurram; Lamas-ṣū; Mānd; Menderes; Merič; Mihrān; al-Mudawwar; Nahr Abī Fuṭrus; Niger; al-Nīl; Ob; Or<u>kh</u>on; Özi; al-Rass; Safīd Rūd; Sakarya; San<u>dj</u>a; Sayḥān; <u>Sh</u>aṭṭ al-ʿArab; <u>Sh</u>ebelle; Si̊r Daryā; Tā<u>dj</u>uh; Ṭarāz; Tarim; Terek; Ṭuna; Turgay; al-Urdunn.1; (al-)Wādī al-Kabīr; Wādī Yāna; Wa<u>kh</u><u>sh</u>; Wardar; Yarmūk.1; Yayi̊ḳ; Ye<u>sh</u>il İrmak; al-Zāb; Zaraf<u>sh</u>ān; Zāyanda-Rūd; <u>Zh</u>ōb; [in Suppl.] Gūmāl
see also Hind.i.j; ʿĪsā, Nahr; Urmiya.2; Zabadānī; *and* → *the section Physical Geography under individual countries*

ROMANIA Bo<u>gh</u>dān; Dobru<u>dj</u>a; Eflāḳ; Erdel; Isakča
see also Bu<u>dj</u>āḳ; Muslimūn.1.B.2
toponyms
districts Deli-Orman
islands Ada Ḳalʿe
towns Babada<u>gh</u>i̊; Bender; Bükre<u>sh</u>; Ibrail; Kösten<u>dj</u>e; Me<u>dj</u>īdiyye; Nagyvárad; Teme<u>sh</u>wār

RUSSIA → EUROPE.EASTERN EUROPE

S

SACRED PLACES Abū Ḳubays; al-Ḥaram al-<u>Sh</u>arīf; Ḥu<u>dj</u>ra; Kaʿba; Karbalāʾ;

Kāẓimayn; al-Khalīl; al-Ḳuds.II; al-Madīna; Makka; al-Muḳaṭṭam; al-Nadjaf; Ṭūbā; Zamzam

see also Ḥawṭa; Ḥimā; Ḳāsiyūn; Mawlāy Idrīs; Mudjāwir; Shāh ʿAbd al-ʿAẓīm al-Ḥasanī; Shayba; Walī; *and* → ARCHITECTURE.MONUMENTS; SAINTHOOD; *for Hindus, see* Allāhābād; Buxar; Djūnāgaṛh; Dwārkā; Ganga; Ḥasan Abdāl; Sūrat; Udjdjayn

pilgrimage to **Ziyāra**

SACRIFICES ʿAḳīḳa; ʿAtīra; Baliyya; Dhabīḥa; Fidya; Hady; Ḳurbān; Shiʿār.2 and 3

see also Ibil; ʿĪd al-Aḍhā; Kaffāra; Nadhr; [in Suppl.] Dam

SAINTHOOD Mawlid

see also ʿAbābda; Mawlā.I; Ziyāra; *and* → CHRISTIANITY; HAGIOGRAPHY; MYSTICISM

saints **Walī**

African Shaykh Ḥusayn

see also Ziyāra.9

Arabic Aḥmad b. ʿĪsā; Aḥmad al-Badawī; Nafīsa

see also Ḳunā; Ziyāra.1 and 2; *and* → MYSTICISM.MYSTICS

North African Abū Muḥammad Ṣāliḥ; Abū Yaʿazzā; ʿĀʾisha al-Mannūbiyya; al-Bādisī.1; al-Daḳḳāḳ; al-Djazūlī, Abū ʿAbd Allāh; Ḥmād u-Mūsā; Ibn ʿArūs; al-Ḳabbāb; Ḳaddūr al-ʿAlamī; al-Khaṣāṣī; Muḥriz b. Khalaf; al-Sabtī; al-Shāwī; [in Suppl.] Ḥamādisha

see also al-Maghrib.VI; Sabʿatu Ridjāl; Walī.2; Ziyāra.4; *and* → MYSTICISM.MYSTICS

Central Asian Aḥmad Yasawī; Uways al-Ḳaranī; Zangī Āta

see also Walī.5; Ziyāra.6; *and* → MYSTICISM.MYSTICS

Indian Abū ʿAlī Ḳalandar; Ashraf Djahāngīr; Badīʿ al-Dīn; Badr; Bahāʾ al-Dīn Zakariyyā; Čishtī; Farīd al-Dīn Masʿūd "Gandj-i Shakar"; Ghāzī Miyān; Gīsū Darāz; Imām Shāh; Khwādja Khiḍr; Maghribī; Makhdūm al-Mulk Manīrī; Masʿūd; Niẓām al-Dīn Awliyāʾ; Nūr Ḳuṭb al-ʿĀlam; Ratan; Shāh Muḥammad b. ʿAbd Aḥmad; [in Suppl.] Bābā Nūr al-Dīn Rishī; Gadāʾī Kambō; Gangōhī; Ḥamīd al-Dīn Ḳāḍī Nāgawrī; Ḥamīd al-Dīn Ṣūfī Nāgawrī Siwālī

see also Ḥasan Abdāl; Pāk Pāṭan; Walī.6; Ziyāra.7; *and* → MYSTICISM.MYSTICS

Indonesian Ziyāra.8

and → MYSTICISM.MYSTICS

Persian ʿAlī al-Hamadānī; Bābā-Ṭāhir

see also Ziyāra.5; *and* → MYSTICISM.MYSTICS

Southeast Asian and Chinese Walī.7 and 8

Turkish Akhī Ewrān; Emīr Sulṭān; Ḥādjdjī Bayrām Walī; Ḥakīm Ata; Ḳoyun Baba; Merkez; Ṣarï Ṣalṭūḳ Dede
see also Walī.4; Ziyāra.6; *and* → MYSTICISM.MYSTICS

terms Abdāl; Ilhām

SAUDI ARABIA (Djazīrat) al-ʿArab; Djarīda.i.A; Djāmiʿa; Dustūr.vii; al-Hidjar; al-Ikhwān; Madjlis.4.A.viii; Maḥkama.4.vii; **al-Suʿūdiyya, al-Mamlaka al-ʿArabiyya**; Wahhābiyya
see also Bā ʿAlawī; Badw; Baladiyya.2; Barakāt; Makka; [in Suppl.] Demography.III; *and* → PRE-ISLAM.IN ARABIAN PENINSULA; TRIBES.ARABIAN PENINSULA

before Islam → PRE-ISLAM.IN ARABIAN PENINSULA

dynasties Hāshimids (2x); Rashīd, Āl; Suʿūd, Āl
and → DYNASTIES.ARABIAN PENINSULA

historians of al-Azraḳī; Daḥlān; al-Fāḳihī; al-Fāsī; Ibn Fahd; Ibn Manda; Ibn al-Mudjāwir; Ibn al-Nadjdjār; al-Samhūdī
see also al-Diyārbakrī

physical geography Nadjd.1

deserts al-Aḥḳāf; al-Dahnāʾ; Nafūd; al-Rubʿ al-Khālī
see also Badw.II; Ḥarra

mountains Djabala; Ḥirāʾ; Ḥufāsh; Raḍwā; al-Sarāt; Thabīr; al-Ṭuwayḳ
see also Adjaʾ and Salmā

plains ʿArafa; al-Dibdiba; al-Ṣammān

wadis al-ʿAtk; al-Bāṭin; Bayḥān; Bayḥān al-Ḳaṣāb; Djayzān; Fāʾw; Ḥamḍ, Wādī al-; al-Rumma; al-Sahbāʾ; Sirḥān; Tabāla; Turaba.1; Wādī Ḥanīfa

waters Dawʿan

population → TRIBES.ARABIAN PENINSULA

toponyms
and → *the section Physical Geography above*

ancient Badr; al-Djār; Fadak; al-Ḥidjr; al-Ḥudaybiya; Ḳurḥ; Madyan Shuʿayb; al-Rabadha; al-Thaʿlabiyya; Wādī 'l-Ḳurā
see also Fāʾw

present-day

districts al-Aflādj; al-Djawf; al-Ḳaṣīm; al-Khardj

islands Farasān

oases al-Dirʿiyya; Dūmat al-Djandal; al-Ḥasā; al-Khurma; al-ʿUyayna

regions ʿAsīr; Bayḥān; al-Ḥāḍina; Ḥaly; al-Ḥawṭa; al-Ḥidjāz; Ḳurayyāt al-Milḥ; Nadjd; Nafūd; Raʾs (al-)Tannūra; al-Rubʿ al-Khālī; Tihāma

towns Abhā; Abḳayḳ; Abū ʿArīsh; Burayda; al-Dammām; al-Djawf; Djayzān; al-Djubayl; al-Djubayla; Djudda; Fakhkh; Ghāmid; Ḥāyil; al-Hufūf; Ḥuraymilā; Ḳarya al-Suflā; Ḳarya al-ʿUlyā; al-Ḳaṣāb; al-Ḳaṭīf; Khamīs Mushayṭ; Khaybar; al-Khubar; al-Ḳunfudha; al-

Madīna; Makka; Minā; al-Mubarraz; Nad̲j̲rān; Rābig̲h̲; al-Riyāḍ;
Tabāla; Tabūk; al-Ṭāʾif; Taymāʾ; Turaba.2 and 3; al-ʿUlā; ʿUnayza;
al-Yamāma; Yanbuʿ; (al-)Z̲ahrān; [in Suppl.] Fayd
see also (D̲j̲azīrat) al-ʿArab; al-ʿĀriḍ; Bīs̲h̲a; Ḍariyya

SCIENCE   **ʿIlm**; Maws̲ūʿa
see also Ibn Abī Uṣaybīʿa; S̲h̲umayyil, S̲h̲iblī; [in Suppl.] al-Bustānī; Ibn al-
Akfānī.3; Ibn Farīg̲h̲ūn; *and* → ALCHEMY; ASTROLOGY; ASTRONOMY; BOTANY;
MATHEMATICS; MECHANICS; MEDICINE; OPTICS; PHARMACOLOGY; ZOOLOGY

SECTS   ʿAd̲j̲ārida; Ahl-i Ḥadīt̲h̲; Ahl-i Ḥaḳḳ; Aḥmadiyya; ʿAlids; Azāriḳa; al-
Bad̲j̲alī; Baḳliyya; Bihʾāfrīd b. Farwardīn; Bohorās; Burg̲h̲ūt̲h̲iyya; D̲j̲abriyya;
D̲j̲ahmiyya; al-D̲j̲anāḥiyya; al-D̲j̲ārūdiyya; Durūz; Farāʾiḍiyya; G̲h̲urābiyya;
Ḥarīriyya; Ḥas̲h̲īs̲h̲iyya; Ḥulmāniyya; Ḥurūfiyya; al-Ibāḍiyya; Ḳarmaṭī;
Karrāmiyya; Kaysāniyya; al-K̲h̲alafiyya; K̲h̲ārid̲j̲ites; K̲h̲as̲h̲abiyya;
K̲h̲aṭṭābiyya; K̲h̲ōd̲j̲a; K̲h̲ūbmesīḥīs; K̲h̲urramiyya; Kuraybiyya; Mahdawīs;
Mansūriyya; al-Mug̲h̲īriyya; Muḥammadiyya; Muk̲h̲ammisa; Muṭarrifiyya; al-
Muʿtazila; Nad̲j̲adāt; Nāwūsiyya; al-Nukkār; Nuḳṭawiyya; Nūrbak̲h̲s̲h̲iyya;
Nuṣayriyya; al-Rāwandiyya; Raws̲h̲aniyya; Salmāniyya; Sārliyya; Satpanthīs;
S̲h̲abak; S̲h̲ābās̲h̲iyya; S̲h̲ayk̲h̲iyya; S̲h̲umayṭiyya; Ṣufriyya; Tablīg̲h̲ī
D̲j̲amāʿat; ʿUlyāʾiyya; ʿUt̲h̲māniyya; Yazīdī; [in Suppl.] D̲h̲ikrīs
see also Abu 'l-Maʿālī; ʿAlī Ilāhī; Bābāʾī; Bābīs; Bāyazīd Anṣārī; Bīs̲h̲arʿ;
Dahriyya; al-D̲h̲ammiyya; Dīn-i Ilāhī; G̲h̲assāniyya; G̲h̲ulāt; Hā-Mīm; Imām
S̲h̲āh; ʿIrāḳ.vi; Kasrawī Tabrīzī; al-Kayyāl; Kāẓim Ras̲h̲tī; Ḳîzîl-bās̲h̲; al-
Malaṭī; Mazdak; Mud̲j̲tahid.III; Sālimiyya; Sulṭān Sehāk; *and* →
MYSTICISM.ORDERS

Alids   ʿAbd Allāh b. Muʿāwiya; Abū ʿAbd Allāh Yaʿḳūb; Abu 'l-Aswad al-Duʾalī;
Abū Hās̲h̲im; Abū Nuʿaym al-Mulāʾī; Abū Salāma al-K̲h̲allāl; Abu 'l-Sarāyā
al-S̲h̲aybānī; ʿAlī b. Muḥammad al-Zand̲j̲ī; **Alids**; al-D̲j̲awwānī; Hāniʾ b.
ʿUrwa al-Murādī; al-Ḥasan b. Zayd b. Muḥammad; Ḥasan al-Uṭrūs̲h̲; Ḥud̲j̲r;
al-Ḥusayn b. ʿAlī, Ṣāḥib Fak̲h̲k̲h̲; Ibrāhīm b. al-As̲h̲tar; K̲h̲idās̲h̲;
Muḥammad b. ʿAbd Allāh (al-Nafs al-Zakiyya); al-Muk̲h̲tār b. Abī ʿUbayd;
Muslim b. ʿAḳīl b. Abī Ṭālib; Sulaym b. Ḳays; Sulaymān b. Ṣurad; al-
Uk̲h̲ayḍir, Banū; Yaḥyā b. ʿAbd Allāh; Yaḥyā b. Zayd; Zayd b. ʿAlī b. al-
Ḥusayn
see also D̲h̲u 'l-Faḳār; al-D̲j̲anāḥiyya; al-D̲j̲ārūdiyya; G̲h̲adīr K̲h̲umm; al-
Maʾmūn; S̲h̲arīf; Zaynab bt. ʿAbd Allāh al-Maḥḍ; *and* → SHIITES

Bābism   Bāb; **Bābīs**; Kās̲h̲ānī; Ḳurrat al-ʿAyn; Maẓhar; Muḥammad ʿAlī
Bārfurūs̲h̲ī; Muḥammad ʿAlī Zand̲j̲ānī; Muḥammad Ḥusayn Bus̲h̲rūʾī; Ṣubḥ-
i Azal
see also al-Aḥsāʾī; Mud̲j̲tahid.III; Nuḳṭat al-Kāf; al-Sābiḳūn

Druzes   → DRUZES

Hindu Barāhima; Ibāḥatiya; Nānak
Ibāḍīs ʿAbd al-ʿAzīz b. al-Ḥādjdj Ibrāhīm; Abū Ghānim al-Khurāsānī; Abū Ḥafṣ ʿUmar b. Djamīʿ; Abū Ḥātim al-Malzūzī (*and* al-Malzūzī); Abu ʾl-Khaṭṭāb al-Maʿāfirī; Abū Muḥammad b. Baraka; Abu ʾl-Muʾthir al-Bahlawī; Abū Zakariyyāʾ al-Djanāwunī; Abū Zakariyyāʾ al-Wardjlānī; Aṭfiyāsh; al-Barrādī; al-Bughṭūrī; al-Dardjīnī; Djābir b. Zayd; al-Djayṭālī; al-Djulandā; **al-Ibāḍiyya**; Ibn Baraka; Ibn Djaʿfar; al-Irdjānī; al-Lawātī; Maḥbūb b. al-Raḥīl al-ʿAbdī; al-Mazātī; al-Nafūsī; al-Shammākhī al-Īfranī; al-Tanāwutī; al-Wisyānī; [in Suppl.] Abū ʿAmmār; al-Ḥārithī
see also ʿAwāmir; Azd; Ḥalḳa; al-Khalafiyya; (Banū) Kharūṣ; *and* → Dynasties.spain and north africa.rustamids; Law; Sects.kharidjites
historians of Abu ʾl-Muʾthir al-Bahlawī; Abū Zakariyyāʾ al-Wardjlānī; al-Barrādī; al-Bughṭūrī; al-Dardjīnī; Ibn al-Ṣaghīr; Ibn Salām; al-Lawātī; Maḥbūb b. al-Raḥīl al-ʿAbdī; al-Mazātī; al-Sālimī
see also al-Nafūsī
Jewish → Judaism
Kharidjites Abū Bayhas; Abū Fudayk; Abū Yazīd al-Nukkārī; al-Ḍaḥḥāk b. Ḳays al-Shaybānī; Ḥurḳūṣ b. Zuhayr al-Saʿdī; ʿImrān b. Ḥiṭṭān; Ḳaṭarī b. al-Fudjāʾa; **Khāridjites**; Ḳurrāʾ; Ḳuʿūd; Mirdās b. Udayya; Nāfiʿ b. al-Azraḳ; al-Nukkār; Shabīb b. Yazīd; ʿUbayd Allāh b. Bashīr; al-Walīd b. Ṭarīf
see also ʿAdjārida; Azāriḳa; Ḥarūrāʾ; al-Ibāḍiyya; Ibn Muldjam; Imāma; Istiʿrāḍ; al-Manṣūr bi ʾllāh; Nadjadāt; Ṣufriyya; al-Ṭirimmāḥ; ʿUbayd Allāh b. Ziyād
Shiite → Shiites

Sedentarism Sārt
see also Shaʿb.1; *and* → Architecture.urban; Geography.urban

Senegal Djolof; **Senegal**
see also Murīdiyya
physical geography Senegal.1
toponyms Ṭūbā; [in Suppl.] Dakar

Sexuality ʿAzl; Bāh; Djins; Khitān; Liwāṭ; Siḥāḳ; [in Suppl.] Bighāʾ
see also Djanāba; Khāṣī; Tanẓīm al-Nasl; *and* → Adultery; Circumcision; Love.erotic
treatises on al-Tīfāshī

Shiites ʿAbd Allāh b. Sabaʾ; ʿAlids; Ghulāt; Imāma; Ismāʿīliyya; Ithnā ʿAshariyya; Sabʿiyya; **Shīʿa**; Taḳiyya; Wilāya.2; Zaydiyya
see also Abu ʾl-Sarāyā al-Shaybānī; ʿAlī b. Abī Ṭālib; ʿAlī Mardān; Madjlis.3;

Taʿziya; [in Suppl.] Batriyya; *and* → Shiites.sects

branches Ismāʿīliyya; Ithnā ʿAshariyya; Ḳarmaṭī; Nizāriyya; Zaydiyya
see also Hind.v.d; Imāma; Sabʿiyya; *and* → Shiites.sects

Carmathians (Djazīrat) al-ʿArab.vii.2; al-Djannābī, Abū Saʿīd; al-Djannābī, Abū Ṭāhir; Ḥamdān Ḳarmaṭ; al-Ḥasan al-Aʿṣam; **Ḳarmaṭī**
see also ʿAbdān; al-Baḥrayn; Baḳliyya; Daʿwa; Shābāshiyya

Ismāʿīliyya ʿAbd Allāh b. Maymūn; Abū ʿAbd Allāh al-Shīʿī; Abu ʾl-Khaṭṭāb al-Asadī; Allāh.iii.1; (Djazīrat) al-ʿArab.vii.2; Bāb; Bāṭiniyya; Dāʿī; Daʿwa; Fāṭimids; Ḥaḳāʾiḳ; Hind.v.d; Ibn ʿAṭṭāsh; Ikhwān al-Ṣafāʾ; Imāma; **Ismāʿīliyya**; Lanbasar; Madjlis.2; al-Mahdī ʿUbayd Allāh; Malāʾika.2; Manṣūr al-Yaman; Maymūn-diz; Sabʿiyya; Shahriyār b. al-Ḥasan; al-Ṭayyibiyya; Yām; Zakarawayh b. Mihrawayh; [in Suppl.] Dawr
see also Ḥawwāʾ; Ikhlāṣ; Maṣyād; Sabʿ; Salamiyya; Ṣulayḥids; Umm al-Kitāb.2; al-Ẓāhir wa ʾl-Bāṭin; *and* → Caliphate.fāṭimids; Shiites.imams

authors Abū Ḥātim al-Rāzī; Abū Yaʿḳūb al-Sidjzī; al-Kirmānī; al-Muʾayyad fi ʾl-Dīn; al-Nasafī.1; Nāṣir-i Khusraw; [in Suppl.] Djaʿfar b. Manṣūr al-Yaman
and → *the sections Mustaʿlī-Ṭayyibīs and Nizārīs below*

Mustaʿlī-Ṭayyibīs Bohorās; al-Ḥāmidī; Luḳmāndjī; al-Makramī; Makramids; Muḥammad b. Ṭāhir al-Ḥārithī; Shaykh Ādam; Sulaymān b. Ḥasan; Sulaymānīs; Ṭāhir Sayf al-Dīn; al-Ṭayyibiyya; [in Suppl.] ʿAlī b. Ḥanẓala b. Abī Sālim; ʿAlī b. Muḥammad b. Djaʿfar; Amīndjī b. Djalāl b. Ḥasan; Ḥasan b. Nūḥ; Idrīs b. al-Ḥasan
see also Ismāʿīliyya

Nizārīs Agha Khān; Alamūt.ii; Buzurg-ummīd; Fidāʾī; Ḥasan-i Ṣabbāḥ; Ḥashīshiyya; Khōdja; Maḥallātī; Nizār b. al-Mustanṣir; **Nizāriyya**; Nūr al-Dīn Muḥammad II; Pīr Ṣadr al-Dīn; Pīr Shams; Rāshid al-Dīn Sinān; Rukn al-Dīn Khurshāh; Sabz ʿAlī; Shāh Ṭāhir; al-Shahrastānī, Abu ʾl-Fatḥ; Shams-al-Dīn Muḥammad; Shihāb al-Dīn al-Ḥusaynī; al-Ṭūsī, Naṣīr al-Dīn
see also Sarkār Āḳā; Satpanthīs

Sevener **Sabʿiyya**
see also Sabʿ

Twelver Imāma; **Ithnā ʿAshariyya**; Mudjtahid.II; Mutawālī; al-Rāfiḍa; Uṣūliyya.1; [in Suppl.] Akhbāriyya
see also Buwayhids; al-Ẓāhir wa ʾl-Bāṭin; *and* → Shiites.imams

authors Ibn Bābawayh(i); al-Māmaḳānī; al-Shahīd al-Thānī; al-Ṭabrisī, Abū Manṣūr; al-Ṭabrisī, Amīn al-Dīn; Ṭabrisī; al-Thaḳafī, Ibrāhīm; al-Ṭihrānī; al-Ṭūsī
and → Shiites.theologians

Zaydiyya al-Djārūdiyya; **Zaydiyya**; [in Suppl.] Batriyya
see also Imāma; Muṭarrifiyya; Rassids; *and* → DYNASTIES.ARABIAN PENINSULA.ZAYDĪS
Zaydīs al-Ḥasan b. Ṣāliḥ b. Ḥayy al-Kūfī; Ibn Abi 'l-Ridjāl; al-Mahdī li-Dīn Allāh Aḥmad; Muḥammad b. Zayd; al-Nāṣir li-Dīn Allāh; al-Rassī; Sulaymān b. Djarīr al-Raḳḳī; al-Thāʾir fi 'llāh; Yaḥyā b. ʿAbd Allāh; Yaḥyā b. Ḥamza al-ʿAlawī; Yaḥyā b. Muḥammad; Yaḥyā b. Zayd; Zayd b. ʿAlī b. al-Ḥusayn; [in Suppl.] Abu 'l-Barakāt; Abu 'l-Fatḥ al-Daylamī; Aḥmad b. ʿĪsā; Djaʿfar b. Abī Yaḥyā; al-Ḥākim al-Djushamī

doctrines and institutions Bāṭiniyya; Djafr; Ḳāʾim Āl Muḥammad; Khalḳ.VII; Madjlis.2 and 3; al-Mahdī; Malāʾika.2; Mardjaʿ-i Taḳlīd; Maẓhar; Maẓlūm; Mudjtahid.II; Mutʿa.V; Radjʿa; Safīr.1; Tanāsukh.2; Taʾwīl; al-Ẓāhir wa 'l-Bāṭin; [in Suppl.] Āyatullāh
see also Adhān; Ahl al-Bayt; ʿAḳīda; Bāb; Ghayba; Ḥudjdja; Imāma; ʿIlm al-Ridjāl; Imām-bārā; Imāmzāda; Mollā; Umm al-Kitāb.2; Ziyāra.1.a and 5; *and* → THEOLOGY.TERMS.SHIITE

dynasties Buwayhids; Fāṭimids; Ṣafawids; Zaydiyya.3
see also Mushaʿshaʿ; al-Ukhayḍir, Banū

imams ʿAlī b. Abī Ṭālib; ʿAlī al-Riḍā; al-ʿAskarī; Djaʿfar al-Ṣādiḳ; (al-)Ḥasan b. ʿAlī b. Abī Ṭālib; (al-)Ḥusayn b. ʿAlī b. Abī Ṭālib; Muḥammad b. ʿAlī al-Riḍā; Muḥammad b. ʿAlī (al-Bāḳir); Muḥammad al-Ḳāʾim; Mūsā al-Kāẓim; Zayn al-ʿĀbidīn
see also Bāb; Ghayba; Imāmzāda; Malāʾika.2; Maẓlūm; Riḍā.2; Safīr.1

jurists al-ʿĀmilī; al-Ḥillī.2; al-Māmaḳānī; al-Mufīd; Muḥammad b. Makkī; al-Shahīd al-Thānī; Shīrāzī; [in Suppl.] Anṣārī; Bihbihānī
see also ʿĀḳila; Madjlisī; Madjlisī-yi Awwal; Mardjaʿ-i Taḳlīd; Mudjtahid.II; Mutʿa.V; Uṣūliyya.1

places of pilgrimage Karbalāʾ; Kāẓimayn; al-Nadjaf; [in Suppl.] ʿAtabāt
see also Shāh ʿAbd al-ʿAẓīm al-Ḥasanī; Ziyāra.1.a and 5

rituals Rawḍa-khʷānī

sects Ahl-i Ḥaḳḳ; ʿAlids; Baḳliyya; Bohorās; Djābir b. Ḥayyān; al-Djanāḥiyya; al-Djārūdiyya; Ghurābiyya; Ḥurūfiyya; Ibāḥa.II; Kaysāniyya; Khashabiyya; Khaṭṭābiyya; Khōdja; Khurramiyya; Kuraybiyya; Manṣūriyya; al-Mughīriyya; Muḥammadiyya; Mukhammisa; Muṭarrifiyya; al-Muʿtazila; Nāwūsiyya; Nūrbakhshiyya; Nuṣayriyya; al-Rāwandiyya; Salmāniyya; Satpanthīs; Shaykhiyya; Shumayṭiyya; Ṭāwūsiyya; ʿUlyāʾiyya; al-Wāḳifa
see also ʿAbd Allāh b. Sabaʾ; Bāṭiniyya; Bayān b. Samʿān al-Tamīmī; Bektāshiyya; Ghulāt; Hind.v.d; Imām Shāh; Ḳaṭʿ; al-Kayyāl; Kāẓim Rashtī; Ḳïzïl-bāsh; Mudjtahid.III; Mushaʿshaʿ; Tawwābūn; [in Suppl.] Ibn Warsand; *and* → BAHAIS; DRUZES; SECTS.ʿALIDS
Kaysāniyya Abū Hāshim; Kaysān; **Kaysāniyya**

see also al-Sayyid al-Ḥimyarī
Khaṭṭābiyya Abu 'l-Khaṭṭāb al-Asadī; Bashshār al-Shaʿīrī; Bazīgh b. Mūsā; **Khaṭṭābiyya**
see also Mukhammisa; al-Ṣāmit
Khurramiyya Bābak; [in Suppl.] Bādhām
Mukhammisa **Mukhammisa**
see also al-Muḥassin b. ʿAlī
Shaykhism al-Aḥsāʾī; Rashtī, Sayyid Kāẓim; **Shaykhiyya**
terms → THEOLOGY.TERMS.SHIITE
theologians al-Dāmād; al-Ḥillī.1; Hishām b. al-Ḥakam; al-Ḥurr al-ʿĀmilī; Ibn Bābawayh(i); Ibn Shahrāshūb; al-Karakī; Kāshif al-Ghiṭāʾ; Khʷānsārī, Sayyid Mīrzā; al-Kulaynī, Abū Djaʿfar Muḥammad; Lāhīdjī.2; Mīr Lawḥī; al-Mufīd; Mullā Ṣadrā Shīrāzī; al-Nasafī.1; Shayṭān al-Ṭāḳ; Ṭabrisī; al-Ṭūsī, Naṣīr al-Dīn; [in Suppl.] Akhbāriyya; Anṣārī; Fayḍ-i Kāshānī; Ibn Abī Djumhūr al-Aḥsāʾī; Ibn Mītham
see also al-ʿAyyāshī; Ḥudjdja; Imāma; Khalḳ.VII; Mollā
20th-century Kāshānī; Khʷānsārī, Sayyid Muḥammad; Khiyābānī, Shaykh Muḥammad; Khurāsānī; Muṭahharī; Nāʾīnī; Sharaf al-Dīn; Sharīʿatī, ʿAlī; Sharīʿatmadārī; [in Suppl.] Āḳā Nadjafī; Burūdjirdī; Ḥāʾirī
traditionists → LITERATURE.TRADITION-LITERATURE.TRADITIONISTS.SHIITES

SIBERIA **Sibīr**
physical geography
waters Ob
see also Tobol
population Bukhārlïk; Tobol
toponyms → EUROPE.EASTERN EUROPE

SICILY Benavert; Kalbids; **Ṣiḳilliya**
see also Aghlabids.iii; Asad b. al-Furāt; Fāṭimids; Ṭarī
local rulers Ibn al-Ḥawwās; Ibn al-Thumna
poets Ibn Ḥamdīs; Ibn al-Khayyāṭ
scholars Ibn al-Birr; Ibn al-Ḳaṭṭāʿ; Ibn Makkī
see also al-Idrīsī
toponyms Balarm; Benavent; Djirdjent; Ḳaṣryānnih; Siraḳūsa
see also al-Khāliṣa

SLAVERY **ʿAbd**; Ghulām; Ḳayna; Khāṣī; Mamlūk; Mawlā; al-Ṣaḳāliba; Umm al-Walad
see also Ḥabash.i; Ḥabshī; Hausa; ʿIdda.5; Istibrāʾ; Khādim; Ḳul; Maṭmūra; Sidi; *and* → MUSIC.SONG.SINGERS
manumission ʿAbd.3.j; ʿItḳnāme; Tadbīr.2

slave revolt Zandj.2

SOMALIA **Somali**
see also Ḥabesh; Muḥammad b. ʿAbd Allāh Ḥassān; Ogādēn; *and* → AFRICA.EAST AFRICA
physical geography Somali.2
religious orders Ṣāliḥiyya
see also Somali.4
toponyms
regions Guardafui
see also Ogādēn
towns Barawa; Berberā; Hargeisa; Maḳdishū; Merka; Shungwaya; Zaylaʿ

SOUTH(-EAST) ASIA → ASIA

SOVIET UNION → CAUCASUS; CENTRAL ASIA.FORMER SOVIET UNION; COMMUNISM; EUROPE.EASTERN EUROPE; SIBERIA

SPAIN Aljamía; Almogávares; al-Burt; al-Bushārrāt; Moriscos
see also Ibn al-Ḳiṭṭ; Ifni; al-ʿIḳāb; *and* → ANDALUSIA; DYNASTIES.SPAIN AND NORTH AFRICA
physical geography al-Andalus.ii and iii.2
see also Wādī.3
mountains al-Sharāt
waters al-Ḥamma; Ibruh; al-Mudawwar; Shaḳūra; Tādjuh; (al-)Wādī al-Kabīr; Wādī Yāna; [in Suppl.] Araghūn
toponyms
ancient Barbashturu; Bulāy; Ḳasṭīliya.1; al-Madīna al-Zāhira; Shadūna; Shaḳunda; Shaḳūra; Shantabariyya; Tākurunnā; Ṭalabīra; Tudmīr; [in Suppl.] Āfrāg; Balyūnash
see also Rayya
present-day
islands al-Djazāʾir al-Khālida; Mayūrḳa; Minūrḳa; Yābisa
regions Ālaba wa ʾl-Ḳilāʿ; Djillīḳiyya; Faḥṣ al-Ballūṭ; Firrīsh; Ḳanbāniya; Ḳashtāla; Navarra; Wādī ʾl-Ḥidjāra; Walba; [in Suppl.] Araghūn
towns Alsh; Arkush; Arnīṭ; Badjdjāna; Balansiya; Bālish; Banbalūna; Barshalūna; al-Basīt; Basta; Baṭalyaws; Bayyāna; Bayyāsa; Biṭrawsh; al-Bunt; Burghush; Dāniya; Djarunda; Djayyān; al-Djazīra al-Khaḍrāʾ; Djazīrat Shuḳr; Finyāna; Gharnāṭa; Ifrāgha; Ilbīra; Ishbīliya; Istidja; Ḳabra; Ḳādis; Ḳalʿat Ayyūb; Ḳalʿat Rabāḥ; Ḳanṭara.2; Ḳarmūna; Ḳarṭādjanna; al-Ḳulayʿa; Ḳūnka; Ḳūriya;

Ḳurṭuba; Labla; Laḳant; Lārida; Lawsha; Liyūn; Lūrḳa; al-Maʿdin; Madīnat Sālim; Madīnat al-Zahrāʾ; Madjrīṭ; Mālaḳa; Mārida; al-Mariyya; Mawrūr; al-Munakkab; Mursiya; Runda; Saraḳusṭa; Shaḳūbiya; Shalamanḳa; Shalṭīsh; Shant Mānkash; Shant Yāḳub; Shantamariyyat al-Sharḳ; Sharīsh; Shāṭiba; Ṭarīfa; Ṭarrakūna; Ṭulayṭula; Ṭurṭūsha; Tuṭīla; Ubbadha; Uḳlīsh; Urdjudhūna; Uryūla; Wādī Āsh; Washḳa; [in Suppl.] Ashturḳa
see also al-Andalus.iii.3; Balāṭ; Djabal Ṭāriḳ; al-Ḳalʿa; *and* → PORTUGAL

SRI LANKA **Ceylon**; Sarandīb
and → INDIA.POPULATION.TAMILS

SUDAN Dār Fūr; Dustūr.xiii; Ḥizb.i; Madjlis.4.A.xvii; al-Mahdiyya; **Sūdān**
see also Baladiyya.2; Fundj; Ḥabesh; Nūba; *and* → AFRICA.EAST AFRICA
Mahdist period ʿAbd Allāh b. Muḥammad al-Taʿāʾishī; Khalīfa.iv; **al-Mahdiyya**; ʿUthmān Diḳna
see also Awlād al-Balad; Dār Fūr; Emīn Pasha; Rābiḥ b. Faḍl Allāh; Taʿāʾisha
modern period
influential persons Ṭāhā, Maḥmūd Muḥammad
see also al-Tūnisī, Muḥammad; al-Tūnisī, Shaykh Zayn al-ʿĀbidīn
physical geography
waters al-Nīl
population ʿAbābda; ʿAlwa; (Banū) ʿĀmir; Baḳḳāra; Barābra; Djaʿaliyyūn; Ghuzz.iii; Nūba.4; Rashāʾida; Shāyḳiyya; Taʿāʾisha; Zaghāwa
see also Bedja; Fallāta
religious orders Mīrghaniyya
toponyms
ancient ʿAydhāb; Sōba
present-day
provinces Baḥr al-Ghazāl.3; Berber.2; Dār Fūr; Fāshōda; Kasala
regions Fāzūghlī; Kordofān
towns Atbara; Berber.3; Dongola; al-Fāshir; Kasala; Ḳerrī; al-Khurṭūm; Omdurman; Sawākin; Shandī; Sinnār; al-Ubayyiḍ; Wad Madanī; Wādī Ḥalfā

SUPERSTITION ʿAyn; Faʾl; Ghurāb; Ḥinnāʾ; Khamsa; Ṣadā
see also ʿAḳīḳ; Bāriḥ; Laḳab

SYRIA Dimashḳ; **al-Shām**
and → LEBANON

architecture → ARCHITECTURE.REGIONS
before Islam → PRE-ISLAM.IN FERTILE CRESCENT
dynasties ʿAmmār; Ayyūbids; Būrids; Fāṭimids; Ḥamdānids; Mamlūks; Umayyads; Zangids
see also [in Suppl.] al-D̲j̲azzār Pas̲h̲a; *and* → DYNASTIES.EGYPT AND THE FERTILE CRESCENT; LEBANON
historians of al-ʿAẓīmī; Ibn Abī Ṭayyiʾ; Ibn al-ʿAdīm; Ibn ʿAsākir; Ibn al-Ḳalānisī; Ibn Kat̲h̲īr; Ibn S̲h̲addād; Kurd ʿAlī; al-Kutubī; al-Yūnīnī
and → DYNASTIES.EGYPT AND THE FERTILE CRESCENT
modern period D̲j̲arīda.i.A; D̲j̲āmiʿa; Dustūr.ix; Ḥizb.i; Ḥukūma.iii; Mad̲j̲lis.4.A.v; Mad̲j̲maʿ ʿIlmī.i.2.a; Maḥkama.4.ii; Mandates; Maysalūn; Salafiyya.2(b); al-S̲h̲ām.2, esp. (b) and (c)
see also Baladiyya.2; Kurd ʿAlī; Mardam.2; [in Suppl.] Demography.III
belletrists
poets al-K̲h̲ūrī; Mardam.2; [in Suppl.] Buṭrus Karāma
statesmen al-K̲h̲ūrī; Mardam.1; al-Zahrāwī, ʿAbd al-Ḥamīd; al-Zaʿīm
physical geography al-S̲h̲ām.1
mountains Ḳāsiyūn; al-Lukkām
waters ʿAfrīn; al-ʿĀṣī; Baradā; al-ʿUtayba; Yarmūk.1; Zabadānī
toponyms
ancient Afāmiya; ʿArbān; al-Bak̲h̲rāʾ; al-Bāra; Barḳaʿīd; Dābiḳ; Diyār Muḍar; Diyār Rabīʿa; al-D̲j̲ābiya; al-D̲j̲azīra; D̲j̲illiḳ; Manbid̲j̲; Namāra.1; al-Raḥba; Raʾs al-ʿAyn; Rīḥā.2; al-Ruṣāfa.3; S̲h̲ayzar
present-day
districts al-Bat̲h̲aniyya; al-D̲j̲awlān
regions al-G̲h̲āb; Ḥawrān; Ḳinnasrīn.2; Lad̲j̲āʾ; al-Ṣafā.2
see also G̲h̲ūṭa
towns Ad̲h̲riʿāt; Bāniyās; Boṣrā; Buzāʿā; Dayr al-Zōr; Dimas̲h̲ḳ; D̲j̲abala; al-D̲j̲abbūl; D̲j̲isr al-S̲h̲ug̲h̲r; Ḥalab; Ḥamāt; Ḥārim; Ḥimṣ; Ḥuwwārīn; Ḳanawāt; Ḳarḳīsiyā; K̲h̲awlān.2; Ḳinnasrīn.1; al-Lād̲h̲iḳiyya; Maʿarrat Maṣrīn; Maʿarrat al-Nuʿmān; Maʿlūlā; Maskana; Maṣyād; al-Mizza; Namāra.2 and 3; al-Raḳḳa; Ṣāfīt̲h̲a; Salamiyya; Ṣalk̲h̲ad; Tadmur; Ṭarṭūs; Zabadānī
see also al-Marḳab

T

TANZANIA Dar-es-Salaam; Kilwa; Mikindani; Mkwaja; Mtambwe Mkuu; **Tanzania**
and → AFRICA.EAST AFRICA
Zanzibar Barg̲h̲as̲h̲; Bū Saʿīd; Kizimkazi; **Zand̲j̲ibār**

see also Tumbatu

TAXATION   Bā<u>dj</u>; **Bayt al-Māl**; Ḍarība; <u>Dj</u>izya; Ḳānūn.ii and iii; <u>Kh</u>arā<u>dj</u>; Taḥrīr;
Taḥṣīl; Taḳsīṭ; ʿU<u>sh</u>r; [in Suppl.] Ḍarība.7
   see also Ḍabṭ; <u>Dj</u>ahba<u>dh</u>; Mā°; Maʾṣir; Raʿiyya; Taḳdīr.2; Taʾrī<u>kh</u>.I.1.viii; Zakāt
collectors   ʿĀmil; Dih<u>k</u>an; Muḥaṣṣil; Mültezim; Musta<u>kh</u>ri<u>dj</u>
   see also Amīr; Taḥṣīl
taxes   ʿArūs Resmi; ʿAwāriḍ; Bād-i Hawā; Badal; Bā<u>dj</u>; Ba<u>sh</u>maḳli̊ḳ; Bennāk;
   Čift-resmi; <u>Dj</u>awālī; <u>Dj</u>izya; Filori; Furḍa; Ispendje; <u>Kh</u>arā<u>dj</u>; Ḳūbčūr;
   Maks; Mālikāne; Mīrī; Muḳāsama; Muḳāṭaʿa; Pī<u>sh</u>ka<u>sh</u>; Resm; Tam<u>gh</u>a;
   Tekālīf; ʿU<u>sh</u>r
   see also Ḥisba.ii; Ḳaṭīʿa; Waẓīfa.1
   land taxes   Ba<u>sh</u>maḳli̊ḳ; Bennāk; Čift-resmi; **<u>Kh</u>arā<u>dj</u>**; Mīrī; Muḳāsama;
   ʿU<u>sh</u>r
      see also Daftar; Daftar-i <u>Kh</u>āḳānī; Ḳabāla; Ḳānūn.iii.1; Rawk; Ustān
tithe-lands   Ḍayʿa; Ī<u>gh</u>ār; Iḳṭāʿ; Iltizām; <u>Kh</u>āliṣa; <u>Kh</u>āṣṣ; Ṣafī; Tīmār; Zamīndār;
   Ziʿāmet
      see also Baʿl.2.b; Dār al-ʿAhd; Fayʾ; Filāḥa.iv; Zaʿīm
treatises on   Abū Yūsuf; al-Ma<u>kh</u>zūmī; al-Tahānawī; Yaḥyā b. Ādam
   see also Abū ʿUbayd al-Ḳāsim b. Sallām

THAILAND   Patani; **Thailand**

THEOLOGY   ʿAḳīda; Allāh; Dīn; <u>Dj</u>anna; **ʿIlm al-Kalām**; Imāma; Īmān; Kalām;
   al-Mahdī; Uṣūl al-Dīn
   see also ʿĀlam.1; Hilāl.i; *and* → ISLAM
disputation   Masāʾil wa-A<u>dj</u>wiba; Munāẓara; Radd; [in Suppl.] ʿIbādat <u>Kh</u>āna
   see also Mubāhala
treatises on   al-Samarḳandī, <u>Sh</u>ams al-Dīn
schools
   Shiite   Ismāʿīliyya; I<u>th</u>nā ʿA<u>sh</u>ariyya; Ḳarmaṭī; Uṣūliyya.1; [in Suppl.]
      A<u>kh</u>bāriyya
         see also Muʿtazila
   Sunni   A<u>sh</u>ʿariyya; Ḥanābila; Māturīdiyya; Muʿtazila
         see also ʿIlm al-Kalām.II; Ḳadariyya; Karāmat ʿAlī; Mur<u>dj</u>iʾa; al-
         Na<u>dj</u><u>dj</u>āriyya
terms   A<u>dj</u>al; A<u>dj</u>r; ʿAdl; ʿAhd; Ahl al-ahwāʾ; Ahl al-kitāb; Ā<u>kh</u>ira; ʿAḳīda; ʿAḳl;
   ʿAḳliyyāt; ʿĀlam.2.; ʿAmal.2; Amr; al-Aṣlaḥ; Ba<u>ʿth</u>; Bāṭiniyya; Bidʿa; Birr;
   Daʿwa; Dīn; <u>Dj</u>amāʿa; <u>Dj</u>azāʾ; <u>Dj</u>ism; Duʿāʾ; Fard.g; Fāsiḳ; Fiʿl; Fitna; Fiṭra;
   al-<u>Gh</u>ayb; <u>Gh</u>ayba; <u>Gh</u>ufrān; Ḥadd; Ḥaḳḳ; Ḥaraka wa-Sukūn.I.2 and 3;
   Ḥisāb; Hu<u>dj</u><u>dj</u>a; Hudū<u>th</u> al-ʿĀlam; Ḥulūl; Iʿ<u>dj</u>āz; Iḍṭirār; I<u>kh</u>lāṣ; I<u>kh</u>tiyār;
   ʿIlla.ii.III; Imāma; Īmān; Islām; ʿIṣma; Istiṭāʿa; Ittiḥād; al-Ḳaḍāʾ wa ʾl-Ḳadar;

Kaffāra; Kāfir; Kalima; Karāma; Kasb; Kashf; Khalḳ; Khaṭīʾa; Khidhlān; Ḳidam; Kumūn; Ḳunūt; Ḳuwwa.3; Luṭf; Maʿād; al-Mahdī; al-Manzila bayn al-Manzilatayn; al-Mughayyabāt al-Khams; al-Munāfiḳūn.2; Murtadd; Muṭlaḳ; Nāfila; Nafs; Nāmūs.1; Nūr Muḥammadī; Riyāʾ; Rizḳ; Rudjūʿ; Ruʾyat Allāh; Sabīl.1; Shubha; Ṣifa.2; Ṭāʿa; Taḥsīn wa-Taḳbīḥ; Taḳlīd; Taklīf; Tanāsukh; Tashbīh wa-Tanzīh; Tawallud; Tawba; Tawfīḳ; Waraʿ; al-Ẓāhir wa ʾl-Bāṭin; Ẓulm; [in Suppl.] Ḥāl

see also Abad; Allāh.ii; In Shāʾ Allāh; ʿInāya; Ṣūra; *and* → ESCHATOLOGY; KORAN.TERMS

Shiite Badāʾ; Ghayba; Ibdāʿ; Kashf; Lāhūt and Nāsūt.5; Maẓhar; Maẓlūm; al-Munāfiḳūn.2; Naḳḍ al-Mīthāḳ; Radjʿa; al-Sābiḳūn; Safīr.1; al-Ṣāmit; Sarkār Āḳā; Tabarruʾ; Tanāsukh.2; Waṣī

and → SHIITES.DOCTRINES AND INSTITUTIONS

theologians ʿUlamāʾ

see also Sharḥ.III

in early Islam Djahm b. Ṣafwān; al-Ḥasan al-Baṣrī; Wāṣil b. ʿAṭāʾ; [in Suppl.] al-Aṣamm; al-Ḥasan b. Muḥammad b. al-Ḥanafiyya; Ibn Kullāb

Ashʿarī al-Āmidī; al-Ashʿarī, Abu ʾl-Ḥasan; al-Baghdādī; al-Bāḳillānī; al-Bayhaḳī; al-Djuwaynī; al-Faḍālī; Fakhr al-Dīn al-Rāzī; al-Ghazālī, Abū Ḥāmid; Ibn Fūrak; al-Īdjī; al-Isfarāyīnī; al-Kiyā al-Harrāsī; al-Ḳushayrī; al-Sanūsī, Abū ʿAbd Allāh; al-Simnānī

see also Allāh.ii; ʿIlm al-Kalām.II.C; Imāma; Īmān; [in Suppl.] Ḥāl

Ḥanbalī ʿAbd al-Ḳādir al-Djīlānī; Aḥmad b. Ḥanbal; al-Anṣārī al-Harawī; al-Barbahārī; Ibn ʿAbd al-Wahhāb; Ibn ʿAḳīl; Ibn Baṭṭa al-ʿUkbarī; Ibn al-Djawzī; Ibn Ḳayyim al-Djawziyya; Ibn Ḳudāma al-Maḳdisī; Ibn Taymiyya; al-Khallāl

see also Īmān; *and* → LAW

Māturīdī ʿAbd al-Ḥayy; Bishr b. Ghiyāth; al-Māturīdī

see also Allāh.ii; ʿIlm al-Kalām.II.D; Imāma; Īmān

Muʿtazilī ʿAbbād b. Sulaymān; ʿAbd al-Djabbār b. Aḥmad; Abu ʾl-Hudhayl al-ʿAllāf; Aḥmad b. Abī Duʾād; Aḥmad b. Ḥābiṭ; ʿAmr b. ʿUbayd; al-Balkhī; Bishr b. al-Muʿtamir; Djaʿfar b. Ḥarb; Djaʿfar b. Mubashshir; Djāḥiẓ; al-Djubbāʾī; Hishām b. ʿAmr al-Fuwaṭī; Ibn al-Ikhshīd; Ibn Khallād; al-Iskāfī; al-Khayyāṭ; Muʿammar b. ʿAbbād; al-Murdār; al-Nāshiʾ al-Akbar; al-Naẓẓām; al-Shaḥḥām; Thumāma b. Ashras; al-Zamakhsharī; [in Suppl.] Abū ʿAbd Allāh al-Baṣrī; Abu ʾl-Ḥusayn al-Baṣrī; Abū Rashīd al-Nīsābūrī; Ḍirār b. ʿAmr; al-Ḥākim al-Djushamī; Ibn Mattawayh

see also Ahl al-Naẓar; Allāh.ii; Ḥafṣ al-Fard; Ibn ʿAbbād, Abu ʾl-Ḳāsim; Ibn Abi ʾl-Ḥadīd; Ibn al-Rāwandī; ʿIlm al-Kalām.II.B; Imāma; Khalḳ.V; Lawn; Luṭf; al-Maʾmūn; al-Manzila bayn al-Manzilatayn; al-Waʿd wa ʾl-Waʿīd; [in Suppl.] al-Aṣamm; Ḥāl

Shiite → Shiites
Wahhābī Ibn ʿAbd al-Wahhāb; Ibn Ghannām
Indo-Muslim ʿAbd al-ʿAzīz al-Dihlawī; ʿAbd al-Ḳādir Dihlawī; Ashraf ʿAlī; Baḥr al-ʿUlūm; al-Dihlawī, Shāh Walī Allāh; al-ʿImrānī; ʿIwaḍ Wadjīh; [in Suppl.] ʿAbd Allāh Sulṭānpūrī; Farangī Maḥall
see also Hind.v.b; al-Maʿbarī; Mappila; Ṣulḥ-i kull; Tablīghī Djamāʿat; ʿUlamāʾ.4
Christian Ibn Zurʿa; Yaḥyā b. ʿAdī; Yaḥyā al-Naḥwī
and → Christianity.denominations
Jewish Ibn Maymūn; Saʿadyā Ben Yōsēf
19th and 20th centuries Muḥammad ʿAbduh; Muḥammad Abū Zayd
see also Sunna.3

Time Abad; Dahr; Ḳidam; **Zamān**
see also Ibn al-Sāʿātī
calendars Djalālī; Hidjra; Nasīʾ; **Taʾrīkh**.I; [in Suppl.] Ilāhī Era
see also Nawrūz; Rabīʿ b. Zayd; Sulaymān al-Mahrī; Taḳwīm; ʿUmar Khayyām
day and night ʿAṣr; ʿAtama; **Layl and Nahār**; al-Shafaḳ; **Yawm**
see also Taʾrīkh.I.1.iii; Zīdj
days of the week Djumʿa; Sabt
months
see also al-Ḳamar
Islamic al-Muḥarram; Rabīʿ; Radjab; Ramaḍān; Ṣafar; Shaʿbān; Shawwāl
see also Taʾrīkh.I.1.iii
Syrian Nīsān; Tammūz; Tishrīn
Turkish Odjaḳ
timekeeping Anwāʾ; al-Ḳamar; Mīḳāt; Mizwala; Sāʿa.1
see also Asṭurlāb; Ayyām al-ʿAdjūz; Hilāl.i; Rubʿ; Taʿdīl al-Zamān

Togo Kabou; Kubafolo; **Togo**

Transport **Naḳl**
and → Animals.camels *and* equines; Hostelry; Navigation
caravans Azalay; **Kārwān**; Maḥmal; ʿUḳayl.2; [in Suppl.] Djammāl
see also Anadolu.iii.5; Darb al-Arbaʿīn; Khān
mountain passes Bāb al-Lān; Bībān; Dār-i Āhanīn; Deve Boynu; Khaybar
see also Chitral
postal service **Barīd**; Fuyūdj; Ḥamām; Posta; Raḳḳāṣ; Ulaḳ; Yām
see also Anadolu.iii.5
stamps **Posta**
railways Ḥidjāz Railway; **Sikkat al-Ḥadīd**

see also Anadolu.iii.5; al-Ḳāhira (442a); Khurramshahr; Zāhidān
wheeled vehicles ʿAdjala; Araba

TRAVEL **Riḥla**; Safar
and → LITERATURE.TRAVEL-LITERATURE
supplies Mifrash
and → NOMADISM

TREASURY **Bayt al-Māl**; Khazīne; Makhzān
and → ADMINISTRATION.FINANCIAL

TREATIES Baḳṭ; Küčük Ḳaynardja; Mandates; Mondros; **Muʿāhada**; Türkmen Čay (i); Zsitvatorok
see also Dār al-ʿAhd; Ḥilf al-Fuḍūl; Mīthāḳ-i Millī; Tudmīr
tributes Baḳṭ; Parias
and → TAXATION

TRIBES ʿĀʾila; ʿAshīra; Ḥayy; **Ḳabīla**; Sayyid
see also ʿAṣabiyya; Ḥilf; Khaṭīb; Sharīf.(1); Shaykh; [in Suppl.] Bisāṭ.iii; *and* → CUSTOM.TRIBAL CUSTOMS; LAW.CUSTOMARY LAW; NOMADISM; *and the section Population under entries of countries*
Afghanistan, India and Pakistan Abdālī; Afrīdī; Bhaṭṭi; Čahar Aymaḳ; Dāwūdpōtrās; Djāṭ; Durrānī; Gakkhaṛ; Gandāpur; Ghalzay; Güdjar; Khaṭak; Khokars; Lambadis; Mahsūd; Mēʾō; Mohmand; Mullagorī; Sammā; Sumerā; Wazīrīs; Yūsufzay; [in Suppl.] Gurčānī
see also Afghān.i; Afghānistān.ii
Africa ʿAbābda; ʿĀmir; Antemuru; Bedja; Beleyn; Bishārīn; Danḳalī; Djaʿaliyyūn; Kunta; Makua; Māryā; Mazrūʿī; Shāyḳiyya; Zaghāwa
see also Diglal; Fulbe; al-Manāṣir; Mande; *for North Africa, see the section Egypt and North Africa below*
Arabian peninsula
ancient ʿAbd al-Ḳays; al-Abnāʾ.I; ʿĀd; ʿAkk; ʿĀmila; ʿĀmir b. Ṣaʿṣaʿa; al-Aws; Azd; Badjīla; Bāhila; Bakr b. Wāʾil; Ḍabba; Djadhīma b. ʿĀmir; Djurhum; Fazāra; Ghanī b. Aʿṣur; Ghassān; Ghaṭafān; Ghifār; Hamdān; Ḥanīfa b. Ludjaym; Ḥanẓala b. Mālik; Ḥārith b. Kaʿb; Hawāzin; Hilāl; ʿIdjl; Iram; Iyād; Kalb b. Wabara; al-Ḳayn; Khafādja; Khathʿam; al-Khazradj; Kilāb b. Rabīʿa; Kināna; Kinda; Khuzāʿa; Ḳuraysh; Ḳushayr; Laʿaḳat al-Dam; Liḥyān.2; Maʿadd; Maʿāfir; Māzin; Muḥārib; Murād; Murra; Naḍīr; Nawfal; Riyām; Saʿd b. Bakr; Saʿd b. Zayd Manāt al-Fizr; Salīḥ; Salūl; Shaybān; Sulaym; Taghlib b. Wāʾil; Tamīm b. Murr; Tanūkh; Ṭasm; Taym Allāh; Taym b. Murra; Thaḳīf; Thamūd; ʿUdhra; ʿUḳayl.1; Yāfiʿ; Yarbūʿ; Yās

see also Asad (Banū); Ḥabash (Aḥābīsh); al-Ḥidjāz; Makhzūm; Mustaʿriba; Mutaʿarriba; Nizār b. Maʿadd; Numayr; Rabīʿa (and Muḍar); Shayba; Thaʿlaba; al-Uḳayṣir; Wabār; Wufūd; Zarḳāʾ al-Yamāma; Zuhayr b. Djanāb; Zuhra; [in Suppl.] Aʿyāṣ

present-day ʿAbdalī; ʿAḳrabī; ʿAwāmir; ʿAwāzim; Banyar; al-Baṭāḥira; Buḳūm; al-Dawāsir; al-Dhīʾāb; Djaʿda (ʿĀmir); al-Djanaba; al-Durūʿ; Ghāmid; Hādjir; Ḥakam b. Saʿd; Hamdān; al-Ḥarāsīs; Ḥarb; Ḥāshid wa-Bakīl; Ḥassān, Bā; Ḥawshabī; Hinā; al-Ḥubūs; Hudhayl; Ḥudjriyya; Hutaym; al-Ḥuwayṭāt; al-ʿIfār; Ḳaḥṭān; Khālid; (Banū) Kharūṣ; Khawlān; Ḳudāʿa; Madhḥidj; Mahra; al-Manāṣir; Mazrūʿī; Murra; Muṭayr; Muzayna; Nabhān; Ruwala; Shammar; Shararāt; Subayʿ; Ṣubayḥī; Sudayri; Ṣulayb; Thaḳīf; ʿUtayba; Wahība; Yām
see also (Djazīrat) al-ʿArab.vi; Badw; al-Ḥidjāz; Shāwiya.2; ʿUtūb; al-Yaman.4

Central Asia, Mongolia and points further north Čāwdors; Dūghlāt; Emreli; Gagauz; Göklän; Ḳarluḳ; Ḳungrāt; Mangi̊t; Mongols; Özbeg; Pečenegs; Salur; Sulduz; Tatar; Tobol; Toghuzghuz; Türkmen; Turks.I.2; Yaghma
see also Ghuzz; Īlāt; Ḳāyi̊; Khaladj; Ḳi̊shlaḳ; Yaylaḳ

Egypt and North Africa ʿAbābda; Ahaggar; al-Butr; Djazūla; Dukkāla; Ifoghas; Khulṭ; Kūmiya; al-Maʿḳil; Mandīl; Riyāḥ; Zmāla
see also Khumayr; *and* → BERBERS

Fertile Crescent

ancient Asad; Bahrāʾ; Djarrāḥids; Djudhām; Lakhm; Muhannā; al-Muntafiḳ.1; Taghlib b. Wāʾil; Ṭayyiʾ; Waththāb b. Sābiḳ al-Numayrī
see also Tanūkh.2; al-Uḳayṣir; Unayf

present-day ʿAnaza; Asad (Banū); Bādjalān; Bilbās; Ḍafīr; Djāf; Djubūr; Dulaym; Hamawand; al-Ḥuwayṭāt; Kurds.iv.A; Lām; al-Manāṣir; al-Muntafiḳ.2; Ṣakhr; Shammar
see also al-Baṭīḥa; Shāwiya.2

Iran Bāzūkiyyūn; Bilbās; Djāf; Eymir.2 and 3; (Banū) Kaʿb; Ḳarā Gözlū; Kurds.iv.A; Lak; Lām; Shāhsewan; Shakāk; Shaḳāḳī; Sindjābī
see also Daylam; Dulafids; Fīrūzānids; Göklän; Īlāt; Shūlistān

Turkey Afshār; Bayat; Bayi̊ndi̊r; Begdili; Čepni; Döger; Eymir.1; Ḳādjār; Ḳāyi̊; Takhtadji̊; Takkalū; Ṭorghud; Yörük; [in Suppl.] Čawdor
see also Shakāk; Shaḳāḳī; Tamgha

TUNISIA Baladiyya.3; Djāmiʿa; Djamʿiyya.iv; Djarīda.i.B; Dustūr.i; Ḥizb.i; Ḥukūma.iv; Istiḳlāl; al-Khaldūniyya; Maʿārif.2.A; Madjlis.4.A.xix; Salafiyya.1(a); **Tunisia;** [in Suppl.] Demography.IV
see also Fallāḳ; Ḥimāya.ii; Khalīfa b. ʿAskar; Ṣafar; [in Suppl.] Inzāl; *and* → BERBERS; DYNASTIES.SPAIN AND NORTH AFRICA

historians of Ibn Abī Dīnār; Ibn Abi ʾl-Ḍiyāf; Ibn ʿIdhārī; [in Suppl.]

ʿAbd al-Wahhāb
see also Ibn al-Raḳīḳ; al-Tidjānī, Abū Muḥammad; *and* → DYNASTIES.SPAIN AND NORTH AFRICA
institutions
educational al-Ṣādiḳiyya; Zaytūna; [in Suppl.] Institut des hautes études de Tunis
see also [in Suppl.] ʿAbd al-Wahhāb
musical al-Rashīdiyya
press al-Rāʾid al-Tūnusī
language ʿArabiyya.A.iii.3; Tunisia.IV
literature Malḥūn; Tunisia.V; *and* → LITERATURE
belletrists Saʿīd Abū Bakr; al-Shābbī; al-Tūnisī, Maḥmūd Bayram; al-Tūnisī, Muḥammad; al-Warghī
nationalists al-Thaʿālibī, ʿAbd al-ʿAzīz; [in Suppl.] al-Ḥaddād, al-Ṭāhir
Ottoman period (1574-1881) Aḥmad Bey; al-Ḥusayn (b. ʿAlī); Ḥusaynids; Khayr al-Dīn Pasha; Muḥammad Bayram al-Khāmis; Muḥammad Bey; Muḥammad al-Ṣādiḳ Bey; Muṣṭafā Khaznadār; Tunisia.II.c; [in Suppl.] Ibn Ghidhāhum
physical geography Tunisia.I.a
pre-Ottoman period ʿAbd al-Raḥmān al-Fihrī; Aghlabids; Ḥafṣids; Ḥassān b. al-Nuʿmān al-Ghassānī; (Banū) Khurāsān; Tunisia.II.b
and → BERBERS; DYNASTIES.SPAIN AND NORTH AFRICA
toponyms
ancient al-ʿAbbāsiyya; Ḥaydarān; Ḳalʿat Banī Ḥammād; Manzil Bashshū; Raḳḳāda; Ṣabra (al-Manṣūriyya); Subayṭila
present-day
districts Djarīd
islands Djarba; Ḳarḳana
regions Djazīrat Sharīk; Ḳasṭīliya.2; Nafzāwa; Sāḥil.1
towns Bādja; Banzart; Ḥalḳ al-Wādī; Ḳābis; al-Kāf; Ḳafsa; Ḳallala; al-Ḳayrawān; al-Mahdiyya; Monastir; Nafṭa; Safāḳus; Sūsa; Ṭabarḳa; Takrūna; Tūnis; Tūzar; Üsküdār

TURKEY Anadolu; Armīniya; Istanbul; Ḳarā Deniz; **Turks**.I.5
see also Libās.iv; *and* → OTTOMAN EMPIRE
architecture → ARCHITECTURE.REGIONS
dynasties → DYNASTIES.ANATOLIA AND THE TURKS; OTTOMAN EMPIRE
language → LANGUAGES.TURKIC
literature → LITERATURE
modern period (1920-) Baladiyya.1; Demokrat Parti; Djāmiʿa; Djarīda.iii; Djümhūriyyet Khalḳ Fïrḳasï; Dustūr.ii; Ḥizb.ii; Ishtirākiyya; Khalḳevi; Köy Enstitüleri; Kurds.iii.C; Madjlis.4.A.ii; Mīthāḳ-i Millī; Shuyūʿiyya.3;

Teraḳḳī-perver Djumhūriyyet Fi̊rḳasi̊; Turks.I.5; [in Suppl.] Demography.III
see also Djamʿiyya.ii; Iskandarūn; Iṣlāḥ.iii; Ittiḥād we Teraḳḳī Djemʿiyyeti; Karakol Djemʿīyyetī; Ḳawmiyya.iv; Kemāl; Kirkūk; Maʿārif.1.i; Māliyye; Nurculuk; Yüzellilikler; *and* → LITERATURE

religious leaders Nursī

statesmen/women Atatürk; Çakmak; Ḥusayn Djāhid; Ileri, Djelāl Nūrī; Kāẓi̊m Karabekir; Khālide Edīb; Köprülü (Mehmed Fuad); Meḥmed ʿĀkif; Menderes; Okyar; Orbay, Ḥüseyin Raʾūf; Shems al-Dīn Günaltay; Sheref, ʿAbd al-Raḥmān; Yeğana, ʿAlī Münīf; Yücel, Ḥasan ʿAlī; [in Suppl.] Adi̊var; Aghaoghlu; Atay; Esendal
see also Čerkes Edhem; Gökalp, Ziya; Hi̊sar; *and* → TURKEY.OTTOMAN PERIOD.YOUNG TURKS

mysticism → MYSTICISM.MYSTICS; SAINTHOOD

Ottoman period (1342-1924) Ḥizb.ii; Istanbul; Ittiḥād-i Muḥammedī Djemʿiyyeti; Ittiḥād we Teraḳḳī Djemʿiyyeti; Maʿārif.1.i; Madjlis.4.A.i; Madjlis al-Shūrā; Maṭbakh.2; **ʿOthmānli̊**; Türk Odjaghi̊; Yeñi ʿOthmānli̊lar
see also Aywaz.1; Derebey; Djamʿiyya.ii; Khalīfa.i.E; [in Suppl.] Demography.II; Djalālī; *and* → OTTOMAN EMPIRE

Young Ottomans and Young Turks **Yeñi ʿOthmānli̊lar**
see also Djamʿiyya; Djewdet; Dustūr.ii; Fāḍil Pasha; Ḥukūma.i; Ḥurriyya.ii; Ittiḥād we Teraḳḳī Djemʿiyyeti
individuals Djawīd; Djemāl Pasha; Enwer Pasha; (Tunali̊) Ḥilmī; Isḥāḳ Sükutī; Kemāl, Meḥmed Nāmi̊ḳ; Mīzāndji̊ Meḥmed Murād; Niyāzī Bey; Ṣabāḥ al-Dīn; Shükrü Bey; Suʿāwī, ʿAlī; Ṭalʿat Bey; Yeğana, ʿAlī Münīf; Yūsuf Aḳčura; Żiyā Pasha

physical geography

mountains Aghri̊ Dagh; Ala Dagh; Aladja Dagh; Beshparmaḳ; Bingöl Dagh; Deve Boynu; Elma Daghi̊; Erdjiyas Daghi̊; Gāwur Daghlari̊; Toros Dağları; Ulu Dāgh
see also Ṭūr ʿAbdīn

waters Boghaz-iči; Čanaḳ-ḳalʿe Boghazi̊; Čoruh.I; Djayḥān; Gediz Čayi̊; Göksu; Ḳi̊zi̊l-irmāḳ; Lamas-ṣū; Marmara Deñizi; Menderes; al-Rass; Sakarya; Sayḥān; Tuz Gölü; Wān.1; Yeshil İrmak

population Yörük; Zāzā; Zeybek; [in Suppl.] Demography.II
see also Muhādjir.2; Türkmen.3

pre-Islamic period → PRE-ISLAM; TURKEY.TOPONYMS

pre-Ottoman period Mengüček
see also Kitābāt.7; *and* → DYNASTIES.ANATOLIA AND THE TURKS; TURKEY.TOPONYMS

toponyms

ancient ʿAmmūriya; Ānī; Arzan; ʿAyn Zarba; Baghrās; Bālis; Beshike; Būḳa; al-Djazīra; Dulūk; Dunaysir; Ḥarrān; Lādhiḳ.1; Shabakhtān; Sīs; Sulṭān

Öñü; Ṭorg̲h̲ud Eli
see also Diyār Bakr; S̲h̲ims̲h̲āṭ
present-day
    districts   S̲h̲amdīnān; Terd̲j̲ān; Yalowa
    islands   Bozd̲j̲a-ada; Imroz
    provinces   Ag̲h̲rî; Čoruh; Diyar Bakr; Hakkārī; Ičil; Kars; Ḳasṭamūnī; K̲h̲anzīt; Ḳod̲j̲a Eli; Mūs̲h̲; News̲h̲ehir; Tund̲j̲eli
    regions   al-ʿAmḳ; Cilicia; Dersim; Diyār Muḍar; D̲j̲ānīk; Mentes̲h̲e-eli; Teke-eli; Ṭūr ʿAbdīn; Tutak
    towns   Ada Pāzārî; Adana; Adiyaman; Afyūn Ḳara Ḥiṣār; Aḳ Ḥiṣār.1 and 2; Aḳ S̲h̲ehir; Ak̲h̲lāṭ; Ala S̲h̲ehir; Alanya; Altîntas̲h̲; Amasya; Anadolu; Anamur; Anḳara; Anṭākiya; Antalya; ʿArabkīr; Ardahān; Artvin; Aya Solūk; Āyās; Aydîn; ʿAynṭāb; Aywalîk; Babaeski; Bālā; Bālā Ḥiṣār; Balāṭ; Bālikesrī; Bālṭa Līmānī; Bandirma; Bāyazīd; Bāybūrd; Baylān; Bergama; Besni; Beys̲h̲ehir; Bidlīs; Bīg̲h̲a; Biled̲j̲ik; Bingöl; Bīred̲j̲ik; Birge; Bodrum; Bolu; Bolwadin; Bozanti; Burdur; Bursa; Čankîrî; Čatāld̲j̲a; Čes̲h̲me; Čölemerik; Čorlu; Čorum; Deñizli; Diwrīgī; Diyār Bakr; Edirne; Edremit; Eğin; Eğridir; Elbistan; Elmalî; Enos; Ereğli; Ergani; Ermenak; Erzind̲j̲an; Erzurum; Eskis̲h̲ehir; Gebze; Gelibolu; Gemlik; Giresun; Göksun; Gördes; Gümüs̲h̲-k̲h̲āne; al-Hārūniyya; Ḥiṣn Kayfā; Iskandarūn; Isparta; Istanbul; Iznīḳ; Ḳarā Ḥiṣār; Ḳarad̲j̲a Ḥiṣār; Kars; Ḳasṭamūnī; Ḳayṣariyya; Kemāk̲h̲; Killiz; Ḳîrḳ Kilise; Kirmāstī; Ḳîrs̲h̲ehir; Ḳoč Ḥiṣār; Konya; Köprü Ḥiṣārî; Ḳoylu Ḥiṣār; Ḳōzān; Ḳūla; Kutāhiya; Lādhiḳ.2 and 3; Lāranda; Lüleburgaz; Mag̲h̲nisa; Malaṭya; Malāzgird.1; Malkara; Maʿmūrat al-ʿAzīz; Marʿas̲h̲; Mārdīn; al-Maṣṣīṣa; Mayyāfāriḳīn; Menemen; Mersin; Merzifūn; Mīlās; Mudanya; Mug̲h̲la; Mūs̲h̲; Naṣībīn; News̲h̲ehir; Nīgde; Nīksār; Nizīb; Orāmār; ʿOt̲h̲mānd̲j̲iḳ; Payās; Rize; al-Ruḥā; Ṣaband̲j̲a; Ṣāmsūn; Ṣart; Sarūd̲j̲; Siʿird; Silifke; Simaw; Sīnūb; Sīwās; Siwri Ḥiṣār; Sögüd; Sumaysāṭ; al-Suwaydiyya; Tall Bās̲h̲ir; Ṭarabzun; Ṭarsūs; Tekirdag̲h̲; Tīre; Tirebolu; Toḳat; Tund̲j̲eli; ʿUs̲h̲āḳ; Wān.2; Wezīr Köprü; Wize; Yalowa; Yeñi S̲h̲ehir; Yes̲h̲ilköy; Yozgat; Zaytūn; Zind̲j̲irli; Zonguldak; [in Suppl.] G̲h̲alaṭa
    see also Fener; Ḳarasî.2; (al-)Ḳusṭanṭīniyya

U

UMAYYADS → CALIPHATE; DYNASTIES.SPAIN AND NORTH AFRICA

UNITED ARAB EMIRATES al-Ḳawāsim; Mad̲j̲lis.4.A.xii; Maḥkama.4.ix; [in

Suppl.] **al-Imārāt al-ʿArabiyya al-Muttaḥida**
population Mazrūʿī
see also Yās; *and* → TRIBES.ARABIAN PENINSULA
toponyms Abū Ẓabī; al-Djiwāʾ; Dubayy; al-Fudjayra; Raʾs al-Khayma; al-Shāriḳa; Ṣīr Banī Yās; Umm al-Ḳaywayn; al-Ẓafra; [in Suppl.] ʿAdjmān
see also (Djazīrat) al-ʿArab; al-Khaṭṭ; Ṭunb; al-ʿUdayd

URBANISM → ARCHITECTURE.URBAN; GEOGRAPHY.URBAN; SEDENTARISM
for rowdy urban groups, see Zuʿʿār; *for urban militia, see* Aḥdāth

(former) USSR → CAUCASUS; CENTRAL ASIA.FORMER SOVIET UNION; COMMUNISM; EUROPE.EASTERN EUROPE; SIBERIA

V

VIRTUES AND VICES
virtues ʿAdl; Ḍayf; Futuwwa; Ḥasab wa-Nasab; Ḥilm; ʿIrḍ; Murūʾa; Ṣabr; Ẓarīf
see also Sharaf; Sharīf *and* → ETHICS; HUMOUR
vices Bukhl
see also Kaffāra; *and* → ADULTERY; DRUGS.NARCOTICS; GAMBLING; LAW.PENAL LAW; OBSCENITY; WINE

W

WEIGHTS AND MEASUREMENTS Aghač; Arpa; Dhirāʿ; Dirham.1; Farsakh; Ḥabba; Iṣbaʿ; Istār; **Makāyil**; Marḥala; Miḳyās; **Misāḥa**; al-Mīzān; Ṣāʿ; Sanadjāt; Tōlā; Tūmān.2; **Wazn**.1; [in Suppl.] Gaz
see also al-Ḳarasṭūn

WINE **Khamr**; Sāḳī
see also Karm
bacchic poetry **Khamriyya**
Arabic Abū Nuwās; Abū Miḥdjan; Abu ʾl-Shīṣ; ʿAdī b. Zayd; Ḥāritha b. Badr al-Ghudānī; (al-)Ḥusayn b. al-Ḍaḥḥāk; Ibn al-ʿAfīf al-Tilimsānī; Ibn Sayḥān; Tamīm b. al-Muʿizz li-Dīn Allāh; Tamīm b. al-Muʿizz; al-Walīd.2
see also al-Babbaghāʾ; Ibn al-Fāriḍ; Ibn Harma; al-Nawādjī; Yamūt b. al-Muzarraʿ
Turkish Rewānī; Riyāḍī
boon companions Ibn Ḥamdūn; al-Ḳāshānī; Khālid b. Yazīd al-Kātib al-Tamīmī

see also Abu 'l-Shīṣ; ʿAlī b. al-Djahm

Women ʿAbd; Ḥarīm; Ḥayḍ; Ḥidjāb.I; ʿIdda; Istibrāʾ; Khafḍ; **al-Marʾa**; Nikāḥ; Siḥāḳ; [in Suppl.] Bighāʾ
see also ʿArūs Resmi; Bashmaḳlïḳ; Khayr; Khiḍr-ilyās; Lithām; Tunisia.VI; ʿUrf.2.II; Zanāna; *and* → Divorce; Life Stages.childbirth *and* childhood; Marriage

and beauty al-Washm
and → Cosmetics

and literature al-Marʾa.1
see also Ḳiṣṣa; Shahrazād

Arabic authors al-Bāʿūni.6; Ḥafṣa bint al-Ḥādjdj; ʿInān; al-Khansāʾ; Laylā al-Akhyaliyya; Mayy Ziyāda; ʿUlayya; Wallāda; al-Yāzidjī.4; [in Suppl.] Faḍl al-Shāʿira
see also ʿAbbāsa; ʿĀtika; Khunātha; Ḳiṣṣa.2; Shilb; Uḳṣūṣa

Persian authors Ḳurrat al-ʿAyn; Mahsatī; Parwīn Iʿtiṣāmī
see also Gulbadan Bēgam; Makhfī

Turkish authors Fiṭnat; Khālide Edīb; Laylā Khānïm (2x); Mihrī Khātūn
see also Ḳiṣṣa.3(b)

and religion Zār

mystics ʿĀʾisha al-Mannūbiyya; Djahānārā Bēgam; Nafīsa; Rābiʿa al-ʿAdawiyya al-Ḳaysiyya
see also Walī.5

concubinage ʿAbd.3.f; Khaṣṣekī; Umm al-Walad

emancipation Ḳāsim Amīn; Malak Ḥifnī Nāṣif; Saʿīd Abū Bakr; Salāma Mūsā; Ṭalāḳ.II.3; [in Suppl.] al-Ḥaddād, al-Ṭāhir
see also Ḥidjāb; Ileri, Djelāl Nūrī; al-Marʾa; Wuthūḳ al-Dawla; al-Zahāwī, Djamīl Ṣidḳī; [in Suppl.] Ashraf al-Dīn Gīlānī

influential women

Arabic ʿĀʾisha bint Ṭalḥa; Asmāʾ; Barīra; Būrān; Hind bint ʿUtba; al-Khayzurān bint ʿAṭāʾ al-Djurashiyya; Khunātha; Shadjar al-Durr; Sitt al-Mulk; Ṣubḥ; Sukayna bt. al-Ḥusayn; Zubayda bt. Djaʿfar; [in Suppl.] Asmāʾ
see also al-Maʿāfirī; Zumurrud Khātūn; *and* → Muḥammad, the Prophet.family of.daughters *and* wives

Indo-Muslim Nūr Djahān; Samrū

Mongolian Baghdād Khātūn; Khān-zāda Bēgum; Töregene Khātūn

Ottoman ʿĀdila Khātūn; Khurrem; Kösem Wālide; Mihr-i Māh Sulṭān; Nīlūfer Khātūn; Nūr Bānū; Ṣafiyye Wālide Sulṭān; Shāh Sulṭān; Shebṣefa Ḳadïn; Ṭurkhān Sulṭān
see also Wālide Sulṭān

Turkish Terken Khātūn; Zumurrud Khātūn

legendary women al-Basūs; Bilḳīs; Hind bint al-Khuss
see also Āsiya; Zarḳā' al-Yamāma
musicians/singers ʿAzza al-Maylā'; Djamīla; Ḥabāba; Rā'iḳa; Sallāma al-Zarḳā'; Shāriya; Siti Binti Saad; ʿUlayya; Umm Kulthūm; [in Suppl.] Badhl al-Kubrā; al-Djarādatān[i]; Faḍl al-Shāʿira; Ḥabba Khātūn
see also ʿĀlima; Ḳayna; Ṭaḳṭūḳa
mystics → *the section And Religion above*

WRITING **Khaṭṭ**
see also Ibn Muḳla; Kitābāt; *and* → ART.CALLIGRAPHY; EPIGRAPHY
manuscripts and books Daftar; Ḥāshiya; **Kitāb**; Muḳābala.2; **Nuskha**; Tadhkira; Taʿlīḳ; Taṣḥīf; Taṣnīf; Tazwīr; ʿUnwān; Warrāḳ; [in Suppl.] Abbreviations
see also Ḳaṭʿ; Maktaba
blockprinting **Ṭarsh**
bookbinding Īlkhāns; Kitāb; Nuskha; ʿOthmānli̊.VII.c
booktitles **ʿUnwān**.2(=3); Zubda
materials Djild; Kāghad; Ḳalam; Khātam; Ḳirṭās; Midād; Papyrus; Raḳḳ; [in Suppl.] Dawāt
see also ʿAfṣ; Afsantīn; Diplomatic; Īlkhāns; Maʿdin.4
scripts Khaṭṭ; Siyāḳat; Tawḳīʿ.2; Tifinagh; Tughra.2(d)
see also Nuskha; Swahili; Taʿlīḳ; Warrāḳ; Zabūr; *and* → ART.CALLIGRAPHY; EPIGRAPHY

Y

YEMEN Djarīda.i.A; Dustūr.viii; Madjlis.4.A.xiv and xv; Maḥkama.4.viii; Yaḥyā b. Muḥammad; **al-Yaman**
see also ʿAsīr; Ismāʿīliyya; Mahrī; Makramids; Ṭāghūt.2; ʿUrf.2.I.A.2; [in Suppl.] Abū Mismār; *and* → DYNASTIES.ARABIAN PENINSULA
architecture → ARCHITECTURE.REGIONS
before Islam al-Abnā'.II; Abraha; Dhū Nuwās; (Djazīrat) al-ʿArab; Ḥabashat; Ḥaḍramawt; Ḳatabān; Ḳayl; Mārib; al-Mathāmina; Saba'; al-Sawdā'; Wahriz; Yazan; [in Suppl.] Ḥaḍramawt
see also [in Suppl.] Bādhām
British protectorate of Ḥaḍramawt period (1839-1967) ʿAdan; Wāḥidī
see also [in Suppl.] Ḥaḍramawt.ii.1
dynasties Hamdānids; Mahdids; Rasūlids; Ṣulayḥids; Ṭāhirids.3; Yuʿfirids; Zaydiyya.3; Ziyādids; Zurayʿids
see also Rassids; *and* → DYNASTIES.ARABIAN PENINSULA
historians of al-Djanadī; al-Khazradjī; al-Mawzaʿī; al-Nahrawālī; al-Rāzī,

Aḥmad b. ʿAbd Allāh; al-S̲h̲arīf Abū Muḥammad Idrīs; al-S̲h̲illī; ʿUmāra al-Yamanī

see also Ibn al-Mud̲j̲āwir

language   al-Yaman.5; [in Suppl.] Ḥaḍramawt.iii

    and → Languages.afro-asiatic.arabic *and* south arabian

Ottoman period (1517-1635)   Maḥmūd Pas̲h̲a; al-Muṭahhar; Özdemir Pas̲h̲a; Riḍwān Pas̲h̲a

    see also Baladiyya.2; K̲h̲ādim Süleymān Pas̲h̲a

physical geography

    mountains   Ḥaḍūr; Ḥarāz; Ḥiṣn al-G̲h̲urāb; al-Sarāt; S̲h̲ahāra; S̲h̲ibām.4

        see also al-Yaman.2

    wadis   Barhūt; al-K̲h̲ārid; al-Saḥūl; Turaba.1

population   ʿAbdalī; ʿAḳrabī; Banyar; Hamdān; Ḥās̲h̲id wa-Bakīl; Ḥaws̲h̲abī; Ḥud̲j̲riyya; Ḳaḥṭān; K̲h̲awlān; Mad̲h̲ḥid̲j̲; Mahra; Yāfiʿ

    see also Yām; al-Yaman.4; Yazan; *and* → Tribes.arabian peninsula

toponyms

    ancient   al-ʿĀra; S̲h̲abwa; Ṣirwāḥ; Ẓafār

        see also Nad̲j̲rān

    present-day

        districts   Abyan; ʿAlawī; ʿĀmiri; ʿAwd̲h̲alī; Dathīna; Faḍlī; Ḥarāz; Ḥarīb; al-Ḥayma; Ḥud̲j̲riyya

        islands   Ḳamarān; Mayyūn; Suḳuṭra

        regions   ʿAwlaḳī; Ḥaḍramawt; Lahd̲j̲; al-S̲h̲iḥr; Tihāma; [in Suppl.] Ḥaḍramawt.ii

        towns   ʿAdan; ʿAt̲h̲r; Bayt al-Faḳīh; D̲h̲amār; G̲h̲alāfiḳa; Ḥabbān; Hadjarayn; Ḥāmī; Ḥawra; al-Ḥawṭa; al-Ḥudayda; Ibb; ʿIrḳa; Ḳaʿṭaba; Kawkabān; Kis̲h̲n; Lahd̲j̲; al-Luḥayya; Mārib; al-Mukallā; al-Muk̲h̲ā; Rayda; Ṣaʿda; al-Saḥūl; Ṣanʿāʾ; Sayʾūn; S̲h̲ahāra; al-S̲h̲ayk̲h̲ Saʿīd; S̲h̲ibām; al-S̲h̲iḥr; Taʿizz; Tarīm; al-Ṭawīla; T̲h̲ulā; Zabīd; Ẓafār; [in Suppl.] ʿĪnāt

        see also (D̲j̲azīrat) al-ʿArab

(former) Yugoslavia   Džabić; K̲h̲osrew Beg; Muslimūn.1.B.6; Pomaks; Riḍwān Begović; **Yugoslavia**; [in Suppl.] Handžić

    see also ʿÖmer Efendi; Ṭopal ʿOt̲h̲mān Pas̲h̲a.2

toponyms

    provinces   [in Suppl.] Dalmatia

    regions   Yeñi Bāzār.1

    republics   Bosna; Ḳaradag̲h̲; Ḳosowa; Māḳadūnyā; Ṣîrb

    towns   Aḳ Ḥiṣār.3; Alad̲j̲a Ḥiṣār; Banjaluka; Belgrade; Eszék; Is̲h̲tib; Ḳarlofča; Livno; Manāṣtir; Mostar; Nis̲h̲; Ok̲h̲rī; Pasarofča; Pirlepe;

Prishtina; Prizren; Raghūsa; Sarajevo; Siska; Travnik; Üsküb; Waradīn; Yeñi Bāzār.2
see also Zenta

Z

ZAIRE Katanga; Kisangani

ZANZIBAR → TANZANIA

ZOOLOGY **Ḥayawān**.7
and → ANIMALS
writers on al-Damīrī; al-Marwazī, Sharaf al-Zamān
see also al-Djāḥiẓ

ZOROASTRIANS Gabr; Iran.vi; **Madjūs**; Mōbadh; Zamzama
see also Bih'āfrīd b. Farwardīn; Ghazal.ii; Gudjarāt.a; Pārsīs; Pūr-i Dāwūd; Sarwistān; Shīz; al-Ṣughd; Sunbādh; Ta'rīkh.I.1.vii; Ustādhsīs; Yazd.1; Zamzam; Zindīḳ
dynasties Maṣmughān
gods Bahrām